Advance praise for *A Women's Lectiona*

"*A Women's Lectionary for the Whole Church* chall our most common readings, upending customar the presence of the feminine Divine. Such upending reveals space in our sacred text not only to see the stories of these women but also to see more deeply our own."

—Rev. Traci D. Blackmon, Associate General Minister,
Justice & Local Church Ministries, The United Church of Christ

"Reading Wil Gafney's work is not unlike listening to a gifted jazz musician. She knows the tradition yet has the ability to weave multiple genres together to create a powerful and beautiful new song."

—Rev. Otis Moss III, Senior Pastor,
Trinity United Church of Christ, Chicago, Illinois

"I did not know how much my soul needed *A Women's Lectionary for the Whole Church* until I began reading it, but now I suspect that I will never prepare another sermon or devotional without consulting it. Every pastor, indeed every Christian, needs this among their collection."

—Chanequa Walker-Barnes, PhD,
author of *I Bring the Voices of My People: A Womanist Vision for Racial Reconciliation* and *Too Heavy a Yoke: Black Women and the Burden of Strength*

"As someone who has learned so much from the Rev. Dr. Wil Gafney, I commend it to every congregation and classroom. It is a prime example of revolutionary scholarship."

—Brian D. McLaren,
author of *Faith After Doubt*

"I could sit at the feet of Wil Gafney for days and soak up her wisdom and knowledge. She has offered the church a treasure in this *Women's Lectionary*, and we would do well to make use of it quickly and thoroughly."

—Rev. Nadia Bolz-Weber, author

"*A Women's Lectionary for the Whole Church* is not only a resource for liturgy and preaching. I believe it is also a tool for contemplation on the mighty works of God on behalf of all people."

—The Rt. Rev. C. Andrew Doyle, Episcopal Bishop of Texas
and author of *Embodied Liturgy*

"Gafney's resource will transform how the Bible gets read and preached in our churches, bringing us closer to the totality of God's love."

—Rev. Karoline M. Lewis, PhD,
The Marbury E. Anderson Chair of Biblical Preaching, Luther Seminary,
and Program Director, *Festival of Homiletics*

"This lectionary is so powerful we will finish each reading saying out loud, 'The word of God! Thanks be to God!'"

—Cláudio Carvalhaes, Associate Professor of Worship,
Union Theological Seminary, New York

"For anyone wanting to read and meditate on scripture and be nurtured by the word without being harmed, this text is indispensable."

—Willie James Jennings, Associate Professor of Systematic Theology
and Africana Studies, Yale Divinity School

"In a predominantly patriarchal world that still diminishes the lives, gifts, contributions, and voices of women, Professor Wil Gafney offers a distinct, bold, women's lectionary for the whole church and academy."

—The Rev. Dr. Luke A. Powery, Dean, Duke University Chapel,
and Associate Professor of Homiletics, Duke Divinity School

"This resource will be a great blessing and useful to all who seek to loose the shackles and set free the voices of the religiously oppressed and suppressed."

—Rev. Dr. Yvette A Flunder, Presiding Bishop,
The Fellowship of Affirming Ministries,
and Senior Pastor, City of Refuge UCC in Oakland, California

YEAR
A

A WOMEN'S LECTIONARY FOR THE WHOLE CHURCH

YEAR
A

A WOMEN'S LECTIONARY FOR THE WHOLE CHURCH

WILDA C. GAFNEY

CHURCH
PUBLISHING
INCORPORATED

Church Publishing
19 East 34th Street
New York, NY 10016

Cover art by Pauline Williamson
Cover design by Tiny Little Hammers
Typeset by Rose Design

Library of Congress Cataloging-in-Publication Data

Names: Gafney, Wilda, 1966- author.
Title: A women's lectionary for the whole church : year A / Wilda C. Gafney.
Description: New York, NY : Church Publishing, [2021-] | Contents: Year A
Identifiers: LCCN 2021007720 (print) | LCCN 2021007721 (ebook) | ISBN 9781640651623 (paperback) | ISBN 9781640651630 (epub)
Subjects: LCSH: Common lectionary (1992) | Lectionaries. | Bible--Feminist criticism.
Classification: LCC BV199.L42 G34 2021 (print) | LCC BV199.L42 (ebook) | DDC 264/.03034--dc23

LC record available at https://lccn.loc.gov/2021007720
LC ebook record available at https://lccn.loc.gov/2021007721

For those who have searched for themselves in the scriptures
and did not find themselves in the masculine pronouns.

CONTENTS

ACKNOWLEDGMENTS

I would like to thank the Louisville Institute for the 2019 Sabbatical Grant for Researchers; the trustees, administration, faculty, and staff of Brite Divinity School for a twelve-month sabbatical in 2019; and the rector, Mike Kinman, vestry, and members of the All Saints Episcopal Church in Pasadena for ongoing material, spiritual, and temporal support during this project and for committing to a year-long trial use of the lectionary in 2020–2021.

Special thanks to the RevGalBlogPal community and Martha Spong for an early hearing of the work and a collaborative digital space in which to try out lesson and translations choices. For valuable feedback, support, and inspiration, many thanks to the women, nonbinary persons, and men who attended collaborative consultation sessions across the country, including Martha Simmons of the African American Lectionary Project. Thanks to Alicia Hager for administrative support in the first year and to NaShieka Knight, my research assistant at Brite.

I remain grateful for translations and translators that have inspired me to take up the text: Marcia Falk, Everett Fox, Hugh Page, and Joel Rosenberg. I am appreciative for the *Wisdom Psalter* by Laura Grimes; it was an early resource and she an early collaborator. The psalms in these volumes are shaped by that interaction.

I am deeply grateful for all who have expressed support and encouragement and impatience for delivery in person, through correspondence, and on social media.

Lastly, I mourn those who will not see this project, especially those who died due to Covid 19 and its complications. They are legion.

ABOUT THE COVER IMAGES

I first saw Wil Gafney in chapel at Candler School of Theology in October of 2016, during a service where Leea Allen read an amazing poem "Heart Matters" and Dr. Gafney preached a sermon entitled "Love God Herself," drawn from Beyoncé's song "Don't Hurt Yourself." I was inspired. I didn't have anything that day other than a regular piece of paper and my colored pens—this was before I unapologetically carted my markers into services, because I do most of my work in situ—but I drew the image of a woman standing proud, brown face crowned with locks of dark hair, clothed in green, and holding up the world. She speaks to me of triumph.

This was not the last time that Dr. Gafney's words would inspire my art.

In a Queer and Feminist Theology course I took, we read Dr. Gafney's article "Don't Hate the Playa, Hate the Game." In it, she refocused our attention on the fullness of Delilah's story, teasing out details and possibilities of connection that reframed both Delilah's motivations and power. If you haven't read it, I suggest you do. It spoke to me of honey, and fire, and memory, and love, and retribution, and these things all shaped the piece I created in response: "Remembering the Fire."

Since then, I've been inspired many times over.

When I was beginning a Lenten series, I read Dr. Gafney's article "Ritualizing Bathsheba's Rape" and drew, in response, "In the Ashes." The piece depicts Bathsheba sitting by a fire in ashes, weeping and cradling her dead child while David laments outside. I also did a series of pieces of the women in Saul's life that were inspired by what Dr. Gafney wrote in her incredible *Womanist Midrash*. Time and time again, I know that if I want to be schooled in a text, brought closer to the nuances and truths contained therein, and inspired by those truths, I will find that wisdom in Dr. Gafney's works. Without a doubt, the volume you currently hold in your hands contains this wisdom, and I hope you are similarly inspired.

My pieces for the *Women's Lectionary* were created in the same theme and seek to center and lift up the power that Black Women have in these stories of salvation. I drew "Queen of Heaven" (the cover image for Volumes A, B, and C) in June of 2017 using Tombow Watercolor Markers on Bristol Vellum paper. It shows Mary, enthroned and crowned with all the planets of the solar system and the wonders of the Universe bearing witness, clothed in life and light and holding the Christ Child in her arms. She is the guardian, and the bearer of God—Theotokos; she is the creation honored by the Creator.

The next work, "No Longer Lost" (the cover image for Volume W), speaks of the parable where God is imaged as a woman, the woman who lost her coin and finds it. She celebrates with all of her neighbors as God celebrates with the host of heaven when the lost ones come home. Surrounding her in these coins are us, connecting, praying, studying, dancing. You can also see the dove, and the lost sheep, and the broom, because some things need cleaning up, not the least of which are our misconceptions and our preconceived notions, which have grown dusty as we have let them sit.

Let the words of the Rev. Dr. Wil Gafney clear up some of those misconceptions and open windows to shed light on truth in a way you have never before seen. Sit with these words. Let them sink in. Feel their power and be empowered by the story of the Good News told in ways you may have never experienced before. May the luminous wisdom of the Word find a home within you, and may it spark your inner fire.

Pauline Williamson, creating as *Seamire*

ABBREVIATIONS

Alter	*The Hebrew Bible: A New Translation with Commentary*, trans. Robert Alter
AYBD	*Anchor Yale Bible Dictionary*
BigS	*Bibel in gerechter Sprache*
BDAG	*A Greek-English Lexicon of the New Testament and Other Early Christian Literature*, revised and edited by Frederick William Danker
BDB	*Brown-Driver-Briggs Hebrew and English Lexicon*
CEB	*Common English Bible*
DCH	*Dictionary of Classical Hebrew*
DSS	Dead Sea Scrolls
Fox	*The Five Books of Moses*, trans. Everett Fox
GSJPS	*A Gender-Sensitive Adaptation of the JPS Translation*
HALOT	*Hebrew and Aramaic Lexicon of the Old Testament*
IB	*The Inclusive Bible*
JPS	Jewish Publication Society *TANAKH*
KJV	King James Version
LXX	Septuagint
MT	Masoretic Text
NRSV	New Revised Standard Version
RCL	Revised Common Lectionary
SP	Samaritan Pentateuch

BIBLICAL RESOURCES

Original Language Texts

Dead Sea Scrolls
Hebrew Masoretic Text
Nestle-Aland Greek New Testament, 28th ed.
Peshitta (both testaments)
Samaritan Pentateuch
Septuagint
Targums
Vulgate

Bibles in Translation

Bishops Bible, 1568
Common English Bible, 2011
Dead Sea Scrolls Bible, 1999
Douay-Rheims Bible, 1582 (NT), 1610 (HB)
The Early Prophets: Joshua, Judges Samuel, Kings, Everett Fox 2014
Five Books of Moses, Everett Fox, 1995
A Gender-Sensitive Adaptation of the JPS Tanakh, 2006
Geneva Bible, 1599
The Hebrew Bible: A Translation with Commentary, Robert Alter, 2018
Inclusive Bible, 2007
Jewish Publication Society Tanakh, 1985
King James Version, 1611
A New English Translation of the Septuagint, 2000
New Revised Standard Version, 1989
Revised Standard Version, 1971
Tyndale's (incomplete) translation, 1525
Wycliffe Bible, 1384

Commentaries

Hermeneia
Jewish Publication Society Torah Commentary
The Torah, A Women's Commentary
The Wisdom Commentary
Women's Bible Commentary
The Yale Anchor Bible Commentary

INTRODUCTION

What does it look like to tell the Good News through the stories of women who are often on the margins of scripture and often set up to represent bad news? How would a lectionary centering women's stories, chosen with womanist and feminist commitments in mind, frame the presentation of the scriptures for proclamation and teaching? How is the story of God told when stories of women's brutalization and marginalization are moved from the margins of canon and lectionary and held in the center in tension with stories of biblical heroines and heroes? More simply, what would it look like if women built a lectionary focusing on women's stories? These were my initial questions when I sat down to draft a proposal for a women's lectionary, a lectionary designed by women—or an individual woman—for the whole church. I do not imagine that my questions and perceptions are the questions and perceptions of all other women. But I do believe that my questions and perceptions invite women, men, and nonbinary readers and hearers to engage the scriptures in new ways and in that engagement, they might find themselves and their questions represented.

The lectionary is a catechetical tool. There are more than two billion Christians in the world according to the Pew Research Center's Forum on Religion and Public Life (Global Religious Landscape). As of 2015, there were nearly 2.3 billion Christians representing slightly more than 31 percent of the world's total population. With Roman Catholics making up an estimated 1.2 billion, and accounting for Orthodox Christians, Anglicans, Episcopalians, Methodists, Presbyterians, Lutherans, and other Reformed traditions along with some Baptist and congregational churches that use a lectionary, the overwhelming majority of Christians receive their scripture mediated through a lectionary; that would be nearly 1.4 billion persons whose customary exposure to the scriptures occurs through a lectionary. Based on the numbers in the Pew Research Center's May 12, 2015, report, "America's Changing Religious Landscape," as many as 60 percent of American Christians attend services in churches that use lectionaries.

The scriptures are androcentric, male-focused, as are the lectionaries dependent upon them. Those lectionaries are not simply *as* androcentric as are the scriptures, but in my experience as a congregant and priest, women are even less well represented in them than they are in the biblical text. For example, there are at a minimum one hundred and eleven named women in the Hebrew Scriptures—which is itself underrepresented in preaching lectionaries and not always preached upon or even read—and that reckoning does not account for the numbers of unnamed women and girls. Yet not many of my students or parishioners can name even ten women in the Hebrew Scriptures or even the entire biblical canon. The extant lectionaries do not introduce us to even a tithe of them. As a result, all many congregants know of the Bible is the texts they hear read from their respective lectionary.

As a biblical scholar, it is my hope to see congregants exposed to the Bible more broadly and deeply and see them equipped to engage the sacred texts of their tradition critically, with nuance. As a Hebrew biblical scholar, it is my hope to see congregations embrace the Hebrew Scriptures as a full and sufficient canon of scripture, revealing God and her word in conversation with, but not subjected to, the Christian scriptures that follow, honoring the ancient texts and *their* contexts. As a professor, priest, and preacher, I am keenly aware that it is the stories of women and girls, female characters and their names (when given), that are most likely to be unknown by congregants and seminarians and, all too often, clergy. A more expansive, more inclusive lectionary will remedy that by introducing readers and hearers of scripture to "woman story" in the scriptures. (Adapted from April D. Westbrook, *"And He Will Take Your Daughters . . .": Woman Story and the Ethical Evaluation of Monarchy in the David Narrative.*)

Biblical women are often generalized as a monolith of oppressed biblical womanhood. In my years teaching in theological classrooms and Jewish and Christian congregations, I find scripture readers unfamiliar with women prophets (the subject of my first book, *Daughters of Miriam: Women Prophets in Ancient Israel*), or the more than twenty named Israelite and Judean queens preserved in the text (addressed in my most recent monograph, *Womanist Midrash: A Reintroduction to the Women of the Torah and the Throne*), or the female assassins who execute their would-be rapists, or many other texts in which women have unexpected power and agency. A significant aim of this project is increased biblical literacy, beginning with scripture's most neglected population.

Recognizing that the scriptures are an androcentric collection of documents steeped in patriarchy, this lectionary grapples with the gender constructs of the text rather than romanticizing admirable heroines. Indeed, it questions "admirable" constructs of womanhood rooted in birthing and mothering. The extent to which women's narratives uphold the patriarchal agendas of the scriptures is held in tension with those passages in which women demonstrate agency, wielding power and authority. Sometimes those are the same texts. The degree to which the scriptures are (and are not) liberating for all of their characters and claimants will be, hopefully, more accessible to preacher and reader and other interpreters and exegetes.

Biblical values and norms around gender occupy a central place in biblical interpretation, providing opportunity for preachers to engage them and their impact on the construction of gender norms in the world in which these texts are interpreted. I believe it is crucial to reframe the texts so that women and girls are at the center of the story, even though they are, to one degree or another, literary creations of premodern men. It is important that women who are often second-class citizens in the text and in the world in which the text is interpreted have a text selection and reading paradigm that centers the interests and voices of women in the text, no matter how constructed. The task of preachers is to proclaim a word—of good news, of liberation, of encouragement, of prophetic power, of God-story, and sometimes, of lament, brokenness, and righteous rage. These lectionaries will provide a framework to do that and attempt to offer some balance to the register in which the word has often been proclaimed.

A significant aspect of the work of shaping a lectionary and preaching from it is hermeneutical. I was (and remain) convinced it ought to be possible to tell the story of God and God's people through the most marginalized characters in the text. That is my practice as a preacher. This project, *A Women's Lectionary for the Whole Church*, intends to do that in a three-year lectionary accompanied by a standalone single-year lectionary. The three-year cycle, Years A, B, and C, will feature the Gospels of Matthew, Mark, and Luke respectively, with John interwoven, as is the case in the Revised Common Lectionary (RCL) and Episcopal Lectionary (similar to the RCL but with the inclusion of deuterocanonical texts not deemed canonical by churches outside of the Anglo-Catholic and Orthodox streams). Year W (for "Women") covers all four Gospels.

Specifically, the *Lectionary* includes:

1. companion texts in the traditional four-fold model, first lesson, generally Hebrew Bible, Psalm (or other Canticle), Christian Testament lesson, and Gospel appropriate to the liturgical season;
2. fresh translation of the lessons for each Sunday, the Principal Feasts, Holy Week, and the Feasts of the Ever-Blessed Virgin Mary and Mary Magdalene, using gender-expansive language and, in the case of the Psalms, explicitly feminine God-language (see "About the Translations");
3. brief text commentaries on each day's lections and,
4. brief preaching commentaries on each day's lections.

The lectionary *does not* include collects. The lack of collects—prayers that tie together the readings that open the Liturgy of the Word—is intentional, that clergy and lay liturgists might develop their own in conversation with the lectionary.

A final word about gendered language: as a women's lectionary, this project specifically and intentionally makes women visible in these lectionary texts. This will inevitably seem strange to some hearers and readers. Some will find it welcome and a signifier of inclusion. Some will find it discordant and I invite those to think deeply about what that discomfiture signifies. These responses may well be multiplied when reading and hearing the psalms using feminine pronouns. And some will find the language in these volumes insufficiently inclusive, particularly with regard to nonbinary and a-gender persons. While there is nonbinary language for human and divine subjects, the purpose of this project is to make women and girls more visible. Nonbinary and inclusive language can obscure women and girls. The commitment to the visibility of women and girls is not in conflict or competition with the commitment to visibility of nonbinary persons; this language, my language, like all language, is simply inadequate to express the fullness of God in and beyond the world or even in human creation.

Most simply, these translations seek to offer and extend the embrace of the scriptures to all who read and hear that they might see and hear themselves in them and spoken to by them. Similarly, taking seriously that we are all created in the image of God, these translations seek to display a God in whose Image we see ourselves reflected and reflecting.

TEXT SELECTION

I crafted lectionaries that centered the telling of the stories of scripture on the stories of women and girls in the text, without regard to whether they are named or voiced in the text or whether their experiences of and with God support the narrative and theological claims made by and on behalf of the text or not. Specifically, I prioritize passages in which women and girls are present whether named or not, whether speaking or not. In addition, I selected passages in which women and girls are present but obscured in plurals and other groupings, e.g., "children," "Israelites," "people," "believers," etc. As is the case with all lectionaries, some passages recur and others are omitted all together. None of the extant Christian lectionaries offers comprehensive reading of any of the canons of scripture. This lectionary is no exception.

My methodology was broadly as follows:

1. First, I established a female canon within the broader canons of scripture by using Accordance Bible Software to identify passages in which there is explicit language for female persons. I designed a Boolean search to capture as many terms as possible in singular and plural constructions and varied grammatical forms (mother* <or> daughter* <or> sister* <or> wom*n <or> wife <or> wives <or> widow* <or>*maid* <or> mistress* <or> lady <or> ladies <or> prostitute* <or> prophetess* <or> princess* <or> queen* <or> sorceress* <OR> womb <OR> pregnan* <or> midwi*e*.) My search terms were not necessarily exhaustive, but they were more than sufficient for the task. I used the *Dictionary of Women in Scripture,* edited by Carol Meyers et al., to supplement this list.
2. Then, beginning with the liturgical season and its themes, I identified Hebrew biblical or deuterocanonical texts from the female canon. (Year W does not use the deuterocanonical texts apart from select readings during one or more of the Principal Feasts, such as Judith during the Great Vigil of Easter).
3. Next, I looked for readings that shared thematic language or specific words that related to the liturgical season and first lesson. I saved my Boolean search results in text groups: Hebrew Bible, Psalms, books that make up the New Testament lesson—Acts, the Epistles, and Revelation—and the Gospels. That meant I did not have to search the entire canon each time I worked on a specific reading. One nontraditional aspect of these lectionaries is that I occasionally use the Acts of the Apostles as the New Testament lesson, expanding the options for readings with female characters.

4. Sometimes a specific passage in a Gospel, Psalm, or Epistle would suggest itself. Other times, I would move through the lesson categories looking for connective language. Most often the selection sequence was Hebrew Bible followed by a psalm then the Gospel and the New Testament lesson last.

Text selection was one of the most time-consuming aspects of the project, second only to translating the text. I was greatly facilitated in this world by collaboration circles, in person in Atlanta, Chattanooga, Chicago, Dallas, Fort Worth, Pasadena, Richmond (VA), and in Kapaa, Kilauea, and Wailua, Kauai (HI) in addition to international trips to Managua (Nicaragua) and a continuing education event for clergy on a Central and South American cruise where the *Lectionary* was one of the teaching topics. There is also an ongoing digital collaboration through a closed Facebook working group.

My conversation partners included sixty-three participants from across the United States, United Kingdom, Scotland, Canada, and New Zealand in one setting, Episcopal parishes in Kauai and Pasadena during separate one-month residencies, and a series of individual and small group consultations, some seventeen collaborations, some of which were composed of multiple sessions. Denominations represented included: African Methodist Episcopal, Anglican, Baptist (of various sorts), Disciples of Christ, Episcopal, the Fellowship of Affirming Ministries, Lutheran, Presbyterian, Unitarian Universalist, United Church of Canada, United Church of Christ, United Church of Scotland, and United Methodist.

I deliberately engaged potential users of the *Lectionary,* including clergy, seminarians, and lay leaders, with a range of gender identities and expressions. I also held a specific session for queer-identifying and nonbinary readers and hearers of the text focusing on the use and implications of binary language, even in service to womanist/feminist work, in an increasingly postbinary world.

I am beyond grateful for the contributions, questions, and suggestions of all of these conversation partners, including their assessment for wording and translation choices in addition to text pairings.

USING *A WOMEN'S LECTIONARY*

The *Women's Lectionary* is designed for congregational and devotional life. It will also serve well in theological classrooms in preaching, worship arts, liturgy, and spiritual formation. The *Lectionary* is also suitable for clergy lectionary study groups. Individuals and congregations will have a number of options for use. Each set of readings is accompanied by text and translation notes and a preaching commentary. In addition, the *Lectionary* comes with a list of the divine names and titles used for God in these translations that might be used in public liturgy and private prayer. There is also an index of all of the passages of scripture in the lectionary, making them available for individual study. Suggested practices for public reading follow in the "About the Translations" section.

CONGREGATIONAL USE

The gender-expansive translations throughout the *Women's Lectionary* and explicit feminine God language in the psalter provide an opportunity for Christian education and formation on matters of biblical authority and translation issues, oft neglected conversations in congregations (beyond creedal statements).

- Adopt the *Lectionary* fully, Years A, B, and C for three years using these lessons in this translation.
- Adopt the *Lectionary* for a single year, using Year W for representation from all four Gospels. This would be especially suitable for churches that do not use a multiyear lectionary.
- Adopt the *Lectionary* to replace a year in the three-year lectionary currently in use.
- Adopt the *Lectionary* readings using another translation of the scriptures for public proclamation. (This may be a useful option in a congregation that might balk at hearing feminine pronouns used for God in scripture proclamation.)
- Use the *Lectionary* for substitute readings for the same day and liturgical season in a particular year (for example, when the Episcopal or RCL lessons are unsatisfactory).
- Use the *Lectionary* for Bible study, whether preaching from the *Lectionary* or not. The preaching prompts may be used as conversation starters.
- Use the list of divine names and titles for God to enrich the theological language of the community in liturgy, corporate, and personal prayer.

DEVOTIONAL USE

The *Lectionary* is designed for oral reading; read it out loud. Use the *Lectionary* for devotional reading, daily or weekly, whether your congregation uses the *Lectionary* or not. The four lessons can be read together every day of the week in their liturgical setting or spread out over the course of the week. The index can be used to identify individual passages for study and the list of divine names in the appendix can be used to augment the vocabulary of prayer.

THEOLOGICAL EDUCATIONAL USE

As a resource in the theological classroom, the *Lectionary* offers a much-needed alternative to the long-standing Episcopal and Revised Common Lectionaries for the study of liturgy and worship planning, offering a relevant and expansive vocabulary at a time when many clergy, congregations, and denominations are looking for liturgical alternatives and some are considering revisions of prayer books and hymnals for this very purpose.

These translations make a specific contribution to the oft-neglected but necessary conversation about the nature, function, and scope of biblical translation beyond the standard rubric of formal literalism and dynamic flexibility.

ABOUT THE TRANSLATIONS

Gender matters. Gender matters in the text, in the world, in the world of the text, and in the world of the translator. Gender matters to me and to countless numbers of women hearers and readers of the biblical text for whom it is Scripture. Gender matters significantly to those who have been and are marginalized because of gender, especially when it is done in the name of God, appealing to the Scriptures. And gender matters to men. Gender matters to hearers and readers of the Scriptures who are privileged to share the gender of the dominant portrayal of God, the majority of biblical characters, the majority of biblical characters who have speaking parts, the majority of translators of biblical texts, and the majority of interpreters of biblical texts.

—Wilda Gafney, *Womanist Midrash: A Reintroduction to the Women of the Torah and the Throne*, 289

While prompted in part by my experience of hearing the scriptures read and proclaimed in nearly exclusively masculine language, multiplied in effect by equally, if not more, male liturgical language, this *Women's Lectionary* is a lectionary for the whole church. Androcentrism, sexism, and misogyny in the scriptures, in their translation and in their preaching and liturgical use, hurts men and boys and nonbinary children and adults as much as it does women and girls. Exclusively masculine language constructs and reinforces the notion that men are the proper image of God and women are secondary and distant. Further, the simple reality that men and boys have always heard their gender identified with God cannot be overlooked as a source of power and authority and security in terms of their place in the divine household and economy. Many, if not most, women and girls have not heard themselves identified by their gender as and with the divine and for those who have had that experience, it has been profoundly moving, rare, and even sometimes profoundly disturbing. The translation choices employed in the *Women's Lectionary* offer an opportunity to hear the scriptures in public and private settings in a different timbre, a feminine vocal register. Specific translation choices are annotated in the text notes that follow each set of readings.

The *Women's Lectionary* is a multilayered work. In addition to the compilation of entirely new lectionary readings for the three-year cycle and composite single year, the production of entirely new gender-expansive translations and in the Psalms, explicitly feminine translations distinguish this lectionary. Gender-expansive means expanding collections of people, e.g., Israelites, children, nations, and even "people" to reflect gendered subgroups such as "the women, children, and men of Israel." (These translations generally place women before men in translation.) In every place where it can be reasonably inferred a group is composed of persons of more than one gender, I reflect that in the translation. Where gender neutral or inclusive language is used, it is used for male subjects; for example, "child" is used preferably to "son."

In genealogies, gender expansiveness means that lineages are presented matrilineally. For example, rather than "the God of Jacob," the *Lectionary* uses "the God of Rebekah's line." When supplemental language is added to establish the maternal genealogy, it is placed in brackets, i.e., "[Rachel-born] Benjamin." In each case, the original reading and translation choices are clearly identified in the text notes. For this project, explicitly feminine language is preferable to inclusive and neuter language, which obscures and erases women and girls. In addition, singular neuter gender and inclusive plurals do not disrupt the learned gender patterns, as many readers and hearers interpret them through their previously learned gender pattern and experience them as male. There is also some nonbinary language for human beings and God throughout the *Lectionary*; erasure of any gendered minority is contrary to the aims of this project.

Because so many readers pray the psalms devotionally, I wanted to offer an opportunity to hear those compositions speaking to, by, and about women and girls primarily and to encounter God in explicitly feminine language so readers of all genders will have the experience of praying to God in the feminine gender. Therefore, these translations of the psalms use feminine pronouns for God primarily, supplemented by nonbinary pronouns.

Following the practice of translators before me, I have adopted the practice of choosing descriptive expressions for the name of God and other divine names and titles. Given the most commonly used title for God in the Hebrew Scriptures, LORD (with the large and small caps indicating it is a substitutionary word for God's unpronounceable Most Holy Name represented by the letters YHWH) is the common male human slave holding title; it is not used for God in the *Lectionary*. The *Lectionary* preserves the ancient biblical and rabbinical practice of substituting something that can be said for that which cannot. (In some places the Hebrew Masoretic text uses Elohim, "God," as a substitute). In rabbinic and subsequent practice, *HaShem*, "the Name," is a common substitution; there are others.

Dr. Joel Rosenberg of Tufts University translated selected psalms for the Kol Haneshamah Reconstructionist prayer book. He renders the divine name using choices such as "THE ETERNAL," "THE ONE," and in Psalm 29, "THE ONE WHO CALLS over many waters." I was deeply impacted by these translations during the time I spent as a member of the Dorshei Derekh Reconstructionist minyan of the Germantown Jewish

Centre in Philadelphia and adopted and expanded the practice in my own translations for teaching, preaching, and publication. The translations in *Lectionary* draw from a robust list of options for naming God listed in an appendix. Some examples include: Ark of Safety, Dread God, Fire of Sinai, Rock Who Gave Us Birth, She Who Is Holy, etc. The list numbers more than one hundred and twenty. I preserve "Lord" for human beings, as that is the origin of the title, respectful address, and functionally the title refers to a slaveholder or other hierarchical role.

Similarly, in the Second Testament, I also reserve "Lord" for human beings—apart from Jesus. There are two sets of divine names and titles for the Christian Testament in the appendix. For Jesus I use: Anointed, God-born, Messiah, Rabbi, Redeemer, Savior, Son of Woman, Teacher, and Woman-Born. Son of Woman and Woman-Born both derive from the expressions previously and commonly translated as "son of man" (in the KJV) and more recently as "Mortal" or "the Human One" in translations like the NRSV and CEB. The underlying Greek expression, *huios tou anthropou*, means "son [male offspring] of a human" ("person of either sex" according to the standard authoritative BDAG lexicon); it also means "humankind" collectively. Whether one speaks or writes from a human, biological perspective or a theological one, the humanity of Jesus stems from his mother. Grammatically, Son of Woman and Woman-Born are both correct. Inasmuch as generic "man" is no longer used to represent humanity in totality, an argument can be made that Son of Woman is more theologically correct. The expression *huios tou anthropou* is not *de novo* to the Second Testament; it occurs in the First Testament in both Hebrew as *ben adam* and the same Greek expression in the LXX. *Ben adam* means son (and generic child) of humanity. In the First Testament and deuterocanonical books, I use woman-born where it is a human title signifying mortality. In at least one occurrence, in a poetic text, I translate it as "children of earth and Eve," given that the root of *adam* is *adamah*, "earth" (soil).

There is a second list of divine titles for God (apart from Jesus) used in the Second Testament. Those names and titles are: Creator, Creator of All, Dread God, Faithful One, Father, Holy One, Living God, Majesty, (our) Maker, Most High, One Parent, Provider, Shepherd-Of-All, Sovereign, and Weaver (of lights). While I do preserve "Father" in some places, I employ it much less frequently than it occurs in the text. I reserve it for places where the parentage of Jesus is being addressed specifically. As it pertains to God's whereabouts and way of being in this world and the world beyond this one, I eschew "king" and "kingdom" in the *Lectionary*. As with all human attempts to describe God, monarchal language is inadequate; it is particularly unsuitable in that it stems from a rather brutal human system of governance that is unnecessary in the space where God is. Instead, I utilize "reign" and "realm" individually or in combination and "majesty." (The latter is feminine in Greek and functions as a divine title in Hebrews 1:3 and 8:1.) When translating from the Hebrew Bible and deuterocanonical texts, I use "ruler" preferentially.

I take special care with translation choices for the Christian Testament because of the long history of anti-Judaism and anti-Semitism in biblical translation and interpretation and, in some cases, in the texts themselves. This lectionary intentionally excludes texts that blame Jews for the death of Jesus. The expression "the Jews" in Christian literature, including scripture, and in broader Christian discourse is very often negative. In the Greek New Testament, *Ioudaioi* can mean Jews, Judeans (people from Judea), or Jewish Christians in distinction from Gentile Christians. I use Judeans preferentially. In addition, because "scribes" can be easily misunderstood as simple copyists, I translate them as "biblical scholars" to make their underlying expertise more readily apparent.

Because scripture is read and heard and understood contextually, I am mindful of the ways in which the Scriptures have been read and heard and understood in the broader Western and specifically American contexts. Across both testaments and the writings in between, slavery is ubiquitous, including on the lips of Jesus. While many translations use "servant" preferentially, I find that to be dishonest given that the persons so named were owned, controlled, raped, impregnated, bred, sold, maimed, and killed. Even when the bondage was of short *durée* or to pay off a debt, the lord and master had complete control of the subjugated person's body and sometimes retained their children after their liberation. So while it is certain to produce discomfort in the reader and hearer, I preserve "slave" and invite the reader and preacher to wrestle with that term and its influence on and in crafting and defending the American slavocracy. Minimizing the footprint of slavery in the scriptures weakens the link between them and subsequent slaveholding societies and the churches that unite them and us. Readers are welcome to replace the word "slave" with "servant" knowing that doing so writes over the degree to which the scriptures are slaveholding texts with no imagination of the possibility of abolition. I would encourage congregations to talk about that language and why they will or will not retain it.

Also bearing in mind the American context in which these translations were produced and the related contexts in which they will be read, I chose to disrupt the traditional biblical language of light and white to mean good and dark and black to mean something negative or even evil. While there is no concept of race in the Hebrew Bible or Christian Testament and people and nations are not assessed based on skin color and physical characteristics, that language has been mapped onto human bodies in the postbiblical world, justifying dehumanizing treatment, including slavery and legalized discrimination, including in the Church. Not all dark/black language in the biblical text is negative. Where it indicates something positive or holy, I retain it; for example, "God dwells in thick darkness" throughout the Scriptures.

In sum, the translations in the *Lectionary*:

- Identify original language and translation choices in accompanying text notes.
- Indicates quoted material from the First Testament in the Christian Testament using italics.
- Identify supplemental expansive translations with brackets.
- Expand people groups to make the presence of women and girls explicit.
- Use feminine and nonbinary pronouns for God in the Psalms.
- List genealogical information maternally.
- Use expansive descriptive language for the name of God instead of "Lord."
- Limit use of "Father" to texts addressing Jesus's parentage.
- Replace "kingdom" with "reign" and "realm" or with "majesty" (ruler is used preferentially in the Hebrew Bible).
- Use "Judeans" rather than "Jews" preferentially where appropriate.
- Maintain slave language rather than weaken or minimize with "servant."
- Modulate "dark/black" negative language as "shadow" and "bleak/ness."

It is my hope that this lectionary will enrich the experience of hearing and reading scripture and invite readers and hearers into deeper study of the scriptures, their translation, and interpretation. It is also my hope that liturgy, the work of the people in service to God, will be a place where all people can experience themselves as fully created in the image of God whose words they hear through the scriptures, and in prayer and preaching.

THE LESSONS WITH COMMENTARY

Year A

ADVENT I

Genesis 1:1–5; Psalm 8; Romans 8:18–25; Matthew 24:32–44

Genesis 1:1 When beginning he, God, created the heavens and the earth, 2 the earth was
shapeless and formless and bleakness covered the face of the deep, while the Spirit of God,
she, fluttered over the face of the waters. 3 Then God said, "Let there be light"; and there was
light. 4 And God saw that the light was good; so God separated the light from the bleakness.
5 Then God called the light Day, and the bleakness God called Night. And there was evening
and there was morning, day one.

Psalm 8

1 WOMB OF LIFE, our Sovereign,
how exalted is your Name in all the earth!
2 Out of the mouths of children and nursing babes
your majesty is praised above the heavens.
3 You have founded a stronghold against your adversaries,
to put an end to the enemy and the avenger.
4 When I consider your heavens, the work of your fingers,
the moon and the stars you have established,
5 What are we that you should be mindful of us?
the woman-born that you attend to them?
6 You have made us a little lower than God;
you adorn us with glory and honor;
7 You give us mastery over the works of your hands;
you put all things under our feet:
8 All sheep and oxen,
even the wild beasts of the field,
9 The birds of the air, the fish of the sea,
and whatsoever walks in the paths of the sea.
10 WOMB OF LIFE, our Sovereign,
how exalted is your Name in all the earth!

Romans 8:18 I consider that the sufferings of this present time are not worth comparing
with the glory about to be revealed to us. 19 For the creation waits with eager longing for the
revealing of the daughters and sons of God; 20 for the creation was subjected to futility, not of

its own will but by the will of the one who subjected it, in hope [21] that the creation itself will be set free from its bondage to decay and will obtain the freedom of the glory of the daughters and sons of God. [22] We know that the whole creation has been groaning in labor pains until now; [23] and not only the creation, but we ourselves, who have the first fruits of the Spirit, groan inwardly while we wait for adoption, the redemption of our bodies. [24] For in hope we were saved. Now hope that is seen is not hope. For who hopes for what is seen? [25] But if we hope for what we do not see, we wait for it with patience.

Matthew 24:32 Jesus said, "From the fig tree learn its lesson: as soon as its branch becomes tender and puts forth its leaves, you know that summer is near. [33] So also, when you see all these things, you know that the Son of Woman is near, at the very gates. [34] Truly I tell you, this generation will not pass away until all these things have taken place. [35] Heaven and earth will pass away, but my words will not pass away.

[36] "But about that day and hour no one knows, neither the angels of heaven, nor the Son, but only the Most High God. [37] For as the days of Noah were, so will be the coming of the Son of Woman. [38] For as in those days before the flood they were eating and drinking, marrying and giving in marriage, until the day Noah entered the ark, [39] and they knew nothing until the flood came and swept them all away, so too will be the coming of the Son of Woman. [40] Then two will be in the field; one will be taken and one will be left. [41] Two women will be grinding meal together; one will be taken and one will be left. [42] Keep awake therefore, for you do not know on what day your Redeemer is coming. [43] But understand this: if the owner of the house had known in what part of the night the thief was coming, the owner would have stayed awake and would not have let the house be broken into. [44] Therefore you also must be ready, for the Son of Woman is coming at an unexpected hour.

PROCLAMATION

Text Notes

In Genesis 1:1, God and God's verb, "create," are grammatically masculine. In Genesis 1:2, the Spirit of God and her verb are grammatically feminine. While this project generally eschews masculine God language with few exceptions, I preserve it here with the feminine language erased by virtually every translation to note God's introduction in the scriptures transcends the singular masculine gender to which God is often reduced.

This Psalter names God in varying forms when rendering the divine Name. In rabbinic practice, God's most holy name most commonly rendered "Lord" is not spelled out—the theoretical spelling is uncertain—it is substituted with a term of reverence that varies in classical literature and liturgical practice: *Adonai* (Lord) and *HaShem* (the Name) are the most common. Following that practice and influenced by developments in liturgical language in Christian and Jewish contexts, the God language here reflects the immediate context. (See the translation of Joel Rosenburg in the *Kol HaNeshamah* seder [prayer book] of the Reconstruction movement in Judaism.) In Psalm 8:5 the text says "a little lower than God," but previous generations of pious translators used "angels" instead.

In the Epistle the inclusive "children" is expanded to "daughters and sons" to make the daughters of God visible and not merely assumed. Two words are used: the masculine plural "sons" functioning as an inclusive plural in verse 19 and the neuter plural "children" in verse 21.

The expressions previously traditionally translated as "Son of Man" in Psalm 8:5, today's Gospel, and throughout the text in Hebrew, Aramaic, and Greek all mean "descended/born of humankind." In each language the expressions include descent from women, as the terms for humanity are inclusive. With regard to Jesus, "Son of Woman" is particularly apt. The title in verse 33 is transposed from verse 30 to concretize the pronoun, "he." "Lord," a hierarchical title used for slaveholders, men with status, and God in the New Testament derives in part from the pious practice of substituting a title for God's name. Its use for Jesus signals his authority and identifies him with God. Here "Redeemer" as the divine title makes explicit the theme that permeates these readings.

Preaching Prompts

All of God's creation is good and beloved; this extends to the earth and her creatures and all of God's children, daughters and sons—and considering the gender-full first human—nonbinary siblings alike. As Advent prepares the Church to receive an incarnate God, the emphasis on the goodness of creation is a powerful reminder that human flesh, particularly womanflesh, is part of that good and beloved creation. Love and longing characterize these texts. God longs for the redemption of the world as, and more than, creation longs to be redeemed. This is an Advent longing. Though we long for the culmination of our redemption, we wait with hope and patience, not knowing the day or hour when Christ will return in the glory that crowned creation at its birth. These Advent readings see women created in the image of God, as the font of the coming incarnate redemption rather than the cause of the world's brokenness. The use of feminine and masculine God-language in the biblical text provides an opportunity to expand our own. Though binary language is the vernacular of the text, the introduction of a God who transcends a single gender category reveals the limitations of those categories for God and for those created in her, hir, his, zir, our, their image.

ADVENT II

Isaiah 54:1–8; Psalm 113; Hebrews 11:8–13; Luke 1:5–17, 24–25

Isaiah 54

1 Sing childless woman,
never-given-birth-woman;
Woman, break out a song and rejoice, woman,
never-in-labor-woman.
For more are the children of the devastated woman
than the children of the espoused woman,
says the Giver of Life.
2 Woman expand the place of your tent, woman
and the curtains of your sanctuary, woman,
extend them—do not hold back, woman!
Woman, lengthen your ropes, woman,
and woman, secure your stakes, woman.
3 For right and left you will break through, woman
and your seed, woman, will inherit nations,
and in devastated cities they will dwell.
4 Do not fear, woman
for you will not be ashamed woman;
do not feel humiliated woman
for you will not be disgraced woman.
For the shame of your youth woman,
you will forget woman,
and the stigma of your widowhood, woman,
you will never remember, woman.
5 For your spouse woman,
is the One who made you woman.
SOVEREIGN-COMMANDER of winged warriors
is God's name.
The Holy One of Israel
will redeem you woman—
who is called God of all the earth.
6 For like a wife abandoned and abject in spirit—
The Faithful God has called you woman—
For you were a rejected young bride,
says your God, woman.

7 For a brief space I abandoned you woman,
but in great mother-love I will gather you woman.
8 For a minute moment
I hid my face briefly from you woman.
But in eternally bonded love
I will mother-love you woman.
Your Redeemer, Woman, has spoken.

Psalm 113

1 Hallelujah! Give praise, you slaves of the MOST HIGH;
praise the Name of the WISDOM OF THE AGES.
2 Let the Name of the HOLY ONE OF OLD be blessed,
from this time forth forevermore.
3 From the rising of the sun to its going down
the Name of the AUTHOR OF LIFE is praised.
4 SHE WHO IS WISDOM is high above all nations,
and her glory above the heavens.
5 Who is like the MOTHER OF ALL our God, who sits enthroned on high,
yet bends down to behold the heavens and the earth?
6 She takes up the weak out of the dust
and lifts up the poor from the ashes.
7 She sets them with the rulers,
with the rulers of her people.
8 She makes the woman of a childless house
to be a joyful mother of children.

Hebrews 11:8 By faith Abraham obeyed when he was called to go out to a place that he
was to receive as an inheritance, so he set out, not knowing where he was going. 9 By faith he
lived as a stranger in the land he had been promised, as in a foreign land, living in tents, as
did Isaac and Jacob, who were joint heirs with him of the same promise. 10 For he was waiting for the city that having foundations, whose architect and builder is God. 11 By faith even
though Sarah herself was barren, she received power to knit together seed in spite of length
of life because Abraham considered God faithful who had promised. 12 Therefore from one
person—and that one practically dead—descendants were born, "as the multitude of the stars
of heaven and as the innumerable grains of sand by the shore of the sea." 13 In faith died these
all without receiving the promises, but from a distance they saw and welcomed them. They
acknowledged that they were strangers and sojourners on the earth.

Luke 1:5 And it was in the days of Herod king of Judea, there was a priest named Zechariah,
who belonged to the lineage of Abijah. His wife was a descendant of Aaron, and her name was

Elizabeth. 6 Both of them were righteous before God, living according to all the commandments and righteous requirements of the Sovereign God blamelessly. 7 Now they had no child because Elizabeth was barren, and they both were advanced in age.

8 And it happened that when Zechariah was serving as priest and his order had the service before God, 9 according to the custom of the priesthood, he was chosen by lot to offer incense and he entered the sanctuary of the Holy God. 10 The whole assembly of the people was praying outside at the time of the incense offering. 11 There appeared to Zechariah a messenger of the Living God, standing to the right of the altar of incense. 12 Now Zechariah was shaken when he saw the messenger and fear overwhelmed him. 13 But the messenger said to him, "Fear not, Zechariah, for your prayer has been heard. Your wife Elizabeth will give birth to a son for you, and you will call his name John. 14 You will have joy and gladness, and many at his birth will rejoice, 15 for he will be great in the sight of the Sovereign God. Wine and strong drink he must not drink. He will be filled with the Holy Spirit from his mother's womb. 16 He will turn many of the women and men of Israel to the Holy One their God. 17 He will go before the Holy God with the spirit and power of Elijah to turn the hearts of parents to their children, and the disobedient to the wisdom of the righteous, to prepare for the Redeeming God a people made ready."

24 After those days Elizabeth his wife conceived, and she hid herself for five months. She said, 25 "This is the Holy God's doing; God has done for me when God looked favorably on me and took away my disgrace among humankind."

PROCLAMATION

Text Notes

My previously published translation of Isaiah 54 above makes visible all of the grammatically feminine words describing and addressing the woman in the passage. There are three to seven of these forms in each verse of the chapter (save the verse in which God speaks in the first person after this lesson). "Sovereign-Commander of winged warriors" in verse 5 communicates that the "hosts" of heaven were understood to be a divine army; later some understood them as angels. Others also identify them with the stars and planets. The verb *racham* conveys feelings that emerge from the *rechem*, the womb in verses 7–8, echoing the relationship between the body part and associated feeling in headache, heartsick, etc. It will be translated as womb-love or mother-love throughout this volume.

Depending on the translation one chooses, either Sarah or Abraham is the subject of Hebrews 11:11 (because Greek verbs are not gendered like Hebrew verbs). In keeping with the aims of this project, women and girls are centered in translation and interpretation.

In Luke 1:15 the Greek presents John's rule of life "from his mother's womb." Both the NRSV and CEB omit mother and womb and use "from before his birth."

This is not only an erasure of Elizabeth, but it disembodies birth, very much at odds with the coming Incarnation. For this reason, I translate both Hebrew Greek verbs for childbirth as "to give birth," rather than "to bear." Lastly, the language around her seclusion is quite strong; "she hid herself," a potentially powerful sermon prompt.

Preaching Prompts

These lessons offer an opportunity to talk about God's promises and faithfulness to and through women in the vernacular of the Hebrew Bible: marriage and children. While the emphasis on pregnancy and birth is a crucial component of the Advent journey, these experiences do not characterize all women and can be heard as essentializing or even stigmatizing in addition to being painful for some. These texts offer space to talk about what God's love and fidelity look like beyond that limited theological frame as we hold Christ's second Advent in conversation with the first.

Some will find the repetition of the word "woman" in Isaiah 54 challenging, which in turn provides opportunity for reflection and discussion: Does it matter that the poet crafted this text using explicit feminine language repetitiously? How and why does that choice affect how the passage is heard when read in conversation with another translation? Focusing on Sarah in Hebrews does not negate how androcentric the list and larger text is. Who is missing from the list and how might they talk about God's fidelity? Luke demonstrates that the Advent of Jesus is a community affair: Elizabeth, Zechariah, John a divine messenger, and God—all before we get to Mary, Joseph, and the Holy Spirit—facilitating a conversation about our work toward the next appearance of the incarnate God in our world.

ADVENT III

Ruth 4:11–17; Psalm 78:1–8; Galatians 4:1–7; Matthew 1:1–16

Ruth 4:11 All the women and men who were at the gate, along with the elders, said, "We
are witnesses. May the FAITHFUL GOD grant that the woman who is coming into your house
be like Rachel and Leah; the two of them built up the house of Israel. May you prosper in
Ephrathah and establish a lineage in Bethlehem; 12 and, may your house, through the children
that the FOUNT OF LIFE will give you by this young woman, be like the house of Perez, whom
Tamar gave birth to for Judah." 13 So Boaz took Ruth as his own for a wife. He came to her and
the SOURCE OF LIFE granted her a pregnancy, and she gave birth to a son. 14 Then the women
said to Naomi, "Blessed be the FAITHFUL GOD, who has not deprived you this day of next-of-
kin; and may the child's name be renowned in Israel! 15 He shall be to you a restorer of life and
a provider in your latter years; for your daughter-in-law has given birth to him, she who loves
you, she who is more to you than seven sons." 16 Then Naomi took the child and laid him in
her bosom, and she fostered him. 17 The neighbor-women gave him a name, saying, "A son

has been born to Naomi." They named him Obed; he became the father of Jesse, the father of David."

Psalm 78

1 Give ear, my people, to my teaching;
incline your ear to the utterances of my mouth.
2 I will open my mouth in a proverb;
I will utter riddles from of old,
3 Which we have heard and known,
and which our mothers and fathers have told us.
4 We will not hide them from their daughters and sons;
we will recount to generations to come
the praiseworthy deeds of SHE WHO SPEAKS LIFE,
and her might, and the wonderful works she has done.
5 She gave her decrees for Rebekah's descendants
and placed teaching among Sarah's offspring,
which she commanded their mothers and fathers
to make known to their daughters and sons.
6 In order that a coming generation, children yet to be, might know,
and will rise up and tell their daughters and sons.
7 Then they will put their confidence in God,
and not forget the works of God, but will keep her commandments;
8 And not be like their ancestors, a stubborn and rebellious generation,
a generation whose heart was not steadfast,
and whose spirit was not faithful to God.

Galatians 4:1 I say that as long as heirs are minors, they are no better than slaves, though they are the masters of all; 2 but they remain under guardians and trustees until the time set by the father. 3 So also for us; while we were minors, we were enslaved by the constitutive elements of the world. 4 But when the fullness of time had come, God sent God's own Son, born of a woman, born under the law, 5 to redeem those who were under the law, so that we might receive adoption like children. 6 And because you are children, God has sent the Spirit of God's own Son into our hearts, crying, "Abba! Father!" 7 So you are no longer a slave but a child, and if a child then also an heir, through God.

Matthew 1:1–16 (alternative)

A genealogy of Jesus Christ, the son of Miriam, the daughter of Anna:
Sarah was the mother of Isaac,
And Rebekah was the mother of Jacob,
Leah was the mother of Judah,
Tamar was the mother of Perez.

The names of the mothers of Hezron, Ram, Amminadab,
Nahshon and Salmon have been lost.
Rahab was the mother of Boaz,
and Ruth was the mother of Obed.
Obed's wife, whose name is unknown, bore Jesse.
The wife of Jesse was the mother of David.
Bathsheba was the mother of Solomon,
Naamah, the Ammonite, was the mother of Rehoboam.
Maacah was the mother of Abijam and the grandmother of Asa.
Azubah was the mother of Jehoshaphat.
The name of Jehoram's mother is unknown.
Athaliah was the mother of Ahaziah,
Zibiah of Beersheba, the mother of Joash.
Jecoliah of Jerusalem bore Uzziah,
Jerusha bore Jotham; Ahaz's mother is unknown.
Abi was the mother of Hezekiah,
Hephzibah was the mother of Manasseh,
Meshullemeth was the mother of Amon,
Jedidah was the mother of Josiah.
Zebidah was the mother of Jehoiakim,
Nehushta was the mother of Jehoiachin,
Hamutal was the mother of Zedekiah.
Then the deportation of Babylon took place.
After the deportation to Babylon
the names of the mothers go unrecorded.
These are their sons:
Jechoniah, Shealtiel, Zerubbabel,
Abiud, Eliakim, Azor and Zadok,
Achim, Eliud, Eleazar,
Matthan, Jacob, and Joseph, the husband of Miriam.
Of her was born Jesus who is called Christ.
The sum of generations is there: fourteen from Sarah to David's mother;
fourteen from Bathsheba to the Babylonian deportation;
and fourteen from the Babylonian deportation to Miriam, the mother of Christ.

("A Genealogy of Jesus Christ" was compiled by Ann Patrick Ware of the Women's Liturgy Group of New York, who has graciously put this text in the public domain for all to use.)

PROCLAMATION

Text Notes

The variety of names for God chosen to express the unpronounceable Name reflect the actions of God throughout. In Ruth 4:14 it is not entirely clear that it is the child whose name will be renowned. There are too many pronouns and not enough nouns with which to clearly identify them. The other option is that God's name will be renowned in verse 14. It is clear that the next verse refers to the child.

In verse 5 of the psalm, Rebekah and Sarah replace Jacob and Israel and "teaching conveys the fullest sense of Torah, rather than "law."

In general, this volume will preserve "Father" in the Gospel when Jesus says it or it pertains specifically to his Sonship/paternity. Likewise, this volume will not whitewash slavery in the text and its world by softening it to servitude. That the enslaved could be beaten, killed, raped, and forced to breed more enslaved persons makes clear that slavery and its vocabulary is the appropriate translation for the assorted terms across the canon. The implications of slave language as normative in the text is something with which readers and hearers must wrestle honestly, particularly in light of the transatlantic trafficking of human persons and legacy of the American slavocracy, including in churches and denominations (discussed further below).

Preaching Prompts

On the third Sunday in Advent, as in Lent, purple (or blue) softens to rose or pink for Rose Sunday, on which it is appropriate to reflect on the ever-blessed Virgin, the tender love of God, and other maternal themes. Naomi's fostering of Obed as her son, replacing those lost to death through Ruth's marriage to a kinsman, can be read in this light if done carefully without romanticizing the relationship between Ruth and Boaz. That relationship is about survival, particularly Naomi's need for security in her latter years. Ruth is at best a willing pawn given her survival is at stake. However, it should not be forgotten that Ruth and her sister-in-law were abducted into Naomi's family on her watch. (The verb that details their unions is an abduction verb and not the regular marriage expression used of Ruth and Boaz.)

Ruth and the Gospel use genealogy to demonstrate the faithfulness of God to Israel through the house of David. Patricia Ware's reframing of the Gospel makes women and their pregnancies and births more visible in the "begots." Yet motherhood remains a challenging category with which to elevate women. Not all women will mother, wish to mother, or were even mothered well. And women who do mother are so much more than their children and their mothering. These lineages point to a coming messiah, a divine visitation whose incarnation sanctifies all human bodies as God-space.

Slave language in the Gospels and Epistles is ugly. It is tempting to soften it to servant, woman servant, maidservant, etc. The blood more than six million Africans spilled in the Middle Passage cries out with the blood of every other enslaved person across time and space. We must confront slavery in the text and in the churches and institutions built on it and its rhetoric. We can retain the image of being adopted by God without a straw comparison to an enslaved person—who cannot even be considered a child according to Paul's rhetoric—to establish our relative worth.

The psalm calls for us to teach the truth of our histories and experiences to our children. And we should without white washing the androcentric, patriarchal, and slaveholding culture of the text—even when grouped around the presence of women.

ADVENT IV

Susanna 31–44; Psalm 34:1–9; Titus 3:4–7; Matthew 1:18–25

(There are two versions of the story of Susanna, the older Septuagint version, LXX, and the one Theodotion revised, traditionally used by the church. Both are below.)

LXX Susanna 31 Now Susanna was an exquisite woman, very much so. [32] Scoundrels commanded her uncovered, so that they might sate their lust on her beauty. [33] Those who were with
her—her mother, father, five hundred enslaved women and men, and her four children—and all
who knew her wept. [34] Then the elders and judges rose before the people; laid their hands on
her head. [35] But her heart trusted in the Holy One her God, and she lifted her head and wept
speaking within herself. "Holy One, everlasting God, you who know all things before their
beginning, you know that I have not done what these men are maliciously alleging against
me." The Holy One heard her plea.

[36] The two elders said, "We were walking around in her husband's garden, [37] and as we
were going around the walkway, we saw this woman reclining with a man. And while we
stood, we saw them having intercourse together. [38] They did not know that we stood there.
Then we agreed among ourselves, saying, 'Let us find out who they are.' [39] We approached and
recognized her, but the young man fled, covered up. [40] Now, we seized this woman; we asked
her, 'Who is the man?' [41] and she would not tell us who he was. These things we testify." And
as they were elders and judges of the people, the whole assembly believed them. [44] Now look
here! There was an angel of God as she was being taken off to be executed.

Theo Susanna 31 Now Susanna was exquisite, very much so, beautiful and shapely.
[32] Scoundrels commanded that she be uncovered—for she was covered—so that they might
sate their lust on her beauty. [33] But those who were with her—her parents, her children, and
all of her relatives—and all who saw her began weeping.

34 Then the two elders stood up in the midst of the people; they put their hands on her
head. 35 Now she wept, looking up to heaven, because her heart trusted in the Holy One.
36 Then the elders said, "We were walking in the garden alone; this woman came in with two
enslaved girls and shut the garden gate and dismissed the enslaved girls. 37 And a young man,
who was hiding, came to her and reclined with her. 38 We were in the corner of the garden;
we saw the lawlessness, we ran to them. 39 And although we saw them having intercourse, we
were not able to overpower him because he was stronger than we, and when he had opened
the gates he ran away. 40 We seized this woman, we asked who the young man was, 41 and she
was not willing to tell us. These things we testify." They were elders of the people and judges;
the assembly believed them and they condemned her to death.

42 Then Susanna cried out with a loud voice and said, "O everlasting God, you are the
one who knows hidden things, who knows all things before their genesis, 43 you know that
they have testified lies against me. See here! I will die, though nothing they have wickedly said
against me have I done!"

44 And the Holy One heeded her voice.

Psalm 34:1–9

1 I will bless She Who is God at all times;
her praise shall ever be in my mouth.
2 I will glory in She Who is Strength;
let the humble hear and rejoice.
3 Proclaim with me the greatness of She Who is Exalted
and let us exalt her Name together.
4 I sought She Who Saves, and she answered me
and delivered me out of all my terror.
5 Look upon her and be radiant,
and let not your faces be ashamed.
6 I called in my affliction and She Who Hears heard me
and saved me from all my troubles.
7 The messenger of She Who Saves encompasses those who revere her,
and she will deliver them.
8 Taste and see that She Who is Delight is good;
happy are they who trust in her!
9 Revere She Who is God, you that are her saints,
for those who revere her lack nothing.

Titus 3:4 When the graciousness and loving kindness of God our Savior appeared, 5 God
saved us through the water of rebirth and renewal by the Holy Spirit, not because of any
works of righteousness that we had done, but according to God's mercy. 6 This Spirit God
poured out on us abundantly through Jesus Christ our Savior, 7 so that, having been justified
by God's grace, we might become heirs according to the hope of life eternal.

Matthew 1:18 Now this is how the birth of Jesus the Messiah happened: When his mother Mary had been betrothed to Joseph, but before they came together, she was found to have a child in her womb from the Holy Spirit. 19 Joseph her husband was a just man and unwilling to shame her; he wanted to divorce her secretly. 20 But when he deliberated this, suddenly an angel of the Most High God appeared to him in a dream and said, "Joseph, son of David, do not be afraid to take Mary as your wife, for in her is conceived a child from the Holy Spirit. 21 She will give birth to a son, and you are to name him Jesus, for he will save his people from their sins." 22 All this happened to fulfill what had been spoken by the Most High God through the prophet: 23 "Look now! The virgin shall conceive a child in her womb and give birth to a son, and they shall call him Emmanuel," which translated means, "God is with us." 24 When Joseph got up from sleep, he did as the angel of the Most High God commanded him. He took her as his wife, 25 yet did not know her sexually until her birthing of a son and named him Jesus.

PROCLAMATION

Text Notes

The story of Susanna is part of the longer Greek tradition of Daniel. The first Bible of the Church included the Septuagint, LXX, accounting for the different sequence of books than the Hebrew Bible and contributing to the number of books resulting in the eighty-book canon of the Episcopal Church shared broadly by other Anglican, Orthodox, and Catholic Christians. The older LXX and the version most commonly used, Theodotion, are above. In the LXX version above, I have added the details of Susanna's retinue in verse 33 from their earlier mention in verse 30.

Biblical Hebrew does not have a word that means simply "divine winged being," what many conceive when they read or hear the word "angel." Instead, Hebrew uses a word, *mal'akh,* that means "messenger," whether the one bearing the message is human or divine. Further, these messengers are distinct from cherubim and seraphim—consider them different species; they are never interchanged—and as in the story of Jacob's ladder, do not have wings. Greek *aggelos* has the same sense of human or divine messenger, and none of the angels of the New Testament are described with wings. There is one distinct angel among the host of heaven, the angel of God (or the Lord) in other translations, here in Psalm 34:7, the angel of Wisdom. Many scholars understand this angel to be God in disguise so that she can be among her people without her holiness harming them. (I say it is God in drag.)

Curiously, "child" is missing from verses 18 and 20 of the Gospel. *Apolusai* has the sense of legally ending a contract or marriage, hence "divorce" in verse 19. Often softened to "quietly," the literal meaning of *lathra* is "secretly"; see Herod calling the magi secretly in the next chapter.

Matthew 1:23 quotes the LXX version of Isaiah 7:14; in the two Greek texts the young woman is a virgin, *parthenos*, and contemporaneously pregnant having a child "in womb," *en gastri*, and will give birth, future tense. This is at odds with the Hebrew text in which the young woman, *almah*, is not specified as virginal, cultural expectations notwithstanding. Further, in Isaiah in Hebrew the young woman is pregnant at the time of Isaiah's speech: he uses the adjective "pregnant," not a verbal form. Christian translations often change the text to support traditional teaching.

Preaching Prompts

The presence of angels all around links these texts and makes them particularly suitable for Advent 4. They also offer space to talk about the ways in which the biblical text and its interpreters are so often fixated on women's bodies and sexuality as well as sexual assault and sexual harassment.

The LXX lesson leaves the reader in suspense. What will happen to the falsely accused Susanna? Will she be executed for adultery? The suspense is deliberate, designed to draw the reader and hearer to the very real consequences faced by Mary with her pregnancy. As with Mary, Susanna is not alone; she is attended by an angel of God. Instead of an angel, in Theodotion's version, the lesson ends with God hearing Susanna cry. Each version gives the reader-hearer the assurance that God attends her daughter and each gives reason to hope that God will intervene. In each we are left with a woman in need of deliverance and dependent on God for that salvific act.

The psalmist offers testimony to those who like Susanna and Mary find themselves in desperate straits and is similarly attended by an angel in her moment of difficulty, verse 7. Susanna's ultimate deliverance, though beyond the lesson, foreshadows the deliverance presented in Titus, a gracious and loving act of a gracious and loving God.

The Gospel treads lightly around the consequences should the betrothed but not married young woman be found to be pregnant, particularly when her intended denied paternity, tantamount to an accusation of adultery. In spite of the stoning provision in the Torah, there are no stories of women or men actually being stoned for adultery in spite of its fairly regular occurrence in the scriptures (not until Jesus breaks up an attempted stoning later). We cannot say with certainty that she would have been stoned, but it was a possibility. Her shame would have made it unlikely for her to marry and therefore be socially and economically vulnerable, relegated to the margins of society.

It is in this context that Jesus is born and named "The Holy One Saves." God's saving work did not begin with Jesus; we see it borne witness to throughout the scriptures. Jesus is the continuation and embodiment of that salvation.

CHRISTMAS I

Isaiah 26:16–19; Psalm 68:4–13; 1 Thessalonians 4:13–18; Luke 2:1–14 or 2:1–20

Isaiah 26:16 HOLY ONE, in distress they sought you,
they pressed out a whispered prayer
when your chastening was on them.
17 Just as an expectant mother
writhes-in-labor and cries out in her pangs
when her birthing time is near;
thus were we because of you, Holy One.
18 We too were expectant, we writhed-in-labor,
but it was as though we birthed only wind.
No victories have we won on earth,
neither do the inhabitants of the world fall.
19 Your dead shall live; their corpses shall rise.
Awake and sing for joy you who dwell in the dust!
For your dew is a radiant dew,
and the earth shall release those long dead.

Psalm 68:4–11

4 Sing to God, sing praises to her Name;
exalt her who rides upon the clouds;
HOLY is her Name, rejoice before her!
5 Mother of orphans and defender of widows,
is God in her holy habitation!
6 God settles the solitary in a home bringing prisoners into prosperity;
while the rebellious shall live in a wasteland.
7 God, when you marched before your people,
when you moved out through the wilderness,
8 the earth shook, even the heavens poured down,
at the presence of God, the One of Sinai,
at the presence of God, the God of Israel.
9 Rain in abundance, God, you showered abroad;
when your heritage grew weary you prepared rest.
10 Your creatures found a dwelling in her;
God, you provided in your goodness for the oppressed.
11 The AUTHOR OF LIFE gave the word;
the women who proclaim the good news are a great army.

1 Thessalonians 4:13 Now we do not want you to be ignorant, sisters and brothers, about those who have fallen asleep, so that you might not grieve as those do who have no hope. 14 For since we believe that Jesus died and rose, even so they who sleep, will God by Jesus, bring with him. 15 For this we declare to you by the word of the Most High God, that we who are alive, who remain until the coming of Jesus, will not precede those who have fallen asleep. 16 For Jesus himself, with a command, in the voice of the archangel and with the trumpet of God, will descend from heaven, and the dead in Christ will rise first. 17 Then we who are alive who are left, together with them, will be caught up in the clouds to meet Jesus in the air; and so we will be with Jesus forever. 18 Therefore comfort one another with these words.

Luke 2:1 Now it happened in those days that a decree went out from Caesar Augustus that all the world should be registered (for taxation). 2 This was the first registration and occurred while Quirinius was governor of Syria. 3 So all went to be registered; each to their own towns. 4 Joseph also went up from Galilee, out of the city of Nazareth in to Judea, to the city of David called Bethlehem, for he was from the house and heritage of David. 5 He went to be registered with Mary, to whom he was betrothed and who was pregnant. 6 So it was, that, while they were there, the time came for her to birth her child. 7 And she gave birth to her firstborn son and swaddled him, and laid him in a manger, because there was no place for them in the inn.

8 Shepherds were in that region there staying in the fields, keeping watch over their flock by night. 9 Then an angel of the Most High God came upon them, and the glory of the Living God shone around them, and they were greatly terrified. 10 But the angel said to them, "Fear not. Look! For I proclaim to you good news of great joy for all the people: 11 For there is born to you this day a Savior who is the Messiah, the Sovereign God, in the city of David. 12 This will be a sign for you: you will find a baby swaddled and lying in a manger." 13 And immediately there was with the angel a multitude of the heavenly array, praising God and saying,

14 "Glory to God in the highest heaven,
and on earth peace among peoples whom God favors!"

15 And it happened when the angels had departed from them into heaven, the shepherds said to one another, "Let us go now to Bethlehem and see this thing that has come to be, which the Sovereign God has made known to us." 16 So they came hurrying and found Mary and Joseph, and the baby lying in the manger. 17 Now seeing this, they made known what had been spoken to them about this child. 18 And all who heard marveled at what was spoken by the shepherds to them. 19 But Mary preserved all these words and pondered them in her heart. 20 The shepherds returned, glorifying and praising God for all they had heard and seen; it was just as it had been told them.

PROCLAMATION

Text Notes

The psalm portion ends with women proclaiming the good news of deliverance using the verbs that will come to mean "proclaim the gospel" in Hebrew and Greek (the LXX uses *euaggelizo*). Unfortunately, NRSV, RSV, CEB, and KJV obscure that this "company of preachers" is exclusively female.

The epistle uses "Lord" repeatedly in such a way that it is not clear whether the author means God or Jesus. The translation above seeks to clarify the referents; however, the reader should be aware of the likely intentional ambiguity.

Preaching Prompts

The Hebrew Scriptures offer a variety of positions on life after death, including "sleep" to which all succumb, and none rise (see Job 14:10–12, 14). This unit of Isaiah uses the language of pregnancy and birth to speak of life beyond death. This first reading for Christmas brings images of a heavily pregnant woman in conversation with the heavily pregnant and laboring Virgin in the Gospel—though the text and tradition gloss over or minimalize her travail. The pregnant woman is the people who have not been able to deliver themselves or have someone to deliver them—rather than a deliverer, they have only produced wind. God is perhaps midwife here. Because of God's response to her people's prayers across the ages, the equally heavily pregnant earth will one day give birth to the dead.

In both the first lesson and psalm, there is water that renews and refreshes dry places. In the regendered psalm, God is the mother of orphans (fatherless children in Hebrew idiom), protector of widows, and provides homes (families) for the lonely. She is also sovereign of the skies, source of rain, and shepherd of her people. The women who functioned as town criers, proclaiming good news of victory in times of war, proclaim the good news of God's providence.

The Epistle takes up the theme of the dead rising and makes it a promise guaranteed by Jesus's own resurrection. Each of these texts with its focus on birth, life, and life beyond frames the Gospel and its presentation of the good news of Mary's child and the portents of his birth which she pondered.

CHRISTMAS II

Isaiah 66:10–13; Psalm 103:1–17; 1 Peter 1:22–2:3; Luke 2:15–20 or 2:1–20

Isaiah 66:10 Rejoice with Jerusalem, and celebrate with her
all you who love her;
rejoice with her in joy,
all who mourn deeply over her;

11 in order that you all may nurse and be satisfied
from her comforting breast;
that you all may drink deeply and delight yourselves
from the glory of her breast.
12 For so says the Holy One of Old:
Watch! I will extend to her flourishing like a river,
and the wealth of the nations like an overflowing stream;
and you all shall nurse and be carried on her arm,
and you all shall be bounced on her knees.
13 As a mother comforts her child,
so will I comfort you all;
you all shall be comforted in Jerusalem.

Psalm 103:1–17

1 Bless the FOUNT OF WISDOM, O my soul,
and all that is within me, bless her holy Name.
2 Bless the FOUNT OF WISDOM, O my soul,
and forget not all her benefits.
3 She forgives all your sins
and heals all your infirmities;
4 She redeems your life from the grave
and crowns you with mercy and lovingkindness;
5 She satisfies you with good things,
and your youth is renewed like an eagle's.
6 SHE WHO IS WISDOM executes righteousness
and judgment for all who are oppressed.
7 She made her ways known to Miriam and Moses
and her works to the children of Israel.
8 WISDOM'S womb is full of love and faithfulness,
slow to anger and overflowing with faithful love.
9 She will not always accuse us,
nor will she keep her anger forever.
10 She has not dealt with us according to our sins,
nor rewarded us according to our wickedness.
11 For as the heavens are high above the earth,
so indomitable is her faithful love upon those who revere her.
12 As far as the east is from the west,
so far has she removed our sins from us.
13 As a mother's love for her children flows from her womb,
so too does WISDOM'S love for those who revere her flow from her womb.

14 For she herself knows whereof we are made;
She remembers that we are but dust.
15 Our days are like the grass;
we flourish like a flower of the field;
16 When the wind goes over it, it is gone,
and its place shall know it no more.
17 But the faithful love of SHE WHO IS WISDOM endures forever
on those who revere her,
and her righteousness on children's children.

1 Peter 1:22 Now that you have purified your souls by your obedience to the truth so that you have the love without pretense of children raised together; from a pure heart love one another persistently. 23 You have been born again, not of corruptible seed but of incorruptible seed through the living and enduring word of God. 24 For:

*"All flesh is like grass**
and all its glory like the flower of grass.
The grass withers,
and the flower falls,
25 *but the word of the Living God abides forever."*

This is the word that was proclaimed to you as good news. 2:1 Lay aside, therefore, all malice, and all deceit, pretense, envy, and all slander. 2 Like newborn babies, long for the pure spiritual milk, so that by it you may grow into salvation—3 if you have tasted that the Sovereign God is good.

See Gospel Reading in Christmas I.

PROCLAMATION

Text Notes

The poet responsible for Isaiah 66 seems to have reached beyond the Hebrew language for the expression "glory of her breast" in verse 11. The underlying expression "teat" or "udder of glory" may well have come from Akkadian and has an Arabic cognate (see the corresponding entry in the *Dictionary of Classical Hebrew*). In verse 12, "flourishing" is a better, less-materialistic reading of *shalom* than "prosperity."

The one comforted by their mother in Isaiah 66:13 is a man; the grammar of his passive comforting relegates his mother to the end of the sentence and makes him the focus: "As a man is comforted by his mother . . ." Common convention (JPS, NRSV, CEB) inverts the sentence, "as a mother comforts. . . ." Mother-love in

* All citations, direct quotes, from the first testament are italicized.

Psalm 103:13 is attributed to a father: "As a father mother-loves his children" (using the verbal form of the noun "womb"). The verse could be translated: "As a father loves his children with a mother's love. . . ." As with Isaiah 66, the maternal image, here womb-love, is also attributed to God.

First Peter 1:22 uses *philadelphia*, sibling-love, where I have translated "children raised together" rather than "sisters and brothers" to avoid excluding reader-hearers who do not identify with a binary understanding of gender. The divine mother's milk is described as "spiritual," a somewhat elliptical rendering of *logikos*, which has to do with "carefully thought through, thoughtful" deliberations particularly in religious contexts. It also connotes "spiritual" in contrast with "literal." (See the corresponding entry in *A Greek-English Lexicon of the New Testament and Other Early Christian Literature* [known as BDAG for its authors]).

Preaching Prompts

These Christmas lessons center an image rarely proffered in liturgy or preaching but common in art and culture, the nursing mother as an icon of love. In Isaiah 66:11, Jerusalem is the nursing mother with abundant "comforting" breasts that are her "glory." (In the CEB she is full-breasted.) In Psalm 103, God's love is womb-love suggesting but not articulating an accompanying abundance of breastmilk (vv. 8, 13). In 1 Peter 2:2–3 God's children are to long for the Gospel as babies long for milk and at the breast of God "taste and see that God is good"—offering a new way to hear that very common refrain. In Luke 2 the newly delivered Virgin Mother nurses her holy child through the visits of mortals and angels without notice in the text.

In Isaiah 66:13, the poet-prophet uses the image of a mother—clearly nursing in light of the earlier verses—as an image of God. This intersects in interesting ways with the parental image in the psalm; mother-love of human and divine parents in verse 8 and 13 provides the lexicon for divine imagery. Even with some masculine grammatical language in the texts, the dominant divine images are feminine, rooted in birthing, nursing, and mothering, a reversal of the more common dominant masculine and male imagery. Similarly, the Gospel presents a woman-born Sovereign God swaddled in human flesh, nourished at his mother's breast. Of all the changes that the Christmas miracle births into the world, the ability to experience and name God more richly can be easily neglected.

The imagery of pregnancy, birthing, nursing, and mothering is integral to the Christmas story. It is also the primary trope for women in the scriptures, often reducing them to one dimension. It is not, however, the universal experience of women, and biblical portrayals of women can be painful for those who cannot mother, were not mothered, or were poorly mothered. These images can also be frustrating for these who choose not to mother.

CHRISTMAS III

Wisdom 9:1–6; 9–11; Psalm 33:1–9; Colossians 1:15–20; John 1:1–14

Wisdom 9:1 "O God of my ancestors and Author of mercy,
who have made all things by your word,
2 and by your wisdom have formed humankind
to govern the creatures you have made,
3 and oversee the world in holiness and righteousness,
and renders judgment as the soul of righteousness:
4 Give me the wisdom that sits by your throne,
and do not reject me from among your children.
5 For I am your slave, the child of your slave girl,
one who is weak and short-lived,
with little understanding of judgment and laws;
6 for even one who is perfect among human beings
will be regarded as nothing without the wisdom that comes from you.
9 With you is Wisdom, she who knows your works
and was present when you made the world;
she knows what is pleasing in your sight
and what is right according to your commandments.
10 Send her forth from the holy heavens,
and from your throne of glory send her,
that she may labor with me,
and that I may learn what is pleasing to you.
11 For she knows and understands all things,
and she will guide me wisely in my actions
and guard me with her glory.

Psalm 33

1 Rejoice in the ALMIGHTY, you righteous;
it is good for the just to sing praises.
2 Praise SHE WHO IS MAJESTY with the harp;
play to her upon the psaltery and lyre.
3 Sing for her a new song;
sound a fanfare with all your skill upon the trumpet.
4 For the word of WISDOM is right,
and all her works are sure.
5 She loves righteousness and justice;
the faithful love of the MOTHER OF ALL fills the whole earth.

6 By the word of WISDOM were the heavens made,
by the breath of her mouth all the heavenly hosts.
7 She gathers up the waters of the ocean as in a waterskin
and stores up the depths of the sea.
8 Let all the earth revere SHE WHO IS WISDOM;
let all who dwell in the world stand in awe of her.
9 For she spoke, and it came to pass;
She commanded, and it stood fast.

Colossians 1:15 Jesus is the image of the invisible God, the firstborn of all creation; 16 for
in him all things in the heavens and on earth were created, things visible and invisible,
whether thrones or dominions or rulers or powers—all things have been created through
him and for him. 17 Jesus himself is before all things, and in him all things hold together.
18 Jesus is the head of the body, the church; he is the beginning, the firstborn from the dead,
so that he might come to have preeminence in everything. 19 For in Jesus all the fullness of
God was well pleased to dwell, 20 and through Jesus God was well pleased to reconcile to
Godself all things, whether on earth or in heaven, by making peace through the blood of
his cross.

John 1:1 In the beginning was the Word, and the Word was with God, and the Word was
God. 2 The Word was with God in the beginning. 3 Everything came into being through the
Word, and without the Word not one thing came into being that came into being. What has
come into being 4 in the Word was life, and that life was the light of all people. 5 The light
shines in the bleakness, and the bleakness did not overtake it.

6 There was a man sent from God, whose name was John. 7 He came as a witness to testify
to the light, so that all might believe through him. 8 He himself was not the light, but he came
to testify to the light. 9 The true light, which enlightens everyone, was coming into the world.

10 He was in the world, and the world was created through him; yet the world did not
know him. 11 To his own he came and his own did not receive him. 12 But to all who did
accept him, who believed in his name, he empowered to become children of God—13 that is,
those who were born, not of blood or of the will of the flesh or of the will of a human person,
but of God.

14 And the Word became flesh and lived among us, and we have seen his glory, glory as of
a parent's only child, full of grace and truth.

PROCLAMATION

Text Notes

The Greek word *pais* used in Wisdom 9:4 means both child and enslaved person. I choose the easier reading here and preserve the slave language in the following verse where two different words for an enslaved person occur.

Colossians uses the masculine pronoun repeatedly and does not include the name of Jesus in the Greek text. I have substituted it for some of the pronouns for smoothness and clarity.

Preaching Prompts

Today's Christmas readings focus on Wisdom and the Word. Both are invoked in the creation of the world; Wisdom in Wisdom 9:2 and Psalm 33:6, and the Word in John 1:1–2. Jesus is the word incarnate, unnamed in the gospel portion. The Colossians reading names Jesus explicitly and links him to the creation of the world. This Sunday has traditionally focused on the preexistent Christ of John's Gospel, a concept expressed in grammatical gender (masculine for the Word and feminine for Wisdom in a similar portrayal), but ontologically beyond gender. These lessons present an opportunity to think about why we and our spiritual ancestors, our languages and theirs, gender things the way we do and what that really means.

The Wisdom reading also offers an opportunity to discuss the ubiquity of slavery in the biblical world and text. The scriptures use the language of slavery as more than a metaphor. Its normalcy is something with which we must contend. Many translations soften slave language to "servant." That seems dishonest given the total control—physical, sexual, reproductive, financial—over the lives and bodies of the persons at stake. Yet, it is hard to use slave language in scripture, prayer, and liturgy; doubly so for Black folk.

FIRST SUNDAY AFTER CHRISTMAS

Proverbs 23:22–25; Psalm 8; 1 John 5:1–5; Luke 2:25–38

(These texts can also be used for the Feast of the Presentation.)

Proverbs 23:22 Listen to your father who begot you,
and do not despise your mother when she is old.
23 Truth, buy and do not sell it;
wisdom, instruction, and understanding as well.
24 The father of the righteous will greatly rejoice;
the one who produces a wise child will be glad in her.
25 Let your mother and father be glad;
let her who birthed you rejoice.

Psalm 8

1 WOMB OF LIFE, our Sovereign,
how exalted is your Name in all the earth!

2 Out of the mouths of infants and children
your majesty is praised above the heavens.
3 You have set up a stronghold against your adversaries,
to quell the enemy and the avenger.
4 When I consider your heavens, the work of your fingers,
the moon and the stars you have set in their courses,
5 What are we that you should be mindful of us?
those born of women that you should seek us out?
6 You have made us a little lower than God;
you adorn us with glory and honor;
7 You give us mastery over the works of your hands;
you put all things under our feet:
8 All sheep and oxen,
even the wild beasts of the field,
9 The birds of the air, the fish of the sea,
and whatsoever walks in the paths of the sea.
10 WOMB OF LIFE, our Sovereign,
how exalted is your Name in all the earth!

1 John 5:1 Everyone who believes that Jesus is the Messiah is born of God, and everyone
who loves the parent loves the child of the parent. 2 By this we know that we love the children
of God, when we love God and undertake God's commandments. 3 For the love of God is
this, that we keep God's commandments. And God's commandments are not difficult, 4 for
anything born of God conquers the world. And this is the victory that conquers the world,
our faith. 5 Who is it that conquers the world but the one who believes that Jesus is the Son
of God?

Luke 2:25 Now, there was a man in Jerusalem whose name was Simeon; this man was righteous and devout, waiting to welcome the consolation of Israel, and the Holy Spirit, she rested
on him. 26 It had been revealed to him by the Holy Spirit that he would not see death before
he had seen the Messiah of the Most High God. 27 Led by the Spirit, Simeon came into the
temple. When the parents brought in the child Jesus, to do for him what was customary under
that which was taught, 28 Simeon took him in his arms and praised God, saying,

29 "You release now your slave in peace, Master,
according to your word;
30 for my eyes have seen your salvation,
31 which you have prepared in the presence of all peoples,
32 a light for revelation to the Gentiles
and for glory to your people Israel."

[33] And the child's mother and father were amazed at what was being said about him.
[34] Then Simeon blessed them and said to his mother Mary, "This child is set for the falling
and the rising of many in Israel, and to be a sign provoking contention; [35] also, your own soul
a sword will pierce so that the true hearts of many will be revealed."
[36] There was also a prophet, Anna the daughter of Phanuel, of the tribe of Asher. She
was of a great age, having lived with her husband seven years after her marriage, [37] then as a
widow to the age of eighty-four. She never left the temple but worshiped there with fasting
and prayer night and day. [38] At that moment she came and began to praise God, and to speak
about the child to all who were looking for the redemption of Jerusalem.

PROCLAMATION

Text Notes

Proverbs 23:24 is "He (or the one who) begets a wise one (masculine singular, missing son/child) will rejoice in him." I use "her" as generic; wisdom is rarely but occasionally credited to women. I have inverted the order of the parents in verse 25 as I do in verse 33 of the Gospel.

Psalm 8:5 uses *ben adam*, literally "child/son of humanity" for humanity. Most often the expression indicates mortality and frailty, see God's repeated address to Ezekiel in chapters 2–5, etc., and Jesus invoking his own mortality in Mark 8:31. More rarely the expression refers to a divine being as in Daniel 7:13 (Aramaic). Jesus also uses it in this way, see Luke 21:27. In Psalm 8:6, humanity is created a little lower than God in Hebrew.

While neuter in Greek, the Spirit is feminine in Hebrew. I retain that gender, reflecting the cultural understanding underneath the literary presentation.

An alternative opening for Simeon's prayer is, "Sovereign, now you are dismissing your servant. . . ." However, that mitigates the explicit slaveholding rhetoric. "Master" here is *despotos*: lord, master, slaveholder.

Most translations place the line about the trauma Mary will experience after the significance of Jesus, as an afterthought. The syntax of the text includes her trauma as part of what unmasks human hearts.

Preaching Prompts

These lessons emphasize the humanity of Jesus, the marvel of the Incarnation in not just human flesh, but child flesh along with his divinity. Proverbs 23:22–25 provides a glimpse into the Israelite home as the locus of social, religious, and ethical formation where that formation results from the teaching of both parents. The psalm keeps us from thinking too lowly of humanity as a container for God. We are the craftwork of God made in the divine image, a little lower than, perhaps barely brushing, the divine. That applies equally to all of us without regard to gender, orientation, or their performance.

In the Epistle, we are enfolded into God's parental embrace; Jesus is not God's only child. We are bound to each other and God by love. That love is transformative; in the militaristic language of the text, it conquers the world. What does that look like? It is for those relegated to the margins of the text and society to say if what we say is love is truly love.

The temple scene involves a creative reading of Israelite traditions: Luke presents the earlier ritual restoration of Mary as "their" restoration, counter to the Torah, which requires the ritual for the new mother and portrays a "presentation" that has no biblical antecedent. Anna's residence in the temple makes sense in light of later rabbinic teaching that there was a special chamber on the temple campus in which women wove the temple curtains. (See the Carta *Illustrated Encyclopedia of the Holy Temple in Jerusalem,* which has a useful section on women's participation in the life of Israelite sanctuaries over time.)

These Christmastide lessons end with the good news of Jesus's birth being preached by an elderly female prophet and the joy of his birth tempered by a word of warning from another elder who is not styled as a prophet. This good news comes at a high cost.

FEAST OF THE HOLY NAME, JANUARY 1

Isaiah 7:3–16; Psalm 89:1–8, 14; Philippians 2:9–13; Luke 2:15–21

Isaiah 7:3 The Holy One said to Isaiah, "Go out now to meet Ahaz, you and She'ar-jashub
your son, at the end of the conduit of the upper pool on the highway to the Fuller's Field,
4 and say to him, 'Watch, hush, and fear not, and let not your heart faint on account of these
two smoldering stumps of firebrands, because of the rage of Rezin and Aram or the son of
Remaliah. 5 For indeed, Aram has plotted evil against you—with Ephraim and the son of
Remaliah—saying, 6 'Let us go up against Judah and cut off Jerusalem and conquer it for ourselves and make the son of Tabeel king in it;' 7 therefore thus says the Sovereign God:

'It shall not stand,
and it shall not come to pass.
8 For the head of Aram is Damascus,
and the head of Damascus is Rezin.'

(In about sixty-five years Ephraim will be shattered, no longer a people.)

9 The head of Ephraim is Samaria,
and the head of Samaria is the son of Remaliah.

If you do not stand firm in faith,
you shall not stand firm at all.'"

10 Again the HOLY ONE spoke to Ahaz, saying, 11 "Ask a sign of the HOLY ONE your God; from the deep of Sheol or the height of what lies above." 12 Yet Ahaz said, "I will not ask, and I will not test the HOLY ONE." 13 Then Isaiah said, "Hear now, House of David! Is it not enough that you exhaust mortals, that you must exhaust my God also? 14 Therefore the selfsame Creator will give you a sign. See, the young woman is pregnant and she shall give birth to a son, and she shall name him Immanu-El. 15 He shall eat curds and honey when he knows how to refuse the evil and choose the good. 16 For before the child knows how to refuse the evil and choose the good, the land before whose two kings you dread will be deserted.

Psalm 89:1–8, 14

1 I will sing of the faithful love of the FOUNT OF LIFE forever;
with my mouth I will make known your faithfulness from across the generations.
2 When I declare that your faithful love is established forever;
your faithfulness is established in the heavens,
3 [you responded,] "I have inscribed a covenant with my chosen one;
I have sworn an oath to the descendants of Bathsheba:
4 'I will establish your line forever,
your throne that I will build, will be to all generations.'"
5 The heavens confess your wonders, O WOMB OF CREATION,
and to your faithfulness in the congregation of the holy ones;
6 For who in the skies can be compared to the WOMB OF LIFE?
who is like the MOTHER OF ALL among the children of the gods?
7 a dread God in the council of the holy ones,
great and terrible above all who surround her.
8 WARRIOR PROTECTRIX, who is mighty like you?
YOU WHO ARE, your faithfulness surrounds you.
14 Righteousness and justice are the foundations of your throne;
enduring love and faithfulness go before your face.

Philippians 2:5 Let the same mind be in you all that was in Christ Jesus,
6 who, though he was in the form of God,
did not regard equality with God
as something to be seized,
7 but emptied himself,
taking the form of a slave,
being born in human likeness;
then being found in human form,

8 he humbled himself
and became obedient to the point of death,
even death on a cross.
9 Therefore God also highly exalted Jesus
and gave him the name
that is above every name,
10 so that at the name of Jesus
every heavenly and earthly knee should bend,
along with those under the earth,
11 and every tongue should confess
that Jesus Christ is Savior,
to the glory of God the Sovereign.

Luke 2:15 And it happened when the angels had departed from them into heaven, the shepherds said to one another, "Let us go now to Bethlehem and see this thing that has come to be,
which the Sovereign God has made known to us." 16 So they came hurrying and found Mary
and Joseph, and the baby lying in the manger. 17 Now seeing this, they made known what had
been spoken to them about this child. 18 And all who heard marveled at what was spoken by
the shepherds to them. 19 But Mary preserved all these words and pondered them in her heart.
20 The shepherds returned, glorifying and praising God for all they had heard and seen; it was
just as it had been told them.

21 After eight days had passed, it was time to circumcise the child; and he was called
Jesus, his name was the name given by the angel before he was conceived in the womb.

PROCLAMATION

Text Notes

Isaiah's son's name means "a remnant will survive." He is a prophetic sign in the text. The stem that means "cut off" in Isaiah 7:6 also means "terrorize." Hebrew hearers would have recognized both meanings. The young woman, an *almah*, in 7:14 is not identified as a virgin, *betulah*. The text does not even stipulate that this is her first child. Many scholars, myself included, consider it possible that she was also the mother of Isaiah's (other) children with equally portentous names, She'ar Yashuv in 7:4 and Maher Shalal Hash Baz in 8:4. The woman's pregnancy is contemporaneous with Isaiah; she *is* pregnant, a descriptive adjective. The word "virgin" and the use of a future tense come from the LXX, rather than the Hebrew text, effectively transforming the text to read more easily as a prediction of Jesus.

In the traditional language of Psalm 89:3, God swears an oath to "David, my servant." Note that Bathsheba indeed has her own throne, symbolically if not literally passed down to the Judean Queen Mothers (see 1 Kings 2:19). The children of the gods refer to any number of divine or semidivine beings, from other gods to angels depending on the age and redaction of the text. Warrior Protectrix in verse 8 is God of "hosts" or warriors.

Preaching Prompts

Biblical prophecy can include prediction, it is at its heart contemporaneous, interpreting the present and speaking to the people for God as well as speaking to God on behalf of the people. While the framers of the New Testament, and likely the followers of Jesus, interpreted Isaiah 7:14 with reference to Jesus, they did not negate its original meaning in its original context. They interpreted it in their contemporary context as we ought, affirming both interpretations.

Read in context, Isaiah 7:14 is not a prediction but demonstration of God's reliable fidelity, available in each generation. The young woman in Isaiah is already pregnant. By the time her child is eating soft foods, the two nations threatening Judah will be gone. The presence of Isaiah's son "A Remnant Shall Survive" is a promise that Judah will not be destroyed while those two nations decline. The promise is faithful as is the God who made it.

Psalm 89 celebrates the eternal faithfulness of God, in this translation, expressing that *through* Bathsheba rather than *to* David. Such a reading does not redeem her rape; it does keep her centered in the story in which she continues to play a part.

Philippians 2 and Luke 2 are each traditional readings for the Feast of the Holy Name of Jesus observed on January 1. They celebrate the majesty of the name given by angels and the humble majesty of its bearer.

SECOND SUNDAY AFTER CHRISTMAS

Hosea 11:1–4, 7–9; Psalm 68:18–20, 22, 24–27, 31–33; Hebrews 11:23–28; Matthew 2:13–18

Hosea 11:1 When Israel was a child, I loved them,
and out of Egypt I called my child.
2 They, the Baals, called to them,
they went out to the Baals;
they sacrificed and to idols,
they offered incense.
3 Yet it was I who walked toddling Ephraim,
taking them by their arms;
yet they did not know that I healed them.

4 I led them with human ties,
with bonds of love.
I was to them like those
who lift babies to their cheeks.
I bent down to them and fed them.
7 My people are bent on backsliding away from me.
To the MOST HIGH they call,
but God does not bring them up altogether.
8 How can I give you up, Ephraim?
How can I hand you over, Israel?
How can I give you up like Admah?
How can I make you like Zeboiim?
My heart recoils within me;
my compassion grows altogether warm.
9 I will not release my raging fury;
I will not again destroy Ephraim;
for I am God and not a mortal,
the Holy One in your midst,
and I will not come in wrath.

Psalm 68:18–20, 22, 24–27, 32–33

18 You have gone up on high and taken captivity captive;
you have taken tribute from the woman-born,
even from those who rebel
against the dwelling of SHE WHO IS, our God.
19 Blessed be SHE who bears us up day by day,
the God of our salvation.
20 Our God is the God of salvation;
The SOURCE OF LIFE is God, to whom belongs escape from death.
22 SHE WHO SAVES has said, "From Bashan I will bring them back;
I will bring them back from the depths of the sea.
24 They see your processions, O God,
the processions of my God and my Sovereign into the holy place.
25 Before go singers, after [them], musicians follow,
in between them young women drum.
26 In great congregations bless God;
bless THE SOURCE OF LIFE, from the fountain of Israel.
27 There is [Rachel-born] Benjamin, the little one, ruling;
then the sons of the royal women of Judah in their crowd;
with royal mothers' sons from Zebulon and Naphtali.

32 Let tribute be brought out of Egypt;
let Nubia stretch out her hands to God.
33 Sing to God, dominions of the earth;
sing praises to SHE WHO IS WORTHY.

Hebrews 11:23 By faith Moses was hidden after his birth by his mother and father for three months, because they saw that the child was beautiful; and they were not afraid of the king's commandment.
24 By faith Moses, after he had grown up, refused to be called a son of Pharaoh's daughter,
25 rather choosing ill-treatment with the people of God than enjoyment of the transitory pleasures of sin.
26 He considered abuse for the sake of the Messiah to be greater wealth than the treasures of Egypt, for he was looking ahead to the reward.
27 By faith he left Egypt, unafraid of the anger of the king; for he persisted as though he saw the unseen.
28 By faith he kept the Passover and the sprinkling of blood, in order that the destroyer of the firstborn would not touch the firstborn daughters and sons of Israel.

Matthew 2:13 Now after the sages had left Herod, an angel of God appeared to Joseph in a dream and said, "Get up, take the child and his mother, and flee to Egypt, and stay there until I tell you; for Herod is about to seek the child, to destroy him."
14 Then Joseph got up, took the child and his mother, and went to Egypt at night,
15 and was there until the death of Herod. This was to fulfill what had been spoken by God through the prophet,

"Out of Egypt I have called my son."

16 When Herod saw that he had been tricked by the sages, he was utterly infuriated, and he sent and killed all the children in Bethlehem and around it who were two years old or under, according to the time that he had learned from the sages.
17 Then was fulfilled what had been spoken through the prophet Jeremiah who said:

18 *"A voice was heard in Ramah,*
wailing and great lamentation,
Rachel weeping for her children,
and she refused to be consoled, because they are no more."

PROCLAMATION

Text Notes

Inconsistencies in the Hebrew, shifts between first and third person, have led to widely variant translations of Hosea 11:2–3. Some shift all the pronouns to "I/my" since God is speaking. Yet the text is sensible, as it is in most cases; where it is, I will preserve it. At this point in Israel's story, Ephraim refers to the separate Northern nation.

The singers and musicians in Psalm 68:25 could have been a mixed gender group; the hand-drum, often mistranslated as a tambourine (or timbrel) was solely a woman's instrument. In verse 27, I offer the option of naming Benjamin in the line of Rachel (which connects with the Gospel) and, have replaced "princes" with the "sons of the royal women/mothers."

The author's use of *tou Christos* in Hebrews 11:27 reads more sensibly theologically as "the Messiah" rather than as "the Christ." It is certainly possible ancient authors imagined Moses had specific knowledge of Jesus as the Messiah; that is not consistent with what is recorded in the Hebrew Bible, nor compatible with the imperative to read the Hebrew Scriptures as authoritative in their own right. Positioning the Hebrew Bible as a prequel to the New Testament denies the integrity of the Hebrew Scriptures and is an anti-Judaistic practice far too common in Christian biblical interpretation. In verse 28 I translate the firstborn inclusively, following Exodus 11:5 and 12:29 where "all the firstborn" were struck.

The number and gender of the sages or magi are indeterminate: grammatically, there is more than one and only one of that number need be male. Matthew 2:15 quotes Hosea 11:1 and verse 18 quotes Jeremiah 31:15. "Tricked" in verse 16 can also mean "mocked."

Preaching Prompts

The Exodus links the lessons, even when used to explain events in the life of Jesus. They offer an opportunity to talk about how Christians can understand Jesus to be the fulfilment of promises made in the Hebrew Bible without denying the meanings of those texts in their own contexts.

Hosea 11 speaks of the calling of Israel as God's child out of Egypt and Matthew 2 uses the same text to speak of God calling Jesus (and his parents) back from Egypt after the death of Herod. Matthew does not deny the content or context of Hosea yet does reinterpret it in the context of the writer. Similarly, Jeremiah 31:15 envisions a Rachel beyond time weeping for the exiled Israelites after Babylonian conquest while Matthew uses the same text to speak of the slaughter of the innocents. In each case both readings stand.

Hosea, famed for using the language of marriage and prostitution to convey God, also portrays God as a tender childcare provider, parent, mother, in Hosea 11:4: God takes the not-yet-toddler by the arms and supports them as they learn to walk. God also bends over to the child and feeds it; arguably God picks the child up and nurses it. Calling her child out of Egypt is the act of a protective mother.

In the psalm, God is not so much parent as savior providing a way out of death, verse 20, though in this context it means deliverance from certain death rather than resurrection. The Epistle portrays the actions of Yocheved, Moses's mother, in saving him along with his own, as acts of faith in the Messiah. The Gospel replaces Moses with Jesus as the savior of his people.

Motherhood abounds in various forms: Rachel the mother of the nation, unnamed Yocheved the mother of Moses, Mary the mother of God, and God the mother of all.

FEAST OF THE EPIPHANY

Isaiah 60:1–6, 11; Psalm 67; 2 Timothy 1:5–10; Matthew 2:1–12

Isaiah 60:1 Arise daughter, shine daughter; for your light has come daughter,
and the glory of the Holy One has risen upon you daughter.
2 For—watch now daughter!—Bleakness shall cover the earth,
and thick bleakness the peoples;
and upon you daughter, the Holy One will arise,
and over you daughter, God's glory will appear.
3 Nations shall come to your light daughter,
and monarchs to the brightness of your dawn daughter.
4 Lift your eyes round about daughter, and see;
all of them gather, they come to you daughter;
daughter, your sons shall come from far away,
and your daughters shall be carried on their nurses' hips.
5 Then daughter, you shall see and be radiant;
your heart, daughter, shall tremble and swell,
because the abundance of the sea shall turn towards you daughter,
the wealth of the nations shall come to you daughter.
6 A multitude of camels shall cover you daughter—
young camels of Midian and Ephah—
all those from Sheba shall come.
They shall bring gold and frankincense,
and shall proclaim the praises of the Holy One.
11 Your gates shall always be open daughter;
day and night they shall not be shut,
so that nations shall bring you their wealth daughter,
being led by their monarchs.

Psalm 67

1 May God be merciful to us and bless us,
show us the light of her countenance and come to us.
2 Let your ways be known upon earth,
your saving health among all nations.
3 Let the peoples praise you, O God;
let all the peoples praise you.

4 Let the nations be glad and sing for joy,
for you judge the peoples with equity
and guide all the nations upon earth.
5 Let the peoples praise you, O God;
let all the peoples praise you.
6 The earth has brought forth her increase;
may God, our own God, give us her blessing.
7 May God give us her blessing,
and may all the ends of the earth stand in awe of her.

2 Timothy 1:5 Considering the recollection of your faith without pretense, a faith that lived
first in your grandmother Lois and your mother Eunice, now I am persuaded that faith lives
in you. 6 For this reason I remind you to reignite the gift of God that is within you through
the laying on of my hands; 7 for God did not give us a spirit of cowardice, but one of power
and of love and of self-control.

8 Be not ashamed, then, of the testimony of our Savior or of me Christ's prisoner, rather
share in suffering for the sake of the gospel, do so through the power of God, 9 who saved us
and called us with a holy calling, not according to our works rather according to God's own
purpose and grace which was given to us in Christ Jesus before the ages began. 10 Now it
has been revealed through the appearing of our Savior Christ Jesus, who negated death and
brought life and immortality to light through the gospel.

Matthew 2:1 Now Jesus was born in Bethlehem of Judea in the days of King Herod; suddenly sages from the East came to Jerusalem, 2 asking, "Where is the one born king of the
Judeans? For we have seen his star at its ascent and have come to reverence him." 3 When
King Herod heard this, he was shaken, and all Jerusalem with him; 4 then calling together all
the chief priests and religious scholars of the people, he inquired of them where the Messiah
would be born. 5 They said to him, "In Bethlehem of Judea; for it has been written by the
prophet:

6 *'And you, Bethlehem, in the land of Judah,*
by no means are least among the rulers of Judah;
for from you shall come a ruler
who is to shepherd my people Israel.'"

7 Then Herod secretly called for the sages and learned from them the time when the
star had appeared. 8 Then he sent them to Bethlehem, saying, "Go, search diligently for the
child, and when you have found him bring me word so that I may also go and reverence him."
9 When they had heard the king, they left, and there suddenly was the star that they had seen
at its ascent going before them until it stopped over the place where the child was. 10 When
they saw that the star had stopped, they rejoiced; their joy was exuberant. 11 On entering the
house, they saw the child with Mary his mother; and they fell down and reverenced him.

Then, opening their treasure, they offered him gifts of gold, frankincense, and myrrh. [12] And having been warned in a dream not to return to Herod, they left for their own country by another road.

PROCLAMATION

Text Notes

Isaiah 60 speaks to a feminine entity, Zion, (meaning Jerusalem) frequently styled as God's daughter; each "you" and "your" is explicitly feminine and singular, rhythmic and repetitive in Hebrew. I have added "daughter" each place this occurs for the English speaker-reader-hearer. The daughters in verse 4 were already delineated; "hips" here is actually "side."

Bleakness: The thick bleakness of Isaiah 60:2 is the same (word) as the thick darkness in which God is veiled in other texts, i.e., Exodus 20:21; Deuteronomy 4:11, 5:22; 2 Samuel 22:10; 1 Kings 8:12.

"Spirit of fear" is a familiar and common translation of 2 Timothy 1:7. *Deilia* is cowardice; an important distinction. Fear is not a failing. It is a natural and healthy response. It is harmful to tell folks not to feel what they feel. What matters is how folk respond to fear.

Grammatically speaking, not all of the *magoi* need be male, only one; note: no number of sages is specified. "Religious scholars" is preferable to scribes, which can suggest copyists. The Gospel famously quotes Micah 5:2 that a ruler with ancient origins shall come from Bethlehem of Judah. There is a variant to that text which states that out of Bethlehem of Judah "one shall not come forth" to rule. It is worth considering that both traditions were known at the times of the setting and production of the Gospel. The line "least among the rulers" is specific to the Gospel; it is among the "thousands," i.e., clans in Hebrew and Aramaic (Targum and Peshitta). A different word for ruler is used in the LXX, *archon* vs. *hegemon*.

The word *Ioudaioi* is regularly translated "Jews" but also means "Judeans" in an age where an ethnic name referred to a people, their land, language, and religion(s). "Judean" is often a preferable reading to "Jew" or "the Jews," which in contemporary discourse have often become an epithet in the mouths of anti-Semites. Further, the distinction is a helpful reminder that the Gospels refer to the Judeans of its world and not the Jewish communities of ours.

Preaching Prompts

These lessons frame a number of epiphanies: God's self-revelation and that of Christ to the world beyond Israel in Isaiah 60 and Psalm 67, in the traditional Epiphany Gospel, Matthew 2, and in 2 Timothy 1. These epiphanies are manifest in or accompanied by light, sometimes set in opposition to darkness, sometimes paired with it, requiring thoughtful exegesis in a world in which darkness and blackness are regularly equated with black and brown people set in opposition to whiteness and white people.

In the commentary on Isaiah 60 in the *Jewish Study Bible,* Benjamin Sommer observes a shift from the traditional pattern centering on a male monarch as a royal figure. Rather God's daughter-city Zion is the locus of liberation wrought by God without human delegation. This is a helpful alternative to the common veneration of monarchy and the fallible members of David's lineage. Similarly, it is God and not a human who judges women and men, "the peoples," with equity, in the psalm.

It is worth asking how the women in and behind these texts experienced and articulated their epiphanies. The promises of restoration and reunification to daughter Jerusalem can be heard as the promises to the daughters of Jerusalem, the mothers, wives, sisters, and daughters of those who are in exile and captivity. Lois and Eunice in 1 Timothy have their own stories of faith. What might they have told us in their own epistle if they had not been relegated to grandmother and mother? (Note the absence of Timothy's male lineage.) These texts offer an opportunity to proclaim the ways in which God is manifest in the world in and beyond the scriptures, in old ways and new.

EPIPHANY I

Isaiah 2:1–5; Psalm 57; 2 Peter 1:16–21; Matthew 3:1–17

Isaiah 2:1 The word that Isaiah son of Amoz envisioned about Judah and Jerusalem:

2 And it will be in coming days,
the mountain of God's home
shall the highest of the mountains,
and shall be elevated beyond the hills,
all the nations shall stream to it.
3 Many peoples shall come and say,
"Let us go and ascend the mountain of the HOLY ONE OF SINAI,
to the home of the God of Jacob [of the line of Rebekah];
that God may teach us God's ways
and that we may walk in God's paths."
For out of Zion shall go forth instruction,
and the word of the HOLY ONE from Jerusalem.
4 God shall judge between the nations,
and shall decide justly for many peoples;

they shall beat their swords into plowshares,
and their spears into pruning hooks;
nation shall not lift up sword against nation,
neither shall they learn war any more.
5 O house of Jacob [line of Rebekah]
come, let us walk
in the light of the HOLY ONE OF OLD!

Psalm 57

1 Grant me mercy, God, grant me mercy, for in you my soul takes refuge;
in the shadow of your wings will I seek refuge
until destruction has passed over.
2 I will call upon the MOST HIGH God,
God who does right by me.
3 She will send from the heavens and save me;
She will rebuke those who trample upon me;
God will send forth her love and her faithfulness.
4 In the midst of lions that devour the woman-born my soul reclines;
their teeth are spears and arrows, their tongue a sharp sword.
5 Be exalted above the heavens, O God,
let your glory be above all the earth.
6 They have set a trap for my feet; my soul was brought low;
they have dug a pit before me but have fallen into it themselves.
7 My heart is firmly fixed, O God, my heart is fixed;
I will sing, I will sing praises.
8 Awake, O my glory! Awake, O lute and harp;
I myself will awaken the dawn.
9 I will give thanks to you among the peoples, FAITHFUL ONE;
I will sing praise to you among the nations.
10 For your faithful love is greater than the heavens,
and your faithfulness reaches to the clouds.
11 Be exalted above the heavens, O God,
let your glory be above all the earth.

2 Peter 1:16 We did not follow manufactured myths when we made known to you the power and coming of our Savior Jesus Christ, but we had been eyewitnesses of his majesty.
17 For he received honor and glory from God the Sovereign when that voice was conveyed to him by the majestic glory, saying, "This is my Son, my Beloved, in whom I am well pleased."
18 We ourselves heard this voice come from heaven, while we were with him on the holy mountain.

19 So we have a reliable prophetic message; you will do well to heed this as you would a
lamp shining in a bleak place, until the day dawns and the morning star rises in your hearts.
20 First this you must understand, that no prophecy of scripture is a matter of an individual's
own interpretation, 21 because no prophecy ever came by human will; rather women and men
moved by the Holy Spirit spoke from God.

Matthew 3:1 In those days John the Baptizer appeared preaching in the wilderness of Judea,
2 and saying, "Repent, for the realm of the heavens is near." 3 This is the one of whom the
prophet Isaiah spoke when he said,

> *"The voice of one crying out in the wilderness:*
> *'Prepare the way of the Most High,*
> *make God's paths straight.'"*

4 Now John had for his clothing camel's hair with a leather belt around his waist, and his food
was locusts and wild honey. 5 Then the women and men of Jerusalem and all Judea were going
out to him, and the whole region of the Jordan, 6 and they were baptized in the river Jordan by
him, confessing their sins.

7 Now when John saw many Pharisees and Sadducees coming for baptism, he said to
them, "You brood of vipers! Who warned you to flee from the coming wrath? 8 Bear fruit
worthy of repentance. 9 And do not presume to say to yourselves, 'We have Abraham as our
ancestor.' For I tell you, God is able from these stones to raise up children to Abraham. 10 The
axe is already lying at the root of the trees; therefore, every tree that does not bear good fruit is
cut down and thrown into the fire.

11 "Indeed, I baptize you with water for repentance, but after me is coming one more
powerful than I; I am not worthy to carry his sandals. He will baptize you with the Holy
Spirit and fire. 12 His winnowing fork is in his hand, and he will clear his threshing-floor and
will gather his wheat into the granary; but the chaff he will burn with unquenchable fire."

13 Then Jesus came from Galilee to John at the Jordan, to be baptized by him. 14 John forbade him, saying, "I need to be baptized by you, yet you come to me?" 15 But Jesus answered
him, "Let it go now; for this way is proper for us to fulfill all righteousness." Then John let
it go. 16 Now when Jesus had been baptized, just as he came up from the water, suddenly the
heavens were opened to him and he saw the Spirit of God, she descended like a dove and came
upon on him. 17 And a voice from the heavens said, "This is my Son, the Beloved, with whom
I am well pleased."

PROCLAMATION

Text Notes

The word "teach" in Isaiah 2:3 provides the root for Torah, which is more teaching than law.

The verb "to pass over" in Psalm 57:1 is the verb at the root of the Passover and the Hebrew for "Hebrew." In verse 2, "God who does right" is most literally "God who completes for (upon) me." JPS has "who is food to me." The *New English Translation of the Septuagint* (NETS) has "my benefactor." The "trap" in verse 6 is a net.

The word "morning" is missing in 2 Peter 1:19.

Matthew 3:3 is famously muddled. Hebrew says: A voice cries, "In the wilderness prepare. . . ." LXX and NT have: A voice cries in the wilderness: "Prepare. . . ." The "people" coming to be baptized in Matthew 3:5 were women and men. It may be a useful exercise to make all of the human plurals explicitly women and men in study and teaching to note how often women are present but buried in the text. "Let it go," in Matthew 3:15 is to release an obligation, including divorce, or here, an objection.

Preaching Prompts

The epiphanies in today's readings include the revelation of God's words from God's own home in Isaiah 2, God's love, faithfulness, and glory in the psalm, and the revelation of Jesus as the Beloved in the Gospel and Epistle. In keeping with the season of Epiphany, these revelations extend beyond the people of Israel to the peoples of the world in Isaiah 2, Psalm 57, and the opening of Matthew 3. There are women experiencing each epiphany and revelation unmarked by the text.

The children of Abraham in Matthew 3:9 include the children of Hagar, Sarah, Keturah, and perhaps other women. This family saga can be an opportunity to talk about the disparities between these matriarchs, the complexity of families, especially blended ones, favoritism and rejection, or the many peoples of the One God. Similarly, the house of Jacob in Isaiah 2:3 is the house of Leah, Bilhah, Zilpah, and Rachel. Both families were built through forced impregnation of enslaved women. Against this background, the ability of women to choose baptism and discipleship matters.

EPIPHANY II

Isaiah 9:2–7; Psalm 36:5–10; Romans 15:8–13; Matthew 4:12–17

Isaiah 9:2 The people—women, children, and men—who walked bleakness
have seen a great light;
those who lived in the land of the shadow of death—
on them light has shined.
3 You have multiplied the nation,
you have magnified its joy;
they rejoice before you
as with joy at the harvest,
as people—women, children, and men—exult when dividing plunder.

4 For the yoke of their burden,
and the staff on their shoulders,
the rod of their oppressor,
you have broken as on the day of Midian.
5 For all the boots of the trampling warriors
and all the garments rolled in blood
shall be burned as fuel for the fire.
6 For a child has been born for us,
a son given to us;
authority rests upon his shoulders;
and his name shall be called:
A Wonder, a Counselor, a Mighty God,
Perpetual Parent, Prince of Peace.
7 His authority shall grow continually,
and there shall be peace without end
for the throne of David and his monarchy.
God will establish and uphold it
with justice and with righteousness
from this time onward and forevermore.
The zeal of God, COMMANDER of heaven's vanguard, will do this.

Psalm 36:5–10

5 HOLY ONE, throughout the very heavens is your faithful love,
your faithfulness beyond the clouds.
6 Your righteousness is like the eternal mountains,
your judgments are like the mighty deep;
you save humankind and animalkind alike, FAITHFUL ONE.
7 How precious is your faithful love, O God!
All the woman-born take shelter in the shadow of your wings.
8 They feast on the abundance of your house,
and you give them drink from the river of your delights.
9 For with you is the fountain of life;
in your light we see light.
10 Extend your faithful love to those who know you,
and your justice to the upright of heart!

Romans 15:8 I tell you that the Messiah has become a servant of the circumcised for the
sake of truth to confirm the promises given to the mothers and fathers,
9 and in order that
the Gentiles might glorify God on account of God's mercy. As it is written,

"Therefore, I will confess you among the Gentiles,
and sing praises to your name,"

10 and again it says,

"Rejoice, O Gentiles, with God's people,"

11 and again,

"Praise the Most High, all you Gentiles,
and let all the peoples praise God,"

12 and again Isaiah says,

"The root of Jesse shall come,
and the one who rises to rule the Gentiles,
in whom the Gentiles shall hope."

13 May the God of hope fill you with all joy and peace in believing, so that you may abound in
hope by the power of the Holy Spirit.

Matthew 4:12 Now when Jesus heard that John had been arrested, he went back to Galilee.
13 Then he left Nazareth behind and settled in Capernaum by the sea, in the territory of
Zebulun and Naphtali, 14 so that what had been spoken through the prophet Isaiah might
be fulfilled:

15 *"Land of Zebulun, land of Naphtali,*
on the sea road, across the Jordan, Galilee of the Gentiles—
16 *the people who sat in bleakness*
have seen a great light,
and for those who sat in the region and shadow of death
light has dawned."

17 From that time Jesus began to preach and say, "Repent, for the realm of the heavens has
come near."

PROCLAMATION

Text Notes

In Isaiah 9:2 "the shadow of death" is the same as in Psalm 23; see its translation in the LXX and in Matthew 4:16. The "day of Midian" in Isaiah 9:4 is most likely a reference to the Midianite War called for in Numbers 25:16–17. It is a very disturbing genocidal war called for against Moses's own in-laws based on a false charge—the Moabites, not the Midianites, were the people of Baal Peor, see Numbers 25. The second charge was the intermarriage of a Midianite woman, Cozbi, to an Israelite man, a marriage that duplicated Moses's own to the Midianite Zipporah. The war ends with Moses's call for a slaughter of the innocents, all the males among the "little ones" along with sexually experienced women and the seizure of prepubescent girls as "booty" for Israelite men in Numbers 31:17–18, 35. It may also refer to Gideon's defeat of Midian in Joshua 7. "Wonder" in Isaiah 9:6 is the noun form, not the adjective "wonderful."

In Romans 15:9–12, Paul quotes Psalm 18:49, Deuteronomy 32:43, Psalm 117:1, and Isaiah 11:10 while Matthew 4:15 quotes and rewrites Isaiah 9:1. In Romans 15:8, *pateron* can be inclusive "ancestors" or gender-specific "fathers." "Mothers and fathers" here expands "ancestors." Throughout the passage, *ethnoi* means non-Israelite/non-Jewish nations, which are by default Gentile, emphasizing Christ's ministry as a "deacon," *diakonon*, to and beyond the circumcised in verse 8.

Preaching Prompts

Isaiah 9 is a classic Epiphany text configuring light and darkness in a binary that is not always helpful. It is joined by Psalm 36 where the shadow of God's wings offers shelter for her people in holy darkness. The joy of the people in Isaiah 9:3 is also complicated. It is compared to the joy of the harvest in which people know they will have food for the time to come and compared to the joy of picking over the dead on a field of battle for plunder, activities which would involve the whole community. War and its aftermath are a very present reality in the text, creating space to talk about the effects of war on women and understandable joy at burning the bloody clothes of warriors and their victims in Isaiah 9:5.

Women are also invoked in the Isaiah text through the special motherhood that will produce the next messiah-king, a fully human king who would restore the earthly Davidic monarchy; in much of Jewish tradition Hezekiah is meant here. Christians have tended to read it with regard to Jesus, while Matthew jettisoned the monarchy language all together, focusing on Jesus's travels that would bring him in contact with Gentiles.

The gift of the Gospel embodied in Jesus and in the early stories marks the Gospel and Epistle as epiphany texts. The theological significance of the Gentiles is radical inclusion in the lexicons of the framers. The Gospel is available to all without regard to nationality, ethnicity, culture, or gender. Romans 15:8 gestures at the intersections of class, ethnicity, and gender by invoking God's promises to the "patriarchs" or "ancestors." God also made and kept promises to the matriarchs Hagar, Sarah, and Rebekah. Their stories including slavery, polygamy, and forced pregnancies paint a more complicated and more honest picture of Israel's past.

FEAST OF THE PRESENTATION, FEBRUARY 2

(The Feast falls variably in early Epiphany. For simplicity and consistency, it is placed after the Second Sunday of Epiphany in these volumes.)

Leviticus 12:1–8; Psalm 48:1–3, 9–14; 1 John 5:1–5; Luke 2:22–38

Leviticus 12:1 The HOLY ONE OF SINAI spoke to Moses, saying: 2 Speak to the women and
men of Israel, saying:
When a woman conceives and gives birth to a male, she shall be taboo seven days; as
during the days of her menstruation, she shall be taboo. 3 On the eighth day the flesh of his
foreskin shall be circumcised. 4 Then, thirty and three days shall she sit in blood purification;
she shall not touch any holy thing, or come into the sanctuary, until the days of her restoration are fulfilled. 5 Now, if she gives birth to a female, she shall be taboo two weeks, as in her
menstruation; her time of blood purification shall be sixty-six days.
6 On completing the days of her purification for a daughter or for a son she shall bring
a yearling lamb for a burnt offering—and a pigeon or a turtledove for a sin offering—to the
priest at the entrance of the tent of meeting. 7 Then he shall offer it before the FIRE OF SINAI
and make atonement on her behalf and she shall be restored from her flow of blood. This is
the teaching for the woman who gives birth to a female or male. 8 If she cannot afford a sheep,
she shall take two turtledoves or two pigeons, one for a burnt offering and the second for a sin
offering; and the priest shall make atonement on her behalf, and she shall be restored.

Psalm 48:1–3, 9–14

1 Great is the AGELESS GOD and greatly praised,
in the city of our God is God's holy mountain.
2 Beautiful in elevation, the joy of all the earth,
Mount Zion, in the far north,
is the city of the great Sovereign.
3 Within her citadels God
has made herself known as a bulwark.
9 We contemplate your faithful love God,
in the midst of your temple.
10 Like your Name, God, your praise,
reaches to the ends of the earth.
Your right hand is filled with righteousness.
11 Let Mount Zion be glad,
let the towns of Judah rejoice
because of your judgments.
12 Go about Zion, go all around her;
count her towers.

13 Set your hearts upon her ramparts;
go through her citadels,
that you may recount to the next generation:
14 For this God is our God, our God forever and ever.
She will be our guide until we die.

1 John 5:1 Everyone who believes that Jesus is the Messiah is born of God, and everyone
who loves the parent loves the child of the parent. 2 By this we know that we love the children
of God, when we love God and undertake God's commandments. 3 For the love of God is
this, that we keep God's commandments. And God's commandments are not difficult, 4 for
anything born of God conquers the world. And this is the victory that conquers the world,
our faith. 5 Who is it that conquers the world but the one who believes that Jesus is the Son
of God?

Luke 2:22 Now when the days of their purification were fulfilled according to the
teaching of Moses, they brought Jesus up to Jerusalem to present him to the Holy One:
23 As it is written in the teaching of the Sovereign God, *"Every male who opens the womb
[as firstborn] shall be called holy to the Sovereign One."* 24 So they offered a sacrifice
according to what is stated in the teaching of the Holy One, *"a pair of turtledoves or two
young pigeons."*

25 Now, there was a man in Jerusalem whose name was Simeon; this man was righteous and devout, waiting to welcome the consolation of Israel, and the Holy Spirit, she
rested on him. 26 It had been revealed to him by the Holy Spirit that he would not see
death before he had seen the Messiah of the Most High God. 27 Led by the Spirit, Simeon
came into the temple. When the parents brought in the child Jesus, to do for him what
was customary under that which was taught, 28 Simeon took him in his arms and praised
God, saying,

29 "You release now your slave in peace, Master,
according to your word;
30 for my eyes have seen your salvation,
31 which you have prepared in the presence of all peoples,
32 a light for revelation to the Gentiles
and for glory to your people Israel."

33 And the child's mother and father were amazed at what was being said about him.
34 Then Simeon blessed them and said to his mother Mary, "This child is set for the falling
and the rising of many in Israel, and to be a sign provoking contention; 35 also, your own soul
a sword will pierce so that the true hearts of many will be revealed."

36 There was also a prophet, Anna the daughter of Phanuel, of the tribe of Asher. She
was of a great age, having lived with her husband seven years after her marriage, 37 then as a
widow to the age of eighty-four. She never left the temple but worshiped there with fasting

and prayer night and day. [38] At that moment she came and began to praise God, and to speak about the child to all who were looking for the redemption of Jerusalem.

PROCLAMATION

Text Notes

The traditional language "clean" and "unclean" is deeply implicated in biased treatment of women and girls, particularly after the onset of menstruation. The language lends itself easily to a debased understanding of women and girls that is inconsistent with full humanity and the image of God. These two distinct words, which are not antonyms, have the sense of being temporarily taboo, not ready to rejoin community, and restoration to a communally appropriate state (see Ilona Rashkow's *Taboo or Not Taboo*). The "purification" requires time, ritual bathing, and an offering. The use of the word "atonement" in verse 8 has made it easier to construct women's bodies and reproductive acts as in some way tainted. However, even moderating the language does not ameliorate the ways in which women and their bodies and reproductive biology are treated as dangerous and in need of control.

In the world of the Hebrew Scriptures, women are impregnated, in verse 2 the Hiphil verb is causative, "she is seeded/caused to bear seed." Contemporary translations tend to use "conceive," reflecting subsequent understanding.

In Psalm 48, Zion's superlatives hail from other cultures identifying their God as God of all the earth using the specific vocabulary of surrounding nations: *nof* signals "elevation" but is also the Egyptian name of Memphis, the capital city (and may also mean "fair," see JPS). Zaphon is the home of the Canaanite gods and is in the farthest northern reach unlike Zion/Jerusalem. In verse 14, God will be our God "until death"; "until we die" makes clear that it is not God who will die.

Luke 2:22 makes Mary's obligation under the Torah "theirs," Joseph's as well; this is counter to the text and practice between Leviticus and Luke and subsequent rabbinic and contemporary Jewish practice.

Preaching Prompts

When overlaid with the androcentrism, patriarchy, and occasional misogyny of the text, the ritual and language for the restoration to the community sounds harsh and discriminatory to many contemporary and non-Jewish ears. It is helpful to remember that biblical Hebrew has a much smaller vocabulary than English and uses some words in ways that extend far beyond their literal meaning. In Leviticus 12, the "purify," "atone," and "sin offering" apply to cleansing the woman and her physical spaces, including the sanctuary, from blood taboo, which was not a matter of sin or transgression. Arguably this period afforded the new mother rest and bonding time;

the additional time for the female infant may account for the occasional vaginal discharge (or appearance of such) observable in newborn girls.

The *Churching of Women* is a Christian rite likely derived from these Leviticus and Luke texts, previously practiced in Catholic and Anglican congregations where a new mother refrained from attending church for four to six weeks and upon her return prayed a prayer of thanksgiving and received a blessing. However, some women experienced isolation and stigma, treated as unclean until they were "churched." The ritual has fallen into disuse.

While all spilled blood requires purification with both ritual and hygienic components, women and girls were subject to blood taboo and purity regulations. Contemporarily, our society seems obsessed with which bodies bleed and bear which organs to categorize gender and assign identities and restrooms. Without either passing judgment on another culture or co-opting the specific practice of another religion, we can make physical and ritual space for human bodies in all of their life-stage changes and welcome and rewelcome folk to and back to the community upon and after significant transitions. This text can provide an opportunity to think about how we reintegrate a transperson into the congregation.

EPIPHANY III

Tobit 13:11–17; Psalm 22:23–31; 1 Timothy 3:14–16; Matthew 4:18–25

Tobit 13:11 A bright light will shine forth to all the ends of the earth;
many peoples from far away will come to you,
inhabitants of the furthest edges of the earth to your holy name,
bearing their gifts in their hands for the Ruler of heaven.
Generation after generation will give joyful praise in you;
the name of the elect city will endure forever.
12 Cursed are all who speak a harsh word against you;
cursed are all who overthrow you
and pull down your walls,
all who topple your towers
and set your homes on fire.
But blessed forever will be all who revere you.
13 Go, then, and rejoice over the daughters and sons of the righteous,
for they will be gathered together
and will praise the Founder of eternity.
14 Blessed are those who love you,
and blessed are those who rejoice in your well-being.
Blessed also are all people who grieve with you

because of all your afflictions;
for in you they will rejoice
and witness all your glory forever.
15 My soul blesses the Sovereign God, the great Ruler!
16 For Jerusalem will be built as God's home for all eternity.
How blessed I will be if a remnant of my descendants should survive
to see your glory and acknowledge the Ruler of heaven.
The gates of Jerusalem will be built with sapphire and emerald,
and all your walls with precious stones.
The towers of Jerusalem will be built with gold,
and their ramparts with pure gold.
The streets of Jerusalem will be paved
with ruby and with stones of Ophir.
17 The gates of Jerusalem will sing hymns of joy,
and all her houses will cry, 'Hallelujah!
Blessed be the God of Israel!'
and the blessed will bless the holy Name forever and ever."

Psalm 22:23–31

23 You who revere the FONT OF LIFE, praise her!
All the offspring of Leah and Rachel, Bilhah and Zilpah glorify her.
Stand in awe of her all you of Rebekah's line.
24 For she did not despise or abhor
the affliction of the afflicted;
she did not hide her face from me,
and when I cried to her, she heard.
25 On your account is my praise in the great congregation;
my vows I will pay before those who revere her.
26 The poor shall eat and be satisfied;
those who seek her shall praise the MOTHER OF ALL.
May your hearts live forever!
27 All the ends of the earth shall remember
and turn to the WELLSPRING OF LIFE;
and all the families of the nations
shall worship before her.
28 For sovereignty belongs to the SHE WHO IS HOLY,
and she rules over the nations.
29 They consume and they bow down, all the fat ones of the earth before her,
they bend their knees, all who go down to the dust,
and cannot save their soul.

[30] Later descendants will serve her;
future generations will be told about our God,
[31] they will go and proclaim her deliverance to a people yet unborn,
saying that she has done it.

1 Timothy 3:14 This to you I write hoping to come to you soon, but I am writing these instructions to you so that, [15] if I am delayed, you may know how one ought to conduct oneself in the house of God, which is the church of the living God, the pillar and foundation of the truth. [16] Without any doubt, the mystery of our religion is great:

One who was made known in flesh,
vindicated in spirit,
seen by angels,
preached among Gentiles,
believed in throughout the world,
taken up in glory.

Matthew 4:18 As Jesus walked by the Sea of Galilee, he saw two brothers, Simon, who is called Peter, and Andrew his brother, casting a net into the sea for they were fisherfolk. [19] And he said to them, "Follow me, and I will make you fish for people—women, children, and men." [20] At once they left their nets and followed him. [21] As Jesus went from there, he saw two other brothers, James son of Zebedee and his brother John, in the boat with their father Zebedee, mending their nets, and he called them. [22] At once they left the boat and their father and followed him.

[23] Jesus went throughout Galilee, teaching in their synagogues and proclaiming the good news of the reign of God and curing every disease and every malady among the people—women, men, and children. [24] So his fame spread throughout all Syria, and they brought to him all the sick, those who were afflicted with various diseases and tormented by pain, demoniacs, epileptics, and paralytics, and he cured them. [25] And great crowds followed him from Galilee, the Decapolis, Jerusalem, Judea, and from beyond the Jordan.

PROCLAMATION

Text Notes

There are two primary Greek manuscripts for Tobit: G^{I}, represented in older Bibles such KJV and RSV, and G^{II}, represented in newer translations, e.g., NRSV and CEB and my own. The latter is longer by some 1,700 words: for example, the first line of Tobit 13:11 is present in G^{II} but not G^{I}. (See Carey Moore's commentary in the *Anchor Bible* series.) Verse numbers vary among the manuscripts; for simplicity I follow NRSV versification.

“Peoples” in Tobit 13:11 refers to Gentile nations. “City” is missing from verse 11; it is implied by the adjective “elect,” which is feminine here, as is “city.” “Revere” in verse 12 is literally “fear.” The “daughters and sons” of the righteous are expanded from “children” in verse 13.

In Psalm 22:23, “the offspring of Jacob” are identified by their mothers/matriarchs, enslaved and free; similarly, “Rebekah’s line” stands in for “the offspring of Israel.” Poverty in verse 24 of the psalm is that which comes from oppression.

I use “realm of God” rather than kingdom in Matthew 4:23 to move away from a violent male human metaphor for God. (Ancient monarchs gained and maintained their crowns through brutality; monarchs were on the front lines, crushing skulls, hacking and bludgeoning opponents to death.)

Preaching Prompts

Women are on the furthest edges of the text of Tobit 13 as they are in so much of the canon: Women are hidden in the “many peoples from far away” and “inhabitants of the furthest edges of the earth.” They are inferred. These women are Gentiles, the persons with the least status in Israel’s scriptures. Yet the epiphanous light of God reaches them.

In the psalm, women are at the fore because the translators chose to name the matriarchs through whom Israel descends rather than the patriarch named in the Hebrew text, Jacob later called Israel. Consider what it means that Jacob’s offspring are born of four women, including enslaved women, and how “offspring of Jacob” renders them unseen and sanitized the story. Identifying Israel as “Rebekah’s line” also evokes the matrilineal practices of her family in which her father was called by his mother’s name, Betheul ben (son of) Milcah (Genesis 24:24).

In 1 Timothy 3, God’s self-revelation in Jesus to the Gentiles is in the past and a pillar of the faith while in Matthew 4 it is ongoing. The Gospel uses inclusive language for those who will be called, “fished,” and those whom Jesus will heal, various words for people and “all.” Specific narratives about women and children are few, but they are always present in the crowds, in the people, in the nation(s), in virtually every collective plural.

Lastly, be aware of what is at stake in the Anglicization of Jewish names throughout the New Testament, how it obscures their Judaism and creates space for anti-Judaism and anti-Semitism, particularly the shift from Ya‘aqov (Jacob) to James and Yochanon (Johanan) to John.

EPIPHANY IV

Isaiah 42:1–5, 10–16; Psalm 107:1–9, 19–22; James 1:17–21; Matthew 8:14–22

Isaiah 42:1 Here is my servant, whom I uphold,
my chosen, the delight of my soul;
I have set my Spirit upon my servant
who will bring forth justice to the nations.
2 My servant will not cry out or raise her voice,
or make it heard in the street.
3 A bruised reed he will not break,
and a dimming wick they will not quench;
my servant shall bring forth true justice.
4 My servant will not be dimmed or bruised
until he has established justice in the earth,
and for her teaching the coastlands wait.
5 Thus says the HOLY GOD,
the One who created the heavens and stretched them out,
who spread out the earth and her progeny,
who gives breath to the people upon her,
and spirit to those who walk in her:
10 Sing to the EVERLASTING GOD a new song:
God's praise from the end of the earth—
Sea-riders and all that fills it—
the coastlands and their denizens.
11 Let the desert and its towns raise their voice,
the villages where Kedar dwells;
let the citizens of Sela sing for joy,
let them shout from the tops of the mountains.
12 Let them give glory to the GOD OF ALL CREATION,
and declare God's praise in the coastlands.
13 The DREAD GOD goes forth like a warrior,
like a combatant God stirs up divine fury;
God shouts, even roars,
showing Godself mighty against the enemies of God.
14 From everlasting have I held myself,
I have kept still and restrained myself;
now I will scream like a birthing woman,
I will gasp, and I will pant at the same time.

15 I will lay waste mountains and hills,
and desiccate all their foliage;
I will turn the rivers into islands,
and I will dry up the pools.
16 I will lead the blind
by a way they do not know,
by paths they have not known
I will guide them.
I will turn the bleakness before them into light,
the rough places into level ground.
These are the things I will do,
and I will not forsake them.

Psalm 107:1–9, 19–22

1 Give thanks to SHE WHO IS MAJESTY, for she is good,
and her faithful love endures forever.
2 Let the redeemed of SHE WHO SAVES proclaim
that she redeemed them from the hand of the foe.
3 And she has gathered them from [all] the lands;
from the east and from the west, from the north and from the south.
4 They wandered in the wilderness, in the desert;
no path to a city fit for settling did they find.
5 They were hungry and thirsty;
their souls fainted within them.
6 Then they cried to SHE WHO HEARS in their trouble,
and from their distress she delivered them.
7 And she led them on a straight path
to a city fit for settling.
8 Let them give thanks to WOMB OF LIFE for her faithful love
and her wonderful works for the woman-born.
9 For she satisfies the thirsty soul
and the hungry souls she fills with goodness.
19 They cried to the MOTHER OF ALL in their trouble,
and she delivered them from their distress.
20 She sent forth her word and healed them
and saved them from their pits.
21 Let them give thanks to the WOMB OF LIFE for her faithful love
and wonderful works for the woman-born.
22 Let them sacrifice sacrifices of thanksgiving
and tell of her acts with shouts of joy.

James 1:17 Every good gift, every perfect gift, is from above, coming down from the Weaver
of lights, with whom there is no variation or changing shadow. 18 In fulfillment of her own
purpose, God gave us birth by the word of truth, so that we would become a kind of first
fruits of her creatures.
19 Understand my beloved kin: let everyone be quick to listen, slow to speak, slow to
anger, 20 for a man's anger does not produce God's righteousness. 21 Therefore rid yourselves
of all impurity and abundance of wickedness, and with meekness welcome the implanted
word that has the power to save your souls.

Matthew 8:14 When Jesus entered Peter's house, he saw his mother-in-law laid out and
fevered, 15 and Jesus touched her hand and the fever left her, and she got up and began to
serve him. 16 That evening they brought Jesus many who were demon-possessed and he cast
out the spirits with a word and healed all the sick 17 in order to fulfill what had been spoken
through the prophet Isaiah, *"He took our infirmities and bore our diseases."*
18 But when Jesus saw a crowd around him, he commanded that they go over to the other
side. 19 A religious scholar then approached and said, "Teacher, I will follow you wherever you
go." 20 And Jesus said to him, "Foxes have dens and birds of the air have nests, but the Son of
Woman has not where to lay his head." 21 Another of his disciples said to him, "Lord, let me first
go and bury my father." 22 But Jesus said to him, "Follow me, and let the dead bury their dead."

PROCLAMATION

Text Notes

The identity of the servants in the Servant Songs range from the nation of Israel to an anonymous prophet or monarch to a messianic figure. Here the servant is unidentified, though the LXX names Jacob. I have used a variety of pronouns to demonstrate that God calls whom God wills, recognizing gender plurality among God's chosen leaders and the reader-hearers who will interpret this text in our time. As is the case throughout the scriptures, "servant" language is "slave" language; I have preserved the more familiar servant here to correspond with the well-known title of the genre, the Servant Songs

The Jewish Publication Society, JPS, offers as an alternative translation for Isaiah 42:3: *A bruised reed, he shall not be broken/A dim wick, he shall not be snuffed out.* "His teaching" in verse 6 is "his torah." The root means "revelation," and "instruction" as well as "law." "Fury" in verse 13 is "jealousy." In verse 11 Kedar, an Ishmaelite kin group, represents one of the furthest edges of the world; Sela, "Rock," was an Edomite stronghold. Together they represent ancient enmity transformed.

In Psalm 107, verses 8 and 20, "woman-born" renders the euphemism for humanity, "human children/children (or sons) of men." Son of Woman for the comparable Greek expression communicates the humanness called for in Matthew 8:20.

The language of birth in James 1:18 drives the translation choices in verse 17–18: Weaver rather than Father, and feminine pronouns. The "implanted word" in verse 20 continues the theme. Verse 19 uses *anthropos*, an inclusive term for humanity, but verse 20 specifies male anger using *andros*.

In Matthew 8:15, Peter's mother-in-law ministers to him, Jesus, in some manuscripts, and them, the disciples, in others. Verse 17 quotes Isaiah 53:4.

Preaching Prompts

God's special servant is revealed as gentle and tender, either a bruised reed or one who will not break a bruised reed, and at the same time reveals God as a dread warrior and a birthing mother. While Christian readers have seen Jesus in Isaiah 42, they have not always attended the multiplicity of images as ways to think about God or Jesus, especially welcome as an alternative to domineering constructions that feed toxic masculinities. Rather than speculating on whether the text can be read as predicting Jesus, hear it as one model for a servant of God on a national and international stage. The language of light and dark (including shadow) are primarily antithetical throughout, yet the holy darkness of God's wombs incubates life. God's work in the first lesson is to lead her people to safety in Isaiah 42:16, a theme continued in Psalm 107.

Each lesson addresses the whole of humanity implicitly or explicitly, Gentile nations in Isaiah 42:1, and coastal peoples and peoples of the Arabian Peninsula in verses 10–11. The peoples of the seacoast may have included Tyre and Phoenicia, the old Philistine territory, who like the Arabians were historically in conflict with Israel. God's justice is for them all. Those on the coast can also be read as emblematic of marginalization; there is no one beyond the reach of God's presence. James 1 and Matthew 8 both address the whole of the anthropological, human project (though James addresses male anger directly in 1:20). Jesus asserts his human identity, one with us, even as his divine nature is revealed in his healing and in the wisdom of his teaching.

The two stories in the Gospel show two different responses to Jesus's self-revelation: the mother of the woman married to Peter turns toward Jesus and Jesus's male pupil turns away. In the *Women's Commentary on the Bible* Amy-Jill Levine notes that the woman's service, *diakonia*, can be seen as continuing the pattern of the *diakonia* of the angels who ministered to Jesus in the wilderness and evokes the ministry of deacons.

While many have commented on the presence of the wife of Peter as affirming marriage and sexual activity among the disciples, few have considered the discipleship of the elder woman and her daughter beyond this scene. Were they among plural undifferentiated disciples? Were they among the "many women" who provided for Jesus in Matthew 27:55?

EPIPHANY V

2 Kings 5:1–4, 9–14; Psalm 30; Acts 16:16–24; Matthew 9:18–26

2 Kings 5:1 Naaman, commander of the army of the ruler of Aram, was a great man in the
sight of his master and highly esteemed, because through him the HOLY ONE had given victory to Aram. The man, a great warrior, was diseased in his skin. 2 Now Aramean troops went
out and took captive from the land of Israel a young girl, and she was placed before Naaman's
wife. 3 She said to her mistress, "If only my lord were with the prophet who is in Samaria! He
would take his skin disease away." 4 So Naaman went in and told his master the girl from the
land of Israel had said this and this.

9 Then Naaman came with his horses and chariot and stood at the entrance of Elisha's house.
10 Elisha sent a messenger to him, who said, "Go, wash in the Jordan seven times, and your flesh
shall be restored, and you shall be unblemished." 11 But Naaman became angry and left saying,
"Look here! I thought that for me he would surely come out and stand and call on the name of
the MOST HIGH, his God, and would wave his hand over the spot, and take away the skin disease! 12 Are not Abana and Pharpar, the rivers of Damascus, better than all the waters of Israel?
Could I not wash in them, and be restored?" Then he turned and went away in a rage. 13 But his
slaves approached and said to him, "My father, were it a great thing the prophet told you to do,
would you not have done it? How much more, when what he said to you was, 'Wash, and be
restored?" 14 So he went down and immersed himself seven times in the Jordan, according to the
word of the man of God; his flesh was renewed like the flesh of a little boy, and he was restored.

Psalm 30

1 I will exalt you, ARK OF SAFETY, because you have pulled me up
and have not let my enemies rejoice over me.
2 HEALING ONE, my God, I cried to you for help,
and you healed me.
3 EVER-LIVING GOD, you brought my soul up from Sheol;
you preserved my life from descent to the Pit.
4 Sing praises to the FAITHFUL GOD, you her faithful;
give thanks remembering her holiness.
5 For her fury is a moment, her favor a lifetime.
Weeping may pass the night, yet in the morning, joy.
6 Now I, I said in my prosperity,
"I shall never be shaken."
7 MAJESTIC ONE by your favor you established me as a mighty mountain;
you hid your face, I was terrified.
8 To you MOST HIGH I call,
and to you my sovereign I appeal:

9 "What profit is there in my [shed] blood, in my descent to the Pit?
Will the dust praise you, declare your faithfulness?
10 Hear, HOLY ONE, and have mercy upon me;
HOLY ONE OF OLD, be my help.
11 You have turned my wailing into dancing;
from me you have taken my sackcloth and you have clothed me with joy.
12 So that my glory might praise you and not keep silent;
GLORIOUS ONE, my God, forever will I praise you.

Acts 16:16 One day, as we were going to the place of prayer, we met an enslaved girl who
had a spirit of divination and brought her masters a great deal of money by fortune-telling.
17 While she followed after Paul and us, she cried out, "These persons are slaves of the Most
High God, who proclaim to you a way of salvation." 18 This she did for many days. But it
bothered Paul, who turned and said to the spirit, "I order you in the name of Jesus Christ to
come out of her." And it came out that hour.

19 Now when her masters saw that their hope of financial gain was gone, they seized Paul
and Silas and into the marketplace they dragged them before the authorities. 20 When they
had brought them before the magistrates, they said, "These persons are disturbing our city;
they are Judeans 21 and are preaching traditions that are not right for us to follow as Romans."
22 The crowd joined against them, and the magistrates had them stripped of their clothing
and ordered them to be beaten with batons. 23 After they had laid many blows on them, they
threw them into prison and commanded the jailer to keep them securely. 24 Receiving these
instructions, he put them in the innermost cell and their feet he fastened in the stocks.

Matthew 9:18 While Jesus was speaking, suddenly a leader [of the synagogue] came in and
prostrated himself, saying, "My daughter has just died; but come and lay your hand on her, and
she will live." 19 And Jesus got up and followed him, along with his disciples. 20 Then suddenly
a woman who had been hemorrhaging for twelve years came up behind him and touched the
fringe on his clothing, 21 for she said to herself, "If I could only touch his clothing, I will be
healed." 22 Jesus turned, and seeing her he said, "Take courage, daughter, your faith has healed
you." And the woman was healed from that hour. 23 Then Jesus came to the leader's house and
saw the flute players and the crowd making a disturbance. 24 He said, "Leave, for the precious
girl is not dead but sleeping." And they laughed at him. 25 But when the crowd had been put
out, he went in and took her by the hand, and the precious girl arose. 26 And the news of this
spread throughout that district.

PROCLAMATION

Text Notes

The specific skin disease mistranslated as leprosy throughout the scriptures does not result in loss of extremities but does infect clothing, houses and walls according to

Leviticus 13:47–59 and 14:54–55, counter to the disease we now call leprosy. The word "lord/master" is used for persons who enslave other persons and for God in the scriptures; it will only be used for human beings in this work. "Lord" appears as the title of Naaman, his commander, and the enslavers of the girl in Acts.

In 2 Kings 5:3, "take away" the disease is literally "gather." The language "clean/unclean" can be stigmatizing and do not accurately convey their wider meanings. In verse 13, the renewal of his flesh is "turned [into] the flesh of a little boy."

Where grammatically and rhetorically possible, I translate the language "slavery" to reflect what was done to persons—being enslaved—rather than identify them by their state as in Acts 16:16. The divining spirit is called a "python," a reference to the python guarding the Delphi Oracle which then became a euphemism for all sorts of vocal performances, including divination and ventriloquism. The word translated as "fortune-telling" can also be translated as "divination" or "prophecy."

Matthew 9:18 is part of a longer discourse. Verse 18 begins, "While he was saying these things to them," connecting this unit to the previous discourse on fasting, the bridegroom, and new and old wineskins. Here Jairus is just "a leader." The synagogue is not mentioned here; it is imported from Mark 5:22 and Luke 8:41. In verse 19, the Greek specifies the fringe that Jewish men and, arguably, women wore as required by Numbers 15:38–39 (counter to some contemporary Jewish practice; women are not prohibited in the text or by its grammar). The language for the girl varies in each account. In verse 24, "girl" is a diminutive of κόρη, one who is the apple of the eye. (Mark 5:41 also preserves an endearment; *talitha* is Aramaic for lamb, see 1 Samuel 7:9; Isaiah 40:11; 65:25).

Preaching Prompts

In these lessons God's power is manifest in healing of the Gentile, Syrian military commander, a beneficence that is not restricted to Israelites. Jesus is manifest as God in human flesh through the same power to heal, in this case a woman with a gynecological hemorrhage and the resurrection of a young girl. The psalm celebrates this fundamental characteristic of God, the one who restores life and health, even from the grasp of the grave. In the Acts lesson, Peter as a disciple of Jesus shares in his healing ministry, but he lacks the grace of Jesus. Peter heals the enslaved girl whose origin is unknown because he is vexed by her, not out of concern for her. In two of these texts, the manifestation of God's awesome power is eclipsed by the banality of unchallenged slavery.

Women and girls abound and stand out in these texts; there are also hidden women among the enslaved persons in 2 Kings 5 and crowds in Acts 16. In addition, the funeral singers and musicians of verse 23 were normally women. There are also violently feminized men present. In Acts 16:22, Paul and Silas are publicly stripped to humiliate them as well as facilitate their flogging. Forcible stripping is a personal violation and sexually violent; imagine the crowd catcalling and hooting, mocking whatever of their anatomy was revealed.

Matthew 9:22 also offers an opportunity to talk about salvation. "Be made well, healed, cured," etc. are all translations of "saved, preserved, delivered." This word is the root of Jesus's name, "He will save his people from their sins" (Matthew 1:21).

EPIPHANY VI

Isaiah 62:1–7, 12; Psalm 146; Revelation 12:1–6, 13–17; Matthew 11:7–19

Isaiah 62:1 For the sake of Zion I will not keep silent,
and for the sake of Jerusalem I will not keep still,
until her vindication shines out like blazing light,
and her salvation like a flaming torch.
2 The nations shall see your vindication, daughter,
and all the monarchs your glory;
and you shall be called by a new name
that the mouth of the LIVING GOD will grant.
3 You, daughter, shall be a crown of beauty in the hand of God MOST HIGH,
and a royal diadem in the hand of your God.
4 Daughter, no more shall you be called Forsaken,
and no more shall your land be called Devastated;
but you shall be called My Delight Is in Her,
and your land, Married;
for the FAITHFUL GOD delights in you,
and your land shall be married.
5 For as a young man marries a virgin girl,
so shall your builder marry you daughter,
and as the bridegroom rejoices over the bride,
so shall your God rejoice over you.

6 Upon your walls, daughter Jerusalem,
I have posted sentinels;
all the day and all the night,
they shall never be silent.
You who remind the GOD WHO SEES,
take no rest for yourselves,
7 and give God no rest
until God establishes Jerusalem
and makes it renowned throughout the earth.

12 They shall call them, "The Holy People,
The Redeemed of the GOD WHO SAVES";
and you, daughter, shall be called, "Sought Out,
A City Not Forsaken."

Psalm 146

1 Hallelujah! Praise the AGELESS ONE, O my soul!
2 I will praise the EVER-LIVING GOD all my life;
I will sing praises to my God throughout my living.
3 Put not your trust in the great, nor in any child of earth,
for there is no help in them.
4 When they breathe their last, they return to earth,
and in that day their thoughts perish.
5 Happy are these for whom the God of Rebekah's line is their help,
whose hope is in the CREATOR OF ALL, their God.
6 Maker of heavens and earth, the seas, and all that is in them;
keeping faith forever.
7 Bringer of justice to the oppressed,
bringer of bread to the hungry;
the COMPASSIONATE GOD sets the prisoners free.
8 The ALL-SEEING GOD opens the eyes of the blind,
the JUST GOD lifts up those who are bowed down;
The RIGHTEOUS GOD loves the righteous.
9 The MOTHER OF ALL cares for the stranger,
orphan and widow she bears up,
but the way of the wicked she confounds.
10 The MAJESTIC ONE shall reign forever,
your God, O Zion, from generation to generation. Hallelujah!

Revelation 12:1 A great sign was seen in heaven: a woman clothed with the sun, with the
moon beneath her feet, and on her head a crown of twelve stars. 2 She had a child in her
womb and was crying out, laboring in pain in the agony of giving birth. 3 Then another
great sign was seen in heaven: See this! a great red dragon, with seven heads and ten horns,
and seven diadems on its heads. 4 Its tail dragged down a third of the stars of heaven and
threw them to the earth. Then the dragon stood before the woman who was about to give
birth, so that it might devour her child as soon as her child was born. 5 And she gave birth
to a son (a male!), who is about to rule all the nations with a rod of iron. But her child was
snatched away and taken to God and to God's throne; 6 and the woman fled into the wilderness, where she has a place prepared by God, so that there she can be nourished for one
thousand two hundred sixty days.

13 Now when the dragon saw that it had been thrown down to the earth, it pursued the
woman who had given birth to the male child. 14 But the woman was given two wings of a great
eagle so that she could fly to her place, where she is nourished for a season, and more seasons, and
half a season, away from the serpent into the wilderness. 15 Then the serpent spewed water like a
river from its mouth after the woman, to engulf and sweep her away. 16 But the earth came to the
help of the woman; she opened her mouth and swallowed the river that the dragon had spewed
from its mouth. 17 Then the dragon was angry with the woman and went off to make war on the
rest of her seed, those who keep the commandments of God and hold the testimony of Jesus.

Matthew 11:7 As John's disciples went away, Jesus began to speak to the crowds about John:
"What did you go out into the wilderness to see? A reed shaken by the wind? 8 But what did
you go out to see? A person dressed in luxurious robes? Look, those who wear luxurious robes
are in royal houses. 9 What then did you go out to see? A prophet? Yes, I tell you, and more
than a prophet. 10 He is the one about whom it is written,

> *'Look, I am sending my messenger ahead of you,*
> *who will prepare your way before you.'*

11 Truly I tell you, no one has arisen among those born of women greater than John the Baptizer; yet the least in the realm of the heavens is greater than he. 12 From the days of John the
Baptizer until now the realm of the heavens endures violence, and the violent seize it. 13 For all
the prophets and the law prophesied until John came; 14 and if you are willing to receive it, he
is Elijah who is to come. 15 Let those with ears hear!
16 "Now to what shall I liken this generation? It is like girls and boys sitting in the marketplaces and calling to one another saying,

> 17 'We played the flute for you, and you did not dance;
> we sang a lament, and you did not mourn.'

18 For John came neither eating nor drinking, and they say, 'He has a demon'; 19 the Son of
Woman came eating and drinking, and they say, 'Look, a glutton and a drunk, a friend of tax
collectors and sinners!' Yet Wisdom is vindicated by her deeds."

PROCLAMATION

Text Notes

The use of "daughter" in Isaiah 62 makes the divine address to a feminine subject, Zion, in verses 1–6, accessible to English readers as it is to those who read in Hebrew. The end of verse 6 addresses the people, or some among them, as a collective.

The poetry of verse 4 is impossible to replicate in English; note the four assonant three-syllable words: *Azuvah, Shamamah, Hephzibah*, and *Beʿulah* (not Beulah) and the corresponding lack of rhyme or rhythm in their translations: "Forsaken,"

"Devastated," "My Delight is in Her," and "Married." The pattern recurs in verse 12 with *D'rushah* and *Ir Lo Ne'etzavah*, "Sought Out," and "A City Not Forsaken."

The verb "marry" in Isaiah 62:4–5 is *ba'al*, which also means "lord/master" as a noun. (It may be familiar as the divine title for the god Ba'al whose proper name, Haddu, is not generally used.) While the verb suggests a very hierarchal understanding of marriage, it is rarely used in the canon, five times for humans and in eleven divine metaphors. Sentinels, as in Isaiah 62:6, are often synonymous for prophets.

In Psalm 146:1, "throughout my living" is derived from "in my continuing" where "continue" is the adverb meaning "longer," *'od*, with the first possessive suffix, "my" attached; a very complex idiomatic saying. The "great" in verse 2 are "nobles," sometimes royal offspring, hence "princes" in other translations. In verse 4 "Rebekah's line" replaces "Jacob." The nature of God's support for widow and orphan in verse 9 is unclear; the verb there is only used there and its derivation is unclear. NRSV's "uphold" derives from the LXX and provides the basis for my "bear up." Similarly, the Peshitta has "nourish/support."

In Matthew 11:8 John's robe is described with a word that can mean "soft," "fancy," or with regard to men, one who sexually penetrated. (I avoid "homosexual" contra to the dominant Greek lexicon, BDAG; that is a contemporary understanding of sexual orientation not applicable to the ancient world.) Verse 10 quotes Malachi 3:1; the word "messenger" here is *aggelos*, otherwise translated "angel," though "messenger" is its primary meaning and covers both human and divine messengers. In verse 19 Wisdom is vindicated or justified by her deeds; in other manuscripts she is justified by her children (hence "children" here in the Vulgate, KJV, and early English translations); the reading "children" endures in Luke 7:35.

Preaching Prompts

These lessons use imagery drawn from the lives and culturally cued social roles for women in ancient Israel continuing through the Greek and Roman periods to frame God's self-revelation and manifestation in and through Jesus. Jerusalem, like most cities in the ancient world is feminine, mothers whose walls protected their children; suburbs were called daughter cities, see Ezekiel 26:6, 8; 30:18.

In Isaiah 62, postdestruction Jerusalem will be rejoiced over as though she were a virgin bride; she, her land, will be married. Remembering that these metaphors are drawn from the experiences of women, this text offers a way to talk about life after trauma, including rape and other dehumanizing acts. Jerusalem's vindication can be read as the vanquishing of shame, the imputed shame of rape.

In Psalm 146, God demonstrates true majesty in her caretaking of the vulnerable: women receive care from the hand of God. Not just widowed women in verse 9 but also women who are oppressed, hungry and imprisoned in verse 7, women who are blind and bowed down in verse 8, and women who are righteous, strangers, sojourners, or immigrants, as well as women who are themselves orphans in verse 9. God's majesty rests on a foundation of righteousness and justice to which no human monarch can ever fully aspire.

In Revelation 12, the maternal construction of women reaches cosmic proportions. The Great Mother is clothed with the sun, crowned with the stars, straddling the moon (my reading), standing and squatting in the face of the primeval dragon—bearing its own feminine history in the Mesopotamian world where it is the form of a number of goddesses. In Egyptian mythology, the devouring serpent Apophis is male (verses 14–15 switches from dragon to serpent, *ophis*). While this woman has been conflated with the Blessed Virgin who bears her iconography—twelve-starred crown and moon underfoot—she is more. She is divine in her own right; there is no parallel for wearing the sun as a garment. Yet she and her child are vulnerable to the dragon-serpent, positioned to snatch the child from her as it emerges from her body, an incredibly violent image. God's care for her is extraordinary: preparing a safe place, nourishing her there, granting her wings to speed her flight. Even the earth wades into the fray on her behalf. It is noteworthy that no human woman in the text receives this level of divine intervention.

Human and divine motherhood come together in Matthew 11. Jesus uses the expression "woman-born" as shorthand for humanity in verse 11, while he is presented in verse 19 as the Son of Woman (my translation), son of humanity, human child, mortal one. The old "Son of Man" translation misses that *anthropos* means "human," not male, and "man" is not generic. Jesus also positions himself as the child of Wisdom; her deeds are his deeds.

EPIPHANY VII

Isaiah 61:1–4, 8–10; Song of Songs 3:1–11; 1 Corinthians 9:1–10; John 2:1–11

Isaiah 61:1 The Spirit of the Sovereign GOD is upon me,
because the HOLY GOD has anointed me.
God has sent me to declare good news to the oppressed,
to bind up the brokenhearted,
to proclaim liberation to the captives,
and freedom to the prisoners;
2 to proclaim a year of the MOST HIGH God's favor,
and the day of vengeance of our God;
to comfort all children, women, and men who mourn;
3 to provide for those women, children, and men who mourn in Zion;
to give them glory instead of ashes,
the oil of gladness instead of mourning,

the mantle of praise instead of a faint spirit.
They will be called oaks of righteousness,
the planting of the MOST HIGH,
for God to display God's own glory.
4 They shall build up the ancient ruins,
they shall raise up the former devastations;
they shall restore the ruined cities,
devastations across generations.
8 For I, the ETERNAL GOD, am the One who loves justice,
and the One who hates robbery sacrificed as a burnt offering;
I will faithfully give them their recompense,
and I will make an everlasting covenant with them.
9 Their descendants shall be known among the nations,
and their offspring among the peoples;
all who see them shall recognize
that they are a people whom the HOLY ONE has blessed.
10 I will greatly rejoice in the MOST HIGH God,
my soul shall exult in my God;
for God has clothed me in garments of salvation,
God has covered me with a robe of righteousness,
as a bridegroom vests himself with a garland,
and as a bride adorns herself with her jewels.

Canticle: Song of Songs 3:1–11

Song 3:1 Upon my bed at night
I sought the one my soul loves;
I sought him, and I found him not;
[I called him, and he gave me no answer.]
2 "Let me rise now; I will go about in the city,
in the streets and in the squares;
I will seek the one my soul loves."
I sought him but found him not.
3 The sentinels found me,
the ones who go about in the city.
"Have you all seen the one my soul loves?"
4 Scarcely had I passed from them,
when I found the one my soul loves.
I held him, and would not let him go
until I brought him into the house of my mother,
and into the chamber of she who conceived me.

5 I need you all to swear, Daughters of Jerusalem,
by the she-gazelles or the does of the field—
Do not stir up or awaken love
until it pleasures!
6 Who is this coming up from the wilderness
like a column of smoke
scented with myrrh and frankincense,
with all the fragrant powders of the merchant?
7 Look! It is his bed! Solomon!
Sixty warriors surround it
from the warriors of Israel.
8 All of them bear swords;
they are learned in war,
each with his sword upon his thigh
because of terror in the night.
9 King Solomon made a palanquin for himself
from the trees of Lebanon.
10 He made its pillars of silver,
its back of gold, its seat of purple;
its interior was bedecked with love from the daughters of Jerusalem.
11 Come out and look, Daughters of Zion,
at the King, Solomon,
at the crown with which his mother crowned him
on the day of his wedding,
on the day of the joy of his heart.

1 Corinthians 9:1 Am I not free? Am I not an apostle? Have I not seen Jesus our Redeemer?
Are you not my work in the Savior? 2 If I am not an apostle to others, surely I am to you, for
you are the seal of my apostleship in the Messiah.

3 This is my defense to those who examine me. 4 Do we not have the right to our food
and drink? 5 Do we not have the right to travel with a sister, a wife, as do the other apostles
and the brothers of the Messiah and Cephas? 6 Or is it only I and Barnabas who have no
right to not work? 7 Who soldiers and pays their own expenses? Who plants a vineyard and
does not eat any of its fruit? Or who shepherds a flock and does not taste any of the milk
of the flock?

8 Do I say this as a human person? Does not the law also say the same? 9 For it is written in the teaching of Moses, "You shall not muzzle a threshing ox." Is it for oxen that God
cares? 10 Or does God not, by all means, speak for our sake? It was indeed written for our
sake, for the one who must plow should plow in hope and whoever threshes should thresh
in hope of partaking.

John 2:1 On the third day there was a wedding in Cana of Galilee, and the mother of Jesus
was there. 2 Jesus and his disciples had also been invited to the wedding. 3 When the wine gave
out, the mother of Jesus said to him, "They have no wine." 4 And Jesus said to her, "Woman,
what concern is that to you and to me? My hour has not yet come." 5 His mother said to the
servants, "Do whatever he tells you." 6 Now standing there were six stone water jars for the
Jewish rites of purification, each holding twenty or thirty gallons. 7 Jesus said to them, "Fill
the jars with water." And they filled them up to the brim. 8 He said to them, "Now draw some
out, and take it to the chief steward." So they took it. 9 When the steward tasted the water that
had become wine, and did not know where it came from (though the servants who had drawn
the water knew), the steward called the bridegroom 10 and said to him, "Everyone serves the
good wine first, and then the inferior wine after the guests have become drunk. But you have
kept the good wine until now." 11 Jesus did this, the first of his signs, in Cana of Galilee, and
revealed his glory; and his disciples believed in him.

PROCLAMATION

Text Notes

In Isaiah 61:1, "vests" has a liturgical sense. The actual verb is a form of the word for priest; the bridegroom dresses himself just as a priest puts on his ornaments.

The last line in Songs 3:1 is not present in the Hebrew text and traditionally added from the LXX. In the last line of verse 5, the chanteuse bids the women of Jerusalem not to disturb love[making] until "that-it-delights" (one word). The NRSV's "do not awaken love until it is ready" reads as an injunction against sexual activity until the proper time, i.e., maturity. That is sage counsel. This passage is actually saying do not disturb the lovers who go to bed in the previous verse until they are pleasured.

In 1 Corinthians 9:5, the "right" to food and drink provided and to marry is expressed as "power" or "authority." Verse 9 quotes Deuteronomy 25:4.

Preaching Prompts

The marriage metaphor that so often symbolizes the relationship between God and Israel and Christ and the Church has its roots in real human relationships. Marriage becomes a sacrament to make manifest the love of God in and between two people within a communal context. Marriage is socially constructed in and out of the Bible: abduction and rape marriages, polygamous marriages, and hierarchal domineering marriages are all biblical but few would call them epiphanies of God's love. Marriage is also heteronormative in the text; our understanding of the human person and sexuality has also evolved since the text and marriage continues to be shaped to make known the wideness of God's love. It is for this reason that the Blessed Virgin chose to reveal her Son's glory at the wedding in Cana.

Reading Isaiah 61 in its own context yields a reminder that God does not just call Jesus to the work of liberation. The poet-prophet says, "The Spirit is upon me" for this same work centuries before Jesus. The work is contextual and concrete. The physical and financial costs of Israelite subjugation will be reversed; liberation is all encompassing, physical as well as spiritual. Likewise, the marriage metaphor provides language for the resulting joy that is physical and includes sexual joy.

The Song of Songs is a riot of sensual and erotic poetry, much of which is placed on the lips of a woman who pursues love and sexual fulfilment shamelessly. (Later Jewish and Christian interpreters would work overtime to strip the Song of its literal meaning in favor of metaphorical and allegorical readings.) God is never mentioned in the text, yet is present in the love and passion of the lovers. Uncomfortably for some, the lovers are not married.

Paul's desire for a companion, a wife, who shares his faith is frank and honest. It is also instructive; depriving people of love, companionship, and sexual fulfilment flies in the face of what it means to be the church of the God who is love and created sex. (His argument in 1 Corinthians 9:9 about whether God cares for oxen *or* humans is short-sighted, as is common with binary claims.)

In John 2, Mary, the mother of Jesus, prompts him to reveal himself in the miracle that is understood as the formal inauguration of his public ministry, verse 3. In so doing, she leaves us with profound instructions for our Christian faith in verse 5, "Do whatever he tells you."

EPIPHANY VIII

Isaiah 6:1–7; Psalm 29; Revelation 4:2–11; John 1:1–5

Isaiah 6:1 In the year that King Uzziah died, I saw the Holy One sitting on a throne, high and
exalted; and the trailing edges, as of God's garment, filled the temple. 2 Seraphs stood attending
God—six wings!—each had six wings! With two they covered their faces, and with two they
covered their groins, and with two they flew. 3 And this one called to that one and said:

> "Holy, holy, holy is the MARSHALL of heaven's armies;
> the whole earth is full of God's glory."

4 The doorposts of the thresholds shook at the voices of those who called, and the house was
filled with smoke. 5 And I said: "Woe is me! I am wrecked, for I am a person of unclean lips,
and I live among a people of unclean lips; yet my eyes have seen the Sovereign, the COMMANDER of the vanguard of heaven!"

6 Then one of the seraphs flew to me, and in its hand a hot coal that with tongs had been
taken from upon the altar. 7 It touched my mouth with it and said: "Look! Now that this has
touched your lips, your guilt has turned aside and your sin atoned."

Psalm 29

1 Render unto SHE WHO IS, O divine ones,
render unto SHE WHO REIGNS, glory and strength.
2 Render to SHE WHO IS GLORY, the glory of her name;
worship SHE WHO IS HOLY in majestic holiness.
3 The voice of SHE WHO THUNDERS is above the waters;
the God of glory thunders,
SHE WHO THUNDERS is above the mighty waters.
4 The voice of SHE WHO IS POWER is powerful;
the voice of SHE WHO IS MAJESTY is full of majesty.
5 The voice of SHE WHO THUNDERS breaks the cedars;
SHE WHO THUNDERS breaks the cedars of Lebanon.
6 She makes Lebanon skip like a calf,
and Sirion like a young wild ox.
7 The voice of SINAI'S FIRE
sunders flames of fire.
8 The voice of SHE WHO THUNDERS
makes the wilderness writhe [as though giving birth];
SHE WHO THUNDERS
makes the wilderness of Kadesh travail [as though giving birth].
9 The voice of SHE WHO SPEAKS CREATION
causes the oaks to arch [as though giving birth],
and strips the forest bare;
and in her temple, all say, "Glory!"
10 SHE WHO IS MAJESTY sits enthroned over the flood;
SHE WHO REIGNS sits enthroned as Sovereign forever.
11 May SHE WHO IS MIGHTY give strength to her people!
May SHE WHO IS PEACE bless her people with peace!

Revelation 4:2 Suddenly I was in the spirit, and there! a throne positioned in heaven, and
upon the throne there was one seated. 3 And the one seated there looks like jasper and
carnelian, and there is a rainbow all around the throne that looks like an emerald. 4 Also, all
around the throne are twenty-four thrones, and on the thrones are twenty-four elders seated,
dressed in white garments, and upon their heads, golden crowns. 5 Coming from the throne
was lightning, and roaring, and thunder, and seven flaming torches in front of the throne
blazed, which are the seven spirits of God; 6 and in front of the throne there is a sea of glass,
like crystal. Around the throne, and on each side of the throne, are four living beings, full of
eyes in front and behind: 7 the first being was like a lion, the second being was like an ox, the
third being had a face like a human being, and the fourth being was like a flying eagle. 8 Now

the four living creatures, each of them had six wings, full of eyes all around and inside. Without ceasing day and night they say,

"Holy, holy, holy,
Sovereign God Almighty,
who was and is and is to come."

9 And when the living beings give glory and honor and thanks to the one seated on the throne, who lives forever and an eternity, 10 the twenty-four elders fall before the one who is seated on the throne and worship the one who lives forever and ever; they cast their crowns before the throne, saying,

11 "Worthy are you, our Savior and God,
to receive glory and honor and power,
for you created all things,
and by your will they existed and were created."

John 1:1 In the beginning was the Word, and the Word was with God, and the Word was
God. 2 The Word was with God in the beginning. 3 Everything came into being through the
Word, and without the Word not one thing came into being that came into being. What has
come into being 4 in the Word was life, and that life was the light of all people. 5 The light
shines in the bleakness, and the bleakness did not overtake it.

PROCLAMATION

Text Notes

This week of Epiphany is optional depending on how late Easter falls; it will be absent some years. Isaiah 6:1 uses the word for seeing with one's eyes to articulate how Isaiah encountered God. It does not use the separate word for "envisioning a vision." The text does not identify the source of God's trailing edges, hems, or trains, just that they are plural. A garment or its semblance is inferred.

The verb articulating the movement of the wilderness, Kadesh, and oak trees in Psalm 29:8–9 also means to writhe or travail in or as in labor during childbirth.

In Revelation 4:2 there is no separate noun or pronoun for the "one" seated upon the throne; the subject is built into the verb. Use of "one" rather than "a person" preserves the understanding that the occupant is not a human person.

Preaching Prompts

There is nothing coy about God's self-revelation to Isaiah. The text doesn't tell us how Isaiah is suddenly in, or able to see into, heaven. He did not get there on his own. While the rest of the text will focus on Isaiah's call into God's service, today's portion functions as an Epiphany text by portraying God as manifestly holy and worthy of awe, as does Psalm 29 and Revelation 4 that follow.

Psalm 29 portrays the majesty and glory of God. In this lectionary that majesty and might is expressed in explicitly feminine terms to forcefully break with the patriarchal hierarchy that identifies power and majesty with male entities and associates female persons and divinities with fertility and nurturance. God is equally majestic and awe-worthy in Revelation 4. John 1 makes the fundamental Christian claim that this great, majestic, awe-inspiring God comes to dwell in this world, embodied and incarnate. The Gospel builds to a dramatic revelation of the identity of the Word later beyond the boundaries of this lesson.

Where are women and the feminine in these lessons? Absent from the heavens if not read in. Here it matters particularly what language and imagery we choose to use for God. Though the seraphs, elders, and seemingly animal-headed beings are grammatically male, it cannot be easily argued that they are biologically male. It may be useful to read them as beyond the gender binary. There is feminine imagery in the psalm; the world writhes like a woman in labor at the sound of the voice of God, easily overlooked or lost in translation. Absent from the Gospel is the woman and the womb in which the Word was prepared.

LAST WEEK OF EPIPHANY (TRANSFIGURATION)

Leviticus 19:1–2, 9–18; Psalm 77:13–20; Romans 12:1–13; Matthew 17:1–9

Leviticus 19:1 The LIVING GOD spoke to Moses, saying:

2 Speak to all the congregation of the women and men of Israel and say to them: You all shall be holy, for I the ETERNAL your God am holy.

9 When you all reap the harvest of your land, it shall not be completed to the very edges
of your field for harvesting, and the gleanings of your harvest shall not be gathered. 10 Your
vineyard you shall not scrape bare, and the fallen grapes of your vineyard you shall not gather; you shall leave them for those oppressed through poverty and for the alien who resides (in your land): I am the Holy One your God.

11 None of you shall steal; none of you shall deceive, and none of you shall lie to a com-
patriot. 12 And none of you shall swear by my Name to a lie and so profane the Name of your God: I am GOD WHOSE NAME IS HOLY.

13 You shall not defraud your neighbor, you shall not steal, and you shall not keep over-
night for yourself the wages of a laborer until morning. 14 You shall not mock the deaf and you shall not put a stumbling block before the blind; you shall fear your God: I am the LIVING GOD.

15 You shall not render justice unjust; you shall not elevate the poor or honor the great;
you shall judge your compatriot rightly. 16 You shall not go around as a slanderer among your
people, and you shall not stand by the blood of your neighbor: I am the Holy God.

17 You shall not hate in your heart your compatriot. Rebuke—yes rebuke!—your compatriot, and do not incur guilt on their account. 18 You shall not take vengeance or nurture
anger against any of your people; you shall love your neighbor as yourself: I am the MOST
HIGH God.

Psalm 77:13–20

13 God, your way is in holiness;
what [other] god is great as [our] God?
14 You are the God who works wonders;
you have made known among the peoples your power.
15 With your [own] arm you have redeemed your people,
the children of Asenath,
and the children of Rachel and Leah, and Bilhah and Zilpah.
16 The waters saw you, O God; the waters saw you
and writhed-as-in-labor;
the very depths were shaken.
17 The clouds poured out water; the skies thundered;
indeed your arrows went about to and fro;
18 The sound of your thunder was in the whirlwind;
your lightnings lit up the world;
the earth trembled and shook.
19 In the sea was your way, and your paths in the many waters,
yet your footsteps were not seen.
20 You led your people like a flock,
by the hand of Miriam, Aaron, and Moses.

Romans 12:1 I urge you therefore, sisters and brothers, because of the mercies of God, to
present your bodies as a living sacrifice, holy and acceptable to God, which is your thoughtful
worship. 2 So do not be conformed to this world, rather be transformed by the renewing of
your minds, so that you may determine what is the will of God, what is good and acceptable
and mature.

3 I say by the grace given to me to each person among you not to think more highly than
you ought to think, but to think soundly; God has assigned each one a measure of faith. 4 For
as in one body we have many parts yet not all the parts have the same function, 5 thus, we
who are many are one body in Christ, and accordingly, we are members of one another. 6 We
have gifts that according to the grace given to us differ: if prophecy, then in proportion to
faith; 7 if ministry, then in ministering; if as the one teaching, then in teaching; 8 if as the one

exhorting, then in exhortation; if as the one giving, then in generosity; if as the one leading, then in commitment; if as the one showing compassion, then in cheerfulness.

9 Let love be without pretense; despise that which is evil, cling fast to what is good. 10 Love one another as children raised together; outdo one another in showing honor. 11 Do not hesitate in diligence, be afire in the Spirit, serve Christ. 12 In hope rejoice, in suffering be patient, in prayer persevere. 13 To the needs of the saints contribute; extend hospitality.

Matthew 17:1 Six days [after Jesus told his disciples that he must go to Jerusalem and undergo great suffering at the hands of the elders and chief priests and biblical scholars, and be killed], Jesus took with him Peter and James and John his brother and brought them up a high mountain, by themselves. 2 And he was transfigured in front of them, and his face shone like the sun, and his clothes became white as light. 3 Then, look! Moses and Elijah appeared to them, talking with him. 4 Peter responded saying to Jesus, "Teacher, it is good for us to be here; if you wish, I will pitch three tents here, one for you, one for Moses, and one for Elijah." 5 He was still speaking when look! A cloud full of light overshadowed them! And then . . . ! A voice from the cloud said, "This is my Son, the Beloved; with him I am well pleased. Listen to him!" 6 When the disciples heard this, they fell upon the ground and were very much afraid. 7 Then Jesus came and touched them, saying, "Get up and do not be afraid." 8 They looked up and they saw no one except Jesus himself alone.

9 As they were coming down the mountain, Jesus instructed them saying, "Tell no one about the vision until the Son of Woman from the dead has been raised."

PROCLAMATION

Text Notes

Often the Torah addresses to a singular representative adult, male, free, Israelite, i.e., "your wife," "your female and male slaves," "the stranger in your (sing.) gates," etc. Leviticus 19:2 addresses to a plural subject including women as recipients of and responsible for this teaching (following verses use both singular and plural forms). When God says, "I am your God," in verse 10, she says I am the God of you *all*, including the women not easily visible in this text. There are many words for poverty in biblical Hebrew, twenty or more. Leviticus 19:10 speaks to a poverty resulting from oppression, including physical as well as economic violence.

In Psalm 77:13, two different words for god/God are used; first *ʾel*, then *ʾelohim*, both of which are used for the God of Israel, *ʾel* is repeated in verse 14, this time meaning Israel's God. Elsewhere *ʾel* is used more broadly for other gods as well. Readers may use one or more of the bracketed terms for clarity. In verse 15, the Egyptian Asenath stands in for her husband Joseph representing the demi-tribes of Manasseh and Ephraim. Leah, Rachel, and the enslaved women, Bilhah and Zilpah, represent Jacob and the rest of his children, including Dinah (known for her rape in Genesis

34) and other daughters (mentioned briefly in Genesis 37:35). The motion of the primordial waters in verse 16 is expressed with the verb that means "to twist," "sometimes is dancing," and "to travail in labor," the former generally indicated by joy.

In Romans 12:1, *logikos* denotes well-reasoned thought out decisions, especially religious ones. In verse 2, *dokimazein*, "prove" or "test," has the sense of "determine" after examination or scientific study; "mature," "complete," and "perfect" are all possible translations of *teleios*; however, "perfection" can represent an unattainable goal unlike complete maturation. Contrary to many translations, thinking highly of oneself is not specified in verse 3. The many parts, *mele*, of the body in verse 4 are like musical parts in a composition; melody is a related term. I use "children raised together" to render *philadelphia*, sibling (brotherly) love in verse 10.

Matthew 16:21 provides the context for "six days after . . ." in 17:1.

Preaching Prompts

I am YHWH; I am a name that is too holy to be pronounced. The divine name is never spelled out with vowels in the Hebrew Bible. Rabbinic annotations call for substitution when the text is read aloud, most often, *adonai*, lord (literally, "my lord). Rabbinic and contemporary literature and liturgy employ a wide variety of names, titles, and descriptions as does this volume.

One of the ways God reveals Godself to the world is through Torah, which Christians have often derided and dismissed as legalistic with few exceptions. Leviticus, the heart of Torah, is often held at great distance. Yet at the heart of this portion of Leviticus 19 is a social justice manifesto in keeping with the Gospel against which law has so often been set in false dichotomy: Verses 9 to 10 offer a communal economic model in which those who have resources share a portion with those who do not. Verse 13 offers an opportunity to talk about wage theft, the practice of some who hire undocumented women and men not only underpaying them but also seizing part of their already impoverished earnings. Verse 15 addresses injustice in the justice system. And verse 16 calls the community to action when blood is spilled. More familiarly, verse 18 calls for love of neighbor. The collection uses the language of community, neighbor, and compatriot, because it is legislation for the community, not because outsiders were expendable.

Leviticus 19 can be read as speaking to what to do when descending from the Mount of Transfiguration. Psalm 77 joins Leviticus 19 in reflecting on God's holiness to inform our own. Romans 12 offers instructions on how Christian women and men are to live out our holiness in our service to God using the gifts she has given. Here there are no strictures on who can prophesy, minister (*diakonia*), teach, exhort, or lead. In Matthew 17, Jesus offers a glimpse of the holiness of God that he embodies.

At the Transfiguration, Moses and Elijah can be interpreted as the ancestral figures whose mantles Jesus inherits and surpasses in teaching and working miracles, or as representing the Torah and the Prophets. One might wish to note the legacies of female prophets that Jesus also embodies: Miriam, who led the people to freedom (Exodus 15:20), Deborah, who won the mountain (Tabor, considered the site of the Transfiguration) in battle (Judges 5:7, 12), and Huldah, who first proclaimed a written word the word of God (2 Kings 22:14–16).

LENT—ASH WEDNESDAY

Joel 2:1, 12–17, 21–22; Psalm 90:1–10, 12;
1 Corinthians 15:45–49; Matthew 6:1–6, 16–18

Joel 2:1 Blow the trumpet in Zion!
Cry the alarm on my holy mountain!
Let all the inhabitants of the land quake,
for the day of the HOLY GOD is coming, it is near.
12 Yet even now, says the HOLY ONE,
return to me with all your hearts,
with fasting, with weeping, and with lamenting.
13 Tear your hearts and not your clothing.
Return to the HOLY ONE, your God,
for God is gracious and loves as a mother,
slow to anger, and abounds in faithful love,
and reluctant to impose harm.
14 Who knows whether God will not turn and relent,
and leave a blessing behind,
for a grain offering and a drink offering
to the HOLY ONE, your God?
15 Blow the trumpet in Zion;
sanctify a fast;
call a solemn assembly.
16 Gather the people:
Sanctify the congregation;
assemble the aged;
gather the children,
even breastfeeding babies.
Let the bridegroom leave his room,
and the bride her canopy.

17 Between the portico and the altar
let the priests, the ministers of the HOLY ONE, weep.
Let them say, "Spare your people, HOLY ONE,
and do not offer your heritage as a mockery,
a byword among the nations.
Why should it be said among the peoples,
'Where is their God?'"
21 Fear not, O land!
Be glad and rejoice,
for the HOLY ONE has done great things!
22 Fear not, O animals of the field!
For the pastures of the wilderness are green;
the tree lifts up its fruit,
the fig tree and vine give their riches.

Psalm 90:1–10, 12

1 MOTHER OF THE MOUNTAINS, you have been our refuge
from one generation to another.
2 Before the mountains were born,
or you writhed the land and the earth into birth,
from age to age you are God.
3 You turn mortal flesh back to the dust and say,
"Turn back, you who are woman-born."
4 For a thousand years in your sight are like yesterday when it is past
and like a watch in the night.
5 You sweep them aside; they are an illusion;
In the morning flourishing and in the evening wilting and withering.
6 In the morning it is green and flourishes;
in the evening it is dried up and withered.
7 For we are consumed in your displeasure;
we are afraid because of your wrathful indignation.
8 Our iniquities you have set before you,
and our hidden sins in the light of your countenance.
9 When you are angry, all our days are gone;
we bring our years to an end like a sigh.
10 The span of our life is seventy years, perhaps in strength even eighty;
yet the sum of them is but labor and sorrow,
for they pass away quickly and we are gone.
12 So teach us to number our days
that we may apply our hearts to Wisdom.

1 Corinthians 15:45 Thus it is written, "The first human, Adam, became a living soul"; the last Adam became a spirit that gives life. 46 But it is not the spiritual that is first, but the physical, and then the spiritual. 47 The first human was from the earth, dust; the second human is from heaven. 48 As was the one of dust, so are those who are of dust; and as is the one of heaven, so are those who are of heaven. 49 Just as we have borne the image of the one of dust, we will also bear the image of the one of heaven.

Matthew 6:1 [Jesus said,] "Now, beware of practicing your justness before other people in order to be seen by them; surely, lest you have no reward from your Creator in heaven.

2 "So when you give alms, do not trumpet before yourself, as the hypocrites do in the synagogues and in the streets, in order that they may be praised by other people. Truly I tell you, they have received their reward. 3 But when you give alms, do not let your left hand know what your right hand is doing, 4 in order that your alms may be secret; and your Creator who sees in secret will reward you.

5 "And when you pray, do not be like the hypocrites; for they love to stand and pray in the synagogues and on the street corners, in order that they may be seen by other people. Truly I tell you, they have received their recompense. 6 But whenever you pray, go into your room and shut the door and pray to your Creator who is in secret; and your Creator who sees in secret will reward you.

16 "And when you fast, do not be sullen like the hypocrites, for they disfigure their faces in order to show other people that they are fasting. Truly I tell you, they have received their reward. 17 But when you fast, put oil on your head and wash your face, 18 in order that your fasting may be seen, not by others, but by your Creator who is in secret, and your Creator who sees in secret will reward you.

PROCLAMATION

Text Notes

Land in Joel 2:1 and 21 is soil, not the nation. The hearts of the people in Joel 2:12–13 form a collective one, "the heart of you all."

In Psalm 90:2, God's grammatical gender is masculine, and the imagery used for God is feminine, birthing imagery (in the cis-gender ancient Israelite world), yielding the name for God in verse 1. "Turn" in verse 3 means both "turn around" and "repent." Also in verse 3, "mortal flesh" renders "man," and "woman-born" renders "children/descendants of humanity/humankind" or "mortals."

First Corinthians 15:47 quotes Genesis 2:7; throughout the passage Paul uses *anthropos*, "human," rather than *aner*, "man," following Genesis where the first earthling is "human," not "man."

In Matthew 6:1, "justness/justice," "uprightness," and "righteousness" are all translations of *dikaiosynēn*. Those righteous acts include far more than the almsgiving, prayer, and fasting in the following verses. The prayer room in verse 6 is an inner one, making one's prayer less likely to be seen.

Preaching Prompts

Joel 2 is a call to solemn assembly in fasting and repentance in response to a locust infestation and resulting economic loss and famine seen as divine punishment. It will be important to unravel the blame language. The text is explicitly inclusive across gender and age categories. The image of God as the mother of the mountains in Psalm 90:2 builds nicely on the maternal imagery present in God's mother-love in Joel 2:13.

The people of the land are to quake at God's power and presence (Joel 2:1), but the land itself (herself) should not fear, verse 21. Notably, God addresses the earth and her creatures in verse 21–22 (excluded from the designated verses in the BCP). God cares for them and whether humanity repents or not, God will care for them.

God's essential characteristics delineated in Joel 2:13—graciousness, loving from her womb (the noun and verb share a root), slow to anger, abounding in faithful love, and being slow to inflict retribution—recur in Exodus 34:6, Deuteronomy 4:31, and Jonah 4:2, and throughout the psalms.

The Epistle makes clear that we are all both earthly dust and the stuff of heaven. We are all equally bearers of the divine image now, and even more so in the age to come. Paul's use of a paradigm distinguishing the spiritual from the physical in 1 Corinthians 15:46 lends itself easily to body/soul dichotomies and hierarchies; it also seems to unhelpfully deemphasize the Incarnation.

As with the Epistle, the implicit gender claims in the Gospel will need to be made explicit. Oiling the head, actually hair, is a common grooming practice for those of African descent like the Afro-Asiatic Israelites and their descendants; it is common in some Asian and other cultures as well. It is less comprehensible in the European culture that has colonized the text and its iconography.

In Matthew 6:6–7, omitted, Jesus tells his disciples not to pray like Gentiles who essentially babble repeatedly, and in that context introduces the Lord's Prayer. It is worth remembering that Jesus initially understood his ministry to be only to "the lost sheep of the house of Israel." (See Matthew 10:6; 15:24.) After his encounter with the Syro-Phoenician woman, his ministry extended to the Gentiles.

A final note, when reciting Psalm 51 in the liturgy of the day, consider recentering Bathsheba's abduction, rape, and forced impregnation along with the murder of her husband.

LENT I

Genesis 2:7–9, 15–17, 21–25; 3:1–7; Psalm 51; Revelation 22:1–5, 16–17; Matthew 3:1–6

Genesis 2:7 The SOVEREIGN God crafted the human from the dust of the humus and
breathed into its nostrils the breath of life, and the human became a living soul. 8 And the
SOVEREIGN God planted a garden in Eden, in the east, and there placed the human whom
God had formed. 9 Out of the ground the SOVEREIGN God made grow every tree pleasant
to the sight and good for food, and the tree of life in the middle of the garden, along with the
tree of the knowledge of good and evil.

15 The SOVEREIGN God took the human and settled it in the garden of Eden to till and
tend it. 16 Then the SOVEREIGN God commanded the human, "From every tree of the garden
you may eat freely, 17 but of the tree of the knowledge of good and evil you shall not eat, for in
the day you eat from it you shall surely die."

21 The SOVEREIGN God caused a deep sleep to fall upon the human, and it slept; then
took one of its sides and closed up its place with flesh in place of it. 22 And the SOVEREIGN
God built the side that had been taken from the human into a woman and brought her to the
human. 23 Then the human said,

> "This time, this one is bone of my bones
> and flesh of my flesh;
> this one shall be called a woman,
> for out of a man this one was taken."

24 Therefore a man leaves his mother and his father and clings to his woman, and they
become one flesh. 25 And they were, the two of them, naked, the man and his woman [or the
woman and her man] and were not ashamed.

3:1 Now the serpent had more naked intelligence than any other animal of the field that
the SOVEREIGN God had made. And it said to the woman, "Indeed, did God say, 'You two
shall not eat from any tree in the garden'?" 2 The woman said to the serpent, "From the fruit
of any tree in the garden we may eat, 3 though of the fruit of the tree that is in the middle of
the garden God said, 'You two shall not eat and shall not touch it lest you two die.'" 4 Then
the serpent said to the woman, "You two will certainly not die, 5 for God knows that when
you eat of it your eyes will be opened, and you two will be like God, knowing good and evil."
6 So when the woman saw that the tree was good for food, and that it was a delight to the eyes,
and that the tree was to be desired to make one wise, she took of its fruit and ate; and she also
gave some to her man, who was with her, and he ate. 7 Then the eyes of both of them were
opened, and they knew that they were naked, and they sewed fig leaves together and made
loincloths for themselves.

Psalm 51

For the music leader: A psalm of David, when the prophet Nathan came to him, after he came to Bathsheba.

1 Have mercy on me, God,
according to your faithful love;
according to your abundant mother-love
blot out my transgressions.
2 Thoroughly wash me from my iniquity,
and from my sin cleanse me.
3 For I know my transgressions,
and my sin is perpetually before me.
4 Against you, against you alone, have I sinned,
and done what is evil in your sight,
therefore, you are justified in your verdict
and blameless in your judgment.
5 Look, I wriggled out in iniquity,
and was a sinner when my mother conceived me.
6 Look, you desire truth in the inward parts;
so teach me wisdom in secret.
7 Purge me with hyssop, and I shall be clean;
wash me, and I shall be whiter than snow.
8 Make me hear joy and gladness;
let the bones that you have crushed rejoice.
9 Hide your face from my sins,
and wipe out all my iniquities.
10 Create a clean heart for me, God,
and implant a new spirit within me.
11 Do not cast me from your presence,
and do not take your holy spirit from me.
12 Restore to me the joy of your salvation,
and sustain me with a generous spirit.
13 I will teach transgressors your ways,
and sinners will return to you.
14 Deliver me from bloodshed, O God,
God of my salvation,
and my tongue will sing with joy of your righteousness.
15 Holy One, open my lips,
and my mouth will declare your praise.

16 For you have no delight in sacrifice;
were I to give a burnt offering, you would not accept.
17 The sacrifices of God are a broken spirit;
a broken and crushed heart, O God, you will not despise.

Revelation 22:1 The angel showed me the river of the water of life, bright as crystal, coming
from the throne of God and of the Lamb 2 through the middle of the street. On each side of
the river is the tree of life with its twelve kinds of fruit, producing its fruit each month, and
the leaves of the tree are for the healing of the nations. 3 There will no longer be any accursed
thing. But the throne of God and of the Lamb will be in it, and God's servants will worship
God; 4 they will see God's face, and God's name will be on their foreheads. 5 And night will be
no more; they need no light of a lamp or of the sun, for the Holy God will be their light, and
they will reign forever and ever.

16 "I, Jesus, sent my angel to you all to testify to this for the churches. I am the root and the descendant of David, the bright morning star."

17 The Spirit and the bride say, "Come."
And let whoever hears say, "Come."
And let whoever thirsts come.
Let whoever wishes take the water of life as a gift.

Matthew 3:1 In those days John the Baptizer appeared preaching in the wilderness of Judea
saying, 2 "Repent, for the realm of the heavens has come near." 3 For this is the one of whom
the prophet Isaiah spoke when he said,

> *"The voice of one crying out in the wilderness:*
> *'Prepare the way of the Holy One,*
> *make straight the paths of God.'"*

4 Now John's clothing was camel's hair with a leather belt around his waist, and his food was
locusts and wild honey. 5 The people of Jerusalem and all Judea were going out to him, along
with the whole region along the Jordan, 6 and they were baptized by him in the river Jordan,
confessing their sins.

PROCLAMATION

Text Notes

God's creation of the human in Genesis 2:7 uses a verb for crafting pottery. "The human," *ha'adam*, is a specific distinct creation; later *adam* will refer to humanity as a whole and serve as the name of the first male human. The earth from which this first earthling was crafted is *ha'adamah*.

I use the pronoun "it," lacking in Hebrew, for the first human that has within it what will be called woman, *isshah*, and man, *ish*. The earth-creature will be divided in half to generate the woman and man. The word *tzela* in Genesis 2:22 means side and not rib, used for the sides of the ark and tabernacle in Exodus, sides of the temple in 1 Kings and Ezekiel, and hillsides in 2 Samuel. It is never translated as rib outside of the creation of woman story. In the LXX, *pleuron* also means side, generally in reference to the human body. There are no distinct words for "wife" and "husband" in Hebrew. The language for woman and man has not changed in the text.

There is a pun between Genesis 2:25 and 3:1, between the words for naked, *arom*, and crafty, *arum*; the serpent also changes the "you shall not eat" to an inclusive plural from masculine singular.

English translations position the first two verses of Psalm 51 separately as a superscription; they are part of the whole. Retaining them ensures Bathsheba is not excised from the text that is dependent on her broken body.

Preaching Prompts

The story of the first woman and the fruit from the tree of knowledge has been translated and interpreted and taught in ways that subordinate and demean women in ways not warranted by the text. (See the classic treatment by Phyllis Trible, *God and the Rhetoric of Sexuality*.)

The primordial human is a pluripotent entity that will be divided into equal halves to form two human persons yielding different theological implications than turning a man's rib into a woman. Inserting "wife" and "husband" in Genesis 2:23–24 has theological and interpretive ramifications: Why would marriage be necessary in paradise with only two people? The text does not mention marriage; the assumption suggests specific understandings of sex and shame.

There is no small amount of irony in David praying for God's mother-love in Psalm 51:3 when his transgression is defiling a woman's womb (*rechem* is "womb," *recham* is love or compassion that emanates from the womb). Situating his crime against God only and not Bathsheba in verse 4 is at odds with contemporary notions of repentance. It conflicts somewhat with the Torah position that sex crimes against women are against their fathers or husbands; Uriah, Bathsheba's husband, is not named here. It is not clear whether David is praying for protection against revenge or to resist his own bloodthirsty impulses in verse 14.

Jesus's self-identification as descended from David in Revelation 22:16 provides an opportunity to talk about God transforming the aftereffects of Bathsheba's rape but certainly not requiring it to bring about redemption. The water of life is a cosmic baptismal font, healing the world of all its brokenness and ills: sexism, misogyny, patriarchy, white supremacy, colonialism, racism, homophobia, transphobia, anti-Semitism, Islamophobia, fat phobia, greed, cruelty, violence, and more.

LENT II

1 Kings 17:8–16; Psalm 111:2–10; 2 Corinthians 9:6–13; Matthew 14:13–21

1 Kings 17:8 The word of the Holy One to Elijah was, 9 “Get up, go to Zarephath, which
is part of Sidon, and settle there; watch now, I have commanded a widow woman there to provide for you.” 10 And Elijah got up and went to Zarephath. Then he came to the gate of the
town, and look! a widow woman was there gathering sticks; so he called to her and said, “Bring
me, please, a little water in a vessel, that I may drink.” 11 She went to bring it, and he called to
her and said, “Bring me, please, a bit of bread in your hand.” 12 Then she said, “As the Holy
One your God lives, if I had a cake. There is only a handful of flour in a jar, and a little oil in
a jug. Now look, I am gathering two sticks, then I will go home and prepare the oil and flour
for myself and for my son; we will eat it, and we will die.” 13 Then Elijah said to her, “Fear not;
go and do as you have said, only make me a little cake of it and bring it to me first, then make
something for yourself and your son afterwards. 14 For thus says the Holy One the God of
Israel: The jar of flour will not empty and the jug of oil will not decrease until the day that the
Holy One grants rain upon the earth.” 15 She went and she did as Elijah said, and she and he,
and her household, ate for many days. 16 The jar of flour did not empty and the jug of oil did
not decrease according to the word of the Holy One that God spoke through Elijah.

Psalm 111:2–10

2 Great are the works of God,
contemplated by all who delight in them.
3 Splendor and majesty are her work,
and her righteousness stands forever.
4 She has gained renown for her wonderful deeds;
the Womb of Life is gracious and abounds in mother-love.
5 She provides fresh meat for those who revere her;
she remembers her covenant perpetually.
6 She has declared the strength of her works to her people,
giving them the heritage of the nations.
7 The works of her hands are truth and justice;
trustworthy are all her precepts.
8 They stand fast forever and ever,
Executed in truth and uprightness.
9 She sent redemption to her people;
she has ordained her covenant forever.
Holy and awesome is her name.
10 Awe of the Ageless God is the beginning of wisdom;
all those who do have good understanding.
Her praise endures forever.

2 Corinthians 9:6 Now hear this: The one who sows sparingly, sparingly will also reap, and the one who sows in abundance, in abundance will also reap. 7 Each one must give as decided in your heart, not out of reluctance or under pressure, for "God loves a cheerful giver." 8 And the power of God is able to grant you all every gift abundantly, so that always having enough of everything, you all may abound in every good work. 9 As it is written,

> *"God scatters generously, and gives to the poor;*
> *God's righteousness endures forever."*

10 The one who supplies seed to the sower and bread for food will supply and multiply your seed and increase the harvest of your righteousness. 11 Enriched in every way for every kind of generosity which will yield through us thanksgiving to God, 12 for the offering of this ministry does not only supply the needs of the saints but also overflows with many thanksgivings to God. 13 Through the character of this ministry you all glorify God by your obedience to the confession of the gospel of Christ and by the generosity of your companionship with them and with all others.

Matthew 14:13 Now when Jesus heard [about the death of John the Baptizer], he withdrew from there in a boat to a deserted place by himself. And when the crowds heard, they followed him on foot from the towns. 14 When he arrived, he saw a great crowd, and he had compassion for them, and healed their sick. 15 Now by evening, the disciples came to him and said, "The place is deserted, and the time has gone; send the crowds away so that they can go into the villages and buy themselves food." 16 Instead, Jesus said to them, "They do not need to leave; you all give them something to eat." 17 They replied to him, "We do not have anything here but five loaves and two fish." 18 Then Jesus said, "Bring them here to me." 19 And he ordered the crowds to sit down on the grass; he took the five loaves and the two fish, looked towards heaven, and blessed and broke them. He gave the loaves to the disciples, and the disciples gave them to the crowds. 20 And all ate and were filled; and they took up the abundance of fragments, twelve baskets full. 21 Now those who ate were women and children, besides about five thousand men.

PROCLAMATION

Text Notes

"The word was/happened to . . ." the prophet; throughout the Hebrew Bible, the word of God "happens" to prophets; it is an encounter.

In Psalm 111:5, the fresh meat, literally prey, is the same as that provided by the warrior-hearted woman in Proverbs 31:15. (For more on that translation, see my *Daughters of Miriam*.)

Second Corinthians 9:7 quotes part of the Greek text of Proverbs 22:8, which differs significantly from the Hebrew: *God blesses a cheerful and generous man*. With the exception of "bless/love" it is an exact quote. Verse 9 cites Psalm 112:9, also from the LXX.

Matthew 14:21 relegates women and children to afterthoughts: *those who ate were about five thousand men, besides women and children.* I have inverted the order of those whom Jesus fed above.

Preaching Prompts

This week, the voluntary privation of Lent is set against the assurance that God provides for her children: the prophet, the widow, and her son in 1 Kings 17, her faithful ones in Psalm 111:5, and those who follow Jesus in Matthew 14. In 2 Corinthians 9, the Christian community does the work of God in sharing what they have received in abundance. In each text, women are recipients of divine largesse. In the first lesson and Epistle, women dispense that largesse.

The widow is desperate and vulnerable. The demand of the prophet of a God she does not claim to give him all she has to feed her child could easily have been exploitative. Contemporarily that is often the case. It's also worth noting neither God nor Elijah requires the woman to make a profession of statement before seeing to her need. And as Jesus will note in Luke 4:26, God's gifts are not limited to those who have a prior standing as God's people.

The psalmist understands God, as any gender, to be the ultimate colonizer, giving Israel the heritage, land, and resources of other nations in verse 6. The following verse emphasizes that God is just in all her works and ways. There is room here to preach on the cost of occupation and colonization to women and other vulnerable populations, and the theological implications of sanctifying it.

Jesus's resort to a desert place is part of what makes this Gospel a Lenten reading, a model for our own journeys. The feeding of the crowd can represent the nourishment we receive from our withdrawal from our lives into our Lenten practices. The casual relegation of women and children to secondary status provides an opportunity to talk about how cultural biases shape the gospel but are not the gospel.

LENT III

Numbers 5:5–10; Psalm 32:1–7; James 5:13–18; Matthew 5:21–26

Numbers 5:5 The HOLY ONE spoke to Moses, saying, [6] "Speak to the daughters and sons of Israel: 'When a man or a woman commits any of the wrongs common to humanity, breaking faith with the HOLY ONE, that person is guilty. [7] Then they shall confess the sin that they committed. The person shall make full restitution of the wrong, they shall add one fifth to the top, and give it to the one wronged. [8] If there is no next of kin to make restitution to for

the wrong, the restitution for the wrong shall go to the Holy One for the priest in addition to the ram of atonement with which atonement is made for the one wronged. 9 And
all the offerings, of all the holy gifts of the daughters and sons of Israel, every gift that they
bring to the priest shall be his. 10 Each priest keeps those holy gifts; each shall keep what
was given to him.'"

Psalm 32

1 Happy is the woman or man whose transgression is forgiven,
whose sin is covered.
2 Happy is the woman or man to whom the Holy One does not reckon iniquity,
and in whose spirit there is no deceit.
3 While I kept silence, my bones wasted away
in my groaning all the day.
4 For day and night your hand was heavy upon me,
my strength melted away as by the heat of summer.
5 My sin I made known to you,
and my iniquity I did not hide.
I said, "I will make known my transgressions to the Gracious One,"
and you forgave the iniquity of my sin.
6 Therefore let all who are faithful
offer prayer to you;
who are found at such a time,
for a rush of mighty waters
shall not touch them.
7 You are a hiding place for me;
you keep me from distress;
you surround me with cries of deliverance.

James 5:13 Are any women or men among you suffering? Then pray. Are any cheerful?
Then sing praise. 14 Are any women or men among you sick? Then call for the elders of the
church and let them pray over them, anointing them with oil in the name of the Messiah.
15 The prayer of faith will save the sick, and the Messiah will raise them up; and sins anyone
has committed will be forgiven them. 16 Therefore confess your sins to one another and pray
for one another that you may be healed. The prayer of the righteous woman or man is powerful and effective. 17 Elijah was a human being like us, and he prayed intensely that it not rain,
and it did not rain on the earth for three years and six months. 18 Then he prayed again, and
the heavens gave rain and the earth yielded its harvest.

Matthew 5:21 Jesus said, "You have heard that it was said to those of old, '*You shall not
murder,*' and 'whoever murders shall be subject to judgment.' 22 But I say to you all that if you
are angry with a sister or brother, you will be liable to judgment, and if you call a sister or

brother an idiot, you will be subject to the council; and if you say, 'You fool,' you will be subject to the hell of fire. [23] Therefore, if you are offering your gift at the altar and you remember that your sister or brother has something against you, [24] leave your gift there before the altar and go; first be reconciled to your sister or brother, and then come and offer your gift. [25] Come to favorable terms quickly with your accuser while you are on the way with them or your accuser may hand you over to the judge, and the judge to the court officer, and you will be thrown into prison. [26] Truly I tell you, you will never get out until you have paid the last penny.

PROCLAMATION

Text Notes

Numbers 5:6 names women explicitly in the text: "when a man or a woman," Israelites, literally "children of Israel," is made explicit, "daughters and sons of Israel" is used, also in verse 9.

Alternately, verse 1–2 of the psalm can be read as "happy is she" for those wishing to experience the psalm as explicitly and exclusively feminine for humanity.

James 5:13–14 asks "are any among you," without specifying person, women, men, believers, etc. Likewise, verse 16 says "the prayer of the righteous" without further delineation. Some have argued that since "righteous" is a masculine adjective, it refers (only) to a male elder; others argue the gender of the adjective represents the widespread practice of using a male subject as a universal referent. Yet the following verse emphasized the humanity (*anthropos*) of Elijah, not his maleness, when commending the efficacity of his prayer.

The Aramaic word *raka* in Matthew 5:22 means "empty-headed." "Gehenna/Hell of fire" acknowledges that the Gehenna they could all see, the Geh Hinnom Valley just south of Jerusalem was not literally hell.

Preaching Prompts

These lessons embody the Lenten themes of self-examination and repentance, confession, and prayer. Notably, Numbers 5 makes clear that repentance is not complete without restitution and when not possible, reparation, often neglected in Christian calls for repentance and reconciliation.

While the culture and language of ancient Israel is male-focused, women did participate in the religious system, bringing their own offerings. They should be read as present and participants in more texts that those that mention them explicitly. To wit, the psalm clearly applies to women as well as men, and in our nonbinary world, to all who are forgiven.

Similarly, the New Testament androcentric language is normative, often subsuming women. The word for "elders" in James 5:14 is a plural that indicates that at least one of an unknown number is male; it can function as an inclusive plural. While it is clear that women served as deacons in the early church, and as presbyters in the early synagogue, it is not clear whether women served as presbyters in the early church. (See Bernadette Brooten's *Women Leaders in the Ancient Synagogue*, and Kate Cooper's *Band of Angels: The Forgotten World of Early Christian Women*.) A further topic for exploration is the notion in James 5:16 that there is a potential causative link between confession and healing, and overly simplistic understandings of prayer.

Jesus's description of reconciliation puts the onus on the one who knows someone has something against them, the one who wronged or is accused of wrong, rather than the one who has been done wrong. This can be read as a disruption of a power curve: It is not up to a victim to demand justice, nor should it be, rather the moral imperative belongs to the one accused of wrong. Unfortunately, this is not the paradigm the church uses in responding to those whom it has injured, particularly marginalized communities: LGBTQI persons, black women and men and other persons of color, women of all races and ethnicities.

LENT IV

Genesis 31:25–27, 43–50; Psalm 144:3–4, 12–15; 1 John 4:13–21; Matthew 12:46–50

Genesis 31:25 Laban overtook Jacob. Now Jacob had pitched his tent in the hill country,
and Laban with his kinsfolk camped in the hill country of Gilead. 26 And Laban said to Jacob,
"What have you done? You have robbed my heart and herded off my daughters like captives
of the sword. 27 Why did you sneak to run away and rob me and not tell me? I would have
sent you away with celebration and singing, with drumming and strumming."

43 Then Laban said to Jacob, "These daughters are my daughters, these children are
my children, these flocks are my flocks, and all that you see, it is mine. Now what can I do
today about these my daughters, or about their children whom they have birthed? 44 Now,
come, let us make a covenant, I and you, and let it be a witness between me and you." 45 So
Jacob took a stone, and set it up as a pillar. 46 Then Jacob said to his kin, "Gather stones,"
and they took stones, and made a *gal*, a heap; and they ate there by the heap. 47 Laban called
it Jegar-sahadutha, but Jacob called it Gal-Ed (Heap of Witness). 48 Laban said, "This heap
is a witness between me and you today." Therefore, he called it Gal-Ed, 49 and the pillar
Mizpah (Watchtower), for he said, "The HOLY ONE watch between me and you, when we
are out of sight of the other. 50 If you treat my daughters violently, or if you take women in
addition to my daughters, though no one else is with us, see, that God is witness between
me and you."

Psalm 144:3–4, 12–15

3 Womb of Life, what is humanity that you even know them,
or the woman-born that you think of them?
4 Humanity is like a breath;
whose days are like a passing shadow.
12 Our sons in their youth
are like plants full grown,
our daughters are like cornerstones,
cut for the building of a palace.
13 Our barns are full,
from produce of every kind;
our sheep have increased by thousands,
many thousands in our surroundings.
14 Our cattle are heavy,
there is no breach in the walls, no exile,
and no cry of distress in our surroundings.
15 Happy are the people to whom such blessings fall;
happy are the people whose God is the Womb of Life.

1 John 4:13 By this we know that we abide in God and God in us, because God has given
us God's own Spirit. 14 And we have seen and so testify that the Father has sent the Son of
God as the Savior of the world. 15 God abides in those who confess that Jesus is the Son
of God, and they abide in God. 16 So we have known and have believed the love that God
has for us.

God is love, and those who abide in love abide in God, and God abides in them. 17 Love
has been perfected among us in order that we may have boldness on the day of judgment,
because as God is, so are we in this world. 18 There is no fear in love, rather perfect love casts
out fear, for fear relates to punishment, and whoever fears has not reached perfection in love.
19 We love because God first loved us. 20 If someone says, "I love God," and hates their sister
or brother, they are a liar; for those who do not love a sister or brother whom they have seen,
cannot love God whom they have not seen. 21 The commandment we have from God is this:
those who love God must love their sisters and brothers also.

Matthew 12:46 While Jesus was still speaking to the crowds, his mother and his siblings
were standing outside, seeking to speak to him. 47 Someone told him, "Look, your mother and
your siblings are standing outside, seeking to speak to you." 48 But to the one who had told
him this, Jesus said, "Who is my mother, and who are my siblings?" 49 And pointing his hand
to his disciples, he said, "Here are my mother and my siblings! 50 For whoever does the will of
my Abba in the heavens is my mother and sister and brother."

PROCLAMATION

Text Notes

Jegar-sahadutha in verse 47 is the Aramaic name for Gal-Ed that also means Heap (of stones) of Testimony. The verb "watch" in verse 49 is from the same root as Mitzpah, *tz-p-h*. "Out of sight" is literally "hidden" from each other in verse 49. In verse 50, the verb *anah* refers to physical affliction and sexual violence; it is a primary indicator of rape, describes Sarah's abuse of Hagar, Egyptian oppression of the Israelites, and the rapes of Dinah, Tamar, and the Levite's low-status wife.

In Psalm 144:3, "woman-born" replaces "children of man."

The abundance of masculine actors (characters or gendered nouns) and masculine pronouns throughout the scriptures regularly makes identifying specific referents difficult. In 1 John 4:21 it is unclear whether the "he" who taught us is intended to be read as God or Jesus. Arguably, either is appropriate.

Jesus's siblings are identified in Matthew 13:55–56 as James, Joseph, Simon, Judas, and an unknown number of sisters. The plural *adelphoi* in Matthew 12:46 encompasses both a mixed group and an all-male group. There is no way to know if *all* of Jesus's siblings were present, or just his brothers, all or some. (Readings that translate *adelphoi* as "relative" making them Jesus's extended family have as a theological goal the perpetual virginity of the Blessed Mother, though they will translate it as brother/sister when not pertaining to Jesus's kin.) Jesus's specific inclusion of sister in verse 50 may indicate only his brothers were present; I have inverted the order of the family in the verse.

Preaching Prompts

The fourth Sunday in Lent is often celebrated as *Laetare* (rejoicing) Sunday, derived from the opening words in Latin of Isaiah 66:10. Many clergy wear rose pink vestments, a color associated with the Virgin Mary. The Sunday can fall in proximity to the Feast of the Annunciation on March 25. This week's readings center on the Virgin Mother and her daughters, along with daughters and sisters in other texts.

It may surprise you that the well-known Mizpah covenant, "May the Lord watch between me and thee" is in actuality a covenant guaranteeing the protection and well-being of women, Leah and Rachel, from spousal abuse and additional wives and children. This is a useful text to address family dynamics, including violence. It should be noted the women are not party to the covenant; they are its patriarchal subjects.

The psalm celebrates human, plant, and animal life in full bloom as the very good gifts of God; one of very few references to daughters in the psalms or larger tradition.

While this volume uses expansive and explicitly feminine God language, it does preserve "Father" in the Gospel when Jesus says it in Matthew 12. The Epistle's claims are rooted in God's paternity of Jesus, so the title is retained there.

First John 4 makes clear that the treatment of women and girls is a fit metric for whether we individually or collectively love God. We cannot love God whom we have seen and hate (abuse, discriminate against) her children. This holds true for all marginalized populations.

Many texts present the believer as the sister or brother of Jesus. Matthew 12:50 makes it possible for some believers to share in the mothering of Jesus. It is more than a statement about discipleship; it is vision of a family system where Jesus willingly subjects himself to the mamas and aunties have something to say to him.

LENT V

Isaiah 40:9–11; Psalm 68:4–11; Romans 16:1–16; Matthew 26:6–13

Isaiah 40:9 Climb a high mountain,
O woman of Zion who proclaims good news!
Raise your voice with power,
O woman of Jerusalem who proclaims good news!
Raise it daughter! Fear not daughter!
Say to the cities of Judah daughter,
"Here is your God!"
10 See, the Sovereign REDEEMER comes with might,
whose arm rules for God;
whose reward is with God,
and God's reparation comes before.
11 She will feed her flock like a shepherd;
she will gather the lambs in her arms,
and carry them in her bosom,
and gently lead the mother sheep.

Psalm 68:4–11

4 Sing to God, sing praises to her Name;
exalt her who rides upon the clouds;
Holy is her Name, rejoice before her!
5 Mother of orphans and defender of widows,
is God in her holy habitation!
6 God settles the solitary in a home, bringing prisoners into prosperity;
while the rebellious shall live in a wasteland.

7 God, when you marched before your people,
when you moved out through the wilderness,
8 the earth shook, even the heavens poured down,
at the presence of God, the One of Sinai,
at the presence of God, the God of Israel.
9 Rain in abundance, God, you showered abroad;
when your heritage grew weary you prepared rest.
10 Your creatures found a dwelling in her;
God, you provided in your goodness for the oppressed.
11 The AUTHOR OF LIFE gave the word;
the women who proclaim the good news are a great army.

Romans 16:1 I commend to you all our sister Phoebe, a deacon of the church in Cenchreae,
2 so that you all may receive her in Christ as is worthy of the saints, and stand by her in
whatever thing she may need of you, for she has been a benefactress of many, and of myself
as well.

3 Greet Prisca and Aquila, my coworkers in Christ Jesus, 4 and who for my life risked
their necks, to whom not only I give thanks, but also all the churches of the Gentiles, 5 and
the church in their house. Greet Epaenetus, my beloved, who was the first fruit in Asia
for Christ. 6 Greet Mary, who has worked much among you all. 7 Greet Andronicus and
Junia, my kin and my fellow prisoners; they are eminent among the apostles, and they
were in Christ before I was. 8 Greet Ampliatus, my beloved in Christ. 9 Greet Urbanus,
our coworker in Christ, and Stachys my beloved. 10 Greet Apelles, who is proven in Christ.
Greet those who belong to Aristobulus. 11 Greet Herodion, my kinsman. Greet those who
belong of Narcissus in Christ. 12 Greet Tryphaena and Tryphosa who toil in Christ. Greet
the beloved Persis who has worked much in Christ. 13 Greet Rufus, chosen in Christ, and
greet his mother who is also mine. 14 Greet Asyncritus, Phlegon, Hermes, Patrobas, Hermas, and the sisters and brothers who are with them. 15 Greet Philologus and Julia, Nereus
and his sister, and Olympas, and all the saints with them. 16 Greet one another with a holy
kiss. All the churches of Christ greet you.

Matthew 26:6 Now Jesus was in Bethany at the house of Simon with the skin disease, 7 a
woman came to him who had an alabaster vessel of extremely valuable balm, and she poured it
on his head as he sat at table. 8 But when the disciples saw it, they were angry and said, "What
purpose does this waste serve? 9 For this could have been sold for much, and the money given
to the poor." 10 But Jesus understanding, said to them, "Why are you making this trouble for
the woman? She has done something good for me. 11 For you always have the poor with you,
but you will not always have me. 12 By pouring this balm on my body she has prepared me for
burial. 13 Truly I tell you, wherever this good news is proclaimed in the whole world, what she
has done will be told in remembrance of her."

PROCLAMATION

Text Notes

To bear good news or "tidings" is to proclaim them, not hold them. The semantic range includes "near news/tidings," usually good, occasionally poor as in loss of a battle/war and "proclaim or preach that news," which can include divine salvation. In Isaiah 40:9, *mebasseret*, "she-who-bears-good-news," has been translated as Zion/Jerusalem being the proclaimer (CEB, NRSV, RSV, KJV, Geneva, and Bishop's Bibles), or as a proclaimer *to* Zion/Jerusalem (the *Dead Sea Scroll Bible*, JPS and Wycliffe Bibles, along with the LXX and Bibles dependent on it, Vulgate and Douay). Grammar dictates that the proclaimer is feminine, as are cities in Hebrew; if not the city, the proclaimer is a woman, likely a prophet. The verb *b-s-r* is *euaggelizo* in Greek and becomes the primary verb for proclaiming the gospel; it is so used in Matthew 26:13 about the woman who anoints Jesus. Isaiah 40:9 could well be translated in part "you good-news-preaching-woman of Zion/Jerusalem"; however, I have endeavored to keep the language more consistent with the context of the Hebrew Bible.

In Isaiah 40:9–10 "daughter" makes plain the feminine imperatives in each place not visible to English readers. The use of feminine pronouns not present in the text for God in verse 11 reflects that shepherding, which can represent God or the caretakers of her people, was a vocation (like prophecy) performed by women and men alike.

The skin disease (or collection of diseases) invoked by "leprosy" in the scriptures, as in Matthew 26:6, does not correspond with the contemporary disease and its symptoms.

Preaching Prompts

These texts trace out a contextual linguistic understanding of women as bearers, proclaimers, and preachers of good news that will become the gospel in Christianity, rooted in the Hebrew Scriptures. This is particularly poignant and relevant scant weeks before the Church commemorates Mary Magdalene, the Apostle to the Apostles, preaching first the good news that Jesus was risen from the dead—even as some attempt to use the latter scriptures to claim that women preachers are "unbiblical."

The story of the woman who anoints Jesus is often the gospel lesson for the last Sunday in Lent. Its irony is that Jesus says what she has done will be told in memory of her wherever the Good News is proclaimed, yet the framers of the text didn't clearly preserve her name. And, in most instances, proclamation of the gospel is not accompanied or preceded by a telling of her story. What seems a deliberate obscuring is easily reckoned as patriarchy, androcentrism, or both. Yet within the pages of scripture there are these women who proclaim good news in Isaiah 40 and Psalm 68. God whose power, might, and tender loving care is not diminished when portrayed as a female rather than male shepherd, and all of the women who built the church with their work and words, not their wombs, are saluted by Paul in Romans 16; among them women he calls deacon and apostle.

Should any have identified sexism and patriarchy in the church as issues over which to repent during Lent and from which to abstain after Lent, these texts point the way to the tomb in which they might be buried never to rise again.

FEAST OF THE ANNUNCIATION, MARCH 25

Zephaniah 3:14–20; Canticle 15, the Magnificat (Luke 1:46–55); 2 Corinthians 6:16b–18; Luke 1:26–38

Zephaniah 3:14 Sing aloud daughter of Zion; shout, all ye Israel!
Rejoice, daughter, and exult with all your heart, daughter of Jerusalem!
15 The JUDGE OF ALL FLESH has taken away the judgments against you,
and has turned away your enemies, daughter.
The sovereign of Israel, CREATOR OF THE HEAVENS AND EARTH,
is in your midst, daughter; no longer shall you fear evil.
16 On that day it shall be said to Jerusalem:
Fear not, Zion; do not let your hands grow weak, daughter.
17 The AGELESS ONE, your God, is in your midst, daughter,
a warrior who will deliver salvation;
who will rejoice over you with gladness, daughter,
God will renew you in love, daughter;
God will exult over you, daughter, with loud singing.
18 Those who are grieved on account of the festivals,
I will remove from you, daughter,
so, daughter, that you will not bear their reproach.
19 I will deal with all your oppressors, daughter, at that time.
And I will save the lame and gather the outcast,
and I will change their shame into praise
and renown in all the earth.
20 At that time I will bring you all home, at the time when I gather all of you;
for I will make you all renowned and praised
among all the peoples of the earth,
when I restore your fortunes before all of your eyes,
says the GOD WHO IS SALVATION.

Canticle 15, the Magnificat, Luke 1:46–55

46 "My soul magnifies the Holy One,
47 and my spirit rejoices in God my Savior,
48 for God has looked with favor on the lowliness of God's own servant.
Surely, from now on all generations will call me blessed;
49 for the Mighty One has done great things for me,
and holy is God's name.
50 God's loving-kindness is for those who fear God
from generation to generation.
51 God has shown the strength of God's own arm;
God has scattered the arrogant in the intent of their hearts.
52 God has brought down the powerful from their thrones,
and lifted up the lowly;
53 God has filled the hungry with good things,
and sent the rich away empty.
54 God has helped God's own child, Israel,
a memorial to God's mercy,
55 just as God said to our mothers and fathers,
to Abraham and Hagar and Sarah, to their descendants forever."

2 Corinthians 6:16 For we are the temple of the living God; as God said:

"I will dwell in them and walk among them,
and I will be their God,
and they shall be my people."
17 Therefore, *"Come out from them,*
and be separate from them," says the Holy One,
and, *"Touch nothing unclean,"*
then, *"I will take you all in."*
18 and, *"I will be your parent,*
and you shall be my daughters and sons,"
says the Almighty Everlasting God.

Luke 1:26 In the sixth month the angel Gabriel was sent by God to a town of Galilee, Nazareth, 27 to a virgin betrothed to a man whose name was Joseph, of the house of David. And the name of the virgin was Mary. 28 And the angel came to Mary and said, "Rejoice, favored one! The Most High God is with you." 29 Now, she was troubled by the angel's words and pondered what sort of greeting this was. 30 Then the angel said to her, "Fear not Mary, for you have found favor with God. 31 And now, you will conceive in your womb and give birth to a son, and you will name him Jesus. 32 He will be great and will be called the Son of the Most

High, and the Sovereign God will give him the throne of his ancestor David. 33 He will reign over the house of Jacob forever, and of his sovereignty there will be no end." 34 Then Mary said to the angel, "How can this be, since I have not known a man intimately?" 35 The angel said to her, "The Holy Spirit, She will come upon you, and the power of the Most High will overshadow you; therefore the one born will be holy. He will be called Son of God. 36 And now, Elizabeth your kinswoman has even conceived a son in her old age, and this is the sixth month for she who was called barren. 37 For nothing will be impossible with God." 38 Then Mary said, "Here am I, the woman-slave of God; let it be with me according to your word." Then the angel left her.

PROCLAMATION

Text Notes

Bat Zion (or Jerusalem) can mean both Daughter Zion, the city *or* a daughter of Zion, a woman from the city. In Isaiah 40:9, reading "daughter of" reveals a female prophet crying out to Jerusalem (compare NRSV and JPS translations). Because the addressee is feminine, all of the verbs to her are also feminine; I reproduce "daughter" in places where English masks the frequency of feminine address. Verse 18 is notoriously difficult to translate: see the discussion in my commentary on Zephaniah in the *Wisdom* series.

In Luke 1:55, the inclusive plural *pateras* can mean ancestors, parents, or fathers. Since God's promises were not just to Abraham and God also made promises to Hagar (Genesis 16:10–13; 21:17–18), and for Sarah (through Abraham in Genesis 17:15–16), I have expanded "Abraham and his descendants" to reflect that. Abraham also had children with Keturah; their offspring would also be beneficiaries of the promises made to Abraham; however, God does not make a promise directly to her in the scriptures.

In Mary's linguistic and cultural world, in Hebrew and Aramaic, the spirit is feminine; the Syriac text uses a feminine verb for the spirit in Luke 1:35. Also in her world, there was no distinction between servant and slave. Mary is not saying she will wait on God hand and foot in verse 38; she is giving God ownership of her body, ownership slaveholders claimed without consent.

Preaching Prompts

In its original context, Daughter Zion was most likely the city. Here I suggest hearing it through the experience of the pregnant Virgin reflecting on her scriptures in light of her experience.

The appointed Epistle is a collection of verse fragments strung together, many out of context. The phrases are inexact quotes, whether looking at Hebrew or Greek antecedents, shaped for deployment here. Leviticus 26:11–12 has the same sense as in 2 Corinthians 6:16. Verse 17 of the Epistle links a fragment found in both Ezekiel 20:34 and 20:41 to a line from Isaiah 52:11 calling for a second Exodus from Egypt. Verse 18 takes God's promise to David for Solomon to be his father in 2 Samuel 7:14 and makes it second person plural, "your all" instead of "his," and adds "daughters" to the altered text in Greek.

Angelic lore is largely pseudepigraphal beginning in 2 Esdras. While Gabriel and Michael appear in the Hebrew Bible (Daniel 8:16; 9:21; 10:13, 21; 12:1), they are not identified as angels. However, Raphael is called an angel in Tobit 5:4.

There is some irony in the pains the Gospel takes to connect Jesus to David and the Hebrew Scriptures, and choice of translators to anglicize the names of the holy family and disciples, undermining their Jewish identity. A further irony is that Jesus's Davidic heritage rests on Joseph's genealogy and the supposition that Mary is from the same tribe as was common but not required. Mary's only relative in the text, Elizabeth, is the wife of a priest. Priests married within the priestly line nearly exclusively, making her likely a *bat cohen*, priest's daughter, as well. What this means for Mary's heritage and that of Jesus is unclear.

PALM SUNDAY—LITURGY OF THE PALMS

Matthew 21:1–11; Psalm 118:19–29

Matthew 21:1 Now they had come near Jerusalem and reached Bethphage on the Mount of
Olives, then Jesus sent two disciples, 2 saying to them, "Go into the village before you, and immediately you will find a donkey tied, and a colt with her; release them and bring them to me. 3 If
anyone says anything to you, just say this, 'The Son of Woman needs them.' And they will send
them immediately." 4 This took place to fulfill what had been spoken through the prophet, saying,

5 "*Tell the daughter of Zion,*
'*Look, your sovereign is coming to you,*
humble, and mounted on a donkey,
and on a colt, the foal of a donkey.'"

6 The disciples went and did just as Jesus had instructed them; 7 they brought the donkey and
the colt, and put their cloaks on them, and he sat on them. 8 A very large crowd spread their
cloaks on the road, and others cut branches from the trees and spread them on the road. 9 The
crowds that were going before him and the one following were shouting, saying:

"*Hosanna to the Son of David!*
Blessed is the one who comes in the name of the Holy One!
Hosanna in the highest!"

10 When Jesus entered Jerusalem, the whole city was shook, asking, "Who is this?" 11 The
crowds were saying, "This is the prophet Jesus from Nazareth in Galilee."

Psalm 118:19–29

19 Open for me the gates of righteousness,
that I may enter them
and give thanks to the LIVING GOD.
20 This is the gate to the HOLY PRESENCE;
the righteous shall enter through it.
21 I thank you that you have answered me
and you have become my salvation.
22 The stone that the builders rejected
has become the chief cornerstone.
23 This is OUR GOD's doing;
it is marvelous in our eyes.
24 This is the day that the FONT OF CREATION has made;
let us rejoice and be glad in it.
25 Ah! HOLY ONE help, save us!
Ah! HOLY ONE haste, deliver us!
26 Blessed is the one who comes in the name of the MOST HIGH GOD.
We bless you from the house of the HOLY ONE.
27 The FAITHFUL ONE is God,
and she has given us light.
Bind the festal offering with ropes of branches,
up to the horns of the altar.
28 You are my God, and I will give thanks to you;
you are my God; I will exalt you.
29 Give thanks to the HOLY ONE, for she is good,
for her faithful love endures forever.

PROCLAMATION

Text Notes

The text has Jesus use the title "Lord" of himself in Matthew 21:3. In keeping with the aims of this volume, expansive and explicitly feminine language for God and humanity, I employ a translation of the messianic title Jesus often uses for himself here. (See commentary on Advent 1, Year A.) In verse 5 the Gospel quotes Zechariah 9:9, seeming not to understand the poetic parallelism that describes the same animal in two ways; he appears to sit on both in verse 7. The Gospel adds an introduction to "*the* daughter of Zion," adding the definite article not common in this expression in Greek, begging the question to whom it is addressed. In verse 9, the crowd chants Psalm 118:26, a procession psalm for entering the temple also recited during Passover.

The assonant and alliterative poetry of Psalm 118:25 (the "Hosanna") is difficult to reproduce: *Ana Ya hoshia na; Ana Ya chatzlicha na.* The "hosanna" pronunciation comes from the Greek transliteration of the Hebrew. Verse 27 is unclear in a number of places: "bind the feast with clouds." Since portions of sacrificial animals were eaten, "festal offering" is likely; and "ropes" and "branches" are each one letter away from "clouds." "God's faithful love endures forever" is one of the oldest liturgical refrains in the Hebrew Bible: see the opening and closing of this psalm and Psalm 118.

Preaching Prompts

While this is not traditionally a preaching occasion, one may choose to frame the liturgy with a brief preface or blurb in the leaflet, or alternately address it in the subsequent sermon (if the liturgy precedes another service).

The ubiquity of monarchy in the scriptures and the worlds from which they emerge reflect more about the humans who received and recorded, and translate and interpret them, than it does about God who inspired and speaks through them. Monarchs were the most powerful persons in those worlds and they and their power, reigns, and regalia provided a vocabulary for talking about God. Jesus subverts that to some degree by reinterpreting that title in such a way as to perplex even those who knew him best.

These lessons provide an opportunity to talk about our language and imagery for God in and out of the Bible (and this lectionary) and its impact on persons in terms of class, gender, the performance of gender, and sexual orientation.

PALM SUNDAY—LITURGY OF THE WORD

Isaiah 49:5–16; Psalm 22:1–11; Galatians 3:23–4:7; Mark 14:32–15:47 (or Mark 14:32–53)

Those who prefer to continue the Gospel through the Passion will find the successive verses in the Good Friday readings.

Isaiah 49:5 And now says the AUTHOR OF LIFE,
who formed me in the womb to be God's slave
to return Jacob back to God,
and that Israel might be gathered to God;

I am honored in the sight of the HOLY ONE OF OLD,
and my God is my strength.
6 God says,
"It is too light a thing that you should be my slave
to raise up the tribes of Jacob [the line of Rebekah],
and to restore the survivors of Israel [born of Rachel and Leah, and Bilhah and Zilpah]?
I will give you as a light to the nations,
for it will be that my salvation reaches to the end of the earth."
7 Thus says the FAITHFUL ONE,
the Redeemer of Israel, God's holy one,
to one despised, abhorred by the nations,
the slave of rulers,
"Queens and kings shall see and arise,
princes and princesses, and they too shall prostrate themselves,
on account of the FIRE OF SINAI, who is faithful,
the Holy One of Israel, who has chosen you."
8 Thus says the MIGHTY GOD:
In a favorable time have I answered you,
on a day of salvation have I helped you;
I have kept you and given you
as a covenant to the people,
to establish the land,
to apportion the desolate portions;
9 saying to the prisoners, "Go free!"
to those who are in darkness, "Let yourselves be seen."
Along the paths they shall pasture,
and on all the bare heights shall be their pasture.
10 They shall not hunger nor shall they thirst,
neither shall heat nor sun strike them down,
for the one who mother-loves them shall lead them,
and by springs of water shall guide them.
11 And I will turn all my mountains into a pathway,
and my highways shall be raised up.
12 Look! These shall come from far away,
and see! These from the north and from the sea to the west,
and these from the southland of Syene.
13 Sing for joy, you heavens, and exult O earth;
let mountains break forth into singing!
For the TENDER LOVING ONE has comforted God's people,
and will mother-love God's suffering ones.

14 But Zion said, "The Everlasting God has forsaken me,
my Sovereign has forgotten me."
15 Can a woman forget her nursing child,
or mother-love for the child of her womb?
Even these may forget,
yet I, no, I will not forget you.
16 See, I have engraved you on the palms of my hands;
your walls are continually before me.

Psalm 22:1–11

1 My God, my God, why have you forsaken me?
Why are you so far from my deliverance, from the words of my groaning?
2 My God, I cry by day, and you do not answer;
and by night, and there I find no rest for me.
3 Yet you are holy,
enthroned on the praises of Israel.
4 In you our mothers and fathers trusted;
they trusted, and you rescued them.
5 To you they cried, and were freed;
in you they trusted, and they were not put to shame.
6 But I am a worm, and not human;
scorned by humankind, and despised by people.
7 All who see me mock me;
they flap their lips at me, they shake their heads:
8 "Commit yourself to the Saving One; let God rescue
and deliver the one in whom God delights!"
9 Yet it was you who drew me from the womb;
keeping me safe on my mother's breast.
10 On you was I cast from birth,
and since my mother's womb you have been my God.
11 Be not far from me,
for trouble is near
and there is none to help.

Galatians 3:23 Now before faith came, we were garrisoned and guarded under the law
until the faith that was coming should be revealed. 24 Therefore the law was our instructor
until Christ came, so that we might be justified by faith. 25 But now that faith has come, we
are no longer subject to an instructor, 26 for in Christ Jesus you are all daughters and sons of
God through faith. 27 So, as many of you as were baptized into Christ are clothed in Christ.
28 There is no Jew or Greek, there is no slave or free, there is no male and female; for all of you

are one in Christ Jesus. 29 And if you belong to Christ, then you are Abraham's [and Sarah's]
offspring, heirs according to the promise.

4:1 I say that as long as heirs are minors, they are no better than slaves, though they are the
masters of all; 2 but they remain under guardians and trustees until the time set by the father.
3 So also for us; while we were minors, we were enslaved by the constitutive elements of the
world. 4 But when the fullness of time had come, God sent God's own Son, born of a woman,
born under the law, 5 to redeem those who were under the law, so that we might receive adoption like children. 6 And because you are children, God has sent the Spirit of God's own Son
into our hearts, crying, "Abba! Father!" 7 So you are no longer a slave but a child, and if a child
then also an heir, through God.

[***Mark 14:32*** Jesus and his disciples went to a place called Gethsemane and he said to his
disciples, "You all sit here while I pray." 33 He took with him Peter and James and John and
began to be deeply moved and distressed. 34 And said to them, "My soul is deeply grieved, to
the point of death; you all stay here, and stay awake." 35 And going a little farther, he threw
himself on the ground and prayed that, if possible, the hour might pass from him. 36 He said,
"Abba, Father, all things are possible for you; remove this cup from me; yet, not what I want,
but what you do." 37 Jesus came and found them sleeping; and he said to Peter, "Simon, are
you sleeping? Could you not stay awake one hour? 38 Stay awake and pray that you all may
not come into the time of trial; the spirit indeed is willing, but the flesh is weak." 39 And again
he went away and prayed, saying the same thing. 40 And once more he came and found them
sleeping, for their eyes were very heavy; and they did not know what to say to him. 41 Jesus
came a third time and said to them, "Are you all sleeping, still, and taking your rest? Enough!
The hour has come. Look! The Son of Woman is betrayed into the hands of sinners. 42 Get
up, let us go. See, my betrayer is at hand."

43 And instantly, while he was still speaking, Judas, one of the twelve, arrived; with him
there was a crowd with swords and clubs from the chief priests, the religious scholars, and the
elders. 44 Now the betrayer had given them a sign, saying, "The one I kiss is he; seize him and
lead him away safely." 45 Then when Judas came, he went up to Jesus immediately and said,
"Rabbi!" and kissed him. 46 Then they laid hands on him and took him. 47 But one of the
bystanders drew his sword and struck the slave of the high priest and cut off his ear. 48 Then
Jesus said to them, "Is it as for a bandit you all have come out with swords and clubs to seize
me? 49 Daily I was with you all in the temple teaching, and you did not seize me. But let
the scriptures be fulfilled." 50 All of them deserted him and fled. 51 A certain young man was
following Jesus, with just a fine cloth on his naked flesh. They caught hold of him, 52 but he
forsook the fine cloth and ran off naked.]

53 They took Jesus to the high priest; and they assembled all the chief priests, the elders,
and the religious scholars. 54 Now Peter followed him from afar into the courtyard of the high
priest and was sitting with the attendants, warming himself at the fire. 55 Now the chief priests
and the whole council sought testimony against Jesus to put him to death but found none.

56 For many gave false testimony against him, yet their testimony did not agree. 57 Some rose
and gave false testimony against him, saying, 58 "Well, we heard him say, 'I will destroy this
hand-made temple, and in three days I will build another, that is not hand-made.'" 59 But even
on this point their testimony did not agree. 60 Then the high priest stood up before them and
said to Jesus, "No response? What are they testifying against you?" 61 But he was silent and
answered nothing. Again, the high priest spoke to him, "Are you the Messiah, the Son of the
Blessed One?" 62 Jesus said, "I am; and

> '*you will see the Son of Woman*
> seated at the right hand of the Power,'
> and '*coming with the clouds of heaven*.'"

63 Then the high priest tore his clothes and said, "Why do we still need witnesses? 64 You
all have heard his blasphemy! How does it appear to you?" All of them condemned him,
"Guilty! This is death!" 65 Some began to spit on him, to blindfold him, and to strike him,
saying to him, "Prophesy!" Then the attendants took him and beat him.

66 While Peter was below in the courtyard, one of the high priest's enslaved girls came
by. 67 When she saw Peter warming himself, she stared at him and said, "You were also with
the Nazarene, Jesus." 68 But Peter denied it, saying, "I do not know or even understand what
you are saying." Then he went out into the front courtyard. Then the cock crowed. 69 And the
enslaved girl, on seeing him, began to say to the bystanders again that this man is one of them.
70 But again he denied it. Then after a little while the bystanders said to Peter again, "Certainly you are one of them, for you are a Galilean." 71 But he began to curse and swore, "I do
not know this person you are talking about." 72 And suddenly the cock crowed for the second
time. Then Peter remembered the thing Jesus had said to him, "Before the cock crows twice,
you will deny me three times." And he threw himself down and sobbed.

15:1 As soon as it was morning, the chief priests took a counsel with the elders and religious scholars and the whole council. They bound Jesus, led him away, and handed him over
to Pilate. 2 Pilate asked him, "Are you the King of the Judeans?" He answered him, saying,
"You say so." 3 Then the chief priests accused him of many things. 4 But Pilate asked him
again, "Have you no reply? See how many charges they bring against you." 5 But Jesus made no
further reply, thus Pilate was amazed.

6 Now at the festival Pilate used to release one prisoner to them, whoever they asked.
7 Now there was a man called Barabbas in prison with the rebels who in the rebellion had
committed murder. 8 So the crowd came and began to ask Pilate to do for them according to
his custom. 9 Then he responded to them saying, "Do you all want me to release the King of
the Judeans to you?" 10 For he recognized that it was out of jealousy that the chief priests had
handed him over. 11 Then the chief priests stirred up the crowd that instead Barabbas might
be released for them. 12 Pilate again responded to them, "What then do you wish me to do
with the one you call the King of the Judeans?" 13 They shouted more [than before], "Crucify him!" 14 Pilate asked them, "Why, for doing what evil?" But they shouted all the more,

"Crucify him!" 15 So Pilate, wanting to satiate the crowd, released Barabbas to them; then he
handed Jesus over for flogging and to be crucified.

16 Then the soldiers led him into the courtyard of the property, which is the military
headquarters, and they called together the entire cohort. 17 And they clothed him in purple,
and they put on him thorns woven into a crown. 18 And they began saluting him, "Hail, King
of the Judeans!" 19 They struck his head with a reed, spat upon him, and knelt in homage to
him. 20 After mocking him, they stripped him of the purple and put his clothes on him. Then
they led him away to crucify him.

21 They compelled a passerby, a certain Simon of Cyrene who was coming from the countryside, to carry his cross; he was the father of Alexander and Rufus. 22 Then they brought
Jesus to the Golgotha place (which means Skull Place). 23 And they offered him myrrh wine,
but he did not take it. 24 And they crucified him, and divided his clothes casting lots among
themselves for what each would take.

25 It was the third hour [past dawn] when they crucified him. 26 The writing above of the
accusation against him read, "The King of the Judeans." 27 And with him they crucified two
revolutionaries, one on his right and one on his left.

29 The passers-by reviled him, shaking their heads and saying, "Ha! You would destroy
the temple and build it in three days—30 save yourself, and come down from the cross!" 31 In
the same way the chief priests, with the religious scholars, mocked him among themselves and
said, "He saved others; himself he is unable to save. 32 The Messiah, the King of Israel! Come
down from the cross now that we may see and believe." Those who were crucified with him
also demeaned him.

33 Now when it was the sixth hour [of the day, or noon], darkness came over the whole
land until the ninth hour [of the day, about three in the afternoon]. 34 At the ninth hour
Jesus cried out with a loud voice, "*Eloi, Eloi, lema sabachthani*?" which means, "My God,
my God, why have you forsaken me?" 35 When some of the bystanders heard it, they said,
"Listen, he is calling Elijah." 36 And someone ran and filled a sponge with vinegary wine, put
it on a stick, and gave it to him to drink, saying, "Wait, let us see whether Elijah will come
to take him down." 37 Then Jesus gave a great cry and breathed out a final time. 38 And the
curtain of the temple was torn in two, from top to bottom. 39 Now when the centurion,
stationed facing him, saw that in this way Jesus breathed out at the end, he said, "Truly this
man was God's Son!"

40 There were also women watching from a distance; among them were Mary the Magdalene, and Mary the mother of James the younger and of Joses, and Salome. 41 These women
followed him and ministered to him when he was in Galilee, and there were many other
women who had come up with him to Jerusalem.

42 When evening had come, since it was the day of Preparation—the day before the
Sabbath—43 Joseph of Arimathea, a respected member of the council, who himself was
also waiting for the reign of God, went boldly to Pilate and requested for the body of Jesus.
44 Then Pilate wondered that Jesus was now dead, and summoning the centurion asked him

whether he had been dead for some time. [45] When he learned it from the centurion, he gave the corpse to Joseph. [46] Then Joseph bought a fine cloth, and taking him down, wrapped him in the fine cloth, and put him in a tomb that had been hewn out of rock. He then rolled a stone against the door of the tomb. [47] Mary the Magdalene and Mary the mother of Joses saw where he was put.

PROCLAMATION

Owing to the length of the Palm Sunday Gospel, the commentary section will be longer than for other readings.

Text Notes

The same word is used in Isaiah 49:5 and 7, yet NRSV, JPS, and CEB all translate Israel as God's "servant" but the nation as the "slave of rulers." "Servant" occludes the expectation of complete domination/submission, including the ability to maim, kill, breed, rape, impregnate, and sell the person without consequence.

Hebrew plurals like "monarchs/kings" and "princes" in Isaiah 49:7 are inclusive. I have expanded both to reflect the presence of female royals in and at the head of some nations. "Go free" in verse 9 uses the primary verb of the exodus. Syene, or Sinim, in verse 12 is an Egyptian town with a record of some Israelite settlement.

In Isaiah 49:5 and 15, "womb" is the more generic "belly" used broadly for women and men; it is also found in Psalm 22:9–10 (verse 10 also uses the more common specific "womb"). In Isaiah 49:13–15, it is paired with "mother-love" (the verb whose root is that same word) and children, including one at the breast, in verse 15. Translating this as "compassion" (NRSV), "pity" (CEB), or just "love" (JPS) eviscerates the intentionally crafted portrait of God as a mother, accomplished despite use of masculine forms.

The second phrase in Psalm 22:3 can also be translated as "you are holy, enthroned, the Praise of Israel." In verse 9, the Divine Midwife "extracts" the baby; she does not just "catch" him, perhaps suggesting a difficult birth.

In Galatians 3:23ff, translation choices can present the law in an antagonistic and ultimately anti-Jewish manner as "prison" and "disciplinarian" (see NRSV). However, *ephrouroumetha* in verse 23 means to set a guard or garrison; that is a protective action. And in verse 24, a *paidagōgos* is a teacher; *torah* itself means "teaching" and "revelation" more than "law."

One of the verbs that describes Jesus's emotions in Mark 14:33 is only used in that place making it difficult to define; suggestions range from "amazed" to "gloomy" to "distressed" to "troubled." In verse 34, Jesus expresses his sorrow using the language of Psalms 42:11 and 43:5 in Greek, "my soul is cast down." Similarly, the description of soldiers gambling for Jesus's clothes matches the wording of Psalm 22:18 in Greek. Judas is concerned that Jesus's arrest be done "safely" in verse 44; he is a complex character with mixed motives. The "attendants" in verse 54 can provide a number of services; the word is more "assistant" than "guard," as is commonly translated. The enslaved "girls" in Mark 14:66–69 could be young women. "Girl" is often used to denote their minor legal status. The criminals crucified with Jesus in Mark 15:27 could have been thieves or highway bandits; the root of *lēstēs* is stolen goods. However, the semantic range includes revolutionaries and insurrectionists. This latter understanding may be what is meant given mention of imprisoned rebels (using a different word, *stasiastēs*) in verse 7. The vinegar wine in verse 36 draws on Psalm 69:21. The nature of the women's ministry to Jesus in 15:41 should be understood as wholistic, spiritual, and material. Many Greek manuscripts use the more explicit *ptōma*, "corpse," rather than *soma*, "body," for Jesus's remains in Mark 15:44.

Preaching Prompts

As Holy Week begins, one may wish to explore God's sorrow over a world that crucifies as well as over a crucified beloved child, a mother's sorrow as well as a father's. In Isaiah 49, God is the divine mother whose love emanates from her womb, most specifically in verse 13 and 14.

Contemporary discomfort with slave language should not overshadow the degree to which it was normative in the biblical text and its theologies. For the biblical ear, "slave of God" and "slave of Sarah" were equally acceptable and nonremarkable. The linguistic distinction between being a "servant" of God and being held in slavery is entirely artificial to the text and permits slave-holding societies to embrace servitude of God as pertaining to them while holding others in bondage in a fictive distinct category.

In Psalm 22, the most obvious divine feminine image is God as midwife and lactation guide in verse 9. There is also the birthing mother who has no voice and makes no cry. In verse 10, God seems to have become a foster parent for a perhaps abandoned child; the child is thrown (away?) on to God. God can be both midwife and foster mother here. We do not know if the birth mother cannot or will not keep her child. She can be preached in conversation with the reminder that women do abandon children in Isaiah 49, yet without demonization. In keeping with Palm Sunday, she can be read as giving her child over to God, whatever his fate.

Galatians 3:23–24 describe the law as a protective, not punitive, garrison and guard. Though addressing a Gentile Church on whom the Torah (or *torah* broadly) was never binding, Paul uses "we" with regard to the law. In a rhetorical flourish, Paul argues that the particularities that characterize individuals and communities no longer exist "in Christ," yet he continues to operate as though those categories continue and are normative. Yet our adoption and kinship does not require us to leave ourselves, our identities behind.

There are very few women and girls in the Passion narratives. Here in Luke there are girls or women held in slavery by the chief priest. There is missing the wife of Simon of Cyrene, the Cross-Bearer; he is named with reference to his sons, but no mention is made of their mother.

The Passion narratives on Palm Sunday and Good Friday have been used to incite lethal physical violence against Jewish communities by the Church and its ministers. They have also been used to craft violent, anti-Semitic theologies that blame Jews for the death of Jesus, demean and defame Judaism, and deem it failed and its covenants replaced. It is important to acknowledge that history, while repudiating it and repenting of it and affirming God's fidelity to all her covenants and all her peoples. It is essential to be in conversation with our Jewish neighbors and listen more than speak. I strongly recommend reading the scriptures in conversation with Jewish scholars (for example, with the *Jewish Study Bible* and *Jewish Annotated New Testament*).

MONDAY IN HOLY WEEK

Jeremiah 31:8–13; Psalm 22:19–31; Hebrews 1:1–9; John 12:1–7

Jeremiah 31:8 Look! I am going to bring them from the land of the north,
and I will gather them from the farthest parts of the earth,
among them blind and lame, pregnant and birthing, together,
a great assembly, they shall return here.
9 With weeping they shall come,
and with consolations I will lead them back,
I will have them walk by streams of water,
on a straight path, they shall not stumble on it;
for I am a parent to Israel,
and Ephraim is my firstborn.
10 Hear the word of the HOLY ONE, you nations,
and declare it in the islands far off;
say, "The One who scattered Israel will gather him,
and will keep him as a shepherd a flock."
11 For the FAITHFUL ONE has ransomed Jacob [of Rebekah's line]
and has redeemed him from hands too strong for him.
12 They shall come and they shall sing on the heights of Zion,
and they shall be radiant over the goodness of the GRACIOUS GOD,
over the grain, and over the new wine, and over the oil,

and over the young of flock and herd;
their souls shall become like a watered garden,
and they shall never languish again.
13 Then shall young women rejoice in dance,
and young men and elders together.
I will turn their mourning to joy;
I will comfort them, and give them joy for sorrow.

Psalm 22:19–31

19 SAVING GOD, be not far away!
My strength, hasten to help me!
20 Deliver my soul from the sword,
my life from the clutch of the dog!
21 Save me from the mouth of the lion!
For on the horns of the wild oxen you have responded to me.
22 I will tell of your name to my sisters and brothers;
in the midst of the congregation, I will praise you:
23 You who revere the FONT OF LIFE, praise her!
all the offspring of Leah and Rachel, Bilhah and Zilpah glorify her.
Stand in awe of her all you of Rebekah's line.
24 For she did not despise or abhor
the affliction of the afflicted;
she did not hide her face from me,
and when I cried to her, she heard.
25 On your account is my praise in the great congregation;
my vows I will pay before those who revere her.
26 The poor shall eat and be satisfied;
those who seek her shall praise the MOTHER OF ALL.
May your hearts live forever!
27 All the ends of the earth shall remember
and turn to the WELLSPRING OF LIFE;
and all the families of the nations
shall worship before her.
28 For sovereignty belongs to the SHE WHO IS HOLY,
and she rules over the nations.
29 They consume and they bow down,
all the fat ones of the earth before her,
they bend their knees,
all who go down to the dust,
and cannot save their soul.

[30] Later descendants will serve her;
future generations will be told about our God,
[31] they will go and proclaim her deliverance
to a people yet unborn,
saying that she has done it.

Hebrews 1:1 Many times and in many ways God spoke to our mothers and fathers through the prophets, female and male. [2] In these last days God has spoken to us by a Son, whom God appointed heir of all there is, and through whom God created the worlds. [3] The Son is the brilliance of God's glory and reproduction of God's very being, and the Son undergirds all there is by his word of power. When the Son had made purification for sins, he sat down at the right hand of the Majesty on high, [4] having become much greater than the angels, as the name he inherited is more excellent than theirs.

[5] For to which of the angels did God ever say,
"*You are my Child; today I have begotten you*"?

Or this,

"*I will be their Parent, and they will be my Child*"?

[6] Then again, when God brings the firstborn into the world, God says,

"*Let all the angels of God worship him.*"

[7] On the one hand, of the angels God says,

"*God makes winds into celestial messengers,*
and flames of fire into God's ministers."

[8] But of the Son God says,

"*Your throne, O God, is forever and ever,*
and the righteous scepter is the scepter of your realm.
[9] *You have loved righteousness and hated lawlessness;*
therefore God, your God, has anointed you
with the oil of gladness beyond your companions."

John 12:1 Now Jesus, six days before the Passover, came to Bethany where Lazarus was who
he raised from the dead. [2] There they gave a dinner for him and Martha served while Lazarus
was one of those at the table with him. [3] Mary took a pound of a balm made of expensive
pure nard, anointed the feet Jesus, and wiped them with her hair. The house was filled with
the scent of the perfume. [4] But Judas Iscariot, one of his disciples, the one who was about to
betray him, said, [5] "Why was this balm not sold for three hundred denarii and the money
given to the poor?" [6] Now he said this not because he cared about the poor, but because he

was a thief; he kept the moneybag and whatever was put into it, he stole. [7] Jesus said, "Leave her alone. It was for the day of my burial that she kept it."

PROCLAMATION

Text Notes

In Jeremiah 31:9, arguably "consolations" became "supplications," the literal reading, when a letter was dropped.

In Psalm 22:23, "the offspring of Jacob" are identified by their mothers/matriarchs, enslaved and free; similarly "Rebekah's line" stands in for "the offspring of Israel."

In keeping with the aims of this work, foremothers and female prophets are made explicit in Hebrews 1:1. *Megalōsynēs*, "Majesty," in Hebrews 1:3, as a feminine noun, marks a rare use of feminine language to describe God or her attributes in the New Testament.

The following verses quote the earlier scriptures widely and often out of context: Hebrews 1:5 quotes Psalm 2:7 where the anonymous psalmist says God told them they were God's begotten child, probably initially heard with regard to David. The next quote is from 2 Samuel 7:14 (and its duplicate, 1 Chronicles 17:13), where the promise of God to be a parent to a future monarch is to one of David's descendants. Given the difficulty of asserting biological gender for heavenly beings, I use the neuter "child" and "parent" in verse 5. Verse 6 quotes Deuteronomy 32:43 and Psalm 97:7 from Greek, where the original "gods" were replaced by "angels" to correct toward a pure monotheism. Verse 7 quotes Psalm 104:4, playing on the primary meaning of angel, "messenger." Verses 8–9 quote Psalm 45:6–7, where the first verse refers to God but the second refers to the king whose wedding psalm it is (Ahab, since Jezebel is the only princess of Tyre to marry into Israel).

Preaching Prompts

A second iteration of the woman who anoints Jesus is traditional on Monday of Holy Week, an earlier version having been read on the last Sunday of Lent. Today the woman is Mary, sister of Martha and the resurrected Lazarus in John. The Jeremiah 31 reading offers the hope of consolation for those who mourn, just as Lazarus's resurrected body at table with Jesus does.

The context of Jeremiah 31 is God's promise to restore Israel after the Babylonian devastation; our reading affirms the faithfulness of God to her people in each generation, building on not replacing the earliest reading. In some ways Jeremiah 31 is an answer to the plea for salvation in Psalm 22. It is important to remember that "salvation" in the Hebrew Scriptures is physical salvation from death or other danger, and normally national or corporate. Paraphrased by Jesus (his recitation does not quite match Hebrew or Greek versions in either Matthew 27:46 or Mark 15:34), Psalm 22 became the Psalm of the Cross, a principal text of Holy Week.

Hebrews 1 calls us back to the fidelity of God who spoke through prophecy but now speaks through her Holy Child. (Some have concluded from this that prophecy came to an end; however, prophets appear scattered throughout the New Testament.) The amount of prooftexting in this short section raises the eyebrows of a biblical scholar, yet reminds us how flexible ancient interpreters found the scriptures. That flexibility enabled them to reinterpret them in light of Jesus while still holding their previous understandings. Christians have all too often abandoned contextual readings, seizing upon this type of exegesis, neglecting other biblical models.

The last line of the Gospel points us to the tomb, where we needs must linger.

TUESDAY IN HOLY WEEK

Isaiah 49:1–6;* Psalm 123; Philippians 3:17–21; Matthew 21:12–17

Isaiah 49:1 Listen to me, you coastlands,
give heed, you peoples from far away!
The LIFE-BREATH OF CREATION called me from the womb,
from the innermost parts of my mother God made my name known.
2 God made my mouth like a sharp sword,
in the shadow of God's own hand did God hide me;
God made me a polished arrow,
in God's own quiver did God hide me away.
3 And God said to me, "You are my slave,
Israel, the one in whom I will be glorified."
4 But I said, "in vain have I labored,
I have spent my strength in futility and vanity;
yet surely my judgment is with the RIGHTEOUS JUDGE,
and my recompense with my God."
5 And now says the AUTHOR OF LIFE,
who formed me in the womb to be God's slave
to return Jacob back to God,
and that Israel might be gathered to God:
I am honored in the sight of the HOLY ONE OF OLD,
and my God is my strength.

* Careful observers may have noticed that both the principal Easter service and Tuesday in Holy Week use the same Isaiah 49 reading. I translated the reading twice, forgetting that I had previously translated it. The two different versions offer a window into the craft and flexibility of translation and the range of choices in some instances.

[6] God says,
"It is too light a thing that you should be my slave
to raise up the tribes of Jacob [the line of Rebekah]
and to restore the survivors of Israel [born of Rachel and Leah, and Bilhah and Zilpah]?
I will give you as a light to the nations,
for it will be that my salvation reaches to the end of the earth."

Psalm 123

[1] To you I lift up my eyes,
the one who is enthroned in the heavens!
[2] See! It is just as the eyes of the enslaved
are toward the hand of their lord,
as the eyes of an enslaved girl
toward the hand of her mistress,
just so our eyes look to the MIGHTY ONE our God,
until God shows us favor.
[3] Have mercy upon us, MERCIFUL ONE, have mercy upon us,
for we have had more than our fill of contempt.
[4] Our soul has had more than its fill
of the scorn of those who are at ease,
of the contempt of the proud.

Philippians 3:17 Become imitators of me together, sisters and brothers, and observe those who
walk according to our example. [18] For many of them—as I have often told you all, and now I tell
you even with tears—walk as enemies of the cross of Christ. [19] Their end is destruction; their
god is the belly; and their glory is in their shame; their minds are set on earthly things. [20] But
our citizenship is in heaven, and it is from there that we are expecting a Savior, Jesus Christ, our
Sovereign, [21] who will transform the body of our humiliation that it may bear the likeness of the
body of his glory, through the force that also enables him to make all things subject to himself.

Matthew 21:12 Then Jesus entered the temple and drove out all who were selling and buying in the temple, and the tables of the moneychangers he overturned, as well as the station of
those who sold doves. [13] He said to them, "It is written,

> *'My house shall be called a house of prayer';*
> *but you all are making it a den of robbers."*

[14] And they came to him in the temple, those who were blind and disabled, and he cured
them. [15] Now when the chief priests and the religious scholars saw the amazing things that
he did, and heard the girls and boys crying out in the temple, "Hosanna to the Son of David,"
they became angry. [16] They said to him, "Do you hear what these are saying?" Jesus said to
them, "Yes; have you never read,

'Out of the mouths of infants and nursing babies
you have prepared praise for yourself'?"

17 He left them, went out of the city to Bethany, and spent the night there.

PROCLAMATION

Text Notes

In Isaiah 49:4, the poet-prophet speaking in the first person emphasizes redundantly, "I, I said" what she or the unidentified servant about whom she is prophesying said to God upon being commissioned in God's service. Writing long past the time of Isaiah proper, the gender and identity of the prophet is unknown. (I discuss the possibility of the author being a woman in *Daughters of Miriam: Women Prophets in Ancient Israel.*)

Psalm 123 makes explicit the psalmist's understanding that God is a slave-master, and we, women and men alike, are God's slaves. This understanding pervades the scriptures. Linguistically, the human slave-master, "lord," in verse 2 is the same word as "LORD," most often used to represent God's unpronounceable name formed of the letters YHVH. This volume eschews that language while wrestling with its lingering theology. Philippians 3:20 uses the Greek equivalent for lord, *kyrion*, for Jesus.

In Philippians 3:19, the belly, *koilia*, the marks of one of the carnal obsessions of the "earthly" believer, can refer to innards broadly or to the womb, thereby perhaps to gluttony or lust.

Where the Greek text has "children" in Matthew 21:15, I have specified "girls and boys"; girls have extremely low visibility in the scriptures but would have been present in the temple. There is no reason to presume that only boys acclaimed him, given the plural form allows for the presence of girls.

Preaching Prompts

These texts emphasize the sovereignty of God and of Christ, calling attention to the great gulf between God and humanity in troubling and troublesome language. At the same time, they frame the story of the One who crossed and closed that gulf, looking more human than divine this week. We may be helped by remembering the Church writes from a position of vulnerability, believing in faith that it won't always be that way. Paul in particular is imprisoned. One might wish to think of the crucified Church looking to its own resurrection.

The various servants in latter Isaiah are sometimes the nation, sometimes a coming monarch, sometimes a messiah, sometimes indeterminate. This passage speaks in messianic terms and was so understood by Christian readers.

As is often the case, the Epistle distinguishes physical, bodily, and earthly from what is spiritual and heavenly. It is worth remembering that there was a widespread belief that Christ's return was imminent and we would soon have little use for this world. It our task to interpret this text in light of our continuing reality and the season, Holy Week, in which the physicality of salvation is made manifest.

Matthew 21:13 fuses Isaiah 56:7 and Jeremiah 7:11 into a single citation. Dr. Amy-Jill Levine helpfully reminds that a "den of robbers" is not a place where there is criminal activity, just as a lion's den is not where lions do their hunting and killing. It is the refuge, or abode, meaning that the moneychangers who were essential to proper functioning of the temple were not robbing people. She suggests that Jesus's rebuke like Jeremiah's before him was that the unrepentant had made the temple a social club rather than a place of prayer; she also notes that the table turning would have been a rather small demonstration given the scale of the complex (*Entering the Passion of Jesus: A Beginner's Guide to Holy Week*, chapter 2, "The Temple: Risking Righteous Anger").

Individual women are hard to locate in the Gospel reading but would have been among the worshippers, praying and making their own offering; some likely would have been among those Jesus healed. Jesus evokes but does not mention women when citing Psalm 8:2/3 in Greek (verse numbers vary by language): women birthed and nurse the infants who offer praise to God.

WEDNESDAY IN HOLY WEEK

Ezekiel 17:22–24; Psalm 36:5–10; 1 John 2:7–14; Matthew 23:37–39

Ezekiel 17:22 Thus says the Sovereign God:
I myself will take a sprig of cedar
from its very top;
and I will place it;
from the topmost of its most tender branch
I will pluck it and I myself will plant it
on a high and lofty mountain.
23 On the mountain height of Israel
I will plant it,
that it may lift up its boughs and bear fruit,
and become a noble cedar.
Under it every kind of bird shall live;
every kind of winged creature shall nest
in the shade of its branches.

24 All the trees of the field shall know
that I am the CREATOR OF ALL.
I bring low the high tree,
I make high the low tree;
I dry up the green tree
and I make the dry tree sprout buds.
I the AGELESS GOD have spoken;
I will make it so.

Psalm 36:5–10

5 HOLY ONE, throughout the very heavens is your faithful love,
your faithfulness beyond the clouds.
6 Your righteousness is like the eternal mountains,
your judgments are like the mighty deep;
you save humankind and animalkind alike, FAITHFUL ONE.
7 How precious is your faithful love, O God!
All the woman-born take shelter in the shadow of your wings.
8 They feast on the abundance of your house,
and you give them drink from the river of your delights.
9 For with you is the fountain of life;
in your light we see light.
10 Extend your faithful love to those who know you,
and your justice to the upright of heart!

1 John 2:7 Beloved, no new commandment do I write you all, but an old commandment
that you have had from the beginning; that commandment is the word that you have heard.
8 Yet, I am writing you all a new commandment that is true in Christ and in you, because
the shadow is passing away and the true light already shines. 9 Whoever says, "I am in the
light," while hating a sister or brother, is in shadow still. 10 Whoever loves a sister or brother
lives in the light, and in such a person there is no occasion for stumbling. 11 But whoever
hates another sister or brother is in shadow, walks in shadow, and does not know where to go,
because the shadow dims the eyes.

12 I am writing to you, little children,
because your sins are forgiven on account of Christ's name.
13 I am writing to you, mothers and fathers,
because you know the one who is from the beginning.
I am writing to you, young women and men,
because you have conquered the evil one.
14 I write to you, children,
because you know the Creator.

I write to you, mothers and fathers,
because you know the one who is from the beginning.
I write to you, young people,
because you are strong
and the word of God abides in you,
and you have overcome the evil one.

Matthew 23:37 "Jerusalem, Jerusalem, that kills the prophets and stones those who are sent to it! How often have I desired to gather your children together as a hen gathers her chicks under her wings, and you were not willing! 38 See, your house is left to you, desolate. 39 For I tell you all, you will not see me again until you say, 'Blessed is the one who comes in the name of the Holy One.'"

PROCLAMATION

Text Notes

In the psalm the noun *el,* God, is used as an adjective describing the mountains in verse 5.

Preaching Prompts

Today's lessons revolve around Jesus's journey to Jerusalem, where even on the way to his death, he expressed his longing to mother Jerusalem through its violent inclinations. In these lessons, birds function as both images for a sheltering God and images for a huddled humanity and are themselves creatures of the natural world for whom God also cares.

Ezekiel 17:22–24 is a highly allegorical text that can be read as a description of a messianic figure who has noble (lofty) origins but is tender rather than hardened. The community founded around and beneath sheltering branches of this "tree" is diverse and flourishing. As in other prophetic texts, God brings low what is high and exalts what is low.

The psalm echoes the theme of God's faithfulness to bird and tree, extending it to all animals and all humanity. Here God is winged, sheltering all life within her wings.

The Epistle exhorts us to replicate the love God has for creation for each other. It also offers a hint that heaviness and shadow of Holy Week will give way to light.

Jesus's embrace of Jerusalem, its history and hopes, ugly realities, looming threats, sacred space, and all of its people, citizens, immigrants, pilgrims, and occupiers was all inclusive. There is room for all in his embrace.

MAUNDY THURSDAY

Exodus 15:11–21; Psalm 136:1–16; Hebrews 11:23–28; Matthew 26:17–56

Exodus 15:11 "Who is like you, MIGHTY ONE, among the gods?
Who is like you, resplendent in holiness,
revered praiseworthy, working wonders?
12 You stretched out your right hand,
the earth swallowed them.
13 You led, in your faithful love, the people whom you redeemed;
you guided them by your strength to your holy abode.
14 The peoples heard, they quaked;
pangs like labor seized the inhabitants of Philistia.
15 Then the chiefs of Edom were dismayed;
the rulers of Moab, trembling seized them;
all the inhabitants of Canaan melted away.
16 Terror and dread fell upon them
by the might of your arm;
they became still as a stone
until your people, REDEEMING GOD, passed by,
until the people whom you acquired passed by.
17 You brought them and planted them on the mountain of your own possession,
the place, SHELTERING GOD, you made for your dwelling,
the sanctuary, Most High God, that your hands have established.
18 The EVERLASTING GOD will reign forever and ever."

19 The horse of Pharaoh and his chariots and charioteers went into the sea, and the MIGHTY GOD turned the waters of the sea back upon them; but the daughters and sons of Israel walked through the sea on dry ground.

20 Then the prophet Miriam, Aaron's sister, took a hand-drum in her hand, and all the
women went out after her with hand-drums and with dancing. 21 And Miriam sang to them,
women and men:

> "Sing to the INDOMITABLE GOD who has triumphed triumphantly;
> horse and rider God has thrown into the sea."

Psalm 136:1–16

1 Give thanks to the FOUNT OF LIFE, who is good,
for her faithful love is everlasting.
2 Give thanks to the God of gods,
for her faithful love is everlasting.

3 Give thanks to the Majesty of Majesties,
for her faithful love is everlasting;
4 who alone does great wonders,
for her faithful love is everlasting;
5 who through insight made the heavens,
for her faithful love is everlasting;
6 to the one who spread out the land upon the waters,
for her faithful love is everlasting;
7 to the one who made the great lights,
for her faithful love is everlasting;
8 the sun to govern the day,
for her faithful love is everlasting;
9 the moon and stars to govern the night,
for her faithful love is everlasting;
10 who struck Egypt through their firstborn daughters and sons,
for her faithful love is everlasting;
11 and brought Israel out from among them,
for her faithful love is everlasting;
12 with a strong hand and an outstretched arm,
for her faithful love is everlasting;
13 who cut the Red Sea in two,
for her faithful love is everlasting;
14 and made Israel pass over through the midst of it,
for her faithful love is everlasting;
15 but churned Pharaoh and his army in the Red Sea,
for her faithful love is everlasting;
16 who walked her people through the wilderness,
for her faithful love is everlasting.

Hebrews 11:23 By faith Moses was hidden after his birth by his mother and father for three months, because they saw that the child was beautiful; and they were not afraid of the king's commandment. 24 By faith Moses, after he had grown up, refused to be called a son of Pharaoh's daughter, 25 rather choosing ill-treatment with the people of God than enjoyment of the transitory pleasures of sin. 26 He considered abuse for the sake of the Messiah to be greater wealth than the treasures of Egypt, for he was looking ahead to the reward. 27 By faith he left Egypt, unafraid of the anger of the king; for he persisted as though he saw the unseen. 28 By faith he kept the Passover and the sprinkling of blood, in order that the destroyer of the firstborn would not touch the firstborn daughters and sons of Israel.

Matthew 26:17 On the first day of Unleavened Bread the disciples came to Jesus, saying, "Where do you want us to prepare for you to eat the Passover?" 18 He said, "Go into the city

to a certain person, and say, 'The Teacher says, My time is near; I will keep the Passover at
your house with my disciples.'" 19 So the disciples did just as Jesus instructed them, and they
prepared the Passover meal.

20 When it was evening, he reclined at table with the twelve, 21 and while they ate, he
said, "Truly I tell you, one of you will betray me." 22 And they became deeply grieved and
each one began to say to him, "Not me, is it Rabbi?" 23 He responded and said, "The one who
dipped his hand into the bowl with me will betray me. 24 Indeed, the Son of Woman goes
away as it is written of him, but woe to the person by whom the Son of Woman is betrayed!
It would have been better for that person not to have been born." 25 Judas, who betrayed him,
responded and said, "It wasn't me was it, Rabbi?" He replied, "You said it."

26 While they were eating, Jesus took a loaf of bread, and blessing it, he broke it, and gave
it to the disciples, saying, "Take, eat; this is my body." 27 Then he took a cup, and giving thanks
he gave it to them, saying, "Drink from it, all of you; 28 for this is my blood of the covenant,
which is poured out for many for forgiveness of sins. 29 I tell you all, I will not drink again of
this fruit of the vine until that day when I drink it new with you all in the realm of my Abba."
30 And when they had sung the hymn, they went out to the Mount of Olives.

31 Then Jesus said to them, "You will all become scandalized to the point of desertion
because of me this night; for it is written,

> '*For I will strike the shepherd,*
> *and the sheep of the flock will be scattered.*'

32 But after I am raised, I will go ahead of you all to Galilee." 33 Peter said to him, "Though all
become scandalized and desert because of you, I will never desert you." 34 Jesus said to him,
"Truly I tell you, this very night, before the cock crows, you will deny me three times." 35 Peter
said to him, "Should it be necessary I die with you, I will not deny you." Then likewise said all
the disciples.

36 Then Jesus came with his disciples to a place called Gethsemane, and he said to them,
"You all sit here while I go pray there." 37 He took Peter and the two sons of Zebedee and began
to be grieved and distressed. 38 Then he said to them, "My soul is deeply grieved, to the point of
death; you all stay here, and stay awake with me." 39 And going on a little, he fell on the ground
and prayed saying, "[My] Abba, if it is possible, let this cup pass from me; nevertheless not
what I want but what you do." 40 Then he came to the disciples and found them sleeping; and
he said to Peter, "So, you all were not strong enough to stay awake with me one hour? 41 Stay
awake and pray that you all may not come into the test; indeed, the spirit is willing, but the
flesh is weak." 42 Again, for the second time, Jesus went away and prayed, saying, "My Abba,
if it is not possible for this to pass lest I drink it, let your will be done." 43 And again he came
and found them sleeping, for their eyes were heavy. 44 So leaving them again, he went away
and prayed for the third time, saying those words again. 45 Then he came to the disciples and
said to them, "Sleep now and take your rest. See, the hour is at hand, and the Son of Woman is
betrayed into the hands of sinners. 46 Get up, let us go. Look, my betrayer is at hand."

47 While Jesus was still speaking, Judas, one of the twelve, came and with him was a large
crowd with swords and clubs from the chief priests and the elders of the people. 48 Now the
betrayer had given them a sign, saying, "The one I kiss is he; take him." 49 At once he came up
to Jesus and said, "Shalom, Rabbi!" and kissed him. 50 Jesus said to him, "Friend, this is why
you have come." Then they came and laid hands on Jesus and took him. 51 Suddenly, someone
with Jesus reached out with his hand, drew his sword, and struck the slave of the high priest,
cutting off his ear. 52 Then Jesus said to him, "Return your sword to its place; for all who
choose the sword will perish by the sword. 53 Do you think I am not able to ask my Abba, who
will at once send me more than twelve legions of angels? 54 How then would the scriptures
be fulfilled, which say it must be thus?" 55 At that hour Jesus said to the crowds, "Is it as for
a bandit you all have come out with swords and clubs to seize me? Daily in the temple I sat
teaching, and you did not arrest me. 56 But all this has happened, so that the scriptures of the
prophets may be fulfilled." Then all the disciples deserted him and fled.

PROCLAMATION

Text Notes

In Exodus 15:13, God's holy "abode" can also be understood as a pasture. The instrument Miriam and the other women play in verse 20 is a hand-drum, traditionally played by women across the ancient Afro-Asiatic world. "Tambourine" is anachronistic; they did not yet exist. In verse 21, Miriam exhorts the entire community or just the men—either can be indicated by the plural verb; however, the women are already following her according to the previous verse.

In Matthew 26:18, the grammar used for the person who hosts Jesus is masculine; it may be generic for "person" as translated above. In verse 22, and elsewhere "Rabbi" replaces "Lord" for direct address. In verse 29 I use "shalom" as the greeting, reflecting the culture of Jesus rather than the literary world of the Greek text. A few manuscripts amend verse 28 to "new" covenant introducing a more firm distinction between the Jesus movement and his ancestral Judaism than may have been warranted at the time. In verse 31, *skandalizo* means "to take offence at/be offended by" (see KJV) and here, to the point of desertion (NRSV). "Scandalized to the point of desertion" includes the full sense and preserves the phonetics of the verb.

Preaching Prompts

Passover and Holy Week and Easter are linked seasonally, thematically, and theologically. In some languages the word for Easter is "Pascha," making the connection more explicit. The two seasons are also connected by violence. In the Exodus and Passover stories, Israel, God's beloved is saved, and God sends their oppressors to their deaths. Painfully, those deaths are celebrated in psalms and songs. In Holy Week, Jesus, God's beloved, is executed by his—still God's beloved—people's oppressors. His death will also be commemorated in songs of praise. Each offers an opportunity to reflect on who we say God is in conversation with the scriptures.

The necessity for Jesus to observe Passover is just one of many reminders that Jesus was a religiously observant Jew who never broke with Judaism. The singular host in Matthew 26:18 seemingly obscures women from the household who would have done or helped with the actual work: cleaning, shopping, meal preparation, cooking, serving, and hosting. Since the more inclusive "disciples" is used rather than presumptively exclusively male "apostles," it is reasonable to expect the presence of women, particularly since these disciples prepared and served the meal, verse 19. Should female and male disciples have been present, it would be likely that children would be present given Passover is a family and community meal. (It should be noted that the form of the Passover meal at the time of Jesus, and even in the literary construction of the evangelists, was not a seder, which form developed later.) The mention of "the twelve" in verse 20 does not foreclose the possibility of a larger group at more than one table.

GOOD FRIDAY

Judges 11:29–40; Psalm 22; Hebrews 12:1–4; Luke 22:14–23:56

Owing to the length of the Passion Gospel, the commentary section will be longer than for other readings.

Judges 11:29 The Spirit of the Holy One, she was upon Jephthah, and he passed through
Gilead and Manasseh. He passed on to Mizpah of Gilead, and from Mizpah of Gilead he
passed on to the Ammonites. [30] And Jephthah vowed a vow to the Holy One of Old, and
said, "If you will give the Ammonites into my hand, [31] then it shall be that the one who comes
out—whoever comes out—of the doors of my house to meet me, when I return having finished with the Ammonites, shall be the Holy One's, I will offer them up as a burnt offering."
[32] Then Jephthah crossed over to the Ammonites to fight against them and the Holy One
gave them into his hand. [33] He smote a mighty smiting on them from Aroer until you come to
Minnith, twenty towns, and as far as Abel-keramim. So, the Ammonites were subdued before
the people of Israel.

[34] Then Jephthah came to his home at Mizpah, and there was his daughter coming out to
meet him with drums and with dancing. Only she, an only child; he had no son or daughter
apart from her. [35] When he saw her, he tore his clothes, and said, "Ah! My daughter, you have
knocked me down; you have become my trouble! I—I opened my mouth to the Holy One,
and I cannot take back my vow." [36] She said to him, "My father, you have opened your mouth
to the Holy One, do to me according to what has gone out of your mouth, after that the
Holy One has taken vengeance through you against your enemies, against the Ammonites."

[37] And she said to her father, "Let be done for me this thing: Release me for two months,
and I will go and go down among the hills, and weep for my virginity, I and my women-
friends." [38] Then he said, "Go," and sent her away for two months. So, she left, she and her
women-friends, and wept over her virginity among the hills. [39] And it was at the end of two
months, she returned to her father, who did to her what he vowed in his vow. She had never
known a man and she became an observance in Israel. [40] Year by year the daughters of Israel
would go out to tell the story of the daughter of Jephthah the Gileadite for four days.

Psalm 22

1 My God, my God, why have you forsaken me?
Why are you so far from my deliverance, from the words of my groaning?
2 My God, I cry by day, and you do not answer;
and by night, and there I find no rest for me.
3 Yet you are holy,
enthroned on the praises of Israel.
4 In you our mothers and fathers trusted;
they trusted, and you rescued them.
5 To you they cried, and were freed;
in you they trusted, and they were not put to shame.
6 But I am a worm, and not human;
scorned by humankind, and despised by people.
7 All who see me mock me;
they flap their lips at me, they shake their heads:
8 "Commit yourself to the SAVING ONE; let God rescue
and deliver the one in whom God delights!"
9 Yet it was you who drew me from the womb;
keeping me safe on my mother's breast.
10 On you was I cast from birth,
and since my mother's womb you have been my God.
11 Be not far from me,
for trouble is near
and there is none to help.
12 Many bulls surround me,
mighty bulls of Bashan encompass me;
13 they open wide their mouths at me,
like a lion, ravaging and roaring.
14 I am poured out like water,
and all my bones are disjointed.
My heart is like wax;
it is melted within my being.

15 My mouth is dried up like a potsherd,
and my tongue cleaves to my jaws;
in the dust of death you lay me down.
16 For dogs are all around me;
a conclave of evildoers encircles me.
Like a lion they ravage my hands and feet.
17 I can count all my bones.
They gloat and stare at me.
18 They divide my clothes among themselves,
and for my clothing they cast lots.
19 SAVING GOD, be not far away!
My strength, hasten to help me!
20 Deliver my soul from the sword,
my life from the clutch of the dog!
21 Save me from the mouth of the lion!
For on the horns of the wild oxen you have responded to me.
22 I will tell of your name to my sisters and brothers;
in the midst of the congregation I will praise you:
23 You who revere the FONT OF LIFE, praise her!
all the offspring of Leah and Rachel, Bilhah and Zilpah glorify her.
Stand in awe of her all you of Rebekah's line.
24 For she did not despise or abhor
the affliction of the afflicted;
she did not hide her face from me,
and when I cried to her, she heard.
25 On your account is my praise in the great congregation;
my vows I will pay before those who revere her.
26 The poor shall eat and be satisfied;
those who seek her shall praise the MOTHER OF ALL.
May your hearts live forever!
27 All the ends of the earth shall remember
and turn to the WELLSPRING OF LIFE;
and all the families of the nations
shall worship before her.
28 For sovereignty belongs to the SHE WHO IS HOLY,
and she rules over the nations.
29 They consume and they bow down, all the fat ones of the earth before her,
they bend their knees, all who go down to the dust,
and cannot save their soul.

30 Later descendants will serve her;
future generations will be told about our God,
31 they will go and proclaim her deliverance to a people yet unborn,
saying that she has done it.

Hebrews 12:1 Therefore, since we are surrounded by so great a cloud of witnesses, let us
also put aside every weight and entangling sin, and with endurance let us run the race that
is set before us, 2 looking to Jesus the originator and perfecter of our faith, who for the sake
of the joy that was set before him endured the cross, its shame disregarding, and at the right
hand of the throne of God has taken his seat.

3 Consider the one who endured such hostility against himself from sinners, so that you
all may not grow weary or your souls grow faint. 4 Not to this point have you all in your strug-
gles against sin resisted to the point of shedding blood.

Luke 22:14 Now when the hour came, he took his place at the table, and the apostles with
him. 15 Then Jesus said to them, "I have greatly desired to eat this Passover with you all before I
suffer. 16 For I tell you all, I will not eat it until it is fulfilled in the realm of God." 17 Then Jesus
took a cup, giving thanks. He said, "Receive this and divide it among yourselves; 18 for I tell
you all that from now on I will not drink of the fruit of the vine until the reign of God comes."
19 Then Jesus took a loaf of bread, giving thanks, he broke it and gave it to them, saying, "This
is my body, which is given for you all. Do this in remembrance of me." 20 And he did the same
with the cup after supper, saying, "This cup that is poured out for you is the new covenant in my
blood. 21 Look, the hand of the one who betrays me is with me, on the table. 22 For indeed the
Son of Woman is going as it has been determined, but woe to the one by whom he is betrayed!"
23 Then they began to ask among themselves, which one of them was about to do this.

24 There was also an argument among them as to which one of them should be considered the greatest. 25 But Jesus said to them, "The royals of the Gentiles lord it over them, and
those who have power over them are called benefactors. 26 But not so with you all, rather the
greatest among you must become like the youngest, and the leader like one who serves. 27 For
who is greater, the one who is at the table or the one who serves? Is it not the one at the table?
Yet I am among you all as one who serves.

28 "You are the ones who have remained with me in my trials, 29 so then I covenant with
you all, just as my Abba has covenanted with me, a royal inheritance, 30 so that you all may eat
and drink at my table in my realm, and you all will sit on thrones governing the twelve tribes
of Israel.

31 "Simon, Simon, listen! The Adversary has demanded to sift all of you like wheat,
32 but I have prayed for you in order that your faith not fail, and you, when you have turned
back, strengthen your brothers." 33 Then he said to Jesus, "Rabbi, I am ready to go with you to
prison and to death!" 34 But Jesus said, "I tell you, Peter, this day the cock will not have crowed
three times, before you deny knowing me."

35 Then Jesus said to them, "When I sent you out without a purse, bag, or sandals, did you lack anything?" They said, "Not a thing." 36 He said to them, "But now, the one who has a purse must take it, and likewise a bag. And the one who does not have one must sell his cloak and buy a sword. 37 For I tell you, this scripture must be fulfilled in me, '*And he was counted among the lawless*,' and indeed that which pertains to me is coming to its completion." 38 So they said, "Rabbi, see, here are two swords." He replied to them, "It is sufficient."

39 Then Jesus came out and went, as was his custom, to the Mount of Olives and the disciples followed him. 40 When he was at the place, he said to them, "Pray that you not enter into testing." 41 Then he withdrew from them about a stone's throw on bended knee and prayed, 42 "Abba, if you are willing, take this cup away from me; yet, not my will but yours be done." 43 [Then an angel from heaven appeared to him and strengthened him. 44 In agony he prayed more earnestly, and his sweat became like drops of blood falling down upon the ground.] 45 When he rose from prayer, he came to the disciples and found them sleeping from grief. 46 And he said to them, "Why are you sleeping? Get up and pray that you not enter into testing."

47 While he was speaking, suddenly there was a crowd, and the one called Judas, one of the twelve, was leading them. He approached Jesus to kiss him. 48 But Jesus said to him, "Judas, is it with a kiss that you betray the Son of Woman?" 49 When those around him saw what was happening, they asked, "Rabbi, should we strike with the sword?" 50 Then one of them struck a person enslaved by the high priest and cut off his right ear. 51 But Jesus responded, saying, "Enough of this!" And he grasped his ear and healed him. 52 Then Jesus said to ones who had come for him, the chief priests, the officers assigned to the temple, and the elders, "Have you all come out with swords and clubs as if I were a bandit? 53 When I was with you daily in the temple, you did not lay hands on me. But this is your hour, and the power of darkness!"

54 Then they seized him and led him away, bringing him into the house of the high priest. But Peter was following from afar. 55 They kindled a fire in the middle of the courtyard and sat down together; Peter sat among them. 56 Then a slave-girl, seeing him near the fire, looked intently at him and said, "This one also was with him." 57 But he denied it, saying, "Woman, I do not know him." 58 After a time someone else, on seeing him, said, "You are one of them too." But Peter said, "Man, I am not!" 59 Then about an hour later another one insisted, "On the truth, this one was with him too, for he is a Galilean." 60 But Peter said, "Man, I do not know what you are talking about!" Immediately, while he was speaking, the cock crowed. 61 The Savior turned and looked at Peter. Then Peter remembered the word of the Messiah, how he had said to him, "Before the cock crows today, you will deny me three times." 62 And Peter went out and wept bitterly.

63 Now the men who were holding Jesus mocked him and beat him; 64 they also blindfolded him and asked him, "Prophesy! Who is it that struck you?" 65 They yelled much other abuse at him.

66 Then when day came, the elders of the people, chief priests and religious scholars,
gathered together and brought him to their council. 67 They said, "If you are the Messiah,
tell us." Jesus replied to them, "If I tell you, you will not believe, 68 and if I ask a question, you
will not answer. 69 But from now on the Son of Woman will be seated at the right hand of the
power of God." 70 They all asked, "Are you, then, the Son of God?" He said to them, "You say
that I am." 71 Then they said, "What further testimony do we need; we have heard it ourselves
from his own lips!"

23:1 Then the assembly rose as a body and brought Jesus before Pilate. 2 They began to
accuse him, saying, "We found this man leading our nation astray, forbidding paying taxes
to the emperor, and saying that he is a messiah, a king." 3 Then Pilate questioned him saying,
"Are you the king of the Judeans?" He answered, "You say so." 4 Then Pilate said to the chief
priests and the crowds, "I find no cause for legal action against this person." 5 But they insisted
saying, "Because he stirs up the people by teaching throughout all Judea, from Galilee to this
very place."

6 Upon hearing this, Pilate asked if the person was a Galilean. 7 Now when he learned
that he was under Herod's authority, he sent him to Herod, who himself was in Jerusalem
at that time. 8 When Herod saw Jesus, he was extremely glad, for he had wanted to see him
for a long time, because he had heard about him and hoped to see him perform some sign.
9 Herod questioned him to his satisfaction, but Jesus answered him nothing. 10 The chief
priests and the religious scholars stood by, vehemently accusing him. 11 Herod and his soldiers
also treated him with contempt and mocked him, and he put a majestic robe on him, and sent
him back to Pilate. 12 That very moment Herod and Pilate became friends with each other;
previously they had been each other's enemy.

13 Pilate then called together the chief priests, the leaders, and the people, 14 and said
to them, "You brought me this person for leading the people astray. Look now, I have examined him in your presence and have not found this person guilty of your charges against him.
15 Nor has Herod, for he sent him back to us. Look here, there is nothing deserving death in
his case. 16 Therefore whip and release him."

18 Then they shouted together saying, "Away with him! Release for us Barabbas!" 19
(Who for a rebellion that had taken place in the city, and for murder, had been put in prison.)
20 Again Pilate addressed them, wanting to release Jesus, 21 but they kept shouting, saying,
"Crucify, crucify him!" 22 A third time he said to them, "Why, what evil has he done? I have
found nothing deserving death in him; I will, therefore, have him whipped and release him."
23 But they insisted with loud shouts that he should be crucified, and their voices prevailed.
24 So Pilate passed sentence to grant their demand. 25 So he released the one in prison for
rebellion and murder who they asked for, and he handed Jesus over as they wished.

26 As they led Jesus away, they seized Simon of Cyrene who was coming from the country, and they laid on him the cross to carry behind Jesus. 27 A great number of people followed
him, and a group of women who were beating their breasts and wailing for him. 28 But Jesus

turned to them and said, "Daughters of Jerusalem, do not weep for me, weep only for yourselves and for your children. 29 Look, the days are surely coming when they will say, 'Blessed
are barren women, and wombs that have never given birth, and breasts that have never nourished.' 30 *Then they will begin to say to the mountains, 'Fall on us'; and to the hills, 'Cover us.'*
31 For if when the wood is green they do this, when it is dry what will happen?"

32 Now two criminals were also led away to be put to death with him. 33 And when they
came to the place called Skull, there they crucified Jesus there with the criminals, one on his
right and one on his left. 34 [And then Jesus said, "Abba, forgive them; for they know not what
they do."] *They divided his clothing by casting lots.* 35 And the people stood there, watching;
but the leaders ridiculed him, saying, "Others he saved; let him save himself if he is the Messiah of God, God's chosen one!" 36 The soldiers also mocked him, coming and offering him
vinegar wine, 37 and saying, "If you are the King of the Judeans, save yourself!" 38 There was
also an inscription above him, "This is the King of the Judeans."

39 One of the criminals who was hanging there derided him, saying, "Are you not the
Messiah? Save yourself and us!" 40 But the other rebuked him, saying, "Do you not fear God,
since you are under the same death sentence? 41 And we indeed justly, for what we have done
merits what we are receiving, but this one has done nothing wrong." 42 Then he said, "Jesus,
remember me when you come into your realm." 43 Jesus replied to him, "Truly I tell you, today
you will be with me in Paradise."

44 And it was now about the sixth hour [of the day, or noon], and darkness came over
the whole land until the ninth hour [of the day, about three in the afternoon]. 45 The sun's
light ceased, and the curtain of the temple was torn in the middle. 46 Then Jesus, crying
with a loud voice, said, "Abba, into your hands I commend my spirit." Saying this then, he
breathed out a final time. 47 Now when the centurion saw what had happened, he praised
God, saying, "This man was indeed innocent." 48 And all the crowds that had gathered for
this spectacle saw what had happened, beating their breasts, they turned back. 49 All those
who knew him stood far off; the women who had followed him from Galilee were watching
these things.

50 Now, take note, there was a man named Joseph, a member of the council, a good man
and a righteous one. 51 He had not agreed with the council and their action. He was from
the Judean town of Arimathea, and he was waiting for the reign of God. 52 This man went to
Pilate and requested the body of Jesus. 53 Then he took it down, wrapped it in a linen cloth,
and laid it in a tomb hewn from rock where no one had yet lain. 54 It was the day of Preparation, and the sabbath was dawning. 55 The women followed, the ones who had come with
him from Galilee, and they saw the tomb and how his body was placed. 56 Then the women
returned, and prepared spices and balms.

On the sabbath they rested according to the commandment.

PROCLAMATION

Text Notes

In Judges 11:31, the word *shalom* is used to indicate completion; the verb is used similarly in Modern Hebrew, for example, to complete a purchase or pay the check. In verse 37 and following, virginity symbolizes a stage of life; the grief is about not reaching the full measure of womanhood in her culture, marrying and mothering. In verse 40, the women gather to memorialize the woman sacrificed by her father; the verb is "recount," not as usually translated, "lament."

The psalmist locates her heart in her "belly" in verse 14. The verb for the violence done to the psalmist's hands and feet is missing. The LXX and traditional Jewish exegesis (Rashi) supply it.

Throughout this passion account in Luke, "Rabbi" replaces "Lord," so as not to further divinize slave language. For third-person references, Messiah, Christ, and Savior will be used. Also, "enslaved person" rather than "slave" distinguishes between a person and their circumstances. The Eucharistic instruction in Luke 22:16 can be translated as "take" or "receive" (this cup). In the Hebrew Scriptures, to judge is to govern, administer, oversee, rule, and render justice. That full sense is intended in Luke 22:30, rather than passing judgment on Israel. The Adversary, the Satan, occurs in verse 31 with the definite article as in Hebrew where the term is a title or description; further contemporary notions of Satan are often postbiblical. Verses 43–44 in chapter 22 and verse 34 in chapter 23 are not present in all manuscripts as indicated by brackets.

In Luke 23:1 and 13, the more common translation "perverting" (rather leading astray here) has an unnecessary sexual connotation in English. Jesus's accusers testify that he says he is *a messiah*; there is no direct object. The term was not unique to Jesus. Hebrew *meshiach* is translated by Greek *christos*; David and Cyrus are each God's messiah, God's christ in the Hebrew and Greek versions of 2 Samuel 23:1 and Isaiah 45:1, which parallel Luke 23:35 where Jesus is disbelieved as the Christ/Messiah of God. The term, otherwise translated "anointed" also applies to monarchs and priests.

The robe with which Jesus was mocked in Luke 23:11 was "bright," or "shiny," suggesting rich embroidery or embellishment. Some less reliable manuscripts include a verse 17 that is generally removed from critical translations: *He had to release one prisoner for them because of the festival.*

Jesus quotes Hosea 10:8, where people ask for the mountains and hills to cover them in Luke 23:30. Verse 34, "Abba, forgive them . . ." is missing in many manuscripts. "Into your hands I commend my spirit" in verse 46 from Psalm 31:5 can also be translated, "Into your hands I place my life." In verse 49, "those who stood" are a mixed gender as indicated by the text (grammatically, an all-male group is also possible); those who were watching were the women, according to the feminine plural verb which excludes males. In contrast, the "they" who rested on the sabbath in verse 56 is inclusive.

A final note, the NRSV translation that Joseph of Arimathea, "who, *though* a member of the council" was "good and righteous" in Luke 23:50 excludes the whole of the Sanhedrin from the possibility of being good and righteous normatively. It is more than an uncharitable reading; it is anti-Judaistic and contributes to the anti-Semitic legacy and practices of the Church.

Preaching Prompts

This lectionary pairs the brutal deaths of Jephthah's daughter and Jesus. Each of their deaths is horrific—at one level, unnecessary slaughter—and each death is believed by someone in their respective story to serve a greater good. The disparate portraits and motives of the two fathers in relation to the death of their sole child offer fruitful space to address the crucifixion beyond the limits of atonement theology. Each of these texts requires us to ask who it is we think God is.

Jephthah, taken from his mother, a sex-worker, by his father Gilead, was rejected by his brothers and his father's wife. The troubled boy is not unrelated to the troubled man. He is desperate for affirmation. Note that God had already given Jephthah victory over the Ammonites in Judges 11:32, before he makes a vow to "ensure" his win. Jephthah's god is familiar to many: rigid and unyielding, apparently incapable of forgiving a rash vow, making human sacrifice the only acceptable appeasement. Jephthah doesn't test his theology; he doesn't bargain with God like Abraham. He doesn't offer himself as recipient of divine rage; he does not fight for the life of his child. His parenthood, like his theology, leaves much to be desired. As is the case in rigid, fundamentalist, patriarchal systems, women's lives hold little value and are expendable. Is spite of the lethal limits of the system in which she finds herself constrained, Jephthah's daughter carves out space for herself and other women, illuminating and memorializing the deficiencies of a god like Jephthah's.

The psalmist's God is lightyears away from the tyrant Jephthah worships, savior rather than destroyer. The psalmist's God is part nurse, part midwife, trustworthy and praiseworthy. In Matthew and Mark, Jesus turns to this psalm and this God on the cross, making it virtually inseparable from Good Friday. In Luke's Passion, Jesus quotes Psalm 31, which shares the theme of trusting a trustworthy God for salvation.

Hebrews calls us to look to Jesus in the company of the faithful. Luke presents a roster of the faithful where women are more fully present than in other accounts. The spaces where women are missing are also instructive, such as a conversation about who is greater and injunction for the greatest to serve the least with apparently no women in the room. How different would the church have looked if that teaching were applied to systemic structural inequities between genders and cultures as a start.

Women are rendered invisible in the crowds that characterize the narrative, visible as enslaved girls, weeping women who accompany Jesus on his death march, and the women who were family, friends, followers, and disciples—some in more than one category—standing watch until the end. In spite of the gruesome horror, Jesus's female companions and followers, family and friends, watched and did not turn away according to Luke 23:49; the text cannot make the same claim of the male apostles and disciples. These women were faithful in and beyond the horror that seemed to mark the end of their shared journey.

HOLY SATURDAY

Job 14:1–14; Psalm 31; Philippians 2:1–8; Matthew 27:57–66

Job 14:1 "Woman-born,
humankind is short of days and full of turmoil.
2 They sprout like a flower and wither,
flee like a shadow and do not endure.
3 Are your eyes, then, open to such a one as this?
Do you bring me into judgment with you?
4 Who can make a clean thing out of an unclean thing?
No one.
5 If their days are fixed,
the number of their months is in your keeping,
it is because you have set their boundaries that they cannot pass.
6 Look away from them, and they sit at ease,
until they complete, like laborers, their days.
7 For there is hope for a tree,
if it is cut down, that it will be renewed,
and that its branches will not fail.
8 Its root grows old in the earth,
and its trunk dies in the dust.
9 At the scent of water it will bud
and put forth branches like a sapling.
10 Mortals die, and are carried away;
the woman-born perish, and where are they?
11 As waters dissipate from a sea,
and a river dries up and is depleted,
12 so a person lies down and does not rise again;
until the heavens are no more,
they will not awake or be stirred from their sleep.

13 Grant that you would hide me in Sheol,
that you would cover me until your wrath is past,
that you would set for me a boundary, and remember me.
14 If a person dies, will they live again?
All the days of my service I would wait
until my change come.

Psalm 31

1 In you, WOMB OF LIFE, I take refuge;
let me not ever be put to shame;
in your righteousness rescue me.
2 Incline your ear to me;
quickly deliver me.
Be for me a rock of refuge,
a stronghold to save me.
3 For you are my rock and my stronghold;
for your name's sake lead me and guide me.
4 Free me from the net that is hidden for me,
for you are my refuge.
5 Into your hand I commit my spirit;
you have redeemed me, ARK OF SAFETY, God of truth.
6 I hate those who attend to worthless vanity,
but in the MOTHER OF ALL I place my trust.
7 I will exult and I will rejoice in your faithful love,
because you have seen my affliction;
you have studied my soul's sorrows.
8 Yet you have not handed me over to the hand of the enemy;
you have set my feet in a broad place.
9 Be gracious to me, MOTHER OF MERCY, for I am in distress;
my eyes waste away with angry tears,
my soul and body too.
10 For my life is spent in sorrow,
and my years in sighing;
because of my iniquity my strength fails,
and my bones waste away.
11 Because of my enemies I am a disgrace to all,
and to my neighbors, more,
an object of dread to those who know me;
those who see me in the street flee from me.

12 I have been forgotten from the heart like one who is dead;
I have become like a ruined vessel.
13 Because I hear the whispering of many,
terror surrounds in their scheming together against me,
as they plot to take my life.
14 Yet I, in you I trust, FAITHFUL GOD;
I declare, "You are my God."
15 My times are in your hand;
deliver me from the hand of my enemies and those who hound me.
16 Let your face shine upon your slave;
save me in your faithful love.
17 GRACIOUS GOD, let me not be put to shame,
for I call upon you;
let the wicked be put to shame;
let them go silent to Sheol.
18 Let lying lips be stilled,
the ones that speak against the righteous,
arrogant with pride and contempt.
19 How great is your goodness
that you have secured for those who fear you,
and that you do for those who take refuge in you,
before all the woman-born.
20 In the shelter of your presence you shelter them
from human plots;
you hide them safe under your shelter
from contentious tongues.
21 Blessed be the MOTHER OF CREATION,
who is marvelous in her faithful love to me,
a city under siege.
22 Now I, I had said in my alarm,
"I am cut off from your sight."
However, you heard my supplications
when I cried to you for help.
23 Love GOD WHOSE NAME IS HOLY, all you her godly ones.
The FAITHFUL GOD preserves the faithful,
and repays with interest the one who acts out of pride.
24 Take courage, and she shall strengthen your hearts,
all you who wait for the MOTHER OF ALL.

Philippians 2:1 If then there is any encouragement in Christ, any consolation from love, any
communion in the Spirit, any tenderness and compassion, 2 make my joy complete. Be wise in
the same way, having the same love, united and sharing the same wisdom. 3 Do nothing from
self-interest, but in humility regard others as better than yourselves. 4 Each of you, look not to
your own interests, but rather to the interests of others. 5 Let the same wisdom be in you all
that was in Christ Jesus,

6 who, though he was in the form of God,
did not regard equality with God
as something to be seized,
7 but emptied himself,
taking the form of a slave,
being born in human likeness;
then being found in human form,
8 he humbled himself
and became obedient to the point of death,
even death on a cross.

Matthew 27:57 When it was evening, a rich person came from Arimathea, Joseph, who was
also a disciple of Jesus. 58 He went to Pilate and requested the body of Jesus; then Pilate commanded it to be given to him. 59 So Joseph took the body and wrapped it in clean linen, 60 and laid
it in his new tomb, which he had hewn in rock. Then he rolled a great stone to the door of the
tomb and departed. 61 Mary Magdalene and the other Mary were there, sitting before the tomb.
62 Now, the next day, which was after the day of Preparation, the chief priests and the
Pharisees gathered before Pilate. 63 They said, "Lord, we remember what that deceiver said
while he was still alive, 'After three days I will rise.' 64 Command, therefore, the tomb be
secured until the third day; otherwise his disciples may go and steal him, and tell the people,
'He has been raised from the dead,' and the last deception would be worse than the first."
65 Pilate said to them, "You may have a squad; go, secure it as you can." 66 So they went with
the guard and secured the tomb, sealing the stone.

PROCLAMATION

Text Notes

Job 14 begins its reflection on mortality using inclusive language, "those born of women," and "humanity" in verse 1, then shifts to masculine language, "(male) warrior" in verses 10 and 14 and "man" in verse 12. I apply inclusive language to the other human references in the passage. Job's address shifts from second to third person in verse 6 and 13. Verse 13 could also begin, "Who will grant . . ." In his book-length legal complaint, Job looks (rhetorically at least) for someone to compel God to do justly by him. That is part of the theological scandal of the book.

In verse 4 of the psalm, "free me" is the "let my people go" verb of the exodus. In verse 9, there is only one "eye" and tears are lacking; "body" is "belly/womb." Somewhat contradictorily, "to go silently to Sheol" can also be "to go weeping to Sheol." "Godly ones" in verse 23 are often translated anachronistically as "saints," importing Christian language and theology into the Hebrew Scriptures.

There is considerable disagreement over the meaning of *eritheian* in Philippians 2:3, translated here as "self-interest"; some other possibilities are: strife, contentiousness, selfishness, or selfish ambition. According to its earlier usage in Aristotle, it may mean "a self-seeking pursuit," for political office in that case. (See the corresponding entry in the *A Greek-English Lexicon of the New Testament and Other Early Christian Literature, BDAG.*)

The use of "Lord" for Pilate serves as a reminder the title was not unique to Jesus, nor a particularly religious one, but one of hierarchy, signifying Pilate's authority as the face of the Roman occupation. Translations like NRSV which preserve it for Jesus but change it for other characters are intentionally misleading.

Preaching Prompts

Holy Saturday may be the most liminal space in the Christian liturgical cycle. Passion has become pathos. The death of Jesus stupefies but the breaking dawn has not dispelled the waking dream. Yet the liturgical remembrance is part of a thousands-year old cycle, and we know what the next dawn brings. We struggle not to anticipate that dawn. These lessons underscore our finitude, our mortality and that of all living things, and the mortality of Jesus, Son of Woman, Son of God, Child of Earth.

Job's reflection on his own mortality comes in the midst of his address to God in chapters 12–14, responding to Zophar's chapter 11 rebuke, blaming Job for the evil that has befallen him. In this lesson Job's ruminations on his inevitable death are accompanied by the reminder that death is part of the cycle of life in nature. Without knowing the hope that Christians hold dear, Job expects a "no" to the question of whether a person who has died will live again. He and the psalmist expect all the dead to go to Sheol (Job 14:13; Psalm 31:17). The psalmist commits her fragile life (verse 5) and finite times (verse 14–15) into God's hands, fully aware of her own mortality. The psalm also includes the remembrance of God's fidelity (verse 7, 19–21, 23) and assurance that God hears the cry of her faithful, verse 22.

As a Holy Saturday text, Philippians 2 presents a Jesus as empty of divinity as his body in the tomb was empty of life. Here Jesus humbles himself to experience the finitude of the human experience, mortality, and one of its most common and most horrific occurrences, a violent death at human hands.

We hold all of these things in our hearts as we wrestle with implications, sitting, watching, and waiting with Miriam, Mary of Magdala, and another woman who also bears the name of Israel's first prophet. They knew not for what they waited. Though we know, we keep vigil with them.

EASTER—THE GREAT VIGIL

At least two of the following lessons are read, of which one is always the lesson from Exodus. After each lesson, the psalm or canticle listed, or some other suitable psalm, canticle, or hymn, is sung.

A God-Crafted Creation: Genesis 1:1–2, 26–27; 2:1–4

Genesis 1:1 When beginning he, God, created the heavens and the earth, 2 the earth was shapeless and formless and bleakness covered the face of the deep, while the Spirit of God, she, fluttered over the face of the waters.

26 And God said, "Let us make humankind in our image, according to our likeness; and let them rule the fish of the sea, and the birds of the heavens, and the animals, and the whole earth, and over every creeping creature that creeps upon the earth."

27 So God created humankind in God's own image,
in God's own image, God created them;
female and male, God created them.

2:1 And the heavens and the earth were complete, along with all their multitude. 2 Then God finished on the seventh day the work that God had done, and rested on the seventh day from all the work that they had done. 3 So God blessed the seventh day and sanctified it, because on it God rested from all the work that God had done in creation.

4 These are the generations of the heavens and the earth when they were created.

Canticle of the Three Young Men: Daniel (LXX) 3:52–60

52 "Let the earth bless the Creator of All;
let her sing hymns to God and highly exalt God forever.
53 Bless the Creator of All, mountains and hills;
sing hymns to God and highly exalt God forever.
54 Bless the Creator of All, all that grows in the ground;
sing hymns to God and highly exalt God forever.
55 Bless the Creator of All, seas and rivers;
sing hymns to God and highly exalt God forever.
56 Bless the Creator of All, you springs;
sing hymns to God and highly exalt God forever.
57 Bless the Creator of All, you sea-monsters and all that swim in the waters;
sing hymns to God and highly exalt God forever.

58 Bless the Creator of All, all birds of the air;
sing hymns to God and highly exalt God forever.
59 Bless the Creator of All, all wild animals and cattle;
sing hymns to God and highly exalt God forever.
60 "Bless the Creator of All, all people on earth;
sing hymns to God and highly exalt God forever.

The Salvation of Hagar and Ishmael: Genesis 21:2, 8–21

Genesis 21:2 Sarah conceived and gave birth to a son for Abraham in his old age, at the set
time of which God had spoken to him.

8 The child grew, and was weaned, and Abraham made a great feast on the day of Isaac's
weaning. 9 Then Sarah saw the son of Hagar the Egyptian woman, whom she had given birth
to for Abraham, playing. 10 So she said to Abraham, "Drive out this slave woman with her
son; for the son of this slave woman shall not inherit with my son, with Isaac." 11 The situation
was evil in Abraham's eyes on account of his son. 12 And God said to Abraham, "See it not as
evil in your eyes on account of the boy and on account of your slave woman. In all that Sarah
says to you, obey her voice, for it is through Isaac that offspring shall be named for you. 13 Yet
even the son of the slave woman I will make a nation also, because he is your offspring." 14 So
Abraham rose early in the morning, and took bread and a skin of water, and gave it to Hagar.
He placed it on her shoulder, along with the child, and sent her away. Then she walked away
and wandered in the wilderness of Beer-Sheba.

15 When the water in the skin was gone, she thrust the child under one of the bushes.
16 Then she went and sat herself down before him some way off, about the distance of a bow-
shot; for she said, "Let me not see the death of the child." So, she sat before him and she lifted
up her voice and she wept. 17 And God heard the voice of the boy, and the messenger of God
called to Hagar from the heavens, and said to her, "What troubles you, Hagar? Fear not; for
God has heard the voice of the boy where he is. 18 Rise, lift the boy and hold him with your
hand, for a great nation of him I will make." 19 Then God opened her eyes and she saw a well
of water. She went, and filled the skin with water, and let the boy drink.

20 God was with the boy, and he grew up; he settled in the wilderness, and became an
archer. 21 He settled in the wilderness of Paran, and his mother acquired a wife for him from
the land of Egypt.

Psalm 27:5–7, 10–14

5 She will shield me in her shelter
when the day is evil;
she will cover me under the cover of her tent;
she will raise me high on a rock.
6 Now my head is raised up
above my enemies surrounding me,

and I will offer in her tent
sacrifices with shouts of joy;
I will sing and make melody to the GOD WHO SAVES.
7 Hear my cry, FAITHFUL ONE, when I cry aloud,
be gracious to me and answer me!
10 If my mother and father forsake me,
the COMPASSIONATE GOD will gather me in.
11 Teach me, RIGHTEOUS ONE, your way,
and lead me on a smooth path
because of my enemies.
12 Do not give me over to the throats of my foes,
for lying witnesses rise against me,
and they breathe violence.
13 If I but believe, I shall see the goodness of SHE WHO IS FAITHFUL
in the land of the living.
14 Wait for the LIVING GOD;
be strong, and let your heart take courage;
wait for GOD WHOSE NAME IS HOLY!

From Slavery to Freedom: Exodus 14:26–29; 15:20–21

Exodus 14:26 Now the HOLY ONE said to Moses, "Stretch out your hand over the sea,
so that the water may come back upon the Egyptians, upon their chariots and charioteers."
27 So Moses stretched out his hand over the sea and the sea turned back; by the break of dawn
it was back to its strength, and the Egyptians fled at its approach. Then the LIVING GOD
shook the Egyptians in the midst of the sea. 28 The waters returned and covered the chariots
and the charioteers, the whole army of Pharaoh that came after them into the sea; not a single
one of them remained. 29 And the women, children, and men of Israel walked on dry ground
through the sea, the waters a wall for them on their right and on their left.

15:20 Then the prophet Miriam, Aaron's sister, took a drum in her hand; and all the
women went out after her with drums and with dancing. 21 And Miriam sang to them:

"Sing to the GOD WHO SAVES, for God has triumphed triumphantly;
horse and rider God has thrown into the sea."

Song of Miriam and Moses: Exodus 15:1–3, 11, 13, 17–18

Exodus 15:1 Moses and the women and men of Israel sang this song to the HOLY ONE OF OLD:

"I will sing to the GOD WHO SAVES, for God has triumphed triumphantly;
horse and rider God has thrown into the sea.
2 The MIGHTY GOD is my strength and my might,
God has become my salvation.

This is my God, whom I will praise,
my mother's God and my father's God, whom I will exalt.
3 The Dread God is a warrior;
Too Holy to be Pronounced is God's name.
11 "Who is like you, Most High, among the gods?
Who is like you, majestic in holiness,
awesome in splendor, working wonders?
13 "In your faithful love you led the people whom you redeemed;
you guided them by your strength to your holy habitation.
17 You brought them in and planted them on the mountain that is your own possession,
the place, Faithful God, that you made your dwelling place,
the sanctuary, Sovereign One, that your hands have established.
18 God who is Majesty will reign forever and ever."

Rahab's Salvation: Joshua 2:1–14; 6:15–17, 22–23

Joshua 2:1 And Joshua son of Nun sent two men, spies, secretly from Shittim, saying, "Go,
surveil the land, surveil Jericho." So, they went, and entered the house of a prostitute—her
name was Rahab—and they lay down there. 2 Now the king of Jericho was told, "Look
now, men have come here tonight from the Israelites to search out the land." 3 Then the
king of Jericho sent to Rahab, "Bring out the men, the ones who came to you, who came
to your house, for they have come to search out the whole of the land." 4 Now the woman
had taken the two men and hid them. Then she said, "True, the men came to me, but I
did not know from where they came. 5 And it was when the gate was to close at dark that
the men went out. I do not know where the men went. Hurry, chase after them, for you
can reach them." 6 However, she had brought them up to the roof and hidden them in the
stalks of flax that she had laid out for herself on the roof. 7 So the men chased after them
along the path of the Jordan up to the fords. The gate was shut as soon as the pursuers had
gone out.

12 [Rahab said,] "Now I bid you all swear to me by the Faithful God—for I have done
faithfully by you all—that you also will do faithfully by my father's household. Give me a
trustworthy sign. 13 Now, spare my mother and my father, my sisters and my brothers, and all
who belong to them, and deliver our lives from death." 14 The men said to her, "Our life for
yours, even unto death! If you do not tell this our business, then when the Faithful God
gives to us the land we will deal faithfully and honestly with you."

6:15 And it happened on the seventh day that they rose early, at the break of dawn, and
circled the city in the same way seven times. Only on that day they circled the city seven times.
16 And it was the seventh time, when the priests blew the ram's horns, Joshua said to the people, "Shout! For the Faithful One has given you the city. 17 The city and all that is in it shall
be devoted to the Holy One. Only Rahab the prostitute, she shall live and all who are with
her in her house because she hid the messengers we sent."

[23] So the youths who were the spies went in and brought Rahab out, along with her mother, her father, her sisters and brothers, and all who belonged to her—all her kinfolk they brought out—and set them outside the camp of Israel.

Canticle: Wisdom 5:1–5; 6:6–7

Wisdom 5:1 The righteous will stand with great confidence
in the presence of those who have oppressed them
and those who make light of their labors.
2 When the unrighteous see, they will be shaken with a terrible fear,
and they will be amazed at the unexpected salvation.
3 They will speak amongst themselves repenting,
and out of distress of spirit they will groan, and say,
4 "These are persons whom we once held in derision
and made the meaning of insult—we were foolish.
We reckoned their lives as madness
and their end without honor.
5 Why have they been numbered among the daughters and sons of God?
And why is their lot among the holy ones?
6:6 For the least may be pardoned in mercy,
but the mighty will be mightily tested.
7 For the Sovereign of all will not draw back from anyone,
or show respect to greatness;
because small and great alike God made,
and God takes thought for all alike.

Deborah Saves the People: Judges 4:1–10, 23

Judges 4:1 And again the men and women of Israel did what was evil in the sight of the HOLY ONE OF SINAI, for Ehud [the Judge] was dead. [2] So the HOLY ONE sold them into the hand of King Jabin of Canaan, who reigned in Hazor; the commander of his army was Sisera, who lived in Harosheth-ha-goiim. [3] Then the women and men of Israel cried out to GOD WHO HEARS; for Jabin had nine hundred chariots of iron, and had oppressed the Israelites with ruthlessness twenty years.

[4] Deborah, a woman, a female prophet, a fiery woman, she was judging Israel at that time. [5] She used to sit under the palm of Deborah between Ramah and Bethel in the hill country of Ephraim; and the women and men of Israel came up to her for judgment. [6] She sent and called for Barak ben Abinoam from Kedesh in Naphtali, and said to him, "Did not the MOST HIGH, the God of Israel, command you? Go! March on Mount Tabor, and take ten thousand men from the tribe of Naphtali and the tribe of Zebulun. [7] I will march towards you to draw to you by the Wadi Kishon Sisera the commander of Jabin's army, with his chariots and his troops; and I will give him into your hand." [8] Then Barak said to her, "If you will go with me,

then I will go; but if you will not go with me, I will not go." 9 And she said, "I will surely go
with you; however, there will be no glory for you on the path you are taking, for the MIGHTY
GOD will sell Sisera into the hand of a woman." Then Deborah got up and went with Barak to
Kedesh. 10 Barak summoned Zebulun and Naphtali to Kedesh; and ten thousand men went
up with him; and Deborah went up with him.

23 And on that day, God subdued King Jabin of Canaan before the women and men of Israel.

Canticle of Deborah: Judges 5:1, 4–7, 12, 24, 31

1 Then Deborah and Barak ben Abinoam sang on that day, saying:

4 "MIGHTY ONE, when you went out from Seir,
when you marched from the field of Edom,
the earth and the heavens dripped,
even the clouds dripped water.
5 The mountains melted before the MOST HIGH, the One of Sinai,
before the ONE GOD, the God of Israel.
6 "In the days of Shamgar son of Anath,
in the days of Jael, caravans ceased
and travelers traversed the byways.
7 The mighty grew fat in Israel,
they grew fat on plunder,
until you arose, Deborah,
you arose as a mother in Israel.
12 "Awake, awake, Deborah!
Awake, awake, utter a song!
Arise, Barak, capture your captives,
ben Abinoam.
24 "Most blessed of women be Jael,
the wife of Heber the Kenite,
of tent-women most blessed.
31 "So perish all your enemies, HOLY ONE OF OLD!
But those who love God will be like the sun rising in its might."
And the land was pacified for forty years.

Jehosheba Saves the King of Judah: 2 Kings 11:1–4, 10–12

2 Kings 11:1 Now Athaliah, Ahaziah's mother, saw that her son was dead, she stood up
and destroyed all the royal offspring. 2 Then Jehosheba, daughter of King Joram, sister of
Ahaziah, took Joash, Ahaziah's son, and she stole him away from among the daughters and
sons of the king who were being killed; she put him and his nurse in a bedroom. Thus,
she hid him from Athaliah, and he was not put to death. 3 [The prince] remained with

Ahaziah six years, hidden in the house of the Ever-Living God, while Athaliah reigned
over the land.
4 But in the seventh year Jehoiada [the High Priest and Josheba's husband] sent for the
captains of the Carites and of the bodyguards and had them come to him in the house of the
Holy One. He made a covenant with them and had them swear it in the house of the Holy
One of Old; then he showed them the son of the king.
10 The priest [Jehoiada] gave to the captains of the hundreds the spears and shields
that had been King David's, which were in the house of the Living God. 11 Then the
guards stood, each with his weapons in his hand, from the south of the temple to the north
of the temple, next to the altar and the temple, around the king on every side. 12 Then he
brought out the son of the king, put the crown on him, and gave Joash the testimony [of
royalty]. They made him king and anointed him; they clapped their hands and shouted,
"Long live the king!"

Psalm 9:1–2, 7–11, 13–14

1 I will give thanks to the God Who Saves with my whole heart;
I will tell of all your wonderful deeds.
2 I will rejoice and exult in you;
I will sing praise to your name, Most High.
7 God who is Majesty sits enthroned forever,
she has established her throne for judgment.
8 She judges the world in righteousness;
she judges the peoples with equity.
9 She Who is Faithful is a stronghold for the oppressed,
a stronghold in times of trouble.
10 They trust you, they who know your name,
for you do not forsake those who seek you Redeeming God.
11 Sing praises to the Holy One enthroned in Zion.
Declare her deeds among the peoples.
13 Be gracious to me, Gracious One.
See what I suffer from those who hate me.
You lift me up from the gates of death,
14 so that I may recount all your praises,
and in the gates of Daughter Zion,
rejoice in your salvation.

Judith Saves Her People: Judith 8:9–10, 32–34; 13:3–14, 17–18

Judith 8:9 Now Judith heard the wicked words of the people against the ruler because they
were disheartened from lack of water, and when she heard all the words that Uzziah said to
them, and how he swore to them to surrender the town to the Assyrians after five days. 10 So

she sent her slave-girl, who was set over all she possessed, to summon Uzziah and Chabris and
Charmis, the elders of her town.
[32] Then Judith said to them, "Hear me and I will do a thing that will go down from
generation to generation of our daughters and sons. [33] You all shall stand at the gate this
night and I shall go out, I along with my slave-girl, and within the days which you have
promised to handover the town to our enemies, the Holy One will visit Israel through my
hand. [34] None of you all should investigate my task; for I will not tell you until I have completed my work."
[13:3] Now Judith had told her slave-girl to stand outside the bedchamber and to wait for
her to come out, as she did other days; for she said she would go out for her prayer. She spoke
to Bagoas these same words. [4] So everyone went out beyond sight, and no one was left in the
bedchamber, either small or great. Then Judith, standing beside his bed, said in her heart,
"Holy God of all power, look with care in this hour on the work of my hands for the exaltation of Jerusalem. [5] Now is the time to help your heritage and to carry out my intention to
destroy the enemies who have risen up against us."
[6] She came to the bedpost at Holofernes's head, and took down his sword from there.
[7] Then she came towards his bed, caught the hair of his head, and said, "Give me strength
today, Holy God of Israel!" [8] And she struck his neck twice with all her might, and cut off
his head. [9] Then she rolled his body off the bed and snatched the canopy from the post. A
little later she went out and gave Holofernes's head to her slave-girl, [10] who placed it in her
food bag.

Then the two women went out together, according to their custom at the time for
prayer. They passed through the encampment, circled the valley, and went up the mountain
to Bethulia, and came to its gates. [11] From a distance Judith called out to the guards at the
gates, "Open! Open the gate! God, our God, is with us, working deeds of power in Israel and
might against our enemies, as God has done today!"
[12] And it happened when the men of her town heard her voice, they rushed to come
down to the gate of the city and summoned the elders of the city. [13] They all ran together,
from small to great, for it was extraordinary to them that she returned. They opened the gate
and welcomed the women. Then they lit a fire to provide light, and gathered around the
women. [14] Then Judith said to them with a loud voice, "Hallelujah! Hallelujah! Praise God,
who did not withdraw mercy from the house of Israel, but has broken our enemies by my
hand this night!"
[17] All the people were completely astounded. They bowed down and worshiped God,
and said with one accord, "Blessed are you our God, who has this day humiliated the
enemies of your people." [18] Then Uzziah said to Judith, "O daughter, you are blessed by
the Most High God above all other women on earth, and blessed be the Holy God, who
created the heavens and the earth, who has guided you to cut off the head of the leader of
our enemies.

The Song of Judith: Judith 16:1–6, 13

Judith 16:1 Judith said:

Begin praise for my God with drums,
sing to my Sovereign with cymbals.
Craft a psalm and a praise for God;
exalt God and call upon God's name.
2 For the Holy One is a God who crushes wars,
whose encampments are in the midst of the people,
who delivered me from the hands of my pursuers.
3 Assyria came down from the mountains of the north;
it came with multitudes of its warriors,
the same multitude blocked up the waterway,
and their cavalry covered the hills.
4 Assyria boasted that it would burn up my territory,
and kill my young men with the sword,
and throw my infants to the ground,
and give my children away as spoils of war,
and despoil my virgins.
5 But the Almighty God dismissed them
with a feminine hand.
6 For their mighty one did not fall by the hands of the young men,
nor did the sons of the Titans strike him down,
nor did tall giants lay him out;
but Judith daughter of Merari
with the beauty of her person undid him.
13 I will sing to my God a new song:
Holy One, you are great and glorious,
wonderful in strength, invincible.

Epistle: Acts 16:13–15

Acts 16:13 On the day of the sabbath we went out the gate by the river, where we thought
there was a place of prayer; and we sat down and spoke to the women who gathered there.
14 Now a certain woman named Lydia, a merchant of purple cloth from the city of Thyatira, a
worshiper of God, was listening to us. The Messiah opened her heart to listen eagerly to what
was said by Paul. 15 As she was baptized along with her household, she urged us, saying, "If you
have judged me to be faithful to Christ, come and stay at my home." And she persuaded us.

Gospel: Matthew 28:1–10

Matthew 28:1 After the sabbath, as the first day of the week was dawning, Mary Magdalene
and the other Mary went to see the tomb. 2 And look! There was a great earthquake, for a

messenger of God, descending from heaven, came and rolled away the stone and sat upon it.
[3] Its appearance was like lightning, and its clothing white as snow. [4] For fear of the messenger,
the guards shook and were as though dead. [5] But the messenger responded to the women and
said, "Fear not; I know that you all are looking for Jesus who was crucified. [6] He is not here;
for he has been raised, just as he said. Come, see the place where he lay. [7] Then go quickly and
tell his disciples, 'He has been raised from the dead, and see, he is on to Galilee ahead of you;
there you all will see him.' This is my message for you." [8] So the women left the tomb quickly
with fear and great joy and ran to tell his disciples the news. [9] Then all of a sudden Jesus met
them and said, "Shalom!" And they came to him, took hold of his feet, and bowed down worshipping him. [10] Then Jesus said to them, "Fear not; go and tell my sisters and brothers to go
to Galilee; there they will see me."

PROCLAMATION

Text Notes

In the very first lines of Genesis, and therefore of the Bible, Jewish or Christian, both masculine and feminine verbs are used for God, masculine for God, feminine for the Spirit. Ultimately God's human creation will reflect their creator as female and male. The translation follows that early pattern and uses pronouns of both genders throughout the passage. In Genesis 2:2 I also use "they" for God, a reminder that God transcends the binary language in which God is disclosed and that some if those created in the image of God are nonbinary.

In Genesis 21:9, the nature of Ishmael's play (or mocking) is not explained. The NRSV and RSV add "with Isaac," which is not in the text, leading to demonization of Ishmael as a child. Some commentators go so far as to accuse him of sexually abusing Isaac based on this fiction. In verse 11, Abraham finds the situation "extremely evil," though the word encodes a range of negativity. Hagar's motion in putting her child under the tree is explosive: "throw" or "cast." The idiomatic expression in verse 17, "What is with you?" sounds harsher to English-speaking ears than the traditional, "What troubles you?"

In Psalm 27:11, "teach" is the verbal form of *torah,* which is more properly "teaching" or "revelation" than law. In verse 12, "throats" translates *nephesh,* "soul." The usage is rare but occurs in Job 24:12, Jeremiah 4:10, and Habakkuk 2:5. In verse 14, the number of grammatically masculine subjects leave open another possible translation, familiar from the King James Version: "Be of good courage and God will strengthen your heart."

The Canticle of the Three Young Men comes from the Greek version of Daniel in the Septuagint. A larger selection of verses occurs in the Song of the Three Young Men used as a canticle in the Book of Common Prayer. In many Protestant Bibles like the NRSV, translations of Greek portions of Daniel and Esther are published in a separate section with the Deuterocanonical/Apocryphal books. In Catholic Bibles like the Inclusive Bible, the Greek-based portions are woven in, resulting in an alternate set of verse numbers. This passage is verses 74–82 in the *New English Translation of the Septuagint* (NETS). The NETS translation was influential in my own here.

In Exodus 15:2 I add "my mother's God." While Moses will have to ask who God is and what is the divine Name, Moses's mother Yocheved, Jochebed, bears the Name in the first syllable of her name and may be the oldest name in the Hebrew Bible including a portion of the Name. In verse 3, God is thoroughly anthropomorphized as "a man of war."

Like Miriam's Song, Judges 5 is one of the oldest works in the Hebrew Bible, replete with translation challenges. In Judges 4:4, Deborah is a woman of *lappidoth*. While many have contrived a husband, the word is the adjective "fiery" or "flaming" with a feminine ending. Further, unlike every male character in the book, *lappidoth* does not have any family information line for Barak son of Abinoam. The feminine singular verb in 5:1 indicates Deborah led the song and Barak followed her lead. An earlier version of the translation of Judges 4–5 and detailed translation notes can be found in *Daughters of Miriam: Women Prophets in Ancient Israel.*

Some details of 2 Kings 11 are filled in with the more detailed account in 2 Chronicles 23.

The sense of the story in Judith is that she dined with the enemy general, maintaining her virtue, got him drunk, and assassinated him. In the critical scene, the tent where Holofernes sleeps is confusingly described as hers in 13:3. Previously 12:1 and following indicate she is staying in his dining tent. In 13:14 I use the traditional "Hallelujah" for the Jewish (woman whose name means just that, a Jewish woman).

In Matthew 28 I have translated the divine messenger in neuter terms, since grammatical gender may not be biologically significant—if the category even applies—to a divine messenger.

Preaching Prompts

While these texts may not be preached on Easter, commentary is offered for those who will choose one for the early service on Easter day. Those preparing for nonlectionary sermons may find the lesson/canticle pairings fruitful. For example, Psalm 27 takes on new meaning when heard from the perspective of Hagar and Ishmael.

In the Exodus account, the God who saves Israelite lives takes Egyptian lives. The scriptures celebrate the liberation and often the deaths of the Egyptians, though later texts will acknowledge that the peoples of Egypt and Israel's other adversaries are also God's. The Exodus Canticle is understood by some scholars to have been Miriam's initially, perhaps just the contents of Exodus 15:21. The longer song in Exodus 15:1–18 then, derives from the shorter.

Note that in Joshua 2 the spies do not surveil the land or Jericho. They head straight for a brothel, and "lay down." That expression is used for sex and for sleeping. "Spend the night" unnecessarily shifts the reader away from the plain understanding of why men go to a brothel. Joshua 6:23 calls them "youth," or "boys," which may contribute to their decision. This text provides an opportunity to talk about sex-work and its criminalization and the (often upstanding) men who buy sex. Tying in Jesus's friendships with sex workers may help frame this text in an Easter sermon.

Note that Rahab's father's household in 2:12 is different from her household in 2:1. She seeks the salvation of her entire family, whether they live with her or not, perhaps, no matter what they think about her line of work. In verse 13, "spare" is less than a command and more than a request. She saves all who are in the house with her in verse 17, the ark of safety she offers may well encompass people who are not related to her. Rahab and her family are delivered using the primary verb of the exodus in Joshua 6:17–18.

Selections from Wisdom chapters 5 and 6 pair with the Rahab story, reminding the reader and hearer that God saves and redeems who God wills, including and particularly those who are thought to be sinful and beyond God's reach and care.

Athaliah is the only woman in the Bible to rule Israel or Judah on her own; functionally she was a king, as neither Israel nor Judah had queens, a title not used by royal wives. Separately, the queen-mothers of Judah were the mothers of the ruling king in Judah and did serve in an official capacity.

While some number of the women who followed Jesus were present at his resurrection in Matthew 28:10, there were certainly more who, like all of his male followers, were not.

EASTER DAY—EARLY SERVICE

The early Easter service traditionally uses lessons from the Great Vigil of Easter. Choose a first lesson from the Vigil and use the psalm, Epistle, and Gospel readings from the Vigil.

EASTER DAY—PRINCIPAL SERVICE

Isaiah 49:1–13; Psalm 18:2–11, 16–19; Hebrews 11:1–2, 23–24, 28–39; Matthew 28:1–10 or John 20:1–10 (11–18)

Isaiah 49:1 Listen you coastlands to me,
And pay heed, you peoples from afar!
The CREATOR OF ALL called me from the womb,
from my mother's belly God made my name known.

2 God made my mouth like a sharpened sword,
and in the shadow of God's own hand, hid me;
God made me like a polished arrow,
in God's own quiver, hid me.
3 And God said to me, "You are my slave,
Israel, in you I am glorified."
4 But I, I said, "in vain have I labored,
I have spent my strength for nothingness and vanity;
surely my judgment is with the FAITHFUL ONE,
and my wages with my God."
5 And now says the AUTHOR OF LIFE,
who formed me in the womb to be God's slave,
to return Jacob back to God,
and that Israel might be gathered to God;
I am honored in the sight of the HOLY ONE OF OLD,
and my God is my strength.
6 God says,
"It is too light a thing that you should be my slave
to raise up the tribes of Jacob [the line of Rebekah],
and to restore the survivors of Israel [born of Rachel and Leah, and Bilhah and Zilpah]?
I will give you as a light to the nations,
for it will be that my salvation reaches to the end of the earth."
7 Thus says the FAITHFUL ONE,
the Redeemer of Israel, God's holy one,
to one despised, abhorred by the nations,
the slave of rulers,
"Queens and kings shall see and arise,
princes and princesses, and they too shall prostrate themselves,
on account of the FIRE OF SINAI, who is faithful,
the Holy One of Israel, who has chosen you."
8 Thus says the MIGHTY GOD:
In a favorable time I have answered you,
on a day of salvation I have helped you;
I have kept you and given you
as a covenant to the people,
to establish the land,
to apportion the desolate portions;
9 saying to the prisoners, "Go free!"
to those who are in darkness, "Let yourselves be seen."

Along the paths they shall pasture,
and on all the bare heights shall be their pasture.
10 They shall not hunger nor shall they thirst,
neither shall heat nor sun strike them down,
for the one who mother-loves them shall lead them,
and by springs of water shall guide them.
11 And I will turn all my mountains into a pathway,
and my highways shall be raised up.
12 Look! These shall come from far away,
and see! These from the north and from the sea to the west,
and these from the southland of Syene.
13 Sing for joy, you heavens, and exult O earth;
let mountains break forth into singing!
For the TENDER LOVING ONE has comforted God's people,
and will mother-love God's suffering ones.

Psalm 18:2–11, 16–19

2 The ROCK WHO GAVE US BIRTH is my rock,
and my fortress, and my deliverer,
my God, my rock in whom I take refuge,
my shield, and the horn of my salvation, my stronghold.
3 I call upon the HOLY ONE, may she be praised,
and from my enemies I shall be saved.
4 The snares of death encompassed me;
the rivers of wickedness assailed me.
5 The snares of Sheol encircled me;
the snares of death confronted me.
6 In my distress I called upon SHE WHO HEARS;
to my God I cried for help.
From her temple she heard my voice,
and my cry came before her, to her ears.
7 Then the earth shuddered and quaked;
the foundations also of the mountains trembled
and were shaken because of her anger.
8 Smoke went up from her nostrils,
and consuming fire from her mouth;
burning coals blazed forth from her.
9 She spread out the heavens, and descended;
thick darkness was under her feet.

10 She mounted up on a cherub, and flew;
she soared upon the wings of the wind.
11 She made darkness her veil around her,
her canopy dark waters and thick clouds.
16 She reached down from on high, she took me;
she drew me out of the multitude of water.
17 She delivered me from my strong enemy,
and from those who hate me;
for they were too mighty for me.
18 They confronted me in the day of my calamity;
yet the Sheltering God was my support.
19 She brought me out into a broad place;
she delivered me, because she delights in me.

Hebrews 11:1 Now faith is the essence of things hoped for, the conviction of that which is
not seen. 2 By faith, indeed, were our ancestors approved.

23 By faith Moses was hidden after his birth by his mother and father for three months,
because they saw that the child was beautiful; and they were not afraid of the king's commandment. 24 By faith Moses, after he had grown up, refused to be called a son of Pharaoh's daughter.

28 By faith he kept the Passover and the sprinkling of blood, in order that the destroyer of
the firstborn would not touch the firstborn daughters and sons of Israel.

29 By faith they passed through the Red Sea as though on dry land, but when the Egyptians chose to try, they were drowned. 30 By faith the walls of Jericho fell when encircled for
seven days. 31 By faith Rahab the prostitute did not perish with those who did not believe,
because she had received the spies in peace.

32 And what more should I say? For time would fail me to tell of Gideon, Barak, Samson,
Jephthah, of David and Samuel and the prophets, female and male, 33 who through faith conquered
realms, administered justice, obtained promises, stopped the mouths of lions, 34 quenched raging
fire, escaped the edge of the sword, were made strong out of weakness, became mighty in war, felled
foreign armies. 35 Women through resurrection received their dead. Other women and men were
tortured, refusing to receive a release, in order to obtain a better resurrection. 36 Yet other women
and men received a trial of mocking and whipping, and even chains and imprisonment. 37 They were
stoned, they were sawed in two, they were slaughtered by sword; they went about in animal-skins,
in sheepskin and goatskin, impoverished, oppressed, tormented. 38 The world was not worthy of
them. They wandered in deserts and mountains, and in caves and holes in the ground.

39 And all these, commended for their faith, did not receive what was promised.

Matthew 28:1–10 is available with commentary in the readings for the Great Vigil of Easter. John 20 is the customary alternative. The reading from the Gospel of John may be read in longer or shorter form.

John 20:1 Now it was the first day of the week, Mary Magdalene came, early on while it was still dark, to the tomb and saw the stone removed from the tomb. 2 So she ran and went to Simon Peter and to the other disciple, the one whom Jesus loved, and said to them, "They have taken the Messiah out of the tomb, and we do not know where they have laid him." 3 Then Peter and the other disciple came and went to the tomb. 4 The two were running together, but the other disciple ran ahead of Peter and reached the tomb first. 5 And bending down to see, saw the linen wrappings lying there, but he did not enter. 6 Then Simon Peter came, following him, and went into the tomb, and he saw the linen wrappings lying there 7 and the facecloth that had been on Jesus's head not lying with the linen wrappings but rolled up separately in another place. 8 Then the other disciple, who reached the tomb first, went in and saw and believed. 9 Indeed they did not understand the scripture, that it was necessary for Jesus to rise from the dead. 10 Then the disciples returned once more to their homes.

[11 Now Mary stood outside, facing the tomb, weeping. As she wept, she bent down to see in the tomb. 12 Then she saw two angels in white sitting, one at the head and the other at the feet, where the body of Jesus had been lying. 13 They said to her, "Woman, why do you weep?" She said to them, "Because, they have taken my Savior, and I do not know where they have laid him." 14 Having said this, she turned around and saw Jesus standing, but she did not know that it was Jesus. 15 Jesus said to her, "Woman, why do you weep? For whom do you look?" Thinking that he was the gardener, she said to him, "Sir, if you have carried him away, tell me where you have laid him, and I will take him away." 16 Jesus said to her, "Mary." She turned and said to him in Aramaic, "Rabbouni!" (which means Teacher). 17 Jesus said to her, "Do not hold me, because I have not yet ascended to the Abba. Rather, go to my brothers and say to them, 'I am ascending to my Abba and your Abba, to my God and your God.'" 18 Mary Magdalene went and announced to the disciples, "I have seen the Savior"; and she told them that he had said these things to her.]

PROCLAMATION

Text Notes

Given there is no concrete present tense in biblical Hebrew, it can be difficult to determine whether an imperfect verb should be translated in present or future tense. In Isaiah 49:3 the question of whether God *is* glorified in Israel or *will be* is open. I have chosen the present to suggest that even in their brokenness, or perhaps because of it, God is glorified in her faithful relationship with an often unfaithful partner. A portion of Isaiah 49 read today overlaps with the one read on Psalm Sunday. See textual and preaching commentary there for further notes.

In Psalm 18:2 I draw the divine name from Deuteronomy 32:18, "You neglected the Rock that gave birth to you; you forgot the God who writhed in birth-labor for you."

The Greek word *hypostasis* means the "essence of a thing," as in the relationship between Jesus and God articulated with this same word earlier in Hebrews 1:2–3; Jesus is the essence of God. In Hebrews 11:1, faith is the essence of that which is hoped for. In 11:2, "to be approved" is the sense of the verb to "be martyred," or "bear witness" when it is the passive voice. The citizens of Jericho in Hebrews 11:31 can be translated as either they who "were disobedient" or "did not believe." Each is problematic in the context of the earlier story. If disobedient, when? To what message? If unbelieving, then to what?

Note that the celestial messengers speak with one voice in John 20:13. In verse 15 Mary addresses Jesus with the honorific given any man of status or used to show respect, "master" or "lord," also used of those who held slaves. It also signifies Jesus's own authority and sovereignty. Her demand that this unknown person tell her where Jesus has been taken is expressed in the imperative, as a command. Exclamation point or period? Does Jesus exclaim her name or call it softly or plainly in verse 16? I imagine the latter.

Hebrew and Aramaic are recognized as distinct languages now, but they were not always so understood; the terms are used interchangeably in the scriptures.

Preaching Prompts

The anonymity of the Servant Songs in Isaiah has led to them being easily interpreted through the story of Jesus. As an Easter reading, the text reminds of the import of the life Jesus lived, not just the death he died, a life that was shaped and molded by scriptures like Isaiah 49.

The psalmist is delivered from certain death in her time by being saved from her enemies and their traps. Yet that is not the limit of the power of the God who harnesses the clouds as her chariot. Psalm 18 also serves as a response to Psalm 22 in the earlier plaintive liturgies of Holy Week and Good Friday, the pleas for deliverance and trust in God are answered by the fact of deliverance. God is able to deliver. God is faithful to deliver. Even to and through death.

The Epistle to the Hebrews forms a bridge to the Gospel. In this Epistle penned to Jewish, and therefore Hebrew, people, the author links that faith to the faith of their people (and collaborators) across time. Yet the list of heroes in Hebrews 11 that recounts that faith reads like a patriarchal revisionist history. For example, Barak replaces Deborah and Jephthah who murdered his own daughter is included in 11:32. (However, since Deborah ruled and delivered in the period mentioned, and other women prophets followed her, and the plural "prophets" includes both genders, I have specified "prophets, female and male.") Ironically, it will be women's faithfulness to Jesus at the cross and tomb that will lead to the first proclamations of his resurrection. As a second lesson, the last line of this reading points forward to a promise realized in that resurrection and its proclamation.

With all of the alleluias, it is hard to remember that Easter morning begins in sorrow. Grieving and dumbfounded, women make their way to the tomb where their friend, teacher, and savior lies. They are not singing alleluia. In John's Gospel, their motivation has been erased; they have been reduced to Mary Magdalene and one "we" in verse 2. They do not enter the tomb, counter to other accounts. They fetch men who go first, then Mary follows them. The male disciples leave and once again Jesus is attended only by women, now just Mary. He reveals himself to her and sends her as his messenger bearing his word.

She announces, *aggellousa*, the good news that Jesus has appeared to her and has a message for the men who were not present. That "announcement" is related to the words for messengers, human or divine ones sometimes called angels, and their message; they share a common root. Interpreters have struggled with what to make of Jesus telling Mary not to touch or hold or hold on to him in John 20:17. Some wince at what they hear as harsh language, as when he asks his mother, "Woman, what concern is that to you and to me?" in John 2:4. I wonder if it is that we do not hear "woman" charitably as a form of address. What may be missed are the parallels to Thomas: Mary sees, hears, speaks with, and touches her savior. Having seen his death, what other than the word of the risen Christ could compel her to let go?

EASTER DAY—EVENING SERVICE

Isaiah 25:6–9; Psalm 118:14–26; 2 Timothy 2:8–13; Luke 24:13–35 (or 24:13–27)

Isaiah 25:6 The COMMANDER of heaven's legions will make for all peoples on this mountain,
a feast of rich food, a feast of well-aged wines,
of rich food prepared with marrow, of refined well-aged wines.
7 And God will destroy on this mountain
the shroud that shrouds all peoples,
the veil that veils all nations.
8 God will swallow up death forever.
Then the SOVEREIGN GOD will wipe away tears from every face,
and will sweep aside the shame of God's people from the whole earth,
for GOD WHOSE NAME IS HOLY has spoken.
9 It will be said on that day,
Look! This is our God; in whom we hope, and who saved us.
This is the CREATOR OF ALL in whom we hope;
let us be glad and rejoice in God's salvation.

Psalm 118:14–26

14 The MIGHTY GOD is my strength and my might
and has become my salvation.
15 The sound of song and of salvation is in the tents of the righteous:
"The right hand of the MOST HIGH is mighty;
16 the right hand of the MIGHTY GOD is exalted;
the right hand of the MOST HIGH is mighty."
17 I shall not die, but I shall live,
and recount the deeds of the ANCIENT OF DAYS.
18 The MERCIFUL GOD has punished me severely,
but to death did not hand me over.
19 Open to me the gates of righteousness,
that I may enter through them
and give thanks to the FOUNT OF JUSTICE.
20 This is the gate of the LIVING GOD;
the righteous shall enter through it.
21 I thank you for you have answered me
and have become my salvation.
22 The stone the builders rejected
has become the chief cornerstone.
23 This is the MIGHTY GOD's doing;
it is marvelous in our eyes.
24 This is the day that the CREATOR OF ALL has made;
let us rejoice and be glad in it.
25 Save us, we pray, SAVING ONE!
GENEROUS ONE, we pray, grant us prosperity!
26 Blessed is the one who comes in the name of GOD WHO IS HOLY.
We bless you from the house of the EVER-LIVING GOD.

2 Timothy 2:8 Remember Jesus Christ, raised from the dead, from the line of David [and
Bathsheba]; that is my gospel, 9 for which I suffer hardship, even to chains, like a criminal. But
the word of God is not chained. 10 Because of this, therefore I endure everything for the sake
of the elect, in order that they may also obtain salvation in Christ Jesus with eternal glory.
11 This is a trustworthy saying:

For if we die together, we will also live together;
12 if we endure, we will also reign together;
if we deny [Christ], he will also deny us;
13 if we are faithless, faithful he remains,
for he cannot deny himself.

Luke 24:13 Now see, two of them on that very day [the first day of the week] were going to a village that was seven miles from Jerusalem; its name was Emmaus. 14 And they talked with each other about all the things that had happened. 15 And it happened while they were talking and questioning that Jesus himself came near and accompanied them. 16 Yet their eyes were kept from recognizing him. 17 And Jesus said to them, "What is this conversation you are having with each other while you journey?" They stood in place, sorrowful. 18 Then one of them, whose name was Cleopas, replied to him saying, "Are you the only foreigner in Jerusalem who does not know the things that have happened there these days?" 19 Jesus asked them, "What kind of things?" They replied, "About Jesus the Nazarene, who was a man, a prophet mighty in deed and word before God and all the people. 20 Also how our chief priests and leaders surrendered him to be sentenced to death and crucified him. 21 But we had hoped that he was the one to soon redeem Israel. Now besides all this, instead, it is now the third day since these things have taken place. 22 Then again, certain women of our community astounded us. They were at the tomb this morning. 23 And when they did not find the body, they came back and told us they had seen a vision of angels who said Jesus was alive. 24 Then some of those who were with us went to the tomb and found it just as the women had said, but they did not see him." 25 Then Jesus said to them, "Oh, foolish souls, and how slow of heart to believe all that the prophets have spoken! 26 Was it not necessary that the Messiah should suffer these things to enter into his glory?" 27 And starting from Moses and from all the prophets, Jesus interpreted to them the things about himself in all the scriptures.

28 When they came near the village to which they were going, Jesus walked ahead as if he were going on. 29 So they urged him strongly, saying, "Stay with us, because it is almost evening and the day is nearly over." Then he went in to stay with them. 30 When Jesus was at the table with them, he took bread, blessed and broke it, and gave it to them. 31 And their eyes were opened, and they recognized him. And he vanished from before them. 32 They said to each other, "Were not our hearts burning within us while he was talking to us on the way, while he was opening up the scriptures to us?" 33 Now that same hour they rose up and returned to Jerusalem, and found the eleven and others with them gathered together. 34 They were saying, "Really! The Savior has risen, and has appeared to Simon!" 35 Then they told what had happened on the way, and how Jesus had been made known to them in the breaking of the bread.

PROCLAMATION

Text Notes

There are regular differences in how biblical passages are broken into verses between translations. In Isaiah 25, the last line of what is verse 7 in some Christian Bibles like NRSV begins verse 8 in Hebrew and in Jewish Bibles and other Christian Bibles, like CEB. I follow the Hebrew and JPS here. In verse 9, the tense of God's salvation can be understood as past or present. God's record of faithfulness makes her trustworthy; pushing these texts into a future time diminishes that past faithfulness.

Psalm 118 is a literary work of art in Hebrew with a lattice of repeating elements that circle from the last line to the beginning. Verse 25 yields "hosanna," an alternate pronunciation for *hoshia-na* in the psalm.

Many translations of 2 Timothy 2:11–13 add "with him" throughout for poetic balance; the object and preposition are not present. Verse 12 requires an object for the verb; I have supplied "Christ" from verse 10.

In Luke 24:25, Jesus says, "Oh foolish X . . ." There is no noun present; the adjective includes object information, masculine or inclusive plural. Common translations are "foolish men," "ones," or "people."

PREACHING PROMPTS

On this Principal Feast of the Resurrection, the Church proclaims that death is not the end. This notion appears intermittently in the Hebrew Bible: Elisha raises a widow's son from death in 2 Kings 4 and Daniel 12:1–2 proclaims an unambiguous resurrection. Frequently cited, Job 19:26 is ambiguous and well-known. Ezekiel 37, the dry bones, represents the resurrection of the nation of Israel, see verse 11. Against this background, Isaiah 25 proclaims that the day is coming when God will destroy death forever, swallowing it up. Belief in resurrection will become normative for most traditions of Judaism, including that of Jesus, for Christians, as well as for Muslims.

Psalm 118 is a festival hymn in the form of a temple liturgy. It is part of the Great *Hallel* (Praise) recited on the major festivals: Passover, Pentecost (*Shavuoth*), and Booths (*Sukkot*). Many understand the Hallel to be the "hymn" that Jesus and the disciples sang after the Last Supper, particularly when it is formed as a Passover meal (though likely not a seder). In these readings, Psalm 118 echoes the theme of salvation in Isaiah 25. In verse 17, the line "I shall not die but live" likely refers to deliverance from death rather than resurrection. Together these collected readings present a God who delivers on both sides of death. While the psalm emphasizes deliverance from death, 2 Timothy offers an ancient hymn for the believer confident in resurrection after death.

It's hard to know what to make of Jesus calling the disciples foolish in Luke 24:25. It sounds like a rebuke but may have been said in humor with a twinkle, the way a text, tweet, or email may sound harsher than intended.

The road to Emmaus stories are Easter evening stories. The travelling disciples have had all day to grapple with incomprehensible claims of resurrection from sister disciples. Notably, they don't doubt the women, rather they find the whole saga—trial, crucifixion, and resurrection claims—simply astounding. This is an important reminder that the terrible images of the crucifixion and the trauma it generated don't simply vanish with proclamation of the good news. The disciples are traumatized and on an emotional rollercoaster.

Jesus, the Bread of Life, confected in the womb of the Blessed Virgin, makes himself known in the breaking of bread. Jesus who is bread offers bread, and Jesus who is the Word interprets the word. When Jesus interprets the scriptures—in Luke 24:27, Torah and Prophets, and in Luke 24:44, Torah, Prophets, and Psalms—the text does not say he shows where the scriptures "predict" him. Reducing the relationship of Jesus with the Hebrew Bible to prediction and fulfillment presents a skewed view of prophecy, scripture more broadly, and Jesus. Rather, I understand him to teach the scriptures that are foundational to him, his identity, his teaching and ministry, after which he patterned himself, which scriptures Christians read through subsequently read through Jesus.

One of the travelers is male; the other is not described. Grammatically, they could have been a woman and man or two men. There were women, children, and men in the village where they stopped absent from the text, as are their hosts. The only women's voices are the echoing proclamations that Christ is risen from the dead.

MONDAY IN EASTER WEEK

1 Peter 1:3–9; Psalm 16:8–11; John 20:19–23

Note: Easter Week services do not traditionally include a Hebrew Bible Reading. In the traditional pattern, the first lesson is a New Testament lesson followed by the psalm and Gospel.

1 Peter 1:3 Blessed be the God and Abba of our Redeemer Jesus Christ who in great mercy
has engendered a new birth for us into a living hope, through the resurrection of Jesus Christ
from the dead, 4 into an inheritance that is incorruptible, undefiled, and unfading, kept in
the heavens for you all, 5 who in the power of God are kept through faith for a salvation ready
to be revealed in the end time. 6 In this you rejoice even when necessary for you to suffer
various trials, 7 in order that the examination of your faith, more precious than gold, which
though perishable is tested by fire, may be found yielding praise and glory and honor when
Jesus Christ is revealed. 8 You have not seen him, yet you love him. You do not see him now,
yet you believe in him and rejoice with a joy glorious and beyond words. 9 You are receiving
the completion of your faith, the salvation of your souls.

Psalm 16:8–11

8 I keep the FAITHFUL ONE before me always;
because she is at my right hand, I shall not be moved.
9 Therefore my heart rejoices, and my inner being delights;
even my body resides in safety.

10 For you will not abandon my soul to Sheol,
or let your faithful one see the Pit.
11 You show me the way of life.
There is fullness of joy in your presence;
delights fill your right hand forevermore.

John 20:19 When it was evening on that day, the first of the week, and the doors of the house
where the disciples were closed for fear of the Judeans, Jesus came and stood in their midst and
said to them, "Peace be with you all." 20 And having said this, Jesus showed them his hands and
his side; then the disciples rejoiced when they saw the Messiah. 21 Jesus said to them again,
"Peace be with you all, just as the God of Peace has sent me, so I send you all." 22 When Jesus had
said this, he breathed on them and said to them, "Receive the Holy Spirit; 23 if you forgive the
sins of any, they are forgiven them; if you retain the sins of any, they are retained."

PROCLAMATION

Text Notes

The reading from 1 Peter has rather long, unwieldly sentences that make for challenging reading, particularly aloud.

In Psalm 16, Sheol, the abode of the dead in the Israelite worldview, was variously described as a place of great gloom, deep below the surface of the (flat) earth. It is an equitable destination, for great and small, righteous and wicked. Presumed to be inescapable except by the rarest of miracles, deliverance from Sheol refers to escape from death and its clutches *before* death. The "Pit" is an occasional synonym for Sheol and the grave.

In the Gospel of John, the disciples in the house are as Jewish as their fellow residents of Judea, as Jewish as Jesus. It would be centuries before there was clear separation between Jews and Christians. Scriptural language pitting Jesus, his disciples, and the early Christians against "the Jews" is one of the more challenging aspects of our faith.

Preaching Prompts

These Easter Week first Lesson readings explore some of the Church's earliest reflections on resurrection. All of the psalms focus on God's deliverance from death, and its abode in the Israelite worldview, Sheol. The Gospel readings center the stories from immediately after the resurrection.

The Epistle addresses believers who, like us, have not seen Jesus yet believe. The active voice in the Epistle emphasizes that the readers and hearers, and we, are being kept by God and that they and we are receiving the salvation of our souls.

Rather than a fixed point at which we "were" saved, we live into our salvation in faith.

The second-person addresses of the Epistle and psalm—the first to the reader, the second to God—do not include gendered language. There are, of course, women among the believers to whom the Epistle is written, and women who would have prayed, and perhaps composed, the psalmist's prayer. We are left to imagine them.

The women are necessarily absent from the Gospel, having proclaimed the good news of Jesus's resurrection to male disciples who still don't quite get it, let alone its implications for a fearless life. They, Mary Magdalene and other women, suggested by the "we" in John 20:2, are arguably still telling the news. What to make of the gift of the Holy Spirit breathed onto those disciples hiding in the house? It matters that the power and authority to forgive and retain sins is connected to the receipt of the Holy Spirit, grammatically and theologically. The text appears to be organizing if not setting up a hierarchy in the community. This early statement of the nascent community's priorities shows them continuing Jesus's radical work, declaring the forgiveness of sins.

TUESDAY IN EASTER WEEK

1 Corinthians 15:3–7; Psalm 18:1–6; Luke 24:36–43

1 Corinthians 15:3 For I handed on to you all as primary what I in turn had received, that
Christ died for our sins in accordance with the scriptures. 4 And, that he was buried, and that
he was raised on the third day in accordance with the scriptures. 5 And that he was seen by
Cephas, then the twelve. 6 Then he was seen by more than five hundred sisters and brothers
together, many of whom remain, though some have died. 7 Then he was seen by James, then
all the apostles.

Psalm 18

1 I love you, MIGHTY ONE, my strength.
2 The ROCK WHO GAVE US BIRTH is my rock,
and my fortress, and my deliverer,
my God, my rock in whom I take refuge,
my shield, and the horn of my salvation, my stronghold.
3 I call upon the HOLY ONE, may she be praised,
and from my enemies I shall be saved.
4 The snares of death encompassed me;
the rivers of wickedness assailed me.
5 The snares of Sheol encircled me;
the snares of death confronted me.
6 In my distress I called upon SHE WHO HEARS;
to my God I cried for help.
From her temple she heard my voice,
and my cry came before her, to her ears.

Luke 24:36 While they [two of Jesus's disciples] were talking about this [his resurrection], he himself stood between them and said to them, "Peace be with you." [37] Now they were frightened and became terrified, and thought they were seeing a spirit. [38] Jesus said to them, "Why are you troubled, because of thoughts rising in your hearts? [39] Look at my hands and my feet; that it is I. Touch me and see; for a spirit does not have flesh and bones as you see I have." [40] And saying this, Jesus showed them his hands and his feet. [41] Yet still disbelieving and in their joy and wondering, he said to them, "Have you any food here?" [42] They gave him a piece of broiled fish, [43] and he took it in their presence and ate.

PROCLAMATION

Text Notes

One of the ways in which the translation of the scriptures is often anti-Judaistic is the intentional changing of Jewish names in the New Testament to Gentile forms. "James" in 1 Corinthian 15:7 is a case in point. His name is Jacob, *Iakob* in Greek; yet translators use "Jacob" for the Hebrew Bible patriarch occurring in the New Testament while treating the Hebrew names of people in the Jesus story differently. Changing *Mariam*, Miriam, to Mary is another example of what is a standard practice. These changes obscure and in some cases erase the primary Jewish identity of the family and followers of Jesus.

The occasion of Psalm 18 is David's escape from Saul; that introduction takes up the first verse in Hebrew. The psalm proper begins with "He said," often included with the introductory verse. David's "love" in what is now verse 1, as Christian translations number the psalms, is *racham*, mother-love, love that is rooted in the womb, *rechem*, and otherwise used only by God to express her love. From David we should perhaps read it as gesturing toward a reciprocal love that originates deep within.

Verse 3 of the psalm has the passive "be praised" without supporting grammar. Other translators have added "*worthy to* be praised." Some translations render verse 3 in the future, see NRSV and KJV, however the introduction makes clear David is reflecting on his past deliverance. The imperfect here is more present, i.e., because of God's faithfulness, whenever I call on God as before, I shall be saved.

The Gospel uses the same word for "spirit" (as in the Holy Spirit) for spirit of the dead, or what we might hear as "ghost" in Luke 24:37 and in verse 39.

Preaching Prompts

Given that the Epistles predate the Gospels, the brief telling of the good news of Jesus's resurrection triumph over the grave is one of the first recorded articulations of the Gospel. It lacks all of the narrative detail and the women evangelists collectively or by name. Not only is Mary Magdalene missing, but there is no mention of Mary the mother of Jesus or the beloved disciple. It lacks the angels and reports only Peter (called Cephas) and the twelve as initial witnesses. The text does go on to position Paul as in the chain of apostles.

The mention of James receiving his own postresurrection appearance is significant. Long understood to be the brother of Jesus, the appearance has been interpreted as confirming James as leader of the emerging church. While the Epistle is invested in hierarchy (hence the lack of women) and continuity, Jesus also takes time to appear to family in the person of his beloved brother. The appearances to the more than five hundred in the plural form that can be inclusive, mixed—with only one male required, or all male—suggest Jesus going to his beloveds to comfort and assure them after his death.

Jesus's evening journey with the pair, or perhaps couple, of disciples on the road to Emmaus reads like an expansion of the note in 1 Corinthians 15 about Jesus's appearances to so many. Even with the scolding of beloved teacher and friend, the account reads as comforting and affectionate. As with the five hundred, only one of these disciples needs must be male grammatically; I chose to read the other as female, likely a spouse.

WEDNESDAY IN EASTER WEEK

1 Corinthians 15:12–20; Psalm 30:1–5; Luke 24:44–53

1 Corinthians 15:12 Now if Christ is preached as raised from the dead, how can some of
you say there is no resurrection of the dead? 13 For if there is no resurrection of the dead, then
Christ has not been raised; 14 and if Christ has not been raised, then our preaching has been
in vain along with your faith. 15 Then we are even found to be false witnesses of God, because
we bore witness of God that God raised Christ—whom God did not raise if the dead are not
raised. 16 For if the dead are not raised, then Christ has not been raised. 17 And if Christ has
not been raised, your faith is useless and you are yet in your sins. 18 And therefore those who
have died in Christ have been destroyed. 19 If for this life we have only hoped in Christ, we are
of all people most pitiable. 20 But now indeed Christ has been raised from the dead, the first
fruits of those who have died.

Psalm 30

1 I will exalt you, Ark of Safety, because you have pulled me up
and have not let my enemies rejoice over me.
2 Healing One, my God, I cried to you for help,
and you healed me.
3 Ever-Living God, you brought my soul up from Sheol;
you preserved my life from descent to the Pit.

4 Sing praises to the FAITHFUL GOD, you her faithful;
give thanks remembering her holiness.
5 For her fury is a moment, her favor a lifetime.
Weeping may pass the night, yet in the morning, joy.

Luke 24:44 Jesus said to [the two disciples], "These are my words that I spoke to you while
I was still with you all, because everything must be fulfilled in the teaching of Moses, the
prophets, and the psalms written about me." 45 Then he opened their minds to understand
the scriptures. 46 Then he said to them, "So it is written, the Messiah is to suffer and to rise
from the dead the third day, 47 and repentance and forgiveness of sins is to be preached in his
name to all nations, beginning from Jerusalem. 48 You are witnesses of these things. 49 Now
look! I am sending you the promise of my Abba. You all stay in the city until you have been
clothed with power from on high."

50 Then Jesus led them out as far as Bethany, and lifting his hands, he blessed them.
51 While he was blessing them, Jesus retreated from them and was carried up into heaven.
52 And they worshiped him, and returned to Jerusalem with great joy; 53 and they were in the
temple every day blessing God.

PROCLAMATION

Text Notes

Both of the readings from 1 Corinthians 15 and Luke 24 continue from the previous day, even though not contiguous.

Preaching Prompts

People have grappled with the Jesus story from the very beginning. Even in a world in which miracles were accepted uncritically, some of the claims about Jesus were astounding—a word that occurs often in the Gospels. As now, there were those for whom a literal resurrection was difficult to believe. Paul's rebuttal draws a straight line from the resurrection to the forgiveness of our sins and our salvation.

The wonder and incredulity of the disciples on the Emmaus road contrasts with doctrinal disputers in Corinth. The disciples are overjoyed and accept the miracle, though they do not seem to understand it. Jesus calls them back to the Jewish scriptures, somewhat fewer than would eventually be canonized: Torah, Prophets, and only psalms from the third traditional division, Writings. (In the Hebrew Bible the Prophets include Joshua, Judges, Samuel, Kings, Isaiah, Jeremiah, Ezekiel, and the Minor Prophets. The Writings include everything else not in the Torah; Daniel is not a prophet in Jewish tradition.) In other passages, the scriptures consist of the Torah (Law) and Prophets suggesting the Writings were still in formation (see Matthew 22:40; Luke 16:16; Acts 13:15; Romans 3:21).

Physical salvation is the theme of the psalm as it is all of Easter Week. Deliverance, salvation, and resurrection are available to all without regard for gender or its performance. However, the scriptures and their writers will try to make these stories make sense in the world they knew with all of its hierarchies in place for the most part.

THURSDAY IN EASTER WEEK

1 Corinthians 15:35–44; Psalm 49:5–15; John 21:4–14

1 Corinthians 15:35 Now then, someone will ask, "How are the dead raised? In what kind
of body do they come?" 36 Fool! What you plant is not brought to life unless it dies. 37 Now
about what you plant, you do not plant the body that will be, but a bare seed, for example,
wheat or of some other grain. 38 Yet God gives it a body as God wills, and to each kind of
seed its own body. 39 Not all flesh is the same flesh, rather there is one flesh for human beings,
another for animals, another for birds, and another for fish. 40 Yet there are heavenly bodies and earthly bodies, while the glory of the heavenly is one kind, and that of the earthly is
another. 41 There is one glory of the sun and another glory of the moon, yet another glory of
the stars, each star even differs in glory.

42 So it is with the resurrection of the dead. What is planted is perishable; what is raised
is imperishable. 43 It is planted in dishonor; it is raised in glory. It is sown in weakness; it is
raised in power. 44 It is planted a physical body; it is raised a spiritual body. If there is a physical body, there is also a spiritual body.

Psalm 49:5–15

5 Why should I fear in evil days,
when iniquity at my heels surrounds me?
6 Those who trust in their wealth
and praise of the abundance of their riches?
7 Certainly, it cannot redeem a person,
or can one give [it] to God as their ransom.
8 For the redemption-price of a soul is costly,
they come to an end, forever.
9 Shall one live eternally
and never see the Pit?
10 For when one sees the wise, they die;
the foolish and ignorant perish together
and leave to others their wealth.
11 Their graves are their homes for all time,
their dwelling places from generation to generation,
though they put their name on lands.

12 Humanity will not recline in grandeur;
rather they are like the animals that perish.
13 This is the way of the foolish,
those pleased with their own words. *Selah*
14 Like sheep they are set for Sheol;
Death shall be their shepherd.
The upright shall rule over them until the morning,
and their form shall waste away;
Sheol shall be their abode.
15 But God will ransom my soul,
for from the grasp of Sheol she will take me. *Selah*

John 21:4 Now when morning came, Jesus stood on the beach; but the disciples did not
know that it was Jesus. 5 Jesus said to them, "Children, do you have any fish prepared?"
They answered him, "No." 6 Then he said to them, "Cast the net to the right side of the
boat, and you will find some." So, they cast it, and they were not able to drag it in because
of the abundance of fish. 7 That disciple whom Jesus loved said to Peter, "It is the Messiah!"
When Simon Peter heard that it was the Messiah, he put on some clothes, for he was naked,
and threw himself into the sea. 8 But the other disciples came in the boat, dragging the net
full of fish, for they were not far from the land, only two hundred cubits [about a hundred
yards] off.

9 As soon as they turned back to land, they saw a fire there, with fish laid over it, and
bread. 10 Jesus said to them, "Bring some of the fish that you have just caught." 11 So Simon
Peter went up and dragged the net to land, full of large fish—one hundred fifty-three—and
with so many the net was not torn. 12 Jesus said to them, "Come and eat." Now none of the
disciples dared to ask him, "Who are you?" because they knew it was the Messiah. 13 Jesus
came and took the bread and gave it to them, and did the same with the fish. 14 Now this was
the third time that Jesus appeared to the disciples after he was raised from the dead.

PROCLAMATION

Text Notes

There are a couple of phrases in the psalm, in verses 7 and 13, that are difficult to translate. I have drawn from the translations of the Jewish Publication Society and Robert Alter, *The Hebrew Bible: A Translation with Commentary*.

Preaching Prompts

Resurrection is the foundation of the Gospel Easter story and even when proclaimed as a certainty, holds a full share of mystery. It seems unreasonable to expect folk to have no questions or to mock them, or call them names (i.e., "fool" in 1 Corinthians 15:36), for asking. The Gospel story, resurrection included, is strong enough to bear the weight of our questions, and God, unlike the apostle, is eternally patient with them.

The psalmist trusts in God for her deliverance, recognizing that wealth is of no avail and there is no price that can be placed on a human life.

John 21 offers a potential narrative response to the questioners mocked in the Epistle. What kind of body do the resurrected have? In this story, one that is solid and tangible, capable of mundane tasks like cooking. One that was recognizable to those who had known the formerly dead. While not putting an end to questions about the resurrection, John 21 demonstrates that the resurrected Jesus has the same demeanor and shows the same care for his disciples that he did in his previous life.

While some forms of fishing were likely performed by women or men, the drag-net fishing indicated by the text, along with Peter's casual nudity, suggest only male disciples were present. This is in keeping with the theme that the male disciples needed to be convinced.

FRIDAY IN EASTER WEEK

Romans 6:5–11; Psalm 86:8–13; Mark 16:9–15, 19–20

Romans 6:5 For if we have been united in a death like Christ's, we will certainly be so in the
resurrection. 6 This we know, that our old self was crucified with him so that the body of sin
might be destroyed, and we might no longer be enslaved to sin. 7 The woman or man who
has died is freed from sin. 8 But if we have died with Christ, we believe that we shall also live
with him. 9 We know that Christ, being raised from the dead, will never die; death no longer
has dominion over him. 10 For dying, he died once to sin, in living, he lives to God. 11 So also
should you consider yourselves dead to sin and alive to God in Christ Jesus.

Psalm 86:8–13

8 There is none like you among the gods, MOST HIGH,
and there are no works like yours.
9 All the nations that you made shall come,
and they shall bow down before you Sovereign One,
and they shall glorify your name.
10 For you are great and work wonders;
you are God, you alone.
11 Teach me, HOLY ONE, your way,
that I may walk in your truth;
let my heart be undivided to revere your name.
12 I give thanks to you, Sovereign One my God, with my whole heart,
and I shall glorify your name forever.

13 For great is your faithful love toward me;
you have delivered my soul from the depths of Sheol.

Mark 16:9 Now after he rose early on the first day of the week, Jesus appeared first to Mary
Magdalene from whom he had cast out seven demons. [10] She went out and she told the ones
mourning and weeping who had been with him. [11] But when they heard that he lives and was
seen by her, they did not believe. [12] After this Jesus was made known in another form to two
of [the disciples] as they were walking into the countryside. [13] And they went back and told
the rest, but they did not believe them. [14] Now later on, while they were sitting at the table,
Jesus appeared to the eleven themselves and he rebuked their lack of faith and stubbornness,
because they did not believe those [the women] who saw Jesus after he had risen. [15] Then
Jesus said to them, "Go into all the world and proclaim the good news to all creation."

[19] And then Jesus the Messiah, after he had spoken to them, was taken up into heaven and
sat down at the right hand of God. [20] And they went out proclaiming the good news everywhere. The Messiah worked with them and confirmed the message by the signs that followed.

PROCLAMATION

Text Notes

Mark's Gospel has a variety of endings that shock many Bible readers who think the scriptures were unchanged from inception. They are missing from the oldest most reliable manuscripts, Sinaticus and Vaticanus, and from more than a hundred Syriac, Coptic, and Armenian manuscripts; in many of the manuscripts in which they are found, they are set off with notations equivalent to an asterisk denoting lack of originality. There is near universal acceptance that verses 1–8 are original. Some scholars further subdivide the remaining verses. The Church (across denominations) treats them as authoritative to varying degrees and they do appear in an abridged form in the lectionary of the Episcopal Church.

In Mark 16:12, the description of Jesus appearing in "another form" to two disciples "walking in the countryside" closely resembles the Emmaus Road story in Luke 24. In verse 14, Jesus "reprimands" or "rebukes" the (presumably male) disciples for not believing "those" who proclaimed his resurrection. I have specified "the women" here, because they were "those" who were not believed: Mary Magdalene, another Mary, and Salome in Mark 16:1.

Preaching Prompts

Whether in spite of or because of being part of the addendum to Mark, 16:14 includes a strong rebuke by Jesus for those who did not believe the gospel of his resurrection from the dead preached by women, perhaps because it was preached by women. It still speaks to those who discount the words and ministries of women. The disciples are sent to preach to all creation and Jesus won't let them be treated like the women: he will work with them, verse 20, providing signs to confirm the message. For the women and the few male disciples, his appearances were the sign. And for some, women and men, surely the women's witness was sufficient. It would have been enough for children. The signs and ascension in verse 19 point to a new reality: Jesus will not continue to appear as he had. And at some point, the signs will come to an end as well. All that will remain will be the proclamation of the gospel by women and men and the faith of those who choose to believe.

SATURDAY IN EASTER WEEK

Acts 13:29–38; Psalm 116:1–9; Matthew 28:8–10, 16–20

Acts 13:29 Now when they had finished doing everything written about him, they took
him down from the tree and laid him in a tomb. 30 But God raised him from the dead. 31 He
appeared for many days to those [women and men] who traveled with him from Galilee to
Jerusalem, and they are now his witnesses to the people. 32 And we proclaim the good news
to you that what God promised to our mothers and fathers 33 God has fulfilled for us, their
children, by raising Jesus; as also it is written in the second psalm,

> "*You are my Son; today I have begotten you.*"

34 Because God raised him from the dead, never to return to corruption, God spoke thusly,

> "*I will give you the holy promises of David.*"

35 Therefore David has also said in another psalm,

> "*You will not let your holy one experience corruption.*"

36 For indeed David, after he had served the purpose of God in his own generation, died, and
was placed beside his mothers and fathers, and experienced corruption; 37 yet the one whom
God raised up saw no corruption. 38 Let it be known to you therefore, my sisters and brothers,
that through this man forgiveness of sins is proclaimed to you.

Psalm 116:1–9

1 I love the God Who Hears,
for God has heard my voice and my supplications.
2 For she opens her ear to me,
whatever day I call.
3 The snares of death encompassed me;
the torments of Sheol took hold of me,
I found distress and sorrow.

4 Then I called on the name of the HOLY ONE OF OLD:
"HOLY ONE, please, save my life!"
5 Gracious is the FOUNT OF JUSTICE, and righteous;
our God loves [like a mother].
6 The FAITHFUL ONE protects the simple;
I was brought low and she saved me.
7 Return, O my soul, to your rest,
for the GRACIOUS ONE has dealt generously with you.
8 For you have delivered my soul from death,
my eyes from tears,
my feet from stumbling.
9 I shall walk before the AUTHOR OF LIFE
in the lands of the living.

Matthew 28:8 So the women left the tomb quickly with fear and great joy and ran to tell his
disciples the news. 9 Then all of a sudden Jesus met them and said, "Shalom!" And they came
to him, took hold of his feet, and bowed down worshipping him. 10 Then Jesus said to them,
"Fear not; go and tell my sisters and brothers to go to Galilee; there they will see me."

16 Now the eleven disciples went to Galilee, to the mountain to which Jesus sent them.
17 And when they saw him, they bowed down worshipping him; but some doubted. 18 Then
Jesus came and said to them, "All authority in heaven and on earth has been given to me. 19 Go
therefore and make disciples of all nations, baptizing them in the name of the Father and of
the Son and of the Holy Spirit, 20 and teaching them to obey everything that I have commanded you. Now look, I am with you always, to the end of the age."

PROCLAMATION

Text Notes

In Acts 13:33–35, Paul cites Psalm 2:7, Isaiah 55:3, and Psalm 16:10 from the LXX (note the psalms are known to be numbered while chapter and verse numbers would not be added for centuries). Paul is in synagogue addressing "Men of Israel, and others who fear God." Women were not excluded from synagogue and would have also been present. "God-fearers" was often language for Gentile worshippers. Paul's language, "men" and "brothers," excludes women and renders them invisible in this passage. Are women to understand themselves included or is Paul specifically addressing men exclusively, figuring they'll pass the good news on to the women in their lives? I read his language as customarily androcentric and patriarchal, as is the bulk of scripture, and make women visible as appropriate.

In Matthew 28:8, the word translated as "authority" also means "power." In verse 10, Jesus tells the women to tell his "siblings" to go to meet him in Galilee. That certainly includes the eleven male disciples but not necessarily limited to them. At some point, the eleven receive other more specific instructions to go to a particular mountain indicated by verse 16.

Preaching Prompts

In Acts 13, Paul tells the Gospel story, adding his own proof-texting exegesis of the Hebrew Scriptures to "prove" that Jesus, who was nothing like the warrior messiah many expected and some scriptures predicted, was nevertheless the fulfillment of the scriptures. Paul is demonstrating the flexibility of the scriptures for reinterpretation in every age; rereading them in light of Jesus yields tantalizing and suggestive readings, which now with full knowledge of the Jesus story seem specifically predictive. These are particularly Christian ways of reading the Hebrew Bible. It is important to remember that Jewish readings, even of passages considered messianic, do not always focus on a single individual. Sometimes the entire nation is the messianic figure, sometimes an individual or specific ruler, sometimes an unknown individual.

In Psalm 116:5, God's love is articulated with the word whose root is "womb," often unhelpfully translated as "merciful" or "compassion."

The Gospel reading combines the resurrection appearances to the women, Mary Magdalene and the "other" Mary, and to the eleven remaining disciples. The women believe immediately and run with joy to tell the news. They are also afraid, perhaps of what this might mean, potentially more violence. The male disciples also bowed down before Jesus, but they do not yet believe. The story of the church will soon become their story as they proclaim the resurrection they first doubted. It might be worthwhile to imagine the evangelism of the women, how the women and men they proclaimed the good news to also became part of the new and expanding Church.

SECOND SUNDAY OF EASTER

Acts 1:3–5, 12–14 (or Sirach 1:14–20); Psalm 111; 1 John 5:1–6; John 20:19–31

The Sundays of Easter traditionally have a choice of readings from the Hebrew Bible and Acts for the first lesson. This lectionary will offer reflections on Wisdom as the alternate to selections from Acts.

Acts 1:3 Jesus presented himself to them, living, after his suffering through many convincing proofs, by appearing to them forty days and speaking about the reign of God. [4] And staying with them, Jesus commanded them not to leave Jerusalem, rather to wait there for the promise of the Faithful One, "what you heard from me. [5] For John baptized with water, but you will be baptized with the Holy Spirit not many days from this one."

12 Then they returned to Jerusalem from the mount called Olivet, which is near Jeru-
salem, a sabbath day's journey away. 13 And when they entered the city, they went upstairs
to the room where they were staying, Peter, and John, and James, and Andrew, Philip and
Thomas, Bartholomew and Matthew, James son of Alphaeus, and Simon the Zealot, and
Judas son of James. 14 All these were persevering in prayer together with women, including
Mary the mother of Jesus, as well as his [sisters and] brothers.

Sirach 1:14–20

14 The beginning of wisdom is awe of the Holy One;
with the faithful in the womb she was created, together with them.
15 With humankind she built her roost, an eternal foundation,
and among their descendants, she will be trusted.
16 The fullness of wisdom is to reverence the Holy One;
she inebriates mortals with her fruits.
17 Every house of theirs she fills whole with desirable things,
and their storehouses with her produce.
18 A crown of wisdom is the awe of the Holy One,
sprouting peace and wholeness, healing.
19 Skill and knowledge, understanding she rained down,
and she exalted the reputation of those who hold her.
20 The root of wisdom is to reverence the Holy One,
and her branches are length of days.

Psalm 111

1 Praise the LIVING GOD!
I will give thanks to the ONE GOD with my whole heart,
in the assembly of the upright, in the congregation.
2 Great are the works of GOD,
contemplated by all who delight in them.
3 Splendor and majesty are her work,
and her righteousness stands forever.
4 She has gained renown for her wonderful deeds;
the WOMB OF LIFE is gracious and abounds in mother-love.
5 She provides fresh meat for those who revere her;
she remembers her covenant perpetually.
6 She has declared the strength of her works to her people,
giving them the heritage of the nations.
7 The works of her hands are truth and justice;
trustworthy are all her precepts.

8 They stand fast forever and ever,
Executed in truth and uprightness.
9 She sent redemption to her people;
she has ordained her covenant forever.
Holy and awesome is her name.
10 Awe of the AGELESS GOD is the beginning of wisdom;
all those who do have good understanding.
Her praise endures forever.

1 John 5:1 Everyone who believes that Jesus is the Messiah is born of God, and everyone who
loves the parent loves the child of the parent. 2 By this we know that we love the children of God,
when we love God and undertake God's commandments. 3 For the love of God is this, that we
keep God's commandments. And God's commandments are not difficult, 4 for anything born of
God conquers the world. And this is the victory that conquers the world, our faith. 5 Who is it
that conquers the world but the one who believes that Jesus is the Son of God?
6 This is the one who came through water and blood, Jesus Christ, not through the water
only but through the water and the blood. And the Spirit is the one that testifies, for the Spirit
is the truth.

John 20:19 When it was evening on that day, the first of the week, and the doors of the
house where the disciples were closed for fear of the Judeans, Jesus came and stood in their midst
and said to them, "Peace be with you all." 20 And having said this, Jesus showed them his hands
and his side, and then the disciples rejoiced when they saw the Messiah. 21 Jesus said to them
again, "Peace be with you all, just as the Living God has sent me, so I send you all." 22 When Jesus
had said this, he breathed on them and said to them, "Receive the Holy Spirit; 23 if you forgive
the sins of any, they are forgiven them; if you retain the sins of any, they are retained."
24 But Thomas, one of the twelve who was called Didymus (the Twin) was not with them
when Jesus came. 25 So the other disciples told him, "We have seen the Messiah." But he said
to them, "Unless I see the mark of the nails in his hands, and put my finger in the mark of the
nails and my hand in his side, I will not believe."
26 And within eight days his disciples were again in the house, and Thomas was with
them. Jesus came, though the doors were shut, and stood among them and said, "Peace be
with you all." 27 Then he said to Thomas, "Put your finger here and look at my hands. Bring
your hand and put it in my side and do not doubt, rather believe." 28 Thomas answered him,
saying, "My Savior and my God!" 29 Jesus said to him, "Was it because you have seen me that
you believed? Blessed are those who have not seen and yet believe."
30 Now Jesus did many other signs in the presence of his disciples, which are not written
in this book. 31 But these are written that you may come to believe Jesus is the Messiah, the
Son of God, and that through believing you may have life in his name.

PROCLAMATION

Text Notes

In Acts 1:12 "a sabbath's day journey" indicates the amount of walking one could do on Sabbath; across time the distance has ranged from one-third to two-thirds of a mile with variables such as whether one is pasturing animals and whether one is still in a city (determined by how far apart are the houses).

In Sirach 1:14 and 18 and Psalm 111:10 I use "awe" rather than the more common "fear" of God; the underlying word includes both as well as reverence for the infinitive form in Sirach 1:16 and 20. Given these options, whether a translator chooses awe/reverence or fear speaks to one's theology, perhaps more so than to who God is. Wisdom is more than personified in Sirach 1. She builds a nest in verse 15, suggesting avian qualities.

Preaching Prompts

In Acts 12:14 women and men who followed Jesus pray together, "persevering in" or "devote themselves to" prayer until Pentecost. Only Mary the mother of Jesus is named among the women. The mention of Jesus's siblings makes it possible that his sisters are there. All that is known of his sisters is that there is more than one and they came with his Mama to get him when they heard he was in trouble, see Matthew 13:56 and Mark 6:3. Other likely candidates are the women who proclaimed his resurrection, Mary Magdalene, the "other" Mary (Matthew 28:1), Mary the mother of James (who may be the former), and Salome (Mark 16:1), Joanna, and the unnamed women in Luke 24:10, and perhaps women who followed and bankrolled Jesus like Susanna (Luke 8:3). These women will be part of the Pentecost spectacle, which Peter will explain in Acts 2:17 by quoting Joel 2:28 where "daughters and sons prophesy."

The identity and divinity of Wisdom, which is fluid in the scriptures and in Jewish and Christian exegesis, is elaborated upon in Proverbs 8 and throughout Sirach and the book of Wisdom, which also elaborates upon Proverbs 8. She is identified with God, as an extension or expression of God, as God's first creation, as God's cocreator, as the Torah, as the Word, and with Jesus. She is the welcoming host of a table of riches. And she offers herself as the chief treasure and companion of humankind. In the psalm, reverence for God is the beginning of Wisdom.

The Gospel and Epistle are beginning the transition from Eastertide to Pentecost. Jesus is still confirming his resurrection, appearing to his disciples, not (merely) to cement a doctrine, but to comfort their hearts. He breathes on them the breath of God, the Holy Spirit, strength and companionship for the journey ahead, and in the words of 1 John 5:6, a perpetual witness to that resurrection.

THIRD SUNDAY OF EASTER

Acts 1:6–8 (or Sirach 4:11–16); Psalm 34:1–14; Hebrews 5:7–14; John 5:25–29

Acts 1:6 When they [the disciples], came together, they asked Jesus, "Rabbi, is this the time
when you will restore sovereignty to Israel?" 7 He replied, "It is not for you to know the times
or seasons that the Creator has set through divine authority. 8 But you will receive power
when the Holy Spirit comes upon you, and you will be my witnesses in Jerusalem, in all Judea
and Samaria, and to the end of the earth."

Sirach 4:11–16

11 Wisdom exalts her children
and takes in those who seek her.
12 The one who loves her loves life,
and those who turn to her early in the morning are filled with joy.
13 The one who takes her hand inherits glory,
and the Holy One blesses the place she enters.
14 Those who worship her worship the Holy One;
the Holy One loves those who love her.
15 The one who obeys her will judge the nations,
and the one who attends to her will dwell securely.
16 If they are faithful, they will inherit her;
and she will be the heritage of their descendants.

Psalm 34:1–14

1 I will bless She Who is God at all times;
her praise shall ever be in my mouth.
2 I will glory in She Who is Strength;
let the humble hear and rejoice.
3 Proclaim with me the greatness of She Who is Exalted
and let us exalt her Name together.
4 I sought She Who Saves, and she answered me
and delivered me out of all my terror.
5 Look upon her and be radiant,
and let not your faces be ashamed.
6 I called in my affliction and She Who Hears heard me
and saved me from all my troubles.
7 The messenger of She Who Saves encompasses those who revere her,
and she will deliver them.
8 Taste and see that She Who is Delight is good;
happy are they who trust in her!

9 Revere SHE WHO IS GOD, you that are her saints,
for those who revere her lack nothing.
10 The young lions suffer want for food and starve,
but those who seek SHE WHO PROVIDES lack no good thing.
11 Come, children, listen to me;
I will teach you the reverence of SHE WHO IS MAJESTY.
12 Who is the woman or man that desires life,
and would love long days to enjoy good?
13 Keep your tongue from evil,
and your lips from speaking deceit.
14 Turn from evil, and do good;
seek peace, and pursue it.

Hebrews 5:7 In the days of his flesh, Jesus offered up prayers and petitions to the one who was able to save him from death, with loud cries and tears, and he was heard because of his reverence. 8 Although he was a Son, he learned obedience through what he suffered; 9 and being made perfect, became the source of eternal salvation for all who obey him. 10 He has been called a high priest according to the order of Melchizedek by God.

11 About this we have more than a word and it is hard to explain because you all have become slow in understanding. 12 Indeed you all ought to be teachers by this time; yet you all need someone to teach you again the foundation elements of the oracles of God. You all need milk, and not solid food. 13 For everyone who consumes milk is unskilled in the word of righteousness, being an infant. 14 But solid food is for the mature, who because of training of their senses practice to distinguish good from evil.

John 5:25 "Truly, truly, I tell you all, the hour is coming, and is now here, when the dead will hear the voice of the Son of God, and those who hear will live. 26 For just as the Living God has life internally, just so God has granted the Son to have life internally. 27 And God has given the Son authority to render justice, because he is the Son of Woman. 28 Do not be astonished at this; for the hour is coming when all who are in their graves will hear his voice
29 and will come out—those who have done good, to the resurrection of life, and those who have done evil, to the resurrection of judgment.

PROCLAMATION

Text Notes

Acts 1 begins by summarizing Jesus's ministry in Luke through instructions given to the apostles in verses 1–3. In the following verses, "they" and "them" seem to refer to a larger group than the first twelve disciples, which becomes clear by verse 14, setting the stage for Pentecost in chapter 2.

The book of Sirach exists in Hebrew and Greek and the Church has tended to use the Greek version corrected against the Hebrew. Given the available Hebrew text is pieced together from various Qumran manuscripts, I will use the Greek as well. Wisdom is personified as a woman and the language used to describe her has implications for women and how they were perceived in the world of the text. In 4:13, one can take wisdom by the hand, grasp, hold, seize, or possess her in the semantic range of the verb *kratōn*. I have eschewed choices that denote violence since there are other legitimate options. In verse 14, synonymous verbs mean both "serve" and "worship." To serve/worship Wisdom is to serve/worship God.

In Hebrews 5:11, "slow" in understanding is also "dull" or "lazy." As a pedagogue, I have chosen the least insulting option (which may well run counter to the aim of the author). In verses 8 and 14, "perfect" and "mature" are the same word, also having the sense of being completed.

In John 5:27, the work of justice is more than passing sentence, rather "judging" or "execute judgment" or "rendering a verdict" are but one dimension of justice work.

Preaching Prompts

In spite of the significant presence of women among Jesus's disciples in Luke, the companion to Acts, particularly at his crucifixion and resurrection, the minimization of women in Acts is surprising and disheartening. Are we to imagine that none of the women from Luke except the Blessed Mother continued with the disciples? The disappearance of women whose names are preserved and appear repeatedly, like Joanna and Mary the mother of James, is perplexing, and the absence of Mary Magdalene is astonishing. That the women who uprooted their lives to follow and support Jesus out of their own means, and in some cases were eyewitnesses to his resurrection, would not make this last trip does not seem credible. In spite of the minimal acknowledgment of women among the disciples and new believers, I read both the disciples and crowds as inclusive even when Peter or Paul addresses the "men of Israel" (see Acts 2:22, 29; 3:12; 5:35; 13:16; 21:28).

The author of Hebrews uses the image of a nursing child—the primary, if not exclusive means of providing infants milk in the era. The child is the new believer, milk, rudiments of the gospel. Who is the nursing mother? Perhaps ultimately God, source of the gospel, but here more likely those who are doing this teaching. Note the author is impatient with the developmental progress of the "children."

In Sirach, Wisdom, who can be read as an extension or expression of God or the Holy Spirit, exalts her children, who seek and serve her. Similarly, the psalmist teaches her children (or students) the reverence of God and rewards of faithfulness. In this Eastertide gospel, God who is worthy of reverence and exaltation shares authority with God's child, the woman-born Jesus to raise the dead in the dual resurrection, to reward and recompense.

FOURTH SUNDAY OF EASTER

Acts 5:12–16 (or Sirach 15:1–6); Psalm 119:97–103; Romans 6:5–11; Matthew 22:23–33

Acts 5:12 Now, many signs and wonders were done among the people through the apostles; they were all together in the Portico of Solomon. 13 None of the others dared to join
them, but the people extolled them. 14 Yet more believers were added to Christ, a multitude of
both women and men. 15 So much so that they even carried the sick into the streets, and laid
them on cots and mats, so that Peter's shadow might overshadow some of them as he passed.
16 Multitudes would also gather from the towns around Jerusalem, bringing the sick and those
tormented by unclean spirits, and they were all made well.

Sirach 15:1–6

1 The one who reveres the Holy One will do this,
the one who embraces the law will embrace Wisdom.
2 She will come to meet them like a mother,
and like a young woman in innocence she will welcome them.
3 She will feed them with the bread of understanding,
and the water of wisdom she will give them to drink.
4 They will be supported by her and not fall,
and will attend her and not be put to shame.
5 She will exalt them above their neighbors,
and in the midst of the assembly she will open their mouths.
6 Joy and a crown of gladness will they find,
and an everlasting name will be their lot.

Psalm 119:97–103

97 How I love your teaching!
All day it is my meditation.
98 Your commandment makes me wiser than my enemies,
for it is always with me.
99 I have more understanding than all my instructors,
for your decrees are my meditation.
100 I understand more than the aged,
for I observe your precepts.
101 I restrain my feet from every evil way,
in order to keep your word.
102 From your decrees I do not turn away,
for you have taught me.

103 How sweet are your words to my taste,
sweeter than honey to my mouth!

Romans 6:5 For if we have been united in a death like Christ's, we will certainly be so in the
resurrection. 6 This we know, that our old self was crucified with him so that the body of sin
might be destroyed, and we might no longer be enslaved to sin. 7 The woman or man who
has died is freed from sin. 8 But if we have died with Christ, we believe that we shall also live
with him. 9 We know that Christ, being raised from the dead, will never die; death no longer
has dominion over him. 10 For dying, he died once to sin; in living, he lives to God. 11 So also
should you consider yourselves dead to sin and alive to God in Christ Jesus.

Matthew 22:23 The same day [that Jesus taught about taxes] some Sadducees came to him,
saying there is no resurrection; and they questioned him, saying, 24 "Teacher, Moses said, 'If a
man dies without having children, his brother shall marry the [widow] woman, and raise up
offspring for his brother.' 25 Now there were seven brothers among us; the first married, and
without having offspring, leaving the woman to his brother. 26 The same for the second, and
the third, to the seventh. 27 After everything the woman died. 28 In the resurrection, then, for
which of the seven will she be wife? For they all had her."

29 Jesus answered them, "You all are wrong, because you know neither the scriptures nor
the power of God. 30 For in the resurrection they neither marry nor are given in marriage,
rather they are like angels in heaven. 31 And about the resurrection of the dead, have you all
not read what was said to you by God, 32 'I am the God of Abraham, the God of Isaac, and the
God of Jacob'? God is God not of the dead, but of the living." 33 And when the crowd heard it,
they were astounded at his teaching.

PROCLAMATION

Text Notes

In Acts 5:13, the "others" in the temple complex would have been other Jews and perhaps Gentiles devoted to the God of Israel. The temple in Jerusalem should be thought of as a campus and not a building; there were multiple interconnected structures on the site. Worship occurred outdoors where the main sacrificial altar was. The primary temple building was entered only by select priests.

In Sirach 15:2, "woman of virginity" from the LXX is understood as "woman/wife of (one's) youth" in two Qumran manuscripts.

The Sadducees cite Deuteronomy 25:5 in Matthew 22:24.

Preaching Prompts

While affirming God is the God of Abraham, Isaac, and Jacob (Matthew 22:32), what is the impact of the claim when including the names of the matriarchs? Can we name them with similar ease? Is it equally true to say God is the God of Hagar, Sarah, Keturah, Rebekah, Rachel, Leah, Bilhah, and Zilpah? Would they make that claim for themselves? Hagar, Bilhah, and Zilpah were enslaved and their surrogacy was not consensual. Bilhah was sexually assaulted by an additional person, and Abraham abandoned Keturah and their children without inheriting them. (For more on them, see my *Womanist Midrash.*) "Marrying and being given in marriage" in verse 30 is framed with women as passive, if not as objects. While their voices are missing, what might the end of such marriages and those endured by their foremothers have meant to them? Might that not be good news?

Romans 6 speaks of the freedom of the believer in generic terms, which I have made explicit for women and men in verse 7. Hindsight makes it easy to see how past generations failed to live in to that freedom. How might Wisdom, mother, sister, beloved, guide us in living into the fullness of resurrection life?

FIFTH SUNDAY OF EASTER

Acts 17:1–4,10–12 (or Wisdom 6:12–19); Psalm 63:1–8; 1 Peter 1:3–9; John 11:17–27

Acts 17:1 Paul and Silas had traveled through Amphipolis and Apollonia. They came to
Thessalonica, where there was a Jewish synagogue. [2] As was his custom Paul went and on
three sabbaths presented to them from the scriptures, [3] explaining and demonstrating it was
necessary for the Messiah to suffer and to rise from the dead: "This is the Messiah, Jesus who I
proclaim to you all." [4] Now, some of [those Jews] were persuaded and joined Paul and Silas, as
did a great many of the devout Greeks and not a few of the prominent women.

[10] Then, the sisters and brothers immediately that night sent Paul and Silas away to
Beroea; when they arrived, they went to the Jewish synagogue. [11] These [persons] were
more high-born and open minded than in Thessalonica; they received the word with great
eagerness. Daily they examined the scriptures to see if these things were so. [12] Thus many
of them therefore believed, including highly respected Greek women and not just a few
[Jewish] men.

Wisdom 6:12–19

12 Luminous and unfading is Wisdom,
and easily discerned by those who love her,
and found by those who seek her.
13 She anticipates those who desire her,
to make herself known in advance.
14 The one who rises early to seek her will not grow weary,
and will find her sitting at the gate.

15 For to fix one's thought on her is perfect understanding,
and the one who remains awake on her account will soon be secure.
16 Those worthy of her she seeks, traveling about,
and in their paths she appears to them, graciously,
and, in every thought she meets them.
17 For her beginning is the true desire for instruction,
and concern for instruction is love of her.
18 Now love of her is keeping her teachings,
and attention to her teachings is assurance of immortality.
19 And immortality brings one near to God.

Psalm 63:1–8

1 God, my God, I seek you, you,
my soul thirsts for you;
my flesh hungers for you,
as in a dry and weary land without water.
2 So in the sanctuary have I beheld you,
seeing your power and glory.
3 Because your faithful love is better than life,
my lips will praise you.
4 Therefore will I bless you by name as long as I live;
while I lift up my hands.
5 As with a rich feast my soul is satisfied,
and with singing lips my mouth will praise you
6 when I recall you upon my bed,
and in the watches of the night meditate on you—
7 for you have been my help—
and in the shadow of your wings I sing for joy.
8 My soul clings to you;
your right hand upholds me.

1 Peter 1:3 Blessed be the God and Father of our Redeemer Jesus Christ who in great mercy
has engendered a new birth for us into a living hope, through the resurrection of Jesus Christ
from the dead, 4 into an inheritance that is incorruptible, undefiled, and unfading, kept in
heaven for you all, 5 who in the power of God are kept through faith for a salvation ready to be
revealed in the end time. 6 In this you rejoice even when necessary for you to suffer various trials, 7 in order that the examination of your faith, more precious than gold, which though perishable is tested by fire, may be found yielding praise and glory and honor when Jesus Christ is
revealed. 8 You have not seen him, yet you love him. You do not see him now, yet you believe
in him and rejoice with a joy glorious and beyond words. 9 You are receiving the completion
of your faith, the salvation of your souls.

John 11:17 When Jesus arrived [in Bethany], he found that for four days Lazarus had already been in the tomb. [18] Now Bethany was near Jerusalem, about two miles away. [19] So, many of the Judeans had come to Martha and Mary to console them about their brother. [20] When Martha heard that Jesus was coming, she met him, however Mary remained at the house. [21] Martha said to Jesus, "Rabbi, if you had been here, my brother would never have died. [22] Yet even now I know that whatever you ask of God, God will give you." [23] Jesus said to her, "Your brother will rise." [24] Martha said to him, "I know that he will rise in the resurrection on the last day." [25] Jesus said to her, "I am the resurrection and the life. The one who believes in me, even though they die, they will live, [26] and everyone who lives and believes in me will never die. Do you believe this?" [27] She said to him, "Yes, Rabbi, I believe that you are the Messiah, the Son of God, the one who comes into the world."

PROCLAMATION

Text Notes

In the world of the text, a "synagogue" is a generic gathering place; it was not yet (nearly) exclusively a place of Jewish worship, hence the need to specify "Jewish" in the text.

"To have words" in Acts 17:2 can mean anything from discussing to disputing; here it is "at" them rather than "with" them, yielding "presented to them." In verse 11, the same word means both "high-born" and the characteristic of being open-minded deriving from that status or accompanying education. While many translations present the women and men as equally high in standing, the adjective is feminine plural and thus refers only to the women; likewise, "Greek" is feminine plural. The men are neither Greek nor of high status. This text is one of very few places where women precede men in the order of their mention.

The second line of Wisdom 6:17 is missing in some manuscripts.

The psalmist "sees" God. While one tradition holds that no one may see God's face and live (Exodus 33:20), a few others see God, like Isaiah (6:1) and Ezekiel (1:1), the elders of Israel in the wilderness (Exodus 24:11), and this anonymous psalmist. Job hopes to see God in Job 19:26.

Preaching Prompts

The new believers in Acts 17:4 include women and men from the Jewish community and Greeks who worship or study with them. It is not clear if the prominent women are prominent in the synagogue and therefore Jewish, or prominent in the Greek city of Thessalonica and therefore more likely to be Greek. Prominent women in the synagogue could include women in leadership, including of the synagogue itself. Bernadette Brooten has demonstrated conclusively that women served as leader of the synagogue (through inscriptions with names and titles in *Women Leaders in the Ancient Synagogue*).

Paul's weekly attendance at synagogue in 17:2 is customary; he is still Jewish and his faith in Jesus is not regarded as a conversion. It will be centuries before Judaism and Christianity were regarded as incompatible by both communities.

Martha's statement to Jesus in John 11:21 is stronger than it has often been translated. Not "my brother would not have died," but "my brother would *never* have died." That same "never" is included by Jesus in his response, "Everyone who lives and believes in me will never die."

SIXTH SUNDAY OF EASTER

Acts 17:22–34 (or Sirach 14:20–27); Psalm 19:7–10; Philippians 3:7–11; Matthew 27:45–54

Acts 17:22 Now Paul stood in the center of the Areopagus and said, "Athenians, I see in
everything how devout you are. 23 For passing through and regarding objects of your worship, I found an altar with the inscription, 'To an unknown god.' What, therefore, you all
worship as unknown, this is what I proclaim to you: 24 The God who made the world and
everything in it, the one who is Sovereign of heaven and earth, does not live in temples
made by human hands. 25 Neither is God served by human hands because of needing anything, since God gives to all life and breath and all things. 26 From one person God made
all nations, all persons [women, men, and children], to inhabit the face of the earth and
God ordered seasons and the boundaries of their habitation, 27 that they would search for
God and perhaps reach for God and find God, yet indeed God is not far from any one of
us. 28 For 'In God we live and move and have our being'; just as some among your poets have
said, 'For we too are the offspring God.'

29 "Since we are the offspring of God, we ought not to think that the divine is like gold, or
silver, or stone, an image formed by the craft and creativity of women and men. 30 At one time
God overlooked ignorance; now God commands all women and men everywhere to repent.
31 For God has fixed a day on which God intends to judge the world in righteousness through
a man whom God has appointed, giving assurance to all by raising him from the dead."

32 They heard of the resurrection of the dead. Some scoffed, yet others said, "We will
hear you again about this." 33 Thus Paul left from their midst. 34 Now some joined him,
believing, including Dionysius the Areopagite and a woman named Damaris, as well as others
with them.

Sirach 14:20–27

20 Happy is the woman or man who meditates on Wisdom
and who in understanding enters discussions.
21 The one who reflects on her ways in their heart
will also ponder her mysteries.

22 Pursue her like a hunter,
and in her paths, wait.
23 The one who peers through her windows
will also listen at her doors.
24 The one who encamps near her house
will also secure a tent-peg to her walls.
25 The one who pitches his tent at her hand,
will lodge in a good-lodging place.
26 They will place their children under her shelter,
and under her boughs will encamp.
27 They will be sheltered by her from heat,
and in her glory will reside.

Psalm 19:7–10

7 The teaching of the HOLY ONE OF OLD is perfect,
restoring the soul;
the decrees of the FOUNT OF WISDOM are trustworthy,
making wise the simple.
8 The precepts of the ALL-KNOWING GOD are right,
rejoicing the heart;
the commandment of the FIRE OF SINAI is clear,
enlightening the eyes.
9 The reverence of the MOST HIGH is pure,
standing forever;
the judgments of the JUST ONE are true
and righteous altogether.
10 They are more desired than gold,
than much fine gold;
sweeter than honey,
and drippings of the honeycomb.

Philippians 3:7 Whatever gains are mine, these things, because of Christ, I regard as loss.
8 More than that, I regard everything as loss because of the excellency of knowing Christ Jesus
my Savior, for his sake I have suffered loss of all things, and regard them as trash, in order that
I may gain Christ 9 and be found in him, not having my own righteousness that comes from
the law, but one that comes through faith in Christ, righteousness from God built on faith.
10 I want to know Christ and the power of Christ's resurrection and the sharing of his sufferings, shaped by his death, 11 that I might in some way attain the resurrection from the dead.

Matthew 27:45 From the sixth hour [of the day, or noon], darkness came over the whole
land until the ninth hour [of the day, about three in the afternoon]. 46 And about the ninth

hour [three o'clock] Jesus cried with a loud voice, "*Eli, Eli, lema sabachthani?*" that is, "*My God, my God, why have you forsaken me?*" [47] When some of the bystanders heard it, they said, "This man is calling for Elijah." [48] And immediately one of them ran and got a sponge, filled it with vinegary wine, put it on a stick, and gave it to him to drink. [49] But the others said, "Hold back, let us see if Elijah will come to save him." [50] Then Jesus cried again with a loud voice and relinquished his spirit. [51] Then, look! The curtain of the temple was torn from top to bottom in two. And the earth was shaken, and the rocks were split. [52] And the tombs were opened, and many bodies of the saints who had fallen asleep were raised. [53] Then after his resurrection they came out of the tombs and entered the holy city and appeared to many. [54] Now when the centurion and those with him, who were standing guard over Jesus, saw the earthquake and what took place, they were terrified and said, "Truly this man was God's Son!"

PROCLAMATION

Text Notes

As is common in Acts, Paul limits his address to men, "You men of Athens . . ." using the gendered term rather than the inclusive term for humanity in 17:22. His rhetorical choices did not keep women from joining the developing church. In verse 34, the text says that "men" joined becoming believers, including Dionysius (a male name) and "a woman named Damaris" (and others). I understand that "men" to be inclusive in meaning though not in form, like "mankind," and that there were other women among the new believers in Athens other than Damaris.

The "sharing" of Christ's suffering in Philippians 3:10 is an intimate thing given the semantic range of *koinōnia*: "fellowship," "communion," and "marital intimacy."

In Matthew 27:50 Jesus relinquishes his *pneuma*, "spirit" or "breath."

Preaching Prompts

Paul seems to argue against the temple tradition of his ancestors in Acts 17:24, yet the temple remains a place of prayer for him (Acts 22:17). Paul also continued to observe festivals at the temple, passing up a trip to Ephesus to observe the Festival of Weeks, Shavuoth in Hebrew, Pentecost in Greek, in Acts 20:16. His remarks more likely reflect the postfall (of Jerusalem) theology, that God was absent from the temple during and after the Babylonian decimation as seen by Ezekiel (10:4, 18-19; 11:23) and not confined or limited to the temple.

Similarly, Sirach 14:20 says, "Happy is the man who . . ." Given some of Sirach's almost comedic misogyny in other passages, such as lamenting the birth of a daughter (22:3), it is unlikely he considered women contemplating wisdom like his literary male subject. Yet looking beyond the confines of his culture, there is no reason to exclude them.

The readings from Acts, Philippians, and Matthew extol the resurrection of Jesus and point to its impact on the world around them. Indeed, the saints at rest in Matthew 27:52 were raised at the moment of Jesus's death, before he himself was raised. Before attaining the resurrection, Sirach 14 and Psalm 19 offer a life enriched by Wisdom and the Torah, teaching, of God.

FEAST OF THE ASCENSION

Acts 1:1–11; Psalm 24; Revelation 3:20–22; Luke 24:46–53

Acts 1:1 In the first writing, I worked on, Theophilus, everything Jesus did and taught from
the beginning 2 until the day he instructed the apostles whom he had chosen through the Holy
Spirit and was taken up to heaven. 3 Jesus presented himself to them, living, after his suffering
through many convincing proofs, by appearing to them forty days and speaking about the reign
of God. 4 And staying with them, Jesus commanded them not to leave Jerusalem, rather to wait
there for the promise of the Faithful God, "what you heard from me." 5 For John baptized with
water, but you will be baptized with the Holy Spirit not many days from this one."

6 When they [the disciples], came together, they asked Jesus, "Rabbi, is this the time
when you will restore sovereignty to Israel?" 7 He replied, "It is not for you to know the times
or seasons that the Sovereign God has set through divine authority. 8 But you will receive
power when the Holy Spirit comes upon you, and you will be my witnesses in Jerusalem, in all
Judea and Samaria, and to the end of the earth."

9 And saying this, as they were watching Jesus was taken up, and a cloud took him out
of their sight. 10 While they were gazing up toward heaven Jesus was going and suddenly two
in white robes stood by them. 11 They said, "Galileans, why are you standing looking up into
heaven? This Jesus, who has been taken up from you into heaven, will come in the way as you
saw him go into heaven."

Psalm 24

1 To the CREATOR OF ALL belongs the earth and all that fills her,
the world, and those who dwell in her.
2 For God upon the seas has founded her,
and on the rivers has established her.
3 Who shall ascend the hill of the HOLY ONE?
And who shall stand in God's holy place?
4 The woman or man who has clean hands and pure hearts,
who does not lift up their [hands] to what is false,
and do not swear deceitfully on their souls.
5 [Instead] they will lift up a blessing from the FAITHFUL GOD,
and what is right from the God of their salvation.

6 Such is the generation of those who seek God,
who seek the face of the God of Rebekah. *Selah*
7 Lift up your heads, you gates!
and be lifted up, you everlasting doors!
that the One of glory may come in.
8 Who is the One of glory?
The FIRE OF SINAI, strong and mighty,
the GOD WHO IS MAJESTY, mighty in battle.
9 Lift up your heads, you gates!
and be lifted up, you everlasting doors!
that the One of glory may come in.
10 Who is this One of glory?
The COMMANDER of heaven's legions,
God is the One of glory. *Selah*

Revelation 3:20 Look! I stand at the door and knock. If you hear my voice and open the door, I will come in to you and dine with you, and you with me. [21] To the one who conquers I will give a place with me on my throne, just as I myself conquered and sat down with my Abba on God's throne. [22] Let anyone who has an ear listen to what the Spirit is saying to the churches."

Luke 24:46 Then Jesus said to them, "So it is written, the Messiah is to suffer and to rise from the dead the third day, [47] and repentance and forgiveness of sins is to be preached in his name to all nations, beginning from Jerusalem. [48] You are witnesses of these things. [49] Now look! I am sending you the promise of my Abba. You all stay in the city until you have been clothed with power from on high." [50] Then Jesus led them out as far as Bethany, and lifting his hands, he blessed them. [51] While he was blessing them, Jesus retreated from them and was carried up into heaven. [52] And they bowed down and worshiped him, and returned to Jerusalem with great joy; [53] and they were in the temple every day blessing God.

PROCLAMATION

Text Notes

The divine beings in Acts 1:10 are described as "men" using the human term. Curiously, there are no female divine beings, messengers, angels, etc., in the canon. It is not clear whether women are present at the Ascension, obscured by masculine grammar. If they are not present, it is worth asking why not when women have been the birthing womb and companion witnesses, participants in and preachers of the entire Christ story. It is tempting to say the women were out in the world proclaiming the gospel while the men still needed one more sign. Yet, there were women with these very men (who are identified as the remaining apostles by name in Acts 1:13). If they were not with them at the Ascension, how did they learn of the meeting place? Since they seemed to have arrived at the same time, they could not have been very far. The texts and the cultures of the biblical world collude to minimize and erase women.

In Psalm 24:1–2 I have retained the feminine grammatical gender of the earth, since it fits well with the contemporary notion of earth as mother. In verse 6, "the God of Rebekah" replaces "the God of Jacob."

Preaching Prompt

Chronologically, the gospel for the Feast of the Ascension goes before the first reading from Acts. It may be useful to reread the Acts account of the Ascension *after* the gospel, perhaps at the beginning of the sermon (if tacking it on to the gospel seems like liturgical heresy). The gospel points to the Ascension in Acts 1, and Acts 1 points to Pentecost, coming soon in the next chapter.

In the Ascension the glory of the resurrection ratchets up another level. The risen Christ appears to followers—addressed as "men" but possibly inclusive—and prepares the burgeoning church for the baptism of the Holy Spirit. The psalm makes clear that God is the One of glory and only the pure-hearted can stand in her presence. The multiple Ascension accounts highlight the divinity of the post-Ascension Christ. Revelation 3 reminds us that the divine, risen, and ascended Christ is not so far away that he cannot come to us. He can and will still meet us at the table; for the Church that is primarily in the Eucharist. Christ also comes to us in communion with one another. That communion, whether at the Eucharist or beyond is communal, not hierarchal, though the scriptures and their authors will continue to assert ancient hierarchies, particularly along class and gender lines.

SEVENTH SUNDAY OF EASTER

Acts 3:18–26 (or Sirach 51:13–21); Psalm 27:1–2, 4–5, 7, 10, 13–14; 1 Peter 3:13–22; Luke 14:7–14

Acts 3:18 In this way [through Jesus] what God had foretold through all the prophets, women and men alike, that God's Messiah would suffer, God has fulfilled.
19 Repent therefore, and turn around that your sins may be wiped out,
20 so that seasons of refreshing may come from the presence of the Most High, and that God may send the Messiah appointed for you all, Jesus,
21 whom it is necessary that heaven receive until the time of the restoration of all things that God announced long ago through women and men, God's holy prophets.
22 Indeed, Moses said, '*The* HOLY ONE *your God will raise up for you all from your own kin a prophet like me. Heed the whole of whatever the prophet speaks to you all.*
23 *And it will be that everyone who does not listen to that prophet will be utterly rooted out of the people.*'

[24] And all the prophets, male and female, from Samuel and those after him, as many as have
spoken, also proclaimed these days. [25] You are the daughters and sons of the prophets and of
the covenant that God gave to your mothers and fathers, saying to Abraham, 'Now in your
descendants all the families of the earth shall be blessed.' [26] First of all, when God raised
up God's child, God sent him to you all, to bless you all by turning each of you from your
wicked ways."

Sirach 51:13 While I was still young, before I wandered,
I sought Wisdom openly in my prayer.
14 Before the temple I petitioned about her,
and until the end I will search for her.
15 From the flower to the ripening grape
my heart rejoiced in her;
my foot is set on the right path;
from my youth I pursued her.
16 I inclined my ear a little and received her,
and I found for myself much instruction.
17 I made progress in her;
to the One who gives Wisdom I will give glory.
18 For I had determined to do all according to her,
and I was zealous for good,
and shall never be disappointed.
19 My soul wrestled with her,
and in my observance of the law I was precise;
I spread out my hands to the heavens,
and lamented ignorance of her.
20 I directed my soul to her,
and in purification I found her.
I obtained a heart joined with her from the beginning;
therefore I will never be forsaken.
21 My depths were stirred to seek her;
therefore I have obtained a treasured possession.

Psalm 27:1–2, 4–5, 7, 10, 13–14

1 The Fire of Sinai is my light and my salvation;
whom shall I fear?
The Ark of Safety is the strength of my life;
whom shall I dread?
2 When evildoers advance against me
to devour my flesh,

my adversaries and my foes,
they shall stumble and fall.
4 One thing I asked of the FOUNT OF LIFE,
that [one thing] will I seek:
to live in the house of the WOMB OF LIFE
all the days of my life,
to behold the beauty of the WELLSPRING OF LIFE,
and to inquire in her temple.
5 She will shield me in her shelter
when the day is evil;
she will cover me under the cover of her tent;
she will raise me high on a rock.
7 Hear my cry, FAITHFUL ONE, when I cry aloud,
be gracious to me and answer me!
10 If my mother and father forsake me,
the COMPASSIONATE GOD will gather me in.
13 If I but believe, I shall see the goodness of SHE WHO IS FAITHFUL
in the land of the living.
14 Wait for the LIVING GOD;
be strong, and let your heart take courage;
wait for GOD WHOSE NAME IS HOLY!

1 Peter 3:13 Now who will harm you if you all are zealots for good? 14 Yet if you suffer
because of righteousness, you all are blessed: "Do not fear what they fear, and do not be intim-
idated." 15 Rather, "sanctify as Sovereign," Christ in your hearts. Always have ready a defense
for anyone who asks from you an account for the hope that is in you. 16 Yet do so with gentleness and reverence, maintaining a good conscience clear, so that when you are maligned, they
who abuse you for a good way of life in Christ may be put to shame. 17 For suffering for doing
good is better, if suffering should be God's will, than to suffer for doing evil. 18 For Christ also
suffered for sins once for all [one] righteous for [those] unrighteous, in order to bring you to
God, on the one hand, being put to death in the flesh, yet being made alive in the spirit, 19 in
which also Christ went and preached to the spirits in prison, 20 who formerly disobeyed while
the patience of God waited in the days of Noah, during the building of the ark, in which a few,
that is, eight souls, were saved through water. 21 And similarly, baptism now saves you, not as
a removal of dirt from the body, but as an appeal to God for a good conscience, through the
resurrection of Jesus Christ, 22 who is at the right hand of God having gone into heaven and,
with angels, authorities, and powers made subject to him.

Luke 14:7 Now Jesus told the guests a parable noticing how they chose the places of honor.
He said to them: 8 "When you are invited by someone to a wedding, do not sit down in the

place of honor lest one more distinguished than you has been invited. 9 Then the one who invited both of you would come and say to you, 'Give this person your place,' and then with shame you would begin to take the lowest place. 10 But when you are invited, go and sit down at the lowest place, so that when the one who invited you comes, your host may say to you, 'Friend, go up higher'; then you will be honored in the presence of all who sit at the table with you. 11 For all who exalt themselves will be humbled, and those who humble themselves will be exalted."

12 Jesus also spoke to the one who had invited him: "When you prepare a dinner or a supper, do not invite your friends or your sisters and brothers or your kin or rich neighbors, so they might invite you in return, and you would be repaid. 13 Rather, when you give a banquet, invite poor, disfigured, disabled, and blind people. 14 And you will be blessed, because they cannot repay you, for you will be repaid at the resurrection of the righteous."

PROCLAMATION

Text Notes

In Acts 3:22–23. Peter cites portions of Deuteronomy 18:15 and 22; some of the phrases match the LXX, some do not. The text is still closer to the Greek than to the Hebrew. However, neither Hebrew nor Greek has "utterly root out" (or destroy). The Hebrew says God will "seek" them out; the Greek says "seek vengeance."

I have made the refences to the prophets in Acts 3 explicitly inclusive since the text refers to "all" the prophets (in a particular timeframe) and those prophets included women. For more on female prophets, see my *Daughters of Miriam: Women Prophets in Ancient Israel.* The NRSV's use of "predicted" in verse 24 unhelpfully reinforces the misunderstanding of prophecy as primarily prediction which can in turn lead to a devaluing of the Hebrew Bible as mere Jesus cypher.

Acts 3:25 cites the promise to Abraham in Genesis 22:16 and 26:4. In Acts 3:26 Jesus is described as God's *pais*, which can be translated as either "slave" or "child," even "boy." Historically, translations have split between "servant," which ameliorates the ubiquitous explicit slave language in the scriptures, and "son," often capitalized.

In Sirach 51:21, the poet's "depths" are "innards," often "belly" or "womb."

The author of 1 Peter quotes Isaiah 8:12 in 3:14. In verse 15, the author rewrites the next verse in Isaiah: instead of "Sanctify the Sovereign Godself," in Isaiah 8:13, the author of the Epistle urges the reader/hearer to sanctify Christ as sovereign.

In Luke 14:8, the wedding is a single event, not a separate banquet as NRSV seems to suggest, a small reminder that words and customs do not mean precisely the same things across time and cultures. I have modified "the crippled, the lame, and the blind" to "disfigured, disabled, and blind people" to not limit people to what their bodies do differently from others.

Preaching Prompts

In this last Sunday of Eastertide, Peter demonstrates in Acts 3 the way in which the nascent Church reread the scriptures, in light of Jesus. Receiving Jesus as the fulfillment of all of God's promises has led to making Jesus the predicate and antecedent of every scripture, even when they are patently about something else. The purpose of this exercise in exegesis is to show how the Jesus story is truly grounded in the words and world of scripture, which were the bulk of what is now the Hebrew Bible. It was to show that Jesus and his teaching and his suffering, death, and resurrection were not some new-fangled idea but the fruit of an ancient tree with deep roots.

The Jerusalem temple figures prominently in Sirach 51 and Psalm 27. In the former, a praying soul seeks Wisdom and petitions for her from the temple courtyard, facing the sanctuary wherein lies the Holy of Holies. In the latter, the praying poet seeks to dwell in the temple complex (not the sanctuary proper), to be as close to God as humanly possible. In Luke 2:36–37, the prophet Hannah bat Phanuel (Anna in Greek) is described as spending her days and nights at the temple crying out to God. There is a rabbinic textual tradition that eighty-two women continuously wove so the temple veil would always be pristine (see Tal Ilan, *Mine and Yours Are Hers: Retrieving Women's History from Rabbinic Literature*).

First Peter 3 and Luke 14 each address the resurrection. The resurrection of Jesus is a mediating event through which we are transformed in 1 Peter 3:21–22, and the point of recompense in Luke 14:13.

PENTECOST VIGIL (OR EARLY SERVICE)

Joel 2:27–32 (or Exodus 19:1–19); Psalm 139:7–14; Acts 2:1–18; John 4:7–26

Joel 2:27 You all shall know that I am in the midst of Israel,
and that I, the HOLY ONE OF SINAI, am your God and there is no other.
And my people shall not be put to shame ever again.
28 And it shall be after that,
I will pour out my Spirit on all flesh;
and your daughters and your sons shall prophesy,
your elders shall dream dreams,
and your youths shall see visions.
29 Even on the enslaved women and men,
in those days, will I pour out my Spirit.

30 I will place portents in the heavens and on the earth, blood and fire and pillars of smoke. 31 The
sun shall be turned to darkness, and the moon to blood, before the great and terrible day of the
DREAD GOD comes. 32 Then it shall be that everyone who calls on the name of the FAITHFUL

GOD shall be saved; for in Mount Zion and in Jerusalem there shall be those who escape, as the
HOLY ONE OF OLD has said, and among the survivors, those whom the GOD WHO SAVES calls.

Exodus 19:1 On the third new moon after the women, children, and men of Israel had
gone out of the land of Egypt, on that day, they entered the wilderness of Sinai. 2 They had
journeyed from Rephidim, entered the wilderness of Sinai, and camped in the wilderness; Israel
camped there in front of the mountain. 3 Then Moses went up to God and the HOLY ONE OF
OLD called to him from the mountain, saying, "Thus you shall say to the house of Jacob, and
tell the women, children, and men of Israel: 4 You all have seen what I did to the Egyptians,
that I raised you all up on the wings of eagles and brought you all to myself. 5 Now, if you all
obey my voice and keep my covenant, you all shall be my treasure from among all peoples, for
the whole earth is mine. 6 And you all shall be for me a sovereignty of priests and a holy nation.
These are the words that you shall speak to the women, children, and men of Israel."

7 So Moses came and called the elders of the people and placed before them all these
words that the HOLY ONE had commanded him. 8 Then the people, women and men, all
answered together: "Everything that the HOLY ONE has spoken we will do." And Moses conveyed the words of the people to the HOLY ONE OF SINAI. 9 Then the HOLY ONE said to
Moses, "I will come to you in an impenetrable cloud, so that the people can hear when I speak
with you and also trust you always." When Moses had told the words of the people to the
HOLY ONE, 10 the HOLY GOD said to Moses:

"Go to the people and have them consecrate themselves today and tomorrow. Have them
wash their clothes, 11 and be prepared for the third day, because on the third day the MOST HIGH
will come down upon Mount Sinai in the sight of all the people. 12 You shall set a boundary
around the people, saying, 'Take heed not to go up the mountain or to touch the edge of it yourselves; anyone who touches the mountain shall surely be put to death. 13 No hand shall touch
them, rather they shall be stoned or shot with arrows; whether animal or human, they shall not
live.' When the ram's horn sounds a long blast, they may go up on the mountain." 14 So Moses
went down from the mountain to the people. He consecrated the people, and they washed their
clothes. 15 And Moses said to the people, "Prepare for the third day; do not go near a woman."

16 And it was on the third day as morning came there was thunder and lightning, as well as
a cloud heavy upon the mountain, and a blast of a trumpet so loud that all the people who were
in the camp trembled. 17 Then Moses brought the people out of the camp to meet God. They
stationed themselves at the base of the mountain. 18 Now Mount Sinai was in smoke, because
the HOLY ONE OF OLD had descended upon it in fire; the smoke ascended like the smoke of a
kiln, while the whole mountain shook violently. 19 And it was that as the sound of the trumpet
grew stronger and stronger, Moses would speak and God would answer him in thunder.

Psalm 139:7–14

7 Where can I go from your spirit?
Or where from your presence can I flee?

[8] If I ascend to the heavens, there you are;
if I recline in Sheol, see, it is you!
[9] If I take up dawn's wings
if I settle at the farthest reaches of the sea,
[10] even there your hand shall lead me,
and your right hand shall hold me fast.
[11] If I say, "Surely darkness shall cover me,
and night will become light behind me,"
[12] even darkness is not dark to you;
night is as daylight,
for dark is the same as light.
[13] For it was you who crafted my inward parts;
you wove me together in my mother's womb.
[14] I praise you, for I am awesomely and marvelously made.
Wondrous are your works;
that my soul knows full well.

Acts 2:1 When the day of Pentecost had come, they were all together in the same place.
[2] And there came suddenly from heaven a sound like the sweeping of a mighty wind, and it
filled the entire house where they were sitting. [3] Then there appeared among them divided
tongues, as of fire, and one rested on each of them. [4] And all of them were filled with the Holy
Spirit and they began to speak in other tongues just as the Spirit gave them to speak.

[5] Now there were dwelling in Jerusalem devout Jews from every nation under heaven.
[6] Now at this sound the crowd gathered and was confused because each heard them speaking
in the native language of each. [7] Amazed and astounded, they asked, "Are not all these who are
speaking Galileans? [8] And how do we hear, each in our own native language? [9] Parthians and
Medes and Elamites, and those who live in Mesopotamia, Judea and Cappadocia, Pontus and
Asia, [10] Phrygia and Pamphylia, Egypt and the parts of Libya adjacent to Cyrene, and visitors
from Rome, both Jews and proselytes, [11] Cretans and Arabs, we hear them speaking in our
own tongues about God's deeds of power." [12] All were amazed and questioning to one another
saying, "What does this mean?" [13] But others mocking said, "They are filled with new wine."

[14] But Peter, standing with the eleven, raised his voice and addressed them, "Judeans
and all who live in Jerusalem, let this be known to you all, and attend to my speech. [15] For
these persons are not drunk as you suppose; it is only the third hour [nine o'clock] in the
morning. [16] No, this is what was spoken through the prophet Joel:

[17] *'In the last days it will be, God declares,*
that I will pour out my Spirit upon all flesh,
and your daughters and your sons shall prophesy,
and your young men shall see visions,
and your elders shall dream dreams.

18 *Even upon my slaves, both women and men,*
in those days I will pour out my Spirit;
and they shall prophesy.'"

John 4:7 A Samaritan woman came to draw water. Jesus said to her, "Give me a drink." 8 Now
his disciples had gone to the city to buy food. 9 The Samaritan woman said to him, "How are
you, a Judean, asking a drink of me, a woman of Samaria?" (Judeans do not share things in
common with Samaritans.) 10 Jesus answered and said to her, "If you knew the gift of God
and who is the one telling to you, 'Give me a drink,' you would have asked him, and he would
have given you living water." 11 The woman said to him, "Sir, you have no bucket, and the well
is deep. From where do you get that living water? 12 Are you greater than our ancestor Jacob,
the one who gave us the well, and with his daughters and sons and his flocks drank from it?"
13 Jesus answered and said to her, "Everyone who drinks of this water will thirst again. 14 But
the one who drinks of the water that I will give will never thirst. The water that I will give will
become in them a fount of water springing up into eternal life." 15 The woman said to him, "Sir,
give me this water, that I may never thirst or keep coming here to draw water."

16 Jesus said to her, "Go, call your husband, and come [back] to this place." 17 The woman
answered and said to him, "I have no husband." Jesus said to her, "You said rightly, 'I have no
husband.' 18 For five husbands have you had, and now the one you have is not your husband.
What you have said is true!" 19 The woman said to him, "Sir, I see that you are a prophet. 20 Our
mothers and fathers worshiped on this mountain, yet you say in Jerusalem is the place where
people must worship." 21 Jesus said to her, "Believe me, woman, the hour is coming when neither on this mountain nor in Jerusalem will you worship the Sovereign God. 22 You all worship
what you do not know; we worship what we know, for salvation is from the Judeans. 23 But the
hour is coming, and now is, when the true worshipers will worship the Sovereign God in spirit
and truth, for these are the worshippers the Sovereign God seeks. 24 God is spirit, and those
who worship God must worship in spirit and truth." 25 The woman said to Jesus, "I know that
Messiah is coming" (the one who is called Christ). "When he comes, he will proclaim all things
to us." 26 Jesus said to her, "I am, the one who is speaking to you."

PROCLAMATION

Text Notes

Verse numbers in Christian Bibles diverge from those (now) in Hebrew and Jewish Bibles. What is Joel 2:28 in Christian texts is 3:1 in Jewish texts such as the JPS *Tanakh* and Hebrew Masoretic Text, as well as other ancient texts, including the LXX and Peshitta. "Elders" in verse 28 is an inclusive plural that grammatically includes women; it can represent chronological age or status. The "elders of Israel" served as an administrative layer (Numbers 16:25; Deuteronomy 27:1, 31:9; Joshua 7:6, 8:10; 1 Samuel 4:3). They are only spoken of as a group, so it is unclear if there were any women among them. In Joel, "elders" is paired with "youth," indicating it should be read chronologically, and therefore, I argue, inclusively.

In Exodus 19:10 and 14, "consecrate" or "sanctify" has a reflexive sense; one does it to oneself, primarily through water, bathing, and washing one's clothing. Scholars from the rabbinic period (Rashi, Ramban, Ibn Ezra, and Nahmanides) understand Moses's sanctification of the people to be a charge to them to sanctify themselves, hence the JPS, "warn them to stay pure."

The use of the masculine pronoun "him" for both a person who transgresses the boundary of the mountain and the mountain itself means that in verse 13 the referent of "no hand shall touch him/it" is unclear.

In Psalm 139:14, "marvelous"" and wondrous" are the same word. I alternate them for alliteration to give a sense of the poetry.

The author limits the multinational Jews in Jerusalem to "devout men" in Acts 2:5 as though there no women or none of the women were devout. The androcentric language discounts women living in the city and women who did make the journey. Yet Deuteronomy 16:11 specifies celebrating the festival with daughters and sons and women and men who are enslaved in the household (no mention of wives). Similarly, Peter addresses "men of Judea" but also "all who live in Jerusalem" in 2:14; I treat both as inclusive.

Preaching Prompts

Pentecost, the fiftieth day, marks the end of the Festival of Weeks, *Shavuoth* (from the Hebrew for "weeks"), originally named the festival of "Harvest" (see Exodus 23:16; Leviticus 23:15–16). The seven weeks follow from Passover and the festivals are entwined. By the time of the New Testament, it was also understood as the anniversary of the revelation of the Torah on Mount Sinai in Exodus 19. These traditions underlie the outpouring of the Holy Spirit on that selfsame day. The Christian observance is inexorably linked to its ancestral Jewish heritage.

Because of its citation in Acts 2, the primary Pentecost narrative, Joel 2 is regarded as fulfilled in the event in Christian interpretation. In Joel, repeated in Acts, "everyone who calls upon the name of the Holy One shall be saved" (or "rescued") means two very different things in each of those contexts. In the Hebrew Bible salvation, rescue, and deliverance are normally corporate (with few exceptions) and relate to physical safety from threats of violence, war, occupation, and even natural and ecological disasters (as is the case in Joel). In the New Testament, the Church has replaced the nation as the frame of reference and to call upon the name, now of Jesus, is to profess faith in him. It is important to tell the Christian story without erasing or rewriting the story of God's faithfulness to Jewish people or their Israelite ancestors.

Exodus 19 is the story of God's covenant with Israel ratified on Sinai with God present in veiled majesty. The language is by turns inclusive and exclusive, inviting reflection on who we understand to be part of and to represent the people of God. The traditional language for Israel, "the sons" or "children of Israel," is both androcentric and inclusive. In verse 8, the people "all" answer, meaning women and men; children would not be subject to a legal agreement like the covenant. ("Children" in the commandments refers to adult children in relation to their parents.) "People" is inclusive and yet is sometimes used as though men are the only ones who count; in verse 15 Moses tells the "people" not to approach women, presumably for sex. In this construction women are not "people." Perhaps more disturbing, Moses *adds* this line to God's instructions and receives no rebuke. (Compare God's directive in verses 10–13 with those of Moses.) The attempts of Moses and his writers notwithstanding, God appears to all the women, children, and men of Israel. Though earlier in Exodus the people see God regularly in the alternating pillars of cloud and fire, God's appearance in verse 15 is perhaps closer than the front of their vanguard and much more dramatic with the addition of thunder and lightning and the sound of God's voice.

Who experiences the touch of the Holy Spirit in Acts 2? Who are the "they"? If they are the upper room community, then they are Mary the mother of Jesus and other unnamed women along with the eleven remaining apostles (Acts 1:13–14), plus a newly elected apostle (who will immediately disappear) (Acts 1:23–26). "They" may also refer to the larger group of one hundred and twenty in the following verse. An intriguing possibility reads the two together, i.e., Mary and an undisclosed number of women together with the twelve apostles constituted the one hundred and twenty. This might explain why Peter chooses Joel to explain the phenomenon, because of its explicit inclusivity.

The *Samarians* were the inhabitants of the northern monarchy of Israel who ultimately fell to Assyria and were largely deported. The land was repopulated with other conquered peoples and their descendants became known as *Samaritans* (see 2 Kings 17:24–34). Judeans held them in low esteem because of their mixed heritage to which they attributed the differences between their worship traditions. Notably, the Samaritan Pentateuch is the entirety of their Bible, nothing else is canonical; that remains the case for Samaritan Jews in the present. (Ἰουδαίοις should be understood as "Judean" in opposition to Samaritan, as both communities are Jewish.) The dispute about the mountain in John 4:20–22 is rooted in one of the many differences between the Samaritan and Judean Torahs: Whether the mountain in Deuteronomy 27:4 on which Joshua (8:30) later built an altar is Ebal (Judeans) or Gerizim (Samaritans). As a result, the Samaritan temple was built on Mt. Gerizim, the "this mountain" of John 4:22. Palestinian Samaritan Jews continue to worship on the mountain, the temple long destroyed by the Romans in 70 CE.

In John 4:12, the woman mentions Jacob and his children (or sons), which I have made explicitly inclusive given Jacob had an unknown number of daughters, including one named Dinah, among his thirty-three children (see Genesis 37:55 and 46:15).

PENTECOST PRINCIPAL SERVICE

Acts 2:1–18 (or Isaiah 44:1–8); Psalm 104:1–4, 10–15, 27–30; Romans 8:14–27; John 14:8–17

Acts 2:1 When the day of Pentecost had come, they were all together in the same place.
2 And there came suddenly from heaven a sound like the sweeping of a mighty wind, and it
filled the entire house where they were sitting. 3 Then there appeared among them divided
tongues, as of fire, and one rested on each of them. 4 And all of them were filled with the Holy
Spirit and they began to speak in other tongues just as the Spirit gave them to speak.

5 Now there were dwelling in Jerusalem devout Jews from every nation under heaven.
6 Now at this sound the crowd gathered and was confused because each heard them speaking
in the native language of each. 7 Amazed and astounded, they asked, "Are not all these who are
speaking Galileans? 8 And how do we hear, each in our own native language? 9 Parthians and
Medes and Elamites, and those who live in Mesopotamia, Judea and Cappadocia, Pontus and
Asia, 10 Phrygia and Pamphylia, Egypt and the parts of Libya adjacent to Cyrene, and visitors
from Rome, both Jews and proselytes, 11 Cretans and Arabs, we hear them speaking in our
own tongues about God's deeds of power." 12 All were amazed and questioning to one another
saying, "What does this mean?" 13 But others mocking said, "They are filled with new wine."

14 But Peter, standing with the eleven, raised his voice and addressed them, "Judeans and
all who live in Jerusalem, let this be known to you all, and attend to my speech: 15 For, these
persons are not drunk as you suppose; it is only the third hour [nine o'clock] in the morning.
16 No, this is what was spoken through the prophet Joel:

17 '*In the last days it will be, God declares,*
that I will pour out my Spirit upon all flesh,
and your daughters and your sons shall prophesy,
and your young men shall see visions,
and your elders shall dream dreams.
18 *Even upon my slaves, both women and men,*
in those days I will pour out my Spirit;
and they shall prophesy.

Isaiah 44:1 Hear now, Jacob [Rebekah's child], my slave,
Israel whom I have chosen!
2 Thus says the Wellspring of Life who made you,
who shaped you in the womb and will help you:
Fear not, Jacob [Rebekah's son], my slave,
Jeshurun whom I have chosen.
3 For I will pour water upon thirsty soil,
and streams upon the dry ground;

I will pour my spirit upon your descendants,
and my blessing on your offspring.
4 They shall spring up in green [places],
like willows by flowing waters.
5 This one will say, "I am God's,"
that one will name the name of Jacob [Born of Rebekah],
another will write on their hand, "This belongs to God,"
and adopt the name of Israel.
6 Thus says the Ageless God, the Sovereign of Israel,
and Israel's Redeemer, the Commander of heaven's legions:
I am the first and I am the last;
apart from me there is no god.
7 Who is like me? Let them proclaim it,
let them declare it and set it out before me.
Who like me from old has laid out things which are coming?
Let them declare to us what will come.
8 Fear not and be not afraid;
have I not from old told you and declared it?
You all are my witnesses!
Is there any god besides me?
There is no rock; I know not one.

Psalm 104:1–4, 10–15, 27–30

1 Bless the Fount of Life, O my soul.
Mother of All, my God, you are very great.
You don honor and majesty,
2 Wrapped in light as a garment,
you stretch out the heavens like a tent-curtain.
3 She who lays on the waters the beams of her upper chambers,
she who makes the clouds her chariot,
she is the one who rides on the wings of the wind.
4 She is the one who makes the winds her celestial messengers,
fire and flame her ministers.
10 She is the one who makes springs gush forth in the torrents;
they flow between the hills.
11 They give drink to every wild animal;
the wild donkeys slake their thirst.
12 By the torrents the birds of the heavens dwell;
among the branches they give voice.

13 She is the one who waters the mountains from her high chambers;
the earth is satisfied with the fruit of your work.
14 She is the one who makes grass to grow for the cattle,
and vegetation for human labor,
to bring forth food from the earth,
15 and wine to make the human heart rejoice,
with oil to make the face shine,
and bread to sustain the human heart.
27 All of these hope in you
to provide their food in due season.
28 You give it to them, they glean it;
you open your hand, they are well satisfied.
29 You hide your face, they are dismayed;
when you collect their breath, they die
and to their dust they return.
30 You send forth your spirit, they are created;
and you renew the face of the earth.

Romans 8:14 Now as many as are led by the Spirit of God are daughters and sons of God.
15 For you all did not receive a spirit of slavery to fall again into fear, but you have received a
spirit of adoption through which we cry, "Abba! Father!" 16 It is that same Spirit who bears
witness with our spirit that we are daughters and sons of God. 17 And if daughters and sons,
then heirs, heirs of God and heirs with Christ, if it is true that we suffer with Christ so that we
may also be glorified with Christ.

18 I consider that the sufferings of this present time are not worth comparing with the
glory about to be revealed to us. 19 For the creation waits with eager longing for the revealing
of the daughters and sons of God; 20 for the creation was subjected to futility, not of its own
will but by the will of the one who subjected it, in hope 21 that the creation itself will be set
free from its bondage to decay and will obtain the freedom of the glory of the daughters and
sons of God. 22 We know that the whole creation has been groaning in labor pains until now;
23 and not only the creation, but we ourselves, who have the first fruits of the Spirit, groan
inwardly while we wait for adoption, the redemption of our bodies. 24 For in hope we were
saved. Now hope that is seen is not hope. For who hopes for what is seen? 25 But if we hope for
what we do not see, we wait for it with patience.

26 Likewise the Spirit helps us in our weakness; for we do not know how to pray as is necessary, but that very Spirit intercedes with sighs too deep for words. 27 And God, who searches
the heart, knows what is the mindset of the Spirit, because the Spirit intercedes for the saints
according to the will of God.

John 14:8 Philip said to Jesus, "Rabbi, show us the Father, and we will be content." [9] Jesus said to him, "Have I been with all of you all this time, Philip, and you still do not know me? The one who has seen me has seen the Father. How can you say, 'Show us the Father'? [10] Do you not believe that I am in the Father and the Father is in me? The words that I speak to you I do not speak on my own; but the Father who dwells in me does the works of God. [11] Believe me that I am in the Father and the Father is in me; but if not, then believe because of the works themselves. [12] Very truly, I tell you all, the one who believes in me will also do the works I do and even will do greater works than these, because I am going to the Father. [13] And whatever you all ask in my name I will do, so that the Father may be glorified in the Son. [14] If you all ask me anything in my name, I will do it.

"If you love me, you will keep my commandments. [16] And I will ask the Father, and God will give you another Advocate, to be with you forever. [17] This is the Spirit of truth, whom the world cannot receive, because it neither sees nor knows the Spirit. You know the spirit, because the Spirit abides with you, and the Spirit will be in you.

PROCLAMATION

Text Notes

See the discussion of the Acts 2 text in the readings for the Pentecost Vigil/Early Service.

Jeshurun, in Isaiah 44:2, is something of a pet name for Israel from Deuteronomy (see verses 32:15; 33:5, 26). In verse 4 there is a missing noun to describe the site of flourishing; I have supplied "places."

Psalm 104 switches between second and third person as is common in the genre. Verses 14–15 use the word that means both "bread" and "food in general" in both senses.

In the Hebrew Bible the Spirit of God (and more broadly) is grammatically feminine. This is not easily visible when reading in English. Translators have historically avoided grammatical constructions that would require a pronoun for the Spirit in the First Testament. Rather, they repeat "the spirit" as the perpetual subject. I have adopted that practice for the translation of John 14:17.

In Greek, in the Septuagint and Christian scriptures, the word for "spirit" is neuter, meaning that in the breadth of the scriptures the spirit is anything and everything but masculine. The deliberate choice to render the spirit in masculine terms in Latin texts such as the Vulgate reflects theological commitments apart from the grammar of the texts. If we were to hear Jesus speak John 14:17 in Aramaic, we would most likely hear: *This is the Spirit of truth, whom the world cannot receive, because it neither sees her nor knows her. You know her, because she abides with you, and she will be in you.*

Preaching Prompts

The outpouring of the Holy Spirit on Pentecost marks the dawn of the Church, but it is not the dawn of the Holy Spirit; she births creation, hovering over her newly hatched brood in Genesis and breathes through the scriptures, celebrated in the final verse of the psalm. Here in Isaiah 44, she is God's promise for coming generations. The God of wind and flame in Psalm 104:4 is the same God, the same Spirit who is the wind and breath of the Pentecostal fire.

Isaiah 44 is significant for its strident monotheism in a largely henotheistic tradition. Henotheism is the worship of one god above others while not denying the existence of the others, i.e., "God of gods," and "choose this day whom you will serve," etc. But in Isaiah 44:8 God says she has never even heard of another god in the rhetoric of her poet-prophet. This is a bold, audacious claim, for the author is not ignorant of the world around her, nor is the God for whom she speaks. Rather, it is both creation and affirmation of a worldview, as is the Pentecost moment.

The psalm is rich with the majesty of creation. And in Romans 8:20 and 22 that same creation waits, longing for us, humanity, to live into the fullness of our glory as the children of God. That same mighty fire swirling spirit prays for us to live up to and into our full potential like the rest of creation, even when we do not know the words to pray. Indeed, when language as we understand it is insufficient, the spirit intercedes, advocates, in sounds, sighs, beyond our capacity to interpret. The gospel promises us that Advocate, Comforter, Intercessor who will be with us forever.

TRINITY SUNDAY

Hosea 11:1–4; Psalm 131:5–6; 132:1–3; 2 Peter 1:16–18; Matthew 28:16–20

Hosea 11:1 When Israel was a child, I loved them,
and out of Egypt I called my child.
2 They, the Baals, called to them,
they went out to the Baals;
they sacrificed and to idols,
they offered incense.
3 Yet it was I who walked toddling Ephraim,
taking them by their arms;
yet they did not know that I healed them.
4 I led them with human ties,
with bonds of love.
I was to them like those

who lift babies to their cheeks.
I bent down to them and fed them.

Psalm 130

5 I wait for the WOMB OF CREATION, my soul waits,
and in her word I hope.
6 My soul keeps watch for the Creator,
more than those who watch for the morning,
more than those who watch for the morning.
7 Israel, hope in the MOTHER OF CREATION!
For with the CREATOR OF ALL there is faithful love,
and with her is abundant redemption.
8 It is she who will redeem Israel
from all their iniquities.

Psalm 131

1 WOMB OF LIFE, my heart is not lifted up,
nor my eyes exalted;
I do not keep company with things
great and too wondrous for me.
2 Rather, I have soothed and quieted my soul,
like a weaned child with her mother;
my soul is like a weaned child within me.
3 Israel, hope in the WELLSPRING OF LIFE
from now until forever.

2 Peter 1:16 For we did not follow sophisticated mythologies when we made known to
you all the power and coming of our Redeemer Jesus Christ, rather we had been eyewitnesses
of his majesty. 17 For Christ from God the Sovereign received honor and glory, a voice came
to him from the Majestic Glory, saying, "This is my Son, my Beloved, with whom I am well
pleased." 18 And we ourselves heard this voice that came from heaven, while we were with him
on the holy mountain.

Matthew 28:16 Now the eleven disciples went to Galilee, to the mountain to which
Jesus sent them. 17 And when they saw him, they bowed down worshipping him; but some
doubted. 18 Then Jesus came and said to them saying, "All authority in heaven and on
earth has been given to me. 19 Go therefore and make disciples of all nations, baptizing
them in the name of the Father and of the Son and of the Holy Spirit, 20 and teaching
them to obey everything that I have commanded you. Now look, I am with you always, to
the end of the age."

PROCLAMATION

Text Notes

In the first line of Hosea 11, "boy," a very ambiguous term, ranges from prepubescent to young adult and can also represent minor or junior status among adults. The passage moves between conceptions of Israel as a singular collective "boy," to a notion of individuals, "them," in the first two verses. In verse 3, "toddling" renders a verb made out of the word for foot, consistent with the child learning to walk and still being nursed, verse 4. Human "ties" in verse 4 is a pun, on ropes and cords and the bonds of human relationships.

In Psalm 130:8 Israel is a singular entity and their sin is also collective and singular here.

Preaching Prompts

The three-fold way in which God has been traditionally named is male in form (Father and Son) and function (the postbiblical construction of the Holy Spirit as male). This rubric which seeks to articulate the essential nature and identity of God to be used in worship and prayer, liturgy and preaching, allows men and boys to hear themselves and their pronouns identified with God along with the exclusion and invisibility of women and girls and nonbinary persons. This exclusion is formative for men and boys in casting gender hierarchy from which they benefit in divine terms. For those who do not hear their pronouns invoke their creation as *imago dei* in the language of the Church, trinitarian language and the observance of Trinity remain a sanctified proclamation of male divinity. For this reason, this project offers more ways to name God, drawn from the scriptures.

While the overwhelming majority of God-language is masculine, there remains a significant collection of feminine imagery for and descriptions of God. The description of the soul as a weaned child in Psalm 131:2 invokes an image of God as the mother upon whose breast it rests.

The Epistle writer uses rare language for God, Majestic Glory, in 2 Peter 1:17. (Hebrews uses "the Majesty" on high in 1:3 and in heaven in 8:1.) The Epistle also comes with a healthy caution for those caught up in the Church's often heated, occasionally violent debates over the Trinity, its Persons, and their relationships, hierarchy, and origins. In disputes about "sophisticated" myths or mythologies—and I add—theologies, philosophies, and church doctrines, the writer turns to their witness to the faith, what they saw and heard. In turn, they pass their testimony down to us.

Matthew 28:19 is the place where what has become the primary Trinitarian formula occurs. (Galatians 4:6 has the same elements but presented discursively: *And because you are children, God has sent the Spirit of God's Son into our hearts, crying, "Abba! Father!"*) While the traditional language will always have a place in the liturgical lexicon, Trinity Sunday offers an opportunity to craft language that draws more widely on the biblical texts and traditions.

Some of mine include:

Sovereign, Savior, and Shelter;
Author, Word, and Translator;
Parent, Partner, and Friend;
Majesty, Mercy, and Mystery;
Creator, Christ, and Compassion;
Potter, Vessel, and Holy Fire;
Life, Liberation, and Love.

SEASON AFTER PENTECOST (29)

The Season after Pentecost runs nearly thirty weeks. It is a season focused on the growth of the Church historically and, contemporarily, the growth of her members. This lectionary will focus on the stories of monarchs and monarchies, providing a curriculum through which those who read and preach these texts will engage in consecutive Bible study through Ruth, Samuel, and Kings after a look at Israel's first, forgotten monarch. We will also continue moving through Matthew. Counter to the traditional lectionary, the Hebrew Bible lesson drives the other choices.

PROPER 1 (CLOSEST TO MAY 11)

Judges 9:1–6, 22, 50–56; Psalm 29; Acts 17:1–7; Matthew 14:1–12

Judges 9:1 Now Abimelech son of [Gideon also called] Jerubbaal, went to Shechem to his
mother's kin and spoke to them and to the entire clan of his maternal grandfather's family: 2
"Please ask in the hearing of all the leaders of Shechem, 'Which is better for you, that seventy men, all of the sons of Jerubbaal, rule over you, or that one rule over you?' Now remember,
I am your bone and your flesh." 3 So his mother's kin spoke all these words about him in the hearing of all the leaders of Shechem, and their hearts inclined to follow Abimelech, for they
said, "He is our kin." 4 They gave Abimelech seventy pieces of silver out of the temple of Ba'al Berith, Ba'al of the Covenant, with which Abimelech hired worthless and reckless men, who
followed him. 5 He went to his father's house in the vicinity of Ophrah, and killed his brothers, the sons of Jerubbaal, seventy men on one stone; yet Jotham, the youngest son of Jerubbaal, survived, for he hid. 6 Then all the leaders of Shechem and all Beth-millo came together,
and they kinged as king Abimelech [whose name means "My Father is King"], by the oak of the pillar at Shechem.

22 Abimelech reigned over Israel three years.
50 Now Abimelech went to Thebez and camped against it and took it. 51 Yet there was
a strong tower within the city, and all the women and men and all the leaders of the city
fled there, and they shut themselves in and went to the roof of the tower. 52 Then Abimelech came against the tower and attacked it. He approached the door of the tower to burn
it with fire. 53 Then a certain woman threw an upper millstone on Abimelech's head, and
crushed his skull. 54 He cried out immediately to the boy who carried his equipment and said
to him, "Draw your sword and kill me, lest people say of me, 'A woman killed him.'" So, his
boy stabbed him, and he died. 55 When each Israelite saw that Abimelech was dead, they
left, each to their home. 56 Thus God repaid the evil of Abimelech that he did against his
father, killing his seventy brothers.

Psalm 29

1 Render unto She Who Is, O divine ones,
render unto She Who Reigns, glory and strength.
2 Render to She Who is Glory, the glory of her name;
worship She Who is Holy in majestic holiness.
3 The voice of She Who Thunders is above the waters;
the God of glory thunders,
She Who Thunders is above the mighty waters.
4 The voice of She Who is Power is powerful;
the voice of She Who is Majesty is full of majesty.
5 The voice of She Who Thunders breaks the cedars;
She Who Thunders breaks the cedars of Lebanon.
6 She makes Lebanon skip like a calf,
and Sirion like a young wild ox.
7 The voice of Sinai's Fire
sunders flames of fire.
8 The voice of She Who Thunders
makes the wilderness writhe [as though giving birth];
She Who Thunders
makes the wilderness of Kadesh travail [as though giving birth].
9 The voice of She Who Speaks Creation
causes the oaks to arch [as though giving birth],
and strips the forest bare;
and in her temple, all say, "Glory!"
10 She Who is Majesty sits enthroned over the flood;
She Who Reigns sits enthroned as Sovereign forever.
11 May She Who Is Mighty give strength to her people!
May She Who Is Peace bless her people with peace!

Acts 17:1 Paul and Silas had traveled through Amphipolis and Apollonia. They came to Thessalonica, where there was a Jewish synagogue. 2 As was his custom Paul went and on three sabbaths presented to them from the scriptures, 3 explaining and demonstrating it was necessary for the Messiah to suffer and to rise from the dead: "This is the Messiah, Jesus who I proclaim to you all." 4 Now, some of [those Jews] were persuaded and joined Paul and Silas, as did a great many of the devout Greeks and not a few of the prominent women.

5 Then the [other] Jews became jealous, and enlisting some immoral men in the marketplaces, they formed a mob and stirred up the city in an uproar and they attacked Jason's house searching for Paul and Silas to bring out to the gathering. 6 Now when they could not find them, they dragged Jason and some believers before the city leaders, shouting, "These are the ones who have disrupted the [entire] world and are now here. 7 This Jason has received them as guests and they are all in opposition to the decrees of the emperor, saying that there is another sovereign named Jesus."

Matthew 14:1 Herod the tetrarch heard the story of Jesus; 2 and he said to his servants, "This is John the Baptizer; he has been raised from the dead and because of this, these powers work through him." 3 For Herod had arrested John, bound him, and put him in prison because of Herodias, the wife of his brother Philip, 4 because John had told him, "It is not permissible for you to have her." 5 Now he wanted to put him to death yet he feared the crowd, because they regarded John as a prophet. 6 Then when Herod's birthday came, the daughter of Herodias danced in their midst, and she pleased Herod. 7 So he swore an oath to grant her whatever she asked. 8 Now, instructed by her mother, "Give me," she said, "here on a platter, the head of John the Baptizer." 9 Grieved, the ruler out of regard for his oaths and for the guests, commanded it be given to her. 10 Herod sent and had John beheaded in the prison. 11 The head was brought on a platter and given to the girl, who brought it to her mother. 12 John's disciples came and took the body and buried it; then they went and told Jesus.

PROCLAMATION

Text Notes

While generally eschewing gendered titles, I use "king" language in Judges 9:6 because of the multilevel word play: the *m-l-k* root for royal persons, places, and rules occurs repeatedly, including in Abimelech's name, *Avimelek*. Everett Fox translates similarly, "They kinged Avimelekh as king." (English lacks the capacity to translate *king, queen, kingdom*, and *reign* with the same root word.) Abimelech's mother's kin in Judges 9:1, and in verse 3, can be understood narrowly as siblings (or just brothers) or, widely, as relatives; context suggests the most inclusive reading. When his brothers are meant in verse 5, they are further identified as his father's sons.

The "leaders," *ba'alim*, of Shechem in Judges 9 share the title *ba'al*, moniker of the Canaanite deity Ba'al Haddu best known as simply Ba'al; the title means "lord," "master," or "husband" and was also used for God over Hosea's objections (see Hosea

2:16). The feminine form occurs rarely, e.g., 1 Kings 17:17 for the female "lord" of her household ("lady" doesn't have the same weight); however the plural form can include women. Gideon becomes known as Jerubbaal, "Let Ba'al contend with (or sue) him," after destroying Ba'al's altar (Judges 6:28–32). Abimelech's "worthless" men are literally "empty," of sense, values, decency, etc.

Ironically, Psalm 29 is widely understood to have originally been a hymn to Ba'al (also known as the Cloud-Rider and Lord of Thunder), converted for service to the God of Israel. It is a fairly common practice for biblical authors to assign the characteristics, names, and even homes of other deities to God.

Jason of Acts 17, possibly the same person mentioned in Romans 16:21, bears a Greek name that may indicate an underlying Hebrew name such as Joshua, suggesting a Jewish follower of Jesus.

Preaching Prompts

There is no small irony that Israel's experiments with monarchy begin with a man named "My Father is King," Abimelech, whose father Gideon/Jerubbaal turned down the throne in Judges 8:23. Abimelech's apple falls far from Gideon's tree; he is a brutal warlord who burns women and men alive. His unnamed mother, a secondary or low status wife (Judges 8:31), facilitates his ascension; her kin are his power base. (The mistranslation "concubine" obscures that secondary—not second—wives were wives; however, their children, who were legitimate, were not entitled to an inheritance.) His story is overlooked by most readers and by those who tell David's story, including in most lectionaries, yet he embodies the same violence that is common to all monarchs of the time, a reminder not to romanticize the text or its context.

These Season after Pentecost readings follow the emergence of Israel's monarchy and the ultimate inadequacy of even the most faithful and well-intentioned human ruler. God's majesty and sovereignty are unmatched. The Second Testament readings present the simple and often perplexing sovereignty of Jesus in contrast to the pomp and circumstance of Roman rulers and their puppets.

The women and men in Shechem choose Abimelech as their sovereign. The women and men in Thessalonica choose Jesus. Abimelech commits atrocities against women and men alike. Ultimately a woman will cost him his life, though he does his best to ensure she does not get the credit. The women and men who choose Jesus in Acts face some lesser violence for their choice. Finally, Matthew presents Herod almost as a parody of a king, yet with all of the lusts and avarice common to those with great power and privilege. Here as in Judges 9, women are the instigators and facilitators of lethal violence, though with widely different motivations and moral valuations in the texts. Herod's solicitation of John's death provides a vivid contrast between him as an earthly monarch and Jesus whose realm is not of this world.

PROPER 2 (CLOSEST TO MAY 18)

Ruth 1:1–14; Psalm 69:1–3, 13–17, 30–34; Acts 2:43–47; Matthew 10:40–42

Ruth 1:1 In the days when the judges judged it happened that there was a famine in the
land, and a man of Bethlehem in Judah went to sojourn in the country of Moab, he and his
wife and their two sons. 2 And the name of the man was Elimelech and the name of his wife
Naomi, and the names of his two sons were Mahlon and Chilion; they were Ephrathites from
Bethlehem in Judah. They went into the country of Moab and remained there. 3 Then Elimelech, the husband of Naomi, died, and she was left, she and her two sons. 4 They abducted
Moabite women for themselves; the name of the one was Orpah and the name of the second,
Ruth. And they lived there about ten years. 5 They also died, both of them, Mahlon and Chil-
ion, and the woman was left without her two sons and without her husband.

6 Then she got up, she and her daughters-in-law, and she returned from the country of
Moab, for she had heard in the country of Moab that the FAITHFUL ONE had considered
God's people and given them food. 7 So she set out from the place where she was while there,
with her two daughters-in-law, and they journeyed on the road to return to the land of Judah.
8 Then Naomi said to her two daughters-in-law, "Go, return, each to your mother's house.
May the HOLY ONE deal kindly with you, as you have done with the dead and with me. 9 The
SAVING GOD grant that you may find security, each in the house of your own husband."
Then she kissed them, and they wept aloud. 10 They said to her, "We will return with you
to your people." 11 Then Naomi said, "Turn back, my daughters, why will you go with me?
Are there yet sons in my belly that may become your husbands? 12 Turn back, my daughters,
go your way, for I am too old to be with a man. Let me say I have hope and even was with a
man tonight and give birth to sons. 13 Would you then wait and hope until they were grown?
Would you then refrain from marrying? No, my daughters, it has been far more bitter for me
than for you, because the hand of the SAVING GOD has turned against me." 14 Then they wept
aloud again. Orpah kissed her mother-in-law, but Ruth clung to her.

Psalm 69:1–3, 13–17, 30–34

1 Save me, God,
for the waters have come to my throat.
2 I sink in deep mire,
there is no foothold;
I come into deep waters,
and the flood overwhelms me.
3 I am weary with my crying;
my throat is parched.
My eyes fail,
waiting for my God.

13 Yet I make my prayer to you, the WISDOM OF THE AGES.
At a favorable time,
God, in the wealth of your faithful love, answer me,
with your certain salvation.
14 Rescue me from the mire,
and let me not sink;
let me be delivered from my enemies
and from the deep waters.
15 Let not the flood waters overwhelm me,
let not the Deep swallow me up;
let not the Pit close its mouth over me.
16 Answer me, GRACIOUS GOD, for your faithful love is good;
according to the wealth of your maternal love, turn to me.
17 Do not hide your face from your slave,
for I am in distress; hurry to answer me.
30 I will praise the name of God with song;
I will magnify her with thanksgiving.
31 This will please the CREATOR OF ALL more than an ox
or a bull with horns and hoofs.
32 Let the oppressed see it and be glad;
you who seek God, let your hearts flourish.
33 For the FAITHFUL GOD hears the needy,
and those who belong to her and are imprisoned,
she does not despise.
34 Let the heavens and earth praise her,
the seas and everything that moves in them.

Acts 2:43 Awe came upon everyone, because many wonders and signs were being done by
the apostles. 44 All who believed were as one and held all things in common. 45 They sold
their possessions and property and distributed the proceeds to all, as any had need. 46 Daily
they continued with the same purpose in the temple; they broke bread at home and ate their
food with gladness and simplicity of heart. 47 They praised God and had the gratitude of all
the people. And day by day the Holy One added to their number those who were being saved.

Matthew 10:40 "The one who welcomes you welcomes me, and the one who welcomes me
welcomes the one who sent me. 41 The one who welcomes a prophet in the name of a prophet
will receive the reward of a prophet; and the one who welcomes a righteous woman or man
in the name of a righteous woman or man will receive the reward of the righteous. 42 And the
one who gives a drink to one of these little ones—even a cup of cold water—in the name of a
disciple, truly I tell you, none of these will lose their reward."

PROCLAMATION

Text Notes

The judges (Ruth 1:1) were rulers or governors in addition to resolving disputes and settling claims. They were the de facto leaders of the people. Verse 2 identifies the children as "his," Elimelech's, not "theirs," though Naomi's maternity will be established later in verse 4. As Hebrew does not have specific words for "wife" and "husband," Naomi is Elimelech's "woman" in verse 2 and he is her "man" in verse 3.

Normally "to take" a wife indicates a consensual union through the verb *l-q-ch*. In Ruth 1:4 the verb is *n-s-'*, which primarily means "lift up"; it indicates abduction here and in other places, such as the abduction of the Shiloh virgins in Judges 21:23. "Marriage" and "marry" reflect the Western world rather than the language of the text. There is a word that signifies marriage, *b-'-l*, which also means to master (the root is the same as Baal and as a noun means "lord" and "master"). It is rarely used and not at all in Ruth.

The Deep and the Pit in Psalm 69:15 are legendary sites associated with death, in some ways parallel to Sheol. In verse 16 God's maternal love is love that emanates from and shares the same root as the womb.

Preaching Prompts

A close reading of Ruth reveals many surprises and challenges the romantic readings common to many; in this way Ruth's story is a fit predecessor to David's story. Ruth and Orpah were trafficked, and may not have been well received upon their return home. Interestingly, Orpah and Ruth come from matrilineal, if not matriarchal, households indicated by "mother's house." (Israelite households include both mother's house/holds and father's house/holds.)

The vulnerability of Naomi and Ruth, and to a lesser degree Orpah, set the stage for the monarchal epic that marks the golden age of ancient Israel. They are part of a mobile population crossing potentially hostile international borders in search of bare sustenance—Moab and Israel were often at war. That human frailty weaves through all of the readings. In the psalm we entrust our fragile, vulnerable places to God. In Acts, it is the community of the church that meets the needs of the people. And in the Gospel, we are reminded that when we relieve the suffering of any human person, we relieve the suffering of Christ.

PROPER 3 (CLOSEST TO MAY 25)

Ruth 1:15–22; Psalm 115:9–18; Acts 4:32–35; Matthew 11:7–19

Ruth 1:15 Naomi said, "Look, your sister-in-law has gone back to her people and to her gods; go back after your sister-in-law." 16 But Ruth said,

"Do not press me to forsake you
or to turn back from following you.
Where you go, I will go,
where you abide, I will abide;
your people shall be my people,
and your God my God.
17 Where you die, I will die,
there will I be buried.
May the HOLY ONE OF OLD do thus and more to me,
if even death parts me from you."

18 When Naomi saw that Ruth had strengthened herself to go with her, she ceased speaking
to her. 19 So the two of them traveled until coming to Bethlehem. When they came to Bethlehem, the whole town was buzzing over them; and the women said, "Is this Naomi?"
20 Naomi
said to the women,

"Call me not Naomi [Pleasant One],
call me Mara [Bitter One]
for Shaddai [the Breasted One] has greatly embittered me.
21 I went away full,
but the HOLY ONE OF SINAI brought me back empty.
Why call me Naomi?
The HOLY ONE has spoken against me,
and Shaddai [the Breasted One] has brought evil upon me."

22 So Naomi returned with Ruth the Moabite woman, her daughter-in-law, with her; she was the one who came back from the country of Moab. They came to Bethlehem at the beginning of the barley harvest.

Psalm 115:9–18

9 O Israel, trust in the FAITHFUL GOD!
God is their help and their shield.
10 O house of Aaron, trust in the FAITHFUL GOD!
God is their help and their shield.
11 You who reverence the HOLY GOD, trust in the HOLY ONE OF OLD!
God is their help and their shield.

12 The Faithful One remembers us and will bless us;
God will bless the house of Israel;
God will bless the house of Aaron;
13 God will bless those who reverence the Holy God,
both small and great.
14 May the Gracious God add to you,
to you and your children.
15 May you be blessed by the Creator of All,
who made the heavens and the earth.
16 The heavens belong to the Most High,
but the earth God has given to the woman-born.
17 The dead do not praise the Ever-Living God,
neither do any that go down into silence.
18 But we will bless the Ancient Of Days
from this time on and forevermore.
Praise the God Whose Name is Holy!

Acts 4:32 Now the whole multitude of those who believed were of one heart and soul, and
no one of them said, of the property they possessed, that it was their own, rather everything
that had been one person's was instead communal. 33 And with great power the apostles gave
testimony to the resurrection of Jesus the Messiah, and great grace was upon them all. 34 Now
there was not a needy person among them, for those who possessed lands or houses sold and
brought the value of what was sold. 35 And they laid it at the apostles' feet, and it was distributed according to the need of each.

Matthew 11:7 As John's disciples went away, Jesus began to speak to the crowds about John:
"What did you go out into the wilderness to see? A reed shaken by the wind? 8 But what did
you go out to see? A person dressed in luxurious robes? Look, those who wear luxurious robes
are in royal houses. 9 What then did you go out to see? A prophet? Yes, I tell you, and more
than a prophet. 10 He is the one about whom it is written,

'*Look, I am sending my messenger ahead of you,*
who will prepare your way before you.'

11 Truly I tell you, no one has arisen among those born of women greater than John the
Baptizer; yet the least in the realm of the heavens is greater than he. 12 From the days of John
the Baptizer until now the realm of the heavens endures violence, and the violent seize it.
13 For all the prophets and the law prophesied until John came; 14 and if you are willing to
receive it, he is Elijah who is to come. 15 Let those with ears hear!

16 "Now to what shall I liken this generation? It is like girls and boys sitting in the marketplaces and calling to one another saying,

[17] 'We played the flute for you, and you did not dance;
we sang a lament, and you did not mourn.'

[18] For John came neither eating nor drinking, and they say, 'He has a demon'; [19] the Son of Woman came eating and drinking, and they say, 'Look, a glutton and a drunk, a friend of tax collectors and sinners!' Yet Wisdom is vindicated by her deeds."

PROCLAMATION

Text Notes

In Ruth 1:20, and in verse 22, God is called *Shaddai*, translated as "Almighty" in most mainline translations; yet the root of the word is not "might" or "strength" but arguably "breast," *shad*. Another argument is that Shaddai is related to Akkadian "mountain" or a class of Arabian deities. Feminist scholars have remarked upon the desire of traditionally trained, primarily male, scholars to find an etymology outside of the obvious cognate. What is not disputed is that Shaddai is invoked in contexts where God is promising or providing fertility, such as Genesis 28:3 and 35:11. Genesis 49:25 offers a blessing from "the God of your father, who shall help you; and by Shaddai, who shall bless you with blessings of the heavens above, blessings of the deep that lies below, blessings of breasts (*shadim*) and womb." (*Shadim* is the plural of *shad*.) There is a possibility that the Akkadian "mountain" is also breast imagery with the mountains as breasts (snow cap as nipple) that nourish the world through their lifegiving water in the desert realm. Bearing these considerations in mind, I translate Shaddai as "Breasted One."

The section of Psalm 115 appointed for this day reads well as an antiphon; I have formatted it for ease of congregational reading.

The Matthew 11 reading also occurs on the Sixth Sunday of Epiphany where text notes and commentary are available.

Preaching Prompts

These readings focus on human needs and divine responsiveness, often through other people. Naomi and Ruth are bereaved and hungry. There is food (*lechem*) in *Bet Lechem*, Bethlehem, the House of Bread. The psalmist urges Israel to trust in God who is faithful. In Acts, it is the nascent church that is faithful across class lines to meet the needs of each member of the community. The life and ministry of Jesus is God's greatest act of generosity; however in the Gospel, God's gift is critiqued as it is not quite as expected: Jesus parties too much for some.

The readings from Ruth and Matthew each use feminine language for God, Shaddai, the Breasted One, and Wisdom. And there is a way in which Naomi's lament can be read as rejection from both "Father God," the Holy One or Lord, and

"Mother God," Shaddai. The psalm and Gospel use traditional masculine language in their original forms, neutral language in translation here. Even in binary language, God reveals Godself to be so much more than our categories.

There is an element of Ruth's story that endures into the Christian Testament, while Ruth is celebrated as David's great-grandmother, she is also perpetually identified as an outsider, "the Moabite woman." There is a difference between affirming the elements of a person's identity and using those elements to identify them as other.

PROPER 4 (CLOSEST TO JUNE 1)

Ruth 2:1-16; Psalm 9; Acts 5:1-11; Matthew 12:46-50

Ruth 2:1 Now Naomi had a relative through her husband, a warrior-hearted man of worth, from the family of Elimelech, and his name was Boaz. 2 And Ruth the Moabite said to Naomi, "Let me go to the field and glean among the ears of grain, behind someone in whose eyes I may find favor." Naomi said to her, "Go, my daughter." 3 And she went, and came and gleaned in the field behind the reapers. As it happened, she happened upon the part of the field that belonged to Boaz, who was from Elimelech's family. 4 Then suddenly, Boaz came from Bethlehem. He said to the reapers, "GOD be with you." They answered, "GOD bless you." 5 Then Boaz said to his boy stationed over the reapers, "To whom does this girl belong?" 6 The boy stationed over the reapers answered, "She is the Moabite, the one who returned with Naomi from the country of Moab. 7 She said, 'Please, let me glean and gather among the sheaves behind the reapers.' So, she came, and she has been standing from the morning until now, only resting in the shelter a little."

8 Then Boaz said to Ruth, "Have you not heard, my daughter? Go not to glean in another field, neither leave this one, thus you will cling to my girls. 9 Keep your eyes on the field that is being reaped, and follow after them [the girls]. Have I not commanded the boys not to touch you? When you thirst, go to the vessels and drink from what the boys have drawn." 10 Then she fell on her face and bowed down to the ground, and said to him, "Why have I found favor in your sight, that you would distinguish me, as I am a foreigner?" 11 And Boaz answered and said to her, "It has been told to me, all that you have done for your mother-in-law after the death of your husband, that you have forsaken your mother and father and your native land and came to a people that you did not know before yesterday. 12 May the HOLY ONE OF OLD reward your works, and may you have a full recompense from the HOLY ONE, the God of Israel, under whose wings you have come for refuge." 13 Then Ruth said, "May I continue to find favor in your eyes, my lord, for you have comforted me and have spoken to the heart to your slave woman, and I, I am not one of your slave women."

14 Boaz said to her when it was time to eat, "Draw near, and eat from this bread, and dip your piece in the vinegar." And she sat beside the reapers, and he handed her some roasted grain; and she ate and was satisfied, and she had some left over. 15 When Ruth got up to glean, Boaz commanded his boys saying, "She may even glean between the sheaves, and do not

humiliate her. 16 You must also pull out some for her from the bundles, and leave them for her to glean, and do not rebuke her."

Psalm 9

1 I will give thanks to the God Who Saves with my whole heart;
I will recount all your marvels.
2 I will be glad and exult in you;
I will sing praise to your name, Most High.
3 When my enemies turn back,
they stumble and perish before your presence.
4 For you judge my cause;
you sit on the throne judging rightly.
5 You rebuke the nations, you destroy the wicked;
their name you blot out forever.
6 The enemy is finished, the ruins everlasting;
their cities you have rooted out; their memory has perished.
7 But the Righteous One sits enthroned forever,
she has established her throne for judgment.
8 She judges the world with righteousness;
she judges the peoples with equity.
9 The Most High is a stronghold for the oppressed,
a stronghold in times of trouble.
10 They trust in you, who know your name,
for you, Faithful One, do not forsake those who seek you.
11 Sing praises to the Holy One of Sinai, who dwells in Zion.
Declare her deeds among the peoples.
12 For the one who avenges blood remembers them;
she does not forget the cry of the afflicted.
13 Be gracious to me, Merciful God;
see my affliction on account of those who hate me.
You are the one who lifts me up from the gates of death,
14 so that I may recount all your praises,
in the gates of Daughter Zion;
I will rejoice in your salvation.
15 The nations have sunk in the pit that they made;
in the net that they hid has their own foot been caught.
16 The Righteous One has made herself known, she has executed judgment;
the wicked are snared in the work of their own hands.
17 The wicked shall depart to Sheol,
all the nations that forget God.

18 For the needy shall not always be forgotten,
nor the hope of the poor perish forever.
19 Rise up, JUST ONE! Do not let those who are only mortal prevail;
let the nations be judged in your presence.
20 Put them in fear, DREAD GOD;
let the nations know that they are only mortal.

Acts 5:1 Now a certain man named Ananias, with his wife Sapphira, sold some property.
2 And he kept back some of the proceeds, with the knowledge of his wife, and brought only
a part and placed it at the feet of the apostles. 3 "Ananias," Peter asked, "why has Satan filled
your heart to lie to the Holy Spirit and to withhold from the proceeds of the land? 4 Was it
not [both of] yours while it remained unsold, and in your power? Why have you contrived
this in your heart? You did not lie to [mere] mortals but to God!" 5 Now when Ananias heard
these words, he fell down dying. And great fear came upon all who heard. 6 The young men
came and wrapped him up, then carried him out and buried him.

7 And it happened after about the space of three hours, his wife came in not knowing
what had happened. 8 Peter said to her, "Tell me whether you two sold the land for such and
such." And she said, "Yes, that was the price." 9 Then Peter said to her, "How is it that you two
have conspired to put the Spirit of the Holy One to the test? Look! The feet of those who
have buried your husband are at the door, and they will carry you out." 10 And she fell down
immediately at his feet and died. Then the young men came in and found her dead, and they
carried her out and buried her beside her husband. 11 And great fear came upon the whole
church and all who heard these things.

Matthew 12:46 While Jesus was still speaking to the crowds [teaching], his mother and his
siblings were standing outside, seeking to speak to him. 47 Someone told him, "Look, your
mother and your siblings are standing outside, seeking to speak to you." 48 But to the one who
had told him this, Jesus said, "Who is my mother, and who are my siblings?" 49 And pointing
his hand to his disciples, he said, "Here are my mother and my siblings! 50 For whoever does
the will of my Abba in the heavens is my mother and sister and brother."

PROCLAMATION

Text Notes

In the field of Boaz, Ruth's material needs are met through his wealth and generosity. In the psalm, the God who judges the nations remembers and provides for the needy and oppressed.

Used for Boaz in Ruth 2:1, *gibor* indicates a man of status, often a warrior. *Chayil* means both warrior and one who holds the values of a warrior, including wealth acquired through military exploits. Boaz will address Ruth as a woman of *chayil* in 3:11. In Proverbs 31, the Queen Mother instructs her son not to give his *chayil* to unworthy women and instructs him on the value of a woman of *chayil*; *chayil* is explicitly martial and refers to armies, e.g., Pharaoh's army in Exodus. "Warrior-hearted" encompasses the full range and does not dilute the meaning for women as do many translations such as "worthy woman/wife," "noble," or the infamous, "Who can find a virtuous woman."

In Ruth 2:5 and following, the text uses diminutive language, "youth/girl/boy," for Boaz's servants and for Ruth. This is the same language Jeremiah uses when he says "I am only a boy" in response to God's call in Jeremiah 1:6. There is a pun in verse 8: Boaz tells Ruth to cling to his girls the way she clung to Naomi, using the same verb. In verse 9, Boaz tells Ruth to follow "them," which in this case is feminine plural and refers to the girls and not the boys.

Psalm 9 is a partial acrostic, one to two verse units begin with successive letters of the Hebrew *aleph-bet* (alphabet) though some are missing. It moves freely between future and past tenses. The use of the present tense in translation holds the two in a common framework. The divine name *elyon*, Most High, occurs in verse 2 of the psalm; it is not in large-and-small capital letters because it is not representing the Unspoken Name as it is in verse 9. The "trouble" in verse 9 is "drought," seemingly metaphorical as no other ecologic details are provided. The invocation for God to "rise up" is the kind of summoning song used to call God to action, particularly in the Psalms, or in the case of 2 Chronicles 6:41, return God to rest after her deliverance.

Since the plural *adelphoi* in Matthew 12:46 encompasses mixed and all-male groups, there is no way to know if Jesus's sisters were present.

Preaching Prompts

There is a lot going on in Boaz's field in terms of gender, class, and identity. It is being worked by women and men who due to their social status relative to Boaz are called girls and boys, very much in the way some used to refer to grown men as house boys, also evoking the racist practice of black women and men being called "gal" and "boy" in (and not just) the south. In verse 9, the boys draw water, a caution against stringent notions of women's and men's work. Curiously neither the narrator nor Boaz use the language of slavery; Boaz's boys and girls may be paid workers. Ruth who does not know their arrangements calls herself and the women slave-women in 2:13. In 2:9, Boaz tells his boys not to touch Ruth—he says nothing about his girls. A charitable reading says his girls were already off-limits, but Ruth was a foreign woman, whom the Israelites tended to view as promiscuous and enticing; she was also hungry, poor, and vulnerable. She may well have been prey without his intervention, which he knew, begging the question if there were other vulnerable women who were not off-limits.

God's wings in Ruth 2:12 suggest a mother bird. The editorial choice to use female pronouns for God where masculine ones occur in the psalms yields portraits of her that are not as nurturing as the sheltering wings. Instead, in Psalm 9:12, she is the one who avenges the blood of her children.

Themes of family and belonging connect the lessons. Ruth has chosen Naomi through whom she is connected to Boaz. God claims all of the peoples in the world in the psalm while holding Jerusalem, Zion, closely as a daughter. And Jesus invites us all into the intimacy of his own family.

PROPER 5 (CLOSEST TO JUNE 8)

Ruth 3:1–18; Psalm 65:5–13; Acts 5:12–16; Matthew 13:31–35

Ruth 3:1 Naomi, Ruth's mother-in-law, said to her, "My daughter, am I not seeking respite
for you, that will be good for you? 2 Now is not Boaz our kin, with whose girls you have been?
Look! He is winnowing barley on the threshing floor tonight. 3 Now bathe and anoint yourself and put on your [best] clothes and go down to the threshing floor; do not make yourself
known to the man until he has finished eating and drinking. 4 When he lies down, note the
place where he lies, and go and uncover his thighs and lie down, and he will tell you what you
should do." 5 Ruth said to Naomi, "All that you tell me I will do."

6 Then Ruth went down to the threshing floor and did just as her mother-in-law commanded her. 7 Now Boaz had eaten and drunk and his heart was content, and he went to lie
down at the end of the heap [of grain]. Then Ruth came in secret and uncovered his thighs
and lay down. 8 At midnight the man trembled and turned and right there a woman was
lying at his thighs! 9 Then Boaz said, "Who are you?" And she said, "I am Ruth, your slave-
woman; spread your cloak over your slave-woman, for you are a kin redeemer." 10 And he
said, "May you be blessed by the Most High my daughter; your most recent act of fidelity
is greater than the first; you have not gone after young men, whether poor or rich. 11 And
now, my daughter, fear not; all that you have spoken, I will do for you, for all the assembly
of my people know you are a warrior-hearted woman. 12 And now, it is true that I am a
kin redeemer, there is a kin redeemer closer than I. 13 Spend the night tonight and when
morning comes, if he will redeem you as kin, good; let him redeem you. If he does not want
to redeem you as kin, then, as the Ageless God lives, I will redeem you as kin myself. Lie
down until the morning."

14 So Ruth lay at his thighs until morning, but got up before one person could recognize
a neighbor for Boaz said [to himself], "Let it not be known that the woman came to the
threshing floor." 15 Then he said, "Bring the cloak you are wearing and hold it out." So she
held it and Boaz measured out six helpings of barley, and put it on her back; then he went into
the city. 16 And Ruth came to her mother-in-law and Naomi asked, "Who are you, my daughter?" And she told her all that the man had done for her. 17 Ruth explained, "He gave these six
helpings of barley to me, for he said, 'Do not go back to your mother-in-law empty-handed.'"

[18] She replied, "Wait, my daughter, until you learn how the matter will shake out, for the man will not rest, but will conclude the matter today."

Psalm 65:5–13

5 Through wondrous deeds you answer us with deliverance,
O God of our salvation,
hope of all the ends of the earth
and of the farthest seas.
6 You established the mountains through your might;
you are girded with strength.
7 The one who silences the roaring of the seas,
the roaring of their waves,
the rumble of the peoples.
8 They who live at the farthest reaches are awed by your signs;
you make the dawnings of morning and evening sing for joy.
9 You attend the earth and water her,
you enrich her greatly;
the river of God is full of water;
you provide the people with grain,
thus you have established it.
10 Irrigating earth's furrows,
smoothing her ridges,
softening her with showers,
and blessing her growth.
11 You crown the year with your goodness;
your paths overflow with fatness.
12 The pastures of the wilderness overflow,
and with joy the hills gird themselves.
13 The meadows are clothed with flocks,
the valleys arrayed in grain,
indeed, they shout for joy.

Acts 5:12 Now, many signs and wonders were done among the people through the apostles; they were all together in the Portico of Solomon. [13] None of the others dared to join
them, but the people extolled them. [14] Yet more believers were added to Christ, a multitude of
both women and men. [15] So much so that they even carried the sick into the streets, and laid
them on cots and mats, so that Peter's shadow might overshadow some of them as he passed.
[16] Multitudes would also gather from the towns around Jerusalem, bringing the sick and those
tormented by unclean spirits, and they were all made well.

Matthew 13:31 Jesus laid out another parable before the crowd: "The realm of the heavens is like a mustard seed that a person took and sowed in their field. [32] Indeed it is the smallest of all the seeds, but when it has grown it is the greatest of plants and becomes a tree, so that the birds of the air come and make nests in its branches." [33] Then Jesus told them another parable: "The realm of the heavens is like yeast that a woman took and mixed in with three scoops of flour until all of it was leavened."

[34] All these things Jesus said to the crowds in parables; without a parable he said nothing to them. [35] This was to fulfill what had been spoken through the prophet:

> *"I will open my mouth to speak in parables;*
> *I will declare what has been hidden from the foundation of the world."*

PROCLAMATION

Text Notes

The text of Ruth uses questions as a narrative device throughout that are often converted to sentences in other translations; KJV tends to preserve the question form (see Judges 4:6 and Ruth 2:8–10). The same expression in Ruth 2:1 means "good for" as well as "good to" you. The word used for the lower extremities in Ruth 3:4 refers to the whole leg and particularly the thighs and genitalia as in childbirth (Deuteronomy 28:57); in Isaiah 7:20 "hair of the feet" refers to pubic hair shaved with other body hair in a ritual of humiliation. All of the slave language in Ruth is Ruth's; the narrator, Boaz, and Naomi all refer to Boaz's agricultural workers as his "girls" and "boys." Ruth refers to them and herself as enslaved (see Ruth 2:3 and 3:9), difficult to observe in translations that use "servant" throughout. Perhaps that communicates something about the harshness and desperation of her character's worldview.

The "kin redeemer," *go'el*, is the nearest adult male who bears responsibility for redeeming, or buying back, their hard-up kin from debt slavery and avenging their blood (Leviticus 25:25–26, 48–49; Numbers 35:12; Deuteronomy 19:6, 12). That language is also used for God redeeming Israel and applied to Jesus in the Christian Testament. Ruth's fidelity in 3:10 is what is usually described as "lovingkindness" or "faithful love" when applied to God. Boaz describes Ruth as a "warrior-hearted" woman using the same description that the narrator uses for him in 2:1 (see discussion on Proper 3). In verse 16 Naomi asked Ruth the same question Boaz asked in verse 9, "who are you," i.e., are you betrothed? Most translations opt for the nonliteral "how is it with you" for the latter. Verses 15 and 17 lack a unit of measure and say simply "six barleys." Similarly, verse 17 lacks "handed," saying merely "empty."

Matthew 13:35 uses a form of Psalm 78:2 that is not found in Hebrew or Greek or in the Syriac Peshitta or Aramaic Targum. In all of those texts the last line is "I will utter riddles from of old."

Preaching Prompts

In all of these texts, God is the one who satiates hunger and provides a home for her people, through the bounty of creation and through human actions, even with complex motives.

Romantic readings of Ruth often ignore Naomi's grooming of her to sexually service Boaz—make herself attractive, wait until he is drunk, uncover his thighs, and do what he tells her—as a survival strategy for them both. Note that once they determine another man has the legal right to wed her, Boaz tells her to lie back down, knowing he has no legal access to her, and tells her to sneak out in the morning when she would have been more visible. It is likely that there was sexual contact between them, which given Ruth's vulnerable status is problematic for contemporary readers. The story of Ruth can easily be read as a story of survival sex, and draws our attention to the plight of vulnerable, hungry, desperate migrant women.

Contrasting the hunger of Ruth and Naomi, one of the marks of goodness and prosperity is "fat" and "fatness" as in verse 11 of the psalm. It does not go too far to say that the Hebrew Scriptures are "fat positive" when it comes to people as well, even with cautions about excess.

In the Gospel reading, Jesus offers diverse and inclusive images of God. In Matthew 13, Jesus uses inclusive language to tell the same parable two ways, once with a person gendered male representing God who created the realm of the heavens and once with a woman as God the creator. (This also happens with the parables of the lost sheep and coin which are also back to back.) Were we to imitate Christ, we could not limit ourselves to just one image for God.

PROPER 6 (CLOSEST TO JUNE 15)

Ruth 4:9–17; Psalm 78:1–8; 1 Timothy 5:1–8; Matthew 15:1–9

Ruth 4:9 Then Boaz said to the elders and all the people, "Today you are witnesses that I am acquiring all that belonged to Elimelech and all that belonged to Chilion and Mahlon from the hand of Naomi. 10 Also, Ruth the Moabite, the wife of Mahlon am I acquiring for myself as a wife to maintain the dead man's name on his inheritance, to reestablish the name of the deceased on his heritable property, that it may not be cut off from his kin and from the gate of his native place; today you are witnesses."

11 All the women and men who were at the gate, along with the elders, said, "We are witnesses. May the FAITHFUL GOD grant that the woman who is coming into your house be like Rachel and Leah; the two of them built up the house of Israel. May you prosper in Ephrathah and establish a lineage in Bethlehem; 12 and, may your house, through the children that the FOUNT OF LIFE will give you by this young woman, be like the house of Perez, whom Tamar

gave birth to for Judah."[13] So Boaz took Ruth as his own for a wife. He came to her and the
SOURCE OF LIFE granted her a pregnancy, and she gave birth to a son. [14] Then the women
said to Naomi, "Blessed be the FAITHFUL GOD, who has not deprived you this day of next-
of-kin; and may the child's name be renowned in Israel! [15] He shall be to you a restorer of life
and a provider in your latter years; for your daughter-in-law has given birth to him, she who
loves you, she who is more to you than seven sons." [16] Then Naomi took the child and laid
him in her bosom, and she fostered him. [17] The neighbor-women gave him a name, saying,
"A son has been born to Naomi." They named him Obed; he became the father of Jesse, the
father of David."

Psalm 78

1 Give ear, my people, to my teaching;
incline your ear to the utterances of my mouth.
2 I will open my mouth in a proverb;
I will utter riddles from of old.
3 Which we have heard and known,
and which our mothers and fathers have told us.
4 We will not hide them from their daughters and sons;
we will recount to generations to come,
the praiseworthy deeds of SHE WHO SPEAKS LIFE,
and her might and the wonderful works she has done.
5 She gave her decrees for Rebekah's descendants
and placed teaching among Sarah's offspring,
which she commanded their mothers and fathers
to make known to their daughters and sons.
6 In order that a coming generation, children yet to be, might know,
and will rise up and tell their daughters and sons.
7 Then they will put their confidence in God,
and not forget the works of God, but will keep her commandments;
8 And not be like their ancestors, a stubborn and rebellious generation,
a generation whose heart was not steadfast,
and whose spirit was not faithful to God.

1 Timothy 5:1 Do not rebuke an elder man, but speak to them as to a father, to those younger,
as brothers, [2] to elder women as mothers, to younger women as sisters, in absolute purity.
[3] Honor widows who are really widows. [4] If a widow has children or grandchildren, let
them learn first to show devotion to their own family and make repayment to their parents;
for this is pleasing in God's sight. [5] Now the real widow, having been left alone, on God she
hopes and continues in supplications and prayers night and day. [6] But she who lives luxuri-
ously is dead even while she lives. [7] In order that they may be blameless, give these commands

as well: [8] Now whoever does not provide for their own, and especially for their household, has
denied the faith and is worse than an unbeliever.

Matthew 15:1 [Now some] Pharisees and religious scholars came to Jesus from Jerusalem
and said, [2] "Why do your disciples transgress the tradition of the elders? For they do not wash
their hands before they eat bread." [3] Then Jesus answered them, "And why do you all break the
commandment of God for the sake of your tradition? [4] For God said, 'Honor your mother
and your father,' and 'Whoever speaks evil of mother or father must die.' [5] But you say that
whoever tells mother or father, 'Whatever benefit you might have had from me is a gift [to
God],' then that person need not honor the mother or father. [6] So, for the sake of your tradition, you make void the word of God. [7] Hypocrites! Well did the prophet Isaiah prophesy of
you, and say:

[8] '*This people honors me with their lips,*
but their hearts are far from me;
[9] *in vain do they worship me,*
teaching human commandments as [authoritative] teaching.'"

PROCLAMATION

Text Notes

In the world of 1 Timothy 5, "widow" signifies more than being bereaved of a husband; it is also a ministerial office in the early church. The term is used both ways in the Epistles (see Annette Bourland Huizenga's discussion in the 1–2 Timothy and Titus volume of the *Wisdom Commentary* and Joanna Dewey's discussion of the passage in the *Women's Bible Commentary*). The ministerial widow could also be a virgin or otherwise unmarried.

Matthew 15:4 quotes Exodus 20:12 (duplicated in Deuteronomy 5:16). Verse 5 appears in different ways in a variety of manuscripts, with some of the text in verse 6 and with and without the final "mother" in the verse. The passage ends with a quote from Isaiah 29:13.

Preaching Prompts

Each of these texts spans or reflects on multiple generations in a community. Ruth's and Naomi's widowhoods are community matters with generational consequences. In the psalm, each generation is responsible for passing on the knowledge of God on to the next. Numerous passages in the Hebrew Scriptures affirm the critical role of mothers' teaching in the community, see Proverbs 1:8 and 6:20. The author of 1 Timothy defines who in the community is vulnerable and merits community resources in his understanding. In the Gospel, ancestral teaching and its interpretation becomes a matter of contention. Jesus models that disputes and differences in interpretation of scripture, faith, and practice vary in community, and their critique is not a matter of losing or breaking faith.

First Timothy 5 challenges us to think about poverty and who we think is deserving of help, and who can serve in the church, and what bearing a minister's family or relationship status has on her service. The author here understands true widows to be bereft of all family and destitute as well in accordance with his preferences, verses 4–6, 16. This is similar to the fatherless children of the Hebrew Bible known as "orphans" while their mothers are present, identified as "widows," see Exodus 22:24 and Lamentations 5:3. The concern is more than preserving the community's resources for those who do not have families who can support them, verses 4, 8. The author is also concerned with regulating the sexual lives of women who serve the church in this way, limiting the ministerial office of the widow to chaste women; he warns that they violate their faith (not "pledge" as in NRSV) if they remarry after widowhood, verses 9, 11. The author believes women who can should bear children and manage households; otherwise, they are "idle," verses 13–14. Then if properly "widowed" they may serve the church at age sixty, verse 9. The author would certainly approve of Ruth's remarriage given she was young enough to bear children. Yet were we to enshrine all of his biases—he says "I would have," not "God said"—we would be deprived of the ministry of a significant portion of the church.

PROPER 7 (CLOSEST TO JUNE 22)

1 Samuel 1:1–6, 9–18; Psalm 113; Colossians 4:10–17; Matthew 15:21–28

1 Samuel 1:1 Now there was a certain man of Ramathaim, a Zuphite from the hill country of Ephraim, whose name was Elkanah son of Jeroham son of Elihu son of Tohu son of Zuph, an Ephraimite. 2 He had two wives; the name of the one was Hannah, and the name of the second, Peninnah. Peninnah had children, but Hannah had no children.

3 Now this man went up year by year from his town to worship and to sacrifice to the SOVEREIGN of heaven's vanguard at Shiloh; there the two sons of Eli, Hophni and Phinehas, were priests of the HOLY ONE OF OLD. 4 And it was, on the day Elkanah sacrificed, he would give to his wife Peninnah and to all her daughters and her sons portions [of the sacrifice]. 5 But to Hannah he gave a double portion, because he loved her, though the WOMB OF LIFE had closed her womb. 6 Her rival used to provoke her severely, to irritate her, because the WELLSPRING OF LIFE had closed her womb.

9 After they had eaten and drunk at Shiloh, Hannah rose and presented herself before the HOLY ONE OF OLD. Now Eli the priest was sitting on the seat beside the doorposts of the temple of the HOLY ONE. 10 Hannah's soul was embittered, and she prayed to the SOURCE

of Life, and she wept profusely. [11] And she vowed a vow and said, “Holy One of heaven’s
legions, if only you would truly look on the affliction of your slave-woman, and remember
me, and not forget your slave-woman, but will give to your slave-woman man-seed, then I
will place him before you as a nazirite all the days of his life. He shall not drink wine or strong
drink, and a razor shall not go upon his head.”

[12] And it was as she increased praying before the Faithful One, Eli was observing her
mouth. [13] Now Hannah, she was speaking in her heart, only her lips moved; her voice was
not heard. So, Eli took her for a drunkard. [14] And Eli said to her, “How long will you remain
drunk? Put your wine away, woman—away from you!” [15] Then Hannah responded and said,
“No, my lord, I am a woman whose spirit has hardened; I have not drunk either wine or strong
drink; I have been pouring out my soul before the God Who Hears. [16] Do not regard your
slave as a worthless woman, for I have been speaking from my great grief and vexation all this
time.” [17] Then Eli answered and said, “Go in peace; the God of Israel grant the petition you
have made to God.” [18] And Hannah said, “May your slave-woman find favor in your eyes.”
Then the woman went on her way to her quarters, ate and drank with her husband, and her
countenance was sad no longer.

Psalm 113

1 Hallelujah! Give praise, you slaves of the Most High;
praise the Name of the Wisdom of the Ages.
2 Let the Name of the Holy One of Old be blessed,
from this time forth forevermore.
3 From the rising of the sun to its going down
the Name of the Author of Life is praised.
4 She Who is Wisdom is high above all nations,
and her glory above the heavens.
5 Who is like the Mother of All our God, who sits enthroned on high,
yet bends down to behold the heavens and the earth?
6 She takes up the weak out of the dust
and lifts up the poor from the ashes.
7 She sets them with the rulers,
with the rulers of her people.
8 She makes the woman of a childless house
to be a joyful mother of children.

Colossians 4:10 Aristarchus my fellow prisoner greets you all, so too Mark the cousin of
Barnabas, about whom you have received instructions, if he comes to you, welcome him.
[11] And Jesus who is called Justus [greets you]. These of the circumcised are my only coworkers
for the realm of God, and they have been a comfort to me. [12] Epaphras, who is one of you, a
slave of the Messiah Jesus, greets you all. He is always fighting for you all in his prayers, so that

you may stand mature and fully assured in everything that is the will of God. 13 For I testify for him that he has [done] much hard labor for you all and for those in Laodicea and in Hierapolis. 14 Luke, the beloved physician, and Demas greet you. 15 Give my greetings to the sisters and brothers in Laodicea, and to Nympha and the church in her house. 16 And when this has been read among you all, make it so that it is read in the Laodicean church; and you all read the one from Laodicea. 17 And say to Archippus, "See that the ministry you have received in the Messiah, that you fulfill it."

Matthew 15:21 Jesus left the place [where he had been teaching] and went back to the regions of Tyre and Sidon. 22 Just then a Canaanite woman from that area came out and shouted, "Have mercy on me, Lord, Son of David; my daughter is badly demon-possessed." 23 But Jesus did not answer her a word. Then his disciples came and implored him, saying, "Send her away, for she keeps shouting after us." 24 Now Jesus answered, "I was not sent to any except the lost sheep of the house of Israel." 25 But she came and knelt before Jesus, saying, "Lord, help me." 26 Then Jesus said, "It is not good to take the children's food and throw it to the dogs." 27 But she said, "Yes, Lord, yet the dogs eat the crumbs that fall from their lord's table." 28 Then Jesus answered her, "Woman, great is your faith! Let it be for you as you wish." And her daughter was healed that moment.

PROCLAMATION

Text Notes

In 1 Samuel 1:5 in Hebrew, Hannah's portion is a "nose" portion, with "double" being construed from context. The alternate equally common meaning for *apayim*, "anger," is not helpful here.

The Dead Sea Scrolls (DSS) versions of 1–2 Samuel offer a significant number of corrections to the text, most of which occur in the NRSV—look for the letter Q in the translation notes at the bottom of the text, present in every NRSV Bible. (Indeed, the NRSV is the first scholarly post-DSS discovery Bible and includes some 100 corrections.) The DSS are authoritative because they are the oldest, most complete manuscripts of the scriptures that have ever been found.

I follow the DSS including "nazirite," "all the days of his life," and "he shall not drink wine or strong drink" in 1:11 from scroll 4QSam^{a}. In verse 11 Hannah asks for the gender-specific "seed of men," here "man-seed," elsewhere "man-child." I also include "she presented herself to the Holy One" in verse 9 and "she went to her quarters, ate and drank with her husband" from the LXX, which shares content with the DSS here.

The presence of "Nympha and the church in her house," attested in what is the oldest most authoritative manuscript that includes the passage, raised questions for early curators of the scriptures, which were not resolved by the change of her name to a male form in later manuscripts, including the *Textus Receptus* used for the KJV where she has been masculinized. The purported masculine form, *Nymphas*, does not exist in the historical or literary record while Nympha occurs some sixty times. (See Ross Kraemer's entry in *Women in Scripture: A Dictionary of Named and Unnamed Women in the Hebrew Bible, the Apocryphal/Deuterocanonical Books, and the New Testament.*) That Colossians also calls for submissive women/wives has led to further speculation, including that Nympha was a widow (see the *Wisdom Commentary* on Colossians by Cynthia Briggs Kittredge and Claire Miller Colombo).

In Matthew 15:23, "send her away" is "loose her," i.e., "cut her loose." Early church interpreters read that to mean the disciples urged Jesus to set her free of the demon, rehabilitating the image of the disciples, though Jesus refuses their request and hers. However, the term also has the sense of "divorce" and therefore, "send away." In verse 26, Jesus infamously uses the word "dogs" (actually "little dogs") in analogy to the woman and her daughter. Many readers hear the word "bitch," female dog, on the lips of Jesus and are disturbed, if not horrified. Others work to ameliorate the comparison to an unclean animal that was used to indicate contempt in the Hebrew Scriptures, see 1 Samuel 17:43; 2 Samuel 3:8; 2 Kings 8:14; Proverbs 26:11. In verse 28, that "moment" is that "hour."

Preaching Prompts

These texts focus on women and their households; in three of the texts, children (or their lack) characterize those homes, not unexpected in the world of the Hebrew Scriptures. However, in the Epistle, the members of Nympha's household are the members of the church in her home, a church that surely she leads.

The first lesson proffers Hannah and her desperate plea for a child. The many biblical accounts of miraculous pregnancies that do not conform to the lived experience of most people can be difficult for women with unwelcome infertility. The text presents Peninnah, demonized in the text and interpretive tradition. It's worth asking what hurts Penninah more as a woman who had fulfilled society's expectation, yet was unloved and unfavored. Note: In the ancient Israelite sacrificial system most offerings (except whole burnt offerings) were split between God and the giver. Select parts could only be offered to God with designated portions for the giver and his or her family; women and men made these offerings.

Psalm 113 shares with Hannah's hymn and Mary's Magnificat the language of reversal, lifting the poor and weak/needy (Psalm 113:7–8; 1 Samuel 2:7–8; Luke 1:52–53). One of the Magnificat's reversals seems to speak more to Hannah than to Mary: a mother of many who is forlorn like Penninah and a previously barren woman who gives birth like Hannah. The psalm affirms that God provides infertile women with children, equated to a proper "home," and some suggest that it was prayed or recited by women living with infertility. There is no broad consensus as to whether the psalm pre- or postdates Samuel. It will be important to affirm dependence on God without demeaning child-free homes and families.

Nympha was most likely Greek, due to her Greek name (young woman or bride or sister-in-law) and due to Paul—commonly agreed upon as the author—stipulating the previous group of addresses as Jewish. The congregation in her home points to her autonomy; it is her home and she is not identified as a widow. Given her support of the church which likely extends beyond providing it a home, she is undoubtably of means. Nympha is clearly the leader of that church; Paul's letter is to her among others. She is a witness to the diversity and inclusivity of the church from its birth, even as some were inscribing hierarchy upon it.

Jesus sought respite by going to the shore. In a shocking scene, Jesus denies a desperate woman and her child the help and healing for which the mother begs, bearing uncomfortable witness to the humanity of Jesus in an unwelcome way. Jesus seems to display ethnocentric bias—a challenging reading for those who understand having and acting on bias to be sinful, which would be incompatible with most Christologies. Yet all of Jesus's comments about Gentiles in Matthew to this point are negative: *Do not even the Gentiles do the same*? (5:47); *do not heap up empty phrases as the Gentiles do* (6:7); *it is the Gentiles who strive for all these things* (6:32); *let such a one be to you as a Gentile and a tax collector* (18:17); and Jesus initially excludes Gentiles from receipt of the gospel: *Go nowhere among the Gentiles, and enter no town of the Samaritans* (10:5), until this conversation. Not only is her daughter healed, but Jesus will withdraw the ethnic limitations he placed on the gospel and send his disciples "into all the world."

The age of the demon-possessed daughter (or what malady her possession might represent) is unknown; it may be useful to allow for the possibilities of the daughter as both a child and an adult and see how each shapes the preaching.

PROPER 8 (CLOSEST TO JUNE 29)

1 Samuel 1:19–28; Canticle of Hannah (1 Samuel 2:1–10); 1 Corinthians 3:1–9; Matthew 15:29–39

1 Samuel 1:19 Hannah and Elkanah rose early in the morning and bowed down and worshiped before the HOLY ONE OF OLD; then they turned back and went to their house at
Ramah. Elkanah knew his wife Hannah, and the HOLY ONE remembered her. [20] And it was
with the turning of the days that Hannah conceived and gave birth to a son. She called his
name Samuel (God hears), for she said, "From the GOD WHO HEARS have I asked him."

[21] Now the man Elkanah went up along with his whole household to offer to the HOLY
ONE the yearly sacrifice, and on account of a vow. [22] Yet Hannah did not go up, for she said

to her husband, "[Not] until the child is weaned, then will I bring him, that he may be seen in the presence of the MOST HIGH and remain there perpetually. I will present him as a nazirite in perpetuity, for all the days of his life."
23 Her husband Elkanah said to her, "Do what is best in your eyes, stay until you have weaned him. May the FAITHFUL GOD establish the words of your mouth." So, the woman remained and nursed her son until she weaned him.
24 And she took him up with her after she had weaned him along with a three-year-old bull, an ephah of flour, and a jug of wine. Hannah brought him to the house of the EVER-LIVING GOD at Shiloh and the boy was just a little boy.
25 Then they slaughtered the bull, and they brought the boy to Eli.
26 And Hannah said, "My lord! As you live, my lord, I am the woman, the one who was standing beside you in this [place] to pray to the GOD WHO HEARS.
27 For this boy I prayed; and the FAITHFUL GOD gave me my asking, what I asked from God.
28 Therefore have I bequeathed him to the GRACIOUS GOD; all his days will he be a bequest to the GOD WHOSE NAME IS HOLY."

So she left him there and she bowed down and worshipped the FAITHFUL GOD.

Canticle of Hannah (1 Samuel 2:1–10)

1 Hannah prayed and she said,
"My heart exults in the HOLY ONE OF OLD;
my horn is lifted up in my God.
My mouth [opens] wide against my enemies,
for I will rejoice in my victory.
2 "There is none holy like the MOST HIGH,
none besides you;
there is no rock like our God.
3 Speak proudly no more, multiplying pride,
nor let arrogance come from your mouth;
for the AGELESS GOD is a God of knowledge,
and by God deeds are accounted.
4 The bows of the mighty are broken,
yet the feeble gird on warrior-strength.
5 Those who were full have hired themselves out for bread,
yet those who were hungry are fat.
She who was barren has birthed seven children,
yet she who has many children languishes.
6 The CREATOR OF ALL kills and gives life;
brings down to Sheol and raises up.
7 The GRACIOUS ONE makes poor and makes rich;
brings low and also lifts up.
8 God raises the poor from the dust,
and lifts the needy from heaps of human waste,
to seat them with nobles and inherit a seat of honor.

For to the Creator belong the pillars of the earth,
and on them God has set the world.
9 God will guard the feet of the faithful who belong to God,
while the wicked perish in shadow;
for it is not by might that one prevails.
10 The Holy One of Sinai!
Those who strive against God shall be shattered;
God thunders against them from heaven.
The Fount of Justice will judge the ends of the earth;
God will give strength to God's ruler,
and exalt the power of the anointed of God."

1 Corinthians 3:1 Now sisters and brothers, I could not speak to you all as spiritual, but
rather as carnal, as infants in Christ. 2 I fed you all with milk, not solid food, for you were
not yet ready for solid food. Even now you are still not ready, 3 for you all are still carnal.
Given there is still jealousy and discord among you, are you not carnal, and going around
as merely human? 4 For when one says, "I am Paul's," and another, "I am Apollos's," are you
not merely human?

5 What then is Apollos? What is Paul? Ministers through whom you came to believe, as
the Messiah granted to each person. 6 I planted, Apollos watered, but God produces growth.
7 Therefore, neither the one who plants nor the one who waters is anything, rather it is God
who produces growth. 8 The one who plants and the one who waters are alike, and each will
receive wages according to their labor. 9 For we are God's coworkers, working together; you
are God's cultivation, God's construction.

Matthew 15:29 After Jesus had left [Tyre and Sidon], he went by the Sea of Galilee, and
he went up the mountain, sitting down there. 30 Great crowds came to him, bringing with
them disabled, blind, and mute people, and people missing body parts along with many others.
Then they put them at his feet, and he healed them 31 so that the crowd was amazed when
they saw mute people speaking, people missing body parts made whole, disabled people walking,
and blind people seeing. And they praised the God of Israel.

32 Then Jesus called his disciples to him and said, "I have compassion for the crowd,
because they have stayed with me for three days now and have nothing to eat, and I do not
want to send them away hungry, for they might collapse on the road." 33 The disciples said to
him, "Where are we to get so much bread in the desert as to feed so great a crowd?" 34 Jesus
asked them, "How many loaves do you have?" They said, "Seven, and a few small fish." 35 Then
ordering the crowd to sit down on the ground, 36 he took the seven loaves and the fish, and giving
thanks he broke them and gave them to the disciples; the disciples gave them to the crowds.
37 And all of them ate and were filled, and they took up the abundance of fragments, seven
baskets full. 38 Those who ate were women and children besides four thousand men. 39 Then
sending away the crowds, he got into the boat and went to the region of Magadan.

PROCLAMATION

Text Notes

I chose "God Who Hears" to render the divine Name in 1 Samuel 1:20 to reiterate the etymology of Samuel's name. Some scholars argue that the etymology belongs more properly to Saul, whose name stems from the verb for "to ask"; the "bequest" of verse 28 is the same spelling and pronunciation of Saul, *Shaul.* Hannah's last line in verse 22, "I will present him . . ." comes from the Qumran scroll 4QSam[a] and is not present elsewhere. According to the older reading supported by the LXX, in verse 23 Elkanah prays that God would establish the words of *Hannah's* mouth; the Masoretic Text has "the words of God's mouth." The same scroll corrects "three bulls" in verse 24 to "three year-old bull." The end of verse 24 is simply the word for "boy" or "youth" repeated twice; the meaning must be reconstructed and construed from context. I use "bequeath/bequest" in verse 28 to mirror the continuing verb "ask" now in a causative form that indicates fulfilling a request. The very last line occurs in two forms: *They bowed down and worshipped God there* from the MT and *she left him there and worshipped* from Qumran. The Dead Sea Scrolls are the oldest, most complete manuscripts of the Hebrew scriptures and generated nearly ninety corrections to the Hebrew Bible, the bulk in Samuel.

Verse 4 of the Canticle uses *chayil,* denoting warrior strength, a warrior's heart, or an army; it is used of Boaz and Ruth and the desirable wife in Proverbs 31 (whose attributes are selected by another woman), and Pharaoh's army. I use "shadow" in verse 9 for "darkness," given the way "dark" has been conflated negatively with "black" and black people in interpretation for harm. "Shattered" in verse 10 also has the sense of being terrified.

In Matthew 15:30–31 I have changed "the mute, the blind . . ." to "mute people, blind people," because people are not their disabilities. In verse 32 "compassion," *splagchnizomai,* emanates from the *splagchnon,* inner organs, similar to the way mother-love comes from the womb. I have inverted the order of the diners in verse 38, removing the women and children from the ancillary position.

Preaching Prompts

According to Targum Onqelos, Hannah worships on her own in 1 Samuel 1:19, without her husband. She names her child in accordance with the broader practice in ancient Israel; the episodes where God or a father name a child should be viewed as exceptions. Hannah's participation in the slaughter of her offering is signaled by the "they" in verse 25; the exact nature of that participation is unclear.

The theology in 1 Corinthians 3:3–4 unhelpfully pits the flesh against the spirit, identifying humanity with the flesh as carnal. This seems very much at odds with the Incarnation. The spirit/flesh dichotomy is fueled by Greek philosophy and will become a gendered hierarchy for some church fathers, with women being identified with the flesh.

Among the ministers who could have been referenced in 1 Corinthians 3:5–6 are the long list of women who served with Paul enumerated in Romans 16, more particularly Priscilla (Prisca), who is named before her husband, signifying leadership, and who corrected Apollos's theology, see Acts 18:18, 26. Verse 9 uses the same language of coworker to describe the relationship between these ministers and God that Paul uses in Romans 16:3 for his female colaborers and elsewhere for men like Timothy.

The healings in today's Gospel immediately follow the healing of the Canaanite woman or girl at her mother's request. Word has gotten out. Has she become an evangelist in the space between two verses? Jesus has traveled back from the shore to an unidentified mountain near the Sea of Galilee; the sea was a bit over twenty miles away as the crow flies. While they are in Galilee, there is no telling from whence the people have come. Jesus sits as though for teaching yet is unclear whether that was his initial purpose; they were there for three days, verse 32, with no mention of teaching at all. Jesus seems to have simply made himself available for whatever needs the people had. Three days at the feet of Jesus, witnessing miracle after miracle. Was that all that happened before the multiplication miracle? Did people visit with Jesus? Did he walk among them, touching, blessing, encouraging, or even playing with the children? The treasure of those three days is made more complicated by a text that reflects the cultural values of its age, that variably abled people need to be fixed, and that wholeness and health look a particular way.

As in the previous story, the disciples fall significantly short of being pastoral. They are not yet shepherds. They do not see the need, and when made aware of it, focus on their limitations and finite resources. There is no little boy and his lunch. The meager resources are either their own or they have collected them, perhaps from mothers who packed a lunch.

PROPER 9 (CLOSEST TO JULY 6)

1 Samuel 2:18–21, 26; Psalm 111; 1 Thessalonians 2:1–8; Matthew 18:23–35

1 Samuel 2:18 Now Samuel was ministering in the presence of the HOLY ONE OF OLD, a boy dressed in a linen ephod. [19] A little robe would his mother make for him and bring up to him year by year, when she went up with her husband to offer the yearly sacrifice. [20] And Eli would bless Elkanah and his wife, and say, "May the HOLY ONE repay you (Elkanah) with seed from this woman in place of the bequest she made to the FOUNT OF LIFE"; and then they would return to their home.

[21] And the FAITHFUL ONE attended Hannah and she conceived and gave birth to two daughters and three sons. And the boy Samuel grew up there in the presence of the LIVING GOD.

[26] Now the boy Samuel went on and grew in goodness with the MOST HIGH and with humanity.

Psalm 111

1 Praise the LIVING GOD!
I will give thanks to the HOLY GOD with my whole heart,
in the company of upright women and men, in the congregation.
2 Great are the works of the CREATOR OF ALL,
diligently sought by all who delight in them.
3 Glorious and majestic is her work,
and her righteousness endures forever.
4 She has made a monument of her own wonders;
the MOTHER OF ALL is gracious and full of mother-love.
5 She provides meat for those who revere her;
she remembers her covenant in perpetuity.
6 The might of her works has she declared to her people,
in giving them the heritage of the nations.
7 The works of her hands are faithful and just,
and all her precepts are trustworthy:
8 Set up for all time,
to be done in faithfulness and uprightness.
9 She sent redemption to her people;
she has commanded her covenant for all time.
Holy and awesome is her name.
10 The beginning of wisdom is the reverence of the EVER-LIVING GOD;
a good understanding have all those who do so.
Her praise endures forever.

1 Thessalonians 2:1 You yourselves know, sisters and brothers, our coming to you was not
in vain. [2] On the contrary, we had suffered previously and been mistreated in Philippi, as you
know; we had courage in our God to declare to you all the gospel of God in spite of much
opposition. [3] For our exhortation is not from deceit or corruption or trickery. [4] Rather, just as
we have been approved by God to be entrusted with the gospel, so do we speak, not to please
women or men, but to please God who tests our hearts. [5] Now, we never came with a word of
flattery as you all know, or with a pretext for greed; God is our witness. [6] Nor did we seek praise
from women and men, whether from you all or from others, [7] though we could have made
demands as apostles of Christ. Rather we were child-like among you, even like a nurse tenderly

caring for her own children. [8] Thus, so caring for you all, it is our pleasure to share with you not only the gospel of God, but also ourselves, because you have become beloved to us.

Matthew 18:21 Peter came and said to Jesus, "Rabbi, if a sister or brother sins against me, how often should I forgive? Up to seven times?" [22] Jesus said to him, "Not seven times, but, I tell you, seventy-seven times.

[23] "For this reason the realm of heaven may be compared to a human ruler who wished to settle matters with their enslaved debtors. [24] When the settlement began, one who owed ten thousand talents was brought forward. [25] Since that one could not pay, the ruler ordered that enslaved person to be sold, together with spouse and children and every possession, and thus to pay. [26] So falling and kneeling before the ruler, the enslaved debtor said, 'Have patience with me, and I will pay you everything.' [27] And out of compassion, the lord of that enslaved person released that one and forgave the debt. [28] But that same enslaved person who was owed a hundred denarii by another enslaved person, upon going out, came upon the debtor; and seizing that one by the throat, said, 'Pay what you owe.' [29] Then the indebted slave fell down and pled, 'Have patience with me, and I will pay you.' [30] But the other enslaved person was not willing and went and threw the debtor into prison until the debt was paid. [31] When those who were also enslaved saw what had happened, they were greatly distressed, and they went and reported to their lord all that had taken place. [32] Then the lord summoned the one whose debt was forgiven saying, 'You wicked slave! I forgave you all that debt because you pleaded with me. [33] Should you not have had mercy on your fellow slave, as I had mercy on you?' [34] And in anger the lord handed that one over to be tortured until the entire debt could be paid. [35] So my heavenly Abba will also do to every one of you, if you do not forgive your sister or brother from your heart."

PROCLAMATION

Text Notes

In 1 Samuel 2:19, all of the action verbs are feminine, they are Hannah's, even when her husband is with her. This is a common feature of biblical Hebrew, a singular verb (any gender) followed by a plural subject indicating that the first person led in the action and the other followed. On the other hand, the blessing of Elkanah in verse 20 is spoken to him alone: May God repay "you," masculine singular. "Repay" comes from the DSS text supported by the LXX. Without the corrections from Qumran, the MT says that Samuel "grew up with God" in verse 21.

In verse 4 of the psalm, "made a monument" renders "made a memory." In the same verse, "mother-love" is the feeling that emerges from the womb with which it shares a grammatical root. It characterizes the love of God but is most often translated "mercy" or "compassion." "Meat" in verse 5 is literally "prey"; the warrior-hearted prospective wife in Proverbs 31 also takes prey in Proverbs 31:15, thoroughly domesticated in most translations.

"Could have made demands" in 1 Thessalonians 2:7 clarifies "able to place weight (or a burden)." In the context of the scriptures, "nurses," as in verse 7 of the Epistle, are childcare providers, often wet-nurses, not healthcare workers.

In Jesus's parable, the ruler and two indebted enslaved persons who feature in it are male and their spouses are women. I've chosen to make the genders of the characters indeterminate to offer a different hearing. While women were particularly vulnerable when enslaved, in this story the economic vulnerability cuts across gender lines. I also translate "slave" as a state of captivity, "enslaved," rather than as a person's identity. However, in the ruler's speech, "slave" is the appropriate epithet. I preserve the use of the title "lord" for the enslaver to help readers and hearers appreciate the full context of its use beyond as a traditional title for God and Jesus.

Preaching Prompts

There is a parenting and provisioning thread that runs through these lessons. Even having "given" Samuel to God, Hannah continues to mother him, spending some portion of the year crafting a robe, a little robe, for her little boy: perhaps purchasing the linen, perhaps growing, harvesting, and weaving it herself. God who mother-loves her people in the psalm provides for them, though the psalmist envisions despoiling others outside of the covenant to do so. In the Epistle, a mother who cares for the children of others as though there were her own is Paul's model of his own apostolic ministry. In the gospel, economic distress—here enslavement and debt—prevents families from providing for themselves and their children.

Hannah is autonomous in her marriage and in her religious practice. She chose to petition for a child and she chose to give him to God (Eli confirms that Samuel was her gift to God in verse 20). Elkanah is not credited with the gift, rather recognized as one to whom compensation is due. Hannah sacrificed to God, along with Elkanah only in some cases. Hannah chose to refrain from traveling for worship until she was finished nursing; Elkanah's assent was not permission. Hannah took her child to God's temporal abode, Shiloh where the Ark was. She invested her time and material resources in clothing her absent child. She went to see him each year. The grammar of Hannah's yearly visit indicated that she led and her husband followed. However, the narrator and Eli assert patriarchal hierarchy by blessing "Elkanah and his wife," putting his name first and omitting hers (until she gives birth again).

Paul's language for the apostolate is maternal in 1 Thessalonians 2:8. To the degree that the contemporary episcopate includes some understandings of the biblical apostolate, it has generally neglected a maternal model.

The spouses of the debtors and their children in the gospel were vulnerable, primarily due to the actions and status of the debtors in the parable. However, the overarching vulnerability is due to the uncontested ubiquitous slavery that not even Jesus challenges. It is certainly possible that the spouses and children were (understood to be) free until one family is sold at the end of the story, though as a teaching story the details do not necessarily reflect a specific reality. Crippling debt, unjust economic structures, and the legacy of slavery imperil families contemporarily, disrupting the ability of parents to provide for their children. While the parable is about mercy and forgiveness, it also speaks to social and economic inequity.

PROPER 10 (CLOSEST TO JULY 13)

1 Samuel 2:12–17, 22–25; Psalm 49:5–15;
1 Timothy 6:6–16; Matthew 19:16–30

1 Samuel 2:12 Now the sons of Eli were worthless; they had no knowledge of the Holy
God. 13 The practice of the priests toward the people was: when any woman or man sacrificed
an offering, the priest's boy came while the meat was boiling, with a three-pronged fork in his
hand. 14 Then he violently shoved it into the pan, or kettle, or caldron, or pot, and all that the
fork brought up the priest took for himself. This is what they did to all the women and men
of Israel who came there, to Shiloh. 15 Even more, before the fat was burned to smoke, the
priest's boy came and said to the one who was sacrificing, "Give up some meat to roast for the
priest; for he will not accept boiled meat from you, but only fresh." 16 And if the woman or
man said to him, "Let them burn the fat to smoke first, and then take for yourself what you
wish," he would say, "No! Now! You will give it, and if not, I will take it by force." 17 Thus the
sin of [Eli's] boys was very great in the sight of the Holy One of Old; for the men treated
the offerings of the Most High with contempt.

22 Now Eli was very old. He heard all that his sons were doing to all Israel, and how they
lay the women who were stationed at the entrance to the tent of meeting. 23 He said to them,
"Why do you do these things I'm hearing—evil things—from all these people? 24 No, my
sons; it is not a good report that I'm hearing the people of the Holy One of Sinai passing
around. 25 If a woman or man sins against another person, God can be entreated but if against
the Holy One someone sins, who can entreat for them?" Yet they would not listen to the
voice of their father; for it was the will of the Dread God to kill them.

Psalm 49:5–15

5 Why should I fear in evil days,
when iniquity at my heels surrounds me?
6 Those who trust in their wealth
and praise of the abundance of their riches?
7 Certainly, it cannot redeem a person,
or give to God as a ransom.

[8] For the redemption-price of a soul is costly,
they come to an end, forever.
[9] Shall one should live eternally
and never see the Pit?
[10] For when one sees the wise, they die;
the foolish and ignorant perish together
and leave to others their wealth.
[11] Their graves are their homes for all time,
their dwelling places from generation to generation,
though they put their name on lands.
[12] Humanity will not recline in grandeur;
rather they are like the animals that perish.
[13] This is the way of the foolish,
those pleased with their own words. *Selah*
[14] Like sheep they are set for Sheol;
Death shall be their shepherd.
The upright shall rule over them until the morning,
and their form shall waste away;
Sheol shall be their abode.
[15] But God will ransom my soul,
for from the grasp of Sheol she will take me. *Selah*

1 Timothy 6:6 Of course, there is great gain in godliness with contentment. [7] For nothing did we bring into the world, so there is nothing we can take out of it. [8] But if we have food and clothing, with these we will be content. [9] Now those who want to be rich fall into temptation and a trap. And many foolish and harmful passions plunge women and men into ruin and destruction. [10] For the root of all evil is the love of money, and some desiring [it] have wandered away from the faith and pierced themselves with many pains.

[11] But as for you, child of God, shun all this; pursue righteousness, godliness, faith, love, endurance, gentleness. [12] Fight the good fight of the faith; take hold of the eternal life, to which you were called and to which you professed the good profession in the presence of many witnesses. [13] I charge you in the presence of God, who enlivens all things, and of Christ Jesus, who in his testimony before Pontius Pilate made the good profession, [14] to keep the commandment without spot or blame until the appearing of our Redeemer Jesus Christ, [15] who God will reveal in God's own time—God who is the blessed and only Sovereign, the Power beyond all powers and Majesty of majesties. [16] It is God alone who has immortality and dwells in light unapproachable, whom no human has seen or can see; to God be honor and everlasting might. Amen.

Matthew 19:16 Someone came to Jesus and said, "Teacher, what good deed must I do to have eternal life?" [17] And Jesus said to him, "Why do you ask me about "goodness"? There is

only one who is good. If you wish to enter into life, keep the commandments." 18 He said to
him, "Which ones?" And Jesus said, "*You shall not murder; You shall not commit adultery; You
shall not steal; You shall not bear false witness;* 19 *Honor your mother and father; also, You shall
love your neighbor as yourself.*" 20 The young man said to him, "I have kept all these; what do
I yet lack?" 21 Jesus said to him, "If you wish to be perfect, go, sell your possessions, then give
to the poor, and you will have treasure in the heavens. Then come, follow me." 22 When the
young man heard this word, he went away grieving, for he had many possessions.

23 Then Jesus said to his disciples, "Truly I tell you all, it will be hard for a rich person to
enter the realm of the heavens. 24 Again I tell you all, it is easier for a camel to go through the
eye of a needle than for someone who is rich to enter the realm of God." 25 When the disciples heard this, they were greatly astounded and said, "Then who can be saved?" 26 And Jesus
looked at them and said, "For mortals it is impossible, but for God all things are possible."

27 Then Peter said to him, "Look, we have abandoned everything and followed you.
What then will we have?" 28 Jesus said to them, "Truly I tell you all, when everything is made
new, when the Son of Woman is seated on the throne of his glory, you all who have followed
me will also sit on twelve thrones, judging the twelve tribes of Israel. 29 And everyone who
has abandoned houses or sisters or brothers or mother or father or children or fields, for my
name's sake, will receive a hundredfold, and will inherit eternal life. 30 But many who are first
will be last, and the last will be first."

PROCLAMATION

Text Notes

Eli's sons were "sons of Belial" or "sons of worthlessness." In verse 13, the worshipper "sacrifices a sacrifice." As the Hannah story among others makes clear, women and men offered sacrifices. "Man" in the texts is generic and usually rendered "person" as in NRSV. The action of the boy on behalf of Eli's sons is physically violent; they "smite" the fork into the pots in verse 14. "Fresh" meat in verse 15 is "living," but of course the animal has been slaughtered, so recently living, i.e., "fresh." In verse 22 Eli's sons "lay," not "lay with" the women they abuse; the preposition is lacking in Hebrew. Often this formulation indicates a lack of consent or inappropriate coupling (see Rueben's rape of Bilhah in Genesis 35:22.) The women's "stationing" is articulated with the verb that describes waging war and as a noun, *tzavaoth*, indicates a military unit, a "host" in older translations, often in regards to God's legions of heavenly warriors—grammatically feminine plural. In Exodus 38:8, the women are in their own *tzavaoth* unit stationed at the tabernacle and donate their mirrors for the sanctuary laver; I relate them to the woman described as "guarding" the temple complex gate in John 18:16–17.

In 1 Timothy 6:10, *odynais* can be either "pains" or "sorrows." While the Epistle is purportedly written to Timothy by Paul (it is among the disputed Epistles), it was also written to the ancient church and received as speaking to us. Therefore, I have changed "man of God," specific to Timothy in verse 11, to "child of God," applicable to him and all future readers.

The question in Matthew 19:17 is "why do you ask me about (the) good?"; other less reliable manuscripts have "why do you call me good?" "Perfect" in Matthew 19:21 is also "whole" and "complete." "Grieving" in verse 22 is also "in pain."

Preaching Prompts

The tangled threads of greed and wealth come together in these lessons. Eli's sons lusted for and reveled in power over the people, stealing their offerings and God's and using their power to manipulate or steal sexual access to women. The psalm warns of trusting in wealth and affirms the infinite value of a soul, of life. We are worthy of God's redemption. The Epistle urges contentment with one's resources and cautions against love for money, not money itself. The Gospel demonstrates how the love of wealth and possessions can prevent some from following Christ.

The story of Eli's family drama raises the question of Eli's wife, the mother of his children, whether she was still in the picture, and if so, how she felt about the condemnation of her children, young men, to death. She can be read back into the story as a mother whose children are caught up in the criminal justice system, whose sons are guilty, but are still her boys. God's intent to kill them prevents them from heeding their father's counsel and perhaps repenting, similar to the hardening of Pharaoh's heart, one of the more challenging biblical worldviews.

The younger priests were entitled to a portion of most sacrifices (including the breast and right thigh); that was their primary provision, see Leviticus 7:28–36 and Numbers 6:20. Leviticus 3:16 declares, "All fat is the Holy One's." Texts calling for the fat to be burned completely as a type of incense offering to God are legion: Exodus 29:13, 22; Leviticus 3:3–4, 9–10, 14–17; 4:8–9, 19, 26, 31, 35; 6:12; 7:3–4, 23–25, 30–31, 33; 8:16, 25–26; 9:10, 19–20, 24; 10:15; 16:25; 17:6; Numbers 18:17.

The claim that no one can or has seen God in 1 Timothy 6:16 is at odds with numerous texts in which Hagar, Moses, Isaiah, and Ezekiel indeed saw God. The sentiment is in accord with later tradition that held persons only saw attributes of God, like her glory.

The image Jesus paints of his Jewish disciples sitting in judgment over other Jews is rife with the potential for misinterpretation and abuse. This is an internal conversation in a complex rabbinic Judaism with multiple internal movements; this text reflects a time (in both its content and production) in which the Jewish followers of Jesus were still seen as Jews and "Christian" was not a separate and distinct category.

Christians have also wrestled with the call to "holy" poverty because of passages like this. Some find a transformative call in these words, but it cannot be forced on a person or community. Indeed, Jesus did not prescribe it for all, but for this particular man with his particular relationship to his possessions. It is also the case that people and societies that hoard resources have tended to sanctify the poverty of others, condemning primarily women and children to poverty as a God-given lot and opportunity for grace. For those who love money and their possessions to heed Jesus and give it all to the poor would primarily benefit children (who lead in homelessness) and women.

PROPER 11 (CLOSEST TO JULY 20)

1 Samuel 8:1, 4–18; Psalm 99; Revelation 19:5–9; Matthew 20:1–16

1 Samuel 8:1 Now it was that when Samuel was old that he made his sons judges over Israel.
4 Then all the elders of Israel gathered themselves together and came to Samuel at
Ramah. 5 They said to him, "Look here! You—you are old, and your sons do not walk in your
ways; now then, set up for us a ruler to judge us, like all the heathen nations." 6 But the thing
was evil in Samuel's sight when they said, "Give us a ruler to judge us." Then Samuel prayed to
the Holy One of Old.

7 And the Holy One said to Samuel, "Hearken to the voice of the people in all that they
say to you; for it is not you they have rejected, but it is me they have rejected from ruling over
them. 8 Like everything else they have done to me, from the day I brought them up out of
Egypt to this very day, forsaking me and serving other gods; they are doing the same to you.
9 Now then, hearken to their voice; but—you shall testify against them, and show them the
judgment of the ruler who shall rule over them."

10 So Samuel relayed all the words of the Holy One to the people who were asking him for a ruler. 11 Samuel said, "This will be the judgment of the ruler who will rule
over you all: your sons he will take and set them aside for himself in his chariots and in
his cavalry, and to run before his chariots. 12 And he will set aside for himself commanders of thousands and commanders of fifties, and some to plow his plowing and to reap his
reaping, and to make his furnishings of war and the furnishings of his chariots. 13 Your
daughters he will take to be apothecaries and cooks and bakers. 14 He will take the best of
your fields and vineyards and olive orchards; he will take and give to those who serve him.
15 One-tenth of your grain and of your vineyards he will take and give to his eunuchs and
those he enslaves. 16 Your male slaves and your female slaves, and the best of your cattle and
donkeys, he will take and put them to his work. 17 Your flocks he will tithe . . . and you
all, you shall be his slaves. 18 And you all will cry out on that day in the face of your sovereign, whom you have chosen for yourselves; and God Whose Name is Holy will not
answer you all on that day."

Psalm 99

1 The EVER-LIVING GOD reigns; let the peoples tremble!
She sits enthroned upon the cherubim; let the earthquake!
2 The HOLY ONE OF OLD is great in Zion;
she is exalted over all the peoples.
3 Let them praise your great and awesome name.
Holy is she!
4 Mighty Majesty, lover of justice,
you have established equity;
you have executed justice
and righteousness among the descendants of Rebekah.
5 Extol the MOTHER OF CREATION, our God;
bow down and worship at her footstool. Holy is she!
6 Moses and Aaron were among her priests [Miriam her prophet],
Samuel [and Hannah] also among those who called on her name.
They cried to the FAITHFUL ONE, and she answered them.
7 In the pillar of cloud she spoke to them;
they kept her decrees,
and the statutes that she gave them.
8 JUST ONE our God, you answered them;
you were a forgiving God to them,
and an avenging one of their doings.
9 Extol the FIRE OF SINAI our God,
Bow down and worship at her holy mountain;
for the CREATOR OF ALL, our God, is holy.

Revelation 19:5 A voice came from the throne saying,

"Praise our God,
all you slaves of God,
and all who fear God,
small and great."

6 Then I heard the sound of a great multitude, like the sound of many waters and like the sound of mighty thunderings, crying out,

"Hallelujah!
For the Holy One our God,
the Almighty reigns.
7 Let us rejoice and revel
and give God the glory,

for the wedding of the Lamb has come,
and his bride has prepared herself.
8 To her it has been granted to be clothed
with fine linen, bright and pure."
(For the fine linen is the righteousness of the saints.)

9 Then the divine messenger said to me, "Write: Blessed are those who are invited to the
wedding supper of the Lamb." And the messenger said to me, "These are true words of God."

Matthew 20:1 [Jesus said,] "The realm of the heavens is like a landowner who went out
in the morning to hire laborers for a vineyard. 2 Agreeing with the laborers for the customary denarius a day, the landowner sent them into the vineyard. 3 The landowner went out
about nine o'clock and saw others standing in the marketplace, idle. 4 And the landowner
said to them, 'You all also go into the vineyard, and I will give you what is right.' 5 Then they
departed. Again, the landowner went out and did the same about the sixth hour, noon, and
about the ninth hour, three [in the afternoon]. 6 Then, about the eleventh hour, five, the landowner went out, found others standing around and said to them, 'Why are you all standing
here idle all day?' 7 They said, 'Because no one has hired us.' The landowner said to them,
'You also go into the vineyard.' 8 Now when it was evening, the owner of the vineyard said to
the manager, 'Call the laborers and give them their pay, beginning with the last group then
the first group.' 9 When those hired at the eleventh hour, five [in the evening], came, each
received a denarius. 10 Now when the first came, they thought they would receive more; but
each of them also received the same denarius. 11 Receiving it, they grumbled against the landowner. 12 They said, 'These last worked only one hour, and you have made them equal to us
who have borne the burden of the day and the scorching heat.' 13 But the owner of the vineyard replied to one of them, 'Friend, I have done you no wrong; did you not agree with me for
a denarius? 14 Take what is yours and go; I choose to give to this last what I gave you. 15 Do I
not have the right to do what I choose with what is mine? Or are your eyes envious because I
am generous?' 16 Thus, the last will be first, and the first will be last."

PROCLAMATION

Text Notes

The people ask Samuel in verse 5 for the same kind of governance he provided, one based in the grammatical root for judges and judging, but they want a monarch rather than another judge. The Hebrew vocabulary for monarchy uses the same root word for noun and verb, i.e., "rulers rule," a common feature of the language. In addition, the word is the same for both genders which does not work for "king," "queen," and "reign." (Think: prophets and prophetesses prophesy prophecy.) "Female and male rulers rule in a realm" may be as close as we can get to preserving both form and function.

Samuel tells the people that a monarch will take their daughters to be "mixers of ointments" in verse 13. In Sirach 38:8 the "mixer" is an apothecary working with a physician. In other texts, the mixer makes scented ointment and incense for use in worship; in yet others, the mixer makes perfume (see Exodus 30:25, 35; 37:29; Ecclesiastes 10:1; 1 Chronicles 9:30; Sirach 49:1). I chose "apothecary" to denote their skill, which could be channeled for either purpose.

"Descendants of Rebekah" replaces "Jacob" in the psalm. "Forgiving" in verse 8 of the psalm is "lifting" or "carrying (away)" sin; though the word "sin" is missing.

The owner of the vineyard in Matthew 20 is described as its "lord" or "master," *kurios*, in verse 8. The end of verse 15 is "are your eyes wicked/evil because I am good."

Preaching Prompts

These lessons offer disparate models of monarchy. There is the human monarch whom Samuel predicts will plunder the people and their resources; scholars understand this passage to be a critique of Solomon. In the psalm, God is a monarch of cosmic proportions, and unlike the greedy human ruler of Samuel, God is just and equitable. Enthroned in majesty in the Revelation, God offers the hospitality of her table, giving rather than taking. In the Gospel, the realm of heaven is a place where its ruler gives so graciously that it infuriates those who think others are undeserving.

There is no small amount of irony in Samuel raising poorly behaved sons like his mentor, Eli. As is the case with Eli's wife, nothing is known of Samuel's wife or their household. Clearly both cohabitated with their wives to some degree, producing children. If the whole family lived at the sacred site, what did that portend for any religious role for the women? Did other women seek them out for counsel or company? I have suggested in *Womanist Midrash* that the daughters and wives of Levites and priests may have, to preserve modesty, checked women for skin disease that could result in quarantine.

The Samuel text discloses skills and occupations for women: apothecary, baker, and cook; each turns on knowledge of plants, herbs, and spices. It would be rare, but certainly possible, for a woman to be a landowner as in the parable, particularly for a widow of means.

Eunuchs in the Bible function as a third gender in many ways. They represent a rupture in the gender binary and provide a space for readers outside of cis- and heterosexual frameworks to see themselves. Broadly understood to have been castrated, in some cases in the Hebrew Bible the term is used to denote a trusted servant who may not be castrated.

FEAST OF MARY MAGDALENE, JULY 22

Genesis 16:10–13; Psalm 68:4–11; Romans 16:1–16; John 20:1–2, 11–18

Genesis 16:10 The messenger of the WELLSPRING OF LIFE said to Hagar, "Greatly will I multiply your seed, so they cannot be counted for multitude." 11 Then the messenger of the FOUNT OF LIFE said to her,

"Look! You are pregnant and shall give birth to a son,
and you shall call him Ishmael (meaning God hears),
for the FAITHFUL ONE has heard of your abuse.
12 He shall be a wild ass of a man,
with his hand against everyone,
and everyone's hand against him;
and he shall live in the sight of all his kin."

13 So Hagar named the LIVING GOD who spoke to her: "You are El-ro'i"; for she said, "Have I really seen God and remained alive after seeing God?"

Psalm 68:4–11

4 Sing to God, sing praises to her Name;
exalt her who rides upon the clouds;
HOLY is her Name, rejoice before her!
5 Mother of orphans and defender of widows,
is God in her holy habitation!
6 God settles the solitary in a home, bringing prisoners into prosperity,
while the rebellious shall live in a wasteland.
7 God, when you marched before your people,
when you moved out through the wilderness,
8 the earth shook, even the heavens poured down,
at the presence of God, the One of Sinai,
at the presence of God, the God of Israel.
9 Rain in abundance, God, you showered abroad;
when your heritage grew weary you prepared rest.
10 Your creatures found a dwelling in her;
God, you provided in your goodness for the oppressed.
11 The AUTHOR OF LIFE gave the word;
the women who proclaim the good news are a great army.

Romans 16:1 I commend to you all our sister Phoebe, a deacon of the church in Cenchreae,
2 so that you all may receive her in Christ as is worthy of the saints, and stand by her in whatever thing she may need of you, for she has been a benefactress of many, and of myself as well.

3 Greet Prisca and Aquila, my coworkers in Christ Jesus, 4 and who for my life risked their necks, to whom not only I give thanks, but also all the churches of the Gentiles, 5 and the church in their house. Greet Epaenetus my beloved, who was the first fruit in Asia for Christ. 6 Greet Mary, who has worked much among you all. 7 Greet Andronicus and Junia, my kin and my fellow prisoners; they are eminent among the apostles, and they were in Christ before I was. 8 Greet Ampliatus, my beloved in Christ. 9 Greet Urbanus, our coworker in Christ, and Stachys my beloved. 10 Greet Apelles, who is proven in Christ. Greet those who belong to Aristobulus. 11 Greet Herodion, my kinsman. Greet those who belong of Narcissus in Christ. 12 Greet Tryphaena and Tryphosa who toil in Christ. Greet the beloved Persis who has worked much in Christ. 13 Greet Rufus, chosen in Christ, and greet his mother who is also mine. 14 Greet Asyncritus, Phlegon, Hermes, Patrobas, Hermas, and the sisters and brothers who are with them. 15 Greet Philologus and Julia, Nereus and his sister, and Olympas, and all the saints with them. 16 Greet one another with a holy kiss. All the churches of Christ greet you.

John 20:1 Now it was the first day of the week, Mary Magdalene came, early on while it was still dark, to the tomb and saw the stone removed from the tomb. 2 So she ran and went to Simon Peter and to the other disciple, the one whom Jesus loved, and said to them, "They have taken the Messiah out of the tomb, and we do not know where they have laid him."

11 Now Mary stood outside, facing the tomb, weeping. As she wept, she bent down to see in the tomb. 12 Then she saw two angels in white sitting, one at the head and the other at the feet, where the body of Jesus had been lying. 13 They said to her, "Woman, why do you weep?" She said to them, "Because they have taken my Savior, and I do not know where they have laid him." 14 Having said this, she turned around and saw Jesus standing, but she did not know that it was Jesus. 15 Jesus said to her, "Woman, why do you weep? For whom do you look?" Thinking that he was the gardener, she said to him, "Sir, if you have carried him away, tell me where you have laid him, and I will take him away." 16 Jesus said to her, "Mary." She turned and said to him in Aramaic, "Rabbouni!" (which means Teacher). 17 Jesus said to her, "Do not hold me, because I have not yet ascended to the Father. Rather, go to my brothers and say to them, 'I am ascending to my Abba and your Abba, to my God and your God.'" 18 Mary Magdalene went and announced to the disciples, "I have seen the Savior"; and she told them that he had said these things to her.

PROCLAMATION

Text Notes

The language of Hagar's annunciation parallels the promise to Abraham in Genesis 13:16 closely; each is promised that their "seed" (or offspring) will be numerous beyond counting. Hagar is the first woman in scripture granted an annunciation, the unnamed mother of Samson follows in Judges 13:3–7, followed in turn by Mary the mother of Jesus. Hagar and Rebekah (Genesis 24:60) are the only women in the canon credited with their own seed/offspring; the language is usually reserved for men. (Rebekah's seed is blessed by her matrilineal family; her father Bethuel ben Milcah bore his mother's name, not his father's.) Notably, God speaks to Abraham *about* Sarah in Genesis 17:15–16, as do the divine messengers in Genesis 18:9–10, even when she is within hearing; none speak to her.

Hagar's abuse or affliction, more rightly, Sarah's abuse of Hagar in verse 11, is articulated with a verb that encodes both physical and sexual violence; the verb is also used of the abuse the Israelites suffered at the hands of the Egyptians. Some translate Ishmael's fate as living "in opposition," i.e., conflict, with his kin rather than "opposite," i.e., in their sight or presence; the verb has both senses.

The "we" in John 20:2 likely refers to other women with Mary Magdalene at the tomb. Other resurrection accounts include Mary the mother of James and Salome from Mark 16:1 and Joanna (with Mary Magdalene and James's mother) in Luke 24:10. Yet other possibilities include Jesus's aunt—the unnamed sister of Mary—with Mary the wife of Clopas, present at his crucifixion in John 19:25, and Susanna, who with other women supported Jesus financially from Luke 8:3.

Mary Magdalene "messages," *aggellō*, the gospel of Christ's resurrection. The verb shares the root of messenger, one who announces, *aggelos*, commonly rendered "angel," though the term is not restricted to divine beings. Both she and the divine messengers she encountered are "angels." See the use of "angel" as church leader in Revelation 2:1, 8, 12, 18, and in 3:1.

Preaching Prompts

For this feast of the disciple Orthodox Christians call the Apostle to the Apostles, the readings focus on women's proclamations to and about God, including their work in shaping the early church that speaks for them. Hagar is the only person in the scriptures to name God. She is a matron saint for this project in which I too name God, using God's characteristics revealed in the texts and in the experiences of its readers and hearers to render the unpronounceable name.

Hagar tells God who She is in her, Hagar's, experience and perception. In Psalm 68:12 at the command of God, an army of women proclaim the good news of God's care for her people. The language for that good news, *basarah* in Hebrew, *euaggelia* in Greek, becomes "gospel" in English, the gospel of the risen Christ that Mary Magdalene proclaimed to the absent male disciples and apostles. The women church leaders acknowledged by Paul spread that good news through Asia though their words are lost to us.

The Magdalene texts are extensive: Matthew 27:55–61; 28:1–10; Mark 15:40–41, 47; 16:1–8 [9–11]; Luke 8:1–3; 23:55–56; 24:1–10; John 19:25; 20:1–2, 11–18. The fifty-seven verses tell a story of discipleship and faith that is virtually without peer among male disciples yet is not unique to this one woman, for there were other women at the cross and tomb who followed Jesus in life, attended him in death, and proclaimed him in resurrection. Yet she is distinguished by the preservation of her name and frequency of appearance. Mary the mother of Jesus and Mary Magdalene are the only women represented in all four Gospels, even considering the difficulty to separate and identify Marys, even with multiple traditions about which Mary anointed Jesus.

Peeling back the traditions accreted around her, some of which—like the red egg—may be useful, she remains a disciple, arguably an apostle, preacher, eyewitness of the Passion, conversant with angels, benefactrix, burial attendant, healed/transformed/exorcised, messenger (angel) of the gospel.

PROPER 12 (CLOSEST TO JULY 27)

1 Samuel 9:1–3, 15–18, 10:1; Psalm 96; Acts 13:16–23; Matthew 4:1–11

1 Samuel 9:1 Now there was a man of Benjamin whose name was Kish son of Abiel son of
Zeror son of Becorath son of Aphiah [himself] a son of a Benjaminite, a warrior-hearted man
of substance. 2 He had a son whose name was Saul, a fine young man. There was not a man
among the people of Israel finer than he; he stood above and beyond everyone else. 3 Now the
female donkeys of Kish, Saul's father, had strayed. So, Kish said to his son Saul, "Take one of
the boys with you, get up and look for the donkeys."

15 Now the Holy One had uncovered the ear of Samuel the day before Saul came, saying: 16 "About this time tomorrow I will send to you a man from the land of Benjamin, and
you shall anoint him to be a leader over my people Israel. He shall save my people from the
hand of the Philistines; for I have seen the humiliation of my people, because their cry has
come to me." 17 When Samuel saw Saul, the Holy One told him, "Here is the man of whom
I spoke to you. He it is who shall govern my people." 18 Then Saul approached Samuel in the
center of the gate, and said, "Tell me, please, where is the house of the seer?"

10:1 Samuel took a vial of oil and poured it on Saul's head, and kissed him, and said, "Has
not the Holy One of Old anointed you leader over God's own heritage?

Psalm 96

1 Sing to the Exalted a new song;
sing to the Creator, all the earth.
2 Sing to the Most High, bless her name;
proclaim from day to day her salvation.
3 Declare among the nations her glory,
among all the peoples, her marvelous works.
4 For great is the Ageless God, and greatly to be praised;
revered is she above all gods.

5 For all the gods of the peoples are idols,
yet the WOMB OF LIFE made the heavens.
6 Splendor and majesty are before her;
strength and beauty are in her sanctuary.
7 Give to the MAJESTIC ONE, you families of the peoples,
give to the MIGHTY ONE glory and strength.
8 Give to the FIRE OF SINAI the glory due her name;
bring an offering and come into her courts.
9 Bow down and worship the SOVEREIGN ONE in majestic holiness;
tremble in her presence, all the earth.
10 Say among the nations, "The EVER-LIVING GOD reigns!
Indeed, the world is firmly established; it shall never be moved.
God will judge the peoples with equity."
11 Let the heavens rejoice, and let the earth be glad;
let the sea roar, along with what fills it.
12 Let the field exult, and all that is in it.
Then shall all the trees of the forest sing for joy
13 before the WISDOM OF THE AGES; for she is coming,
for she is coming to judge the earth.
She will judge the world with righteousness,
and the peoples with her truth.

Acts 13:16 Standing and waving his hand, Paul spoke:

"People of Israel, and others who fear God, listen. 17 The God of this people Israel chose our mothers and fathers and made the people great during their sojourn in the land of Egypt, and with God's own outstretched arm God led them out of Egypt. 18 For about forty years God put up with them in the wilderness. 19 After God overthrew seven nations in the land of Canaan, God gave them their land as their lot, 20 for about four hundred fifty years. After that God gave them judges until the time of the prophet Samuel. 21 Then they asked for a ruler and God gave them Saul son of Kish, a man of the tribe of Benjamin for forty years. 22 When God had removed Saul, God made David their ruler. In God's testimony about David God said, 'I have found David, son of Jesse, to be a man after my heart, who will carry out all my wishes.' 23 From this seed God has brought to Israel a Savior, Jesus, as promised."

Matthew 4:1 Jesus was led up by the Spirit into the wilderness to be tempted by the devil.
2 He fasted forty days and forty nights, and afterwards he was hungry. 3 The tempter came and said to him, "If you are the Son of God, tell these stones to become loaves of bread." 4 But Jesus answered, "It is written,

'Not by bread alone does humanity live,
but by every word that comes out of the mouth of God.'"

[5] Then the devil took Jesus to the holy city and placed him on the pinnacle of the temple,
[6] and said to him, "If you are the Son of God, throw yourself down; for it is written,

'God will command God's own angels concerning you' and
'On their hands they will take you up,
so that you will not strike your foot against a stone.'"

[7] Jesus said to it, "Again it is written, *'Do not put the Holy One your God to the test.'*"
[8] Again, the devil took him to a very high mountain and showed him all the dominions
of the world and their glory. [9] And it said to him, "All these I will give you, if you will fall
down and worship me." [10] Jesus said to it, "Away with you, Satan! for it is written,

'Worship the Holy One your God,
and serve only God.'"

[11] Then the devil left him, and suddenly angels came and waited on Jesus.

PROCLAMATION

Text Notes

Gibor chayil indicates a man of significance or substance in 1 Samuel 9:1, translated as "mighty (*gibor*) warrior and warrior-hearted (*chayil*)" or often "mighty man of valor," also includes "man of means" with the sense that wealth is ennobling. Saul is "fine" ("good"), which in African American vernacular means both "good" and "good-looking." The verb *galah* means "uncover" and therefore "reveal." God's revelation to Samuel in verse 15 appears to be auditory. In verse 16 God "sees" the people in the MT; in the LXX she sees the "humiliation" of her people, making the verse correspond with Exodus 3:7.

Using a verb that means "restrain" for "govern" in verse 17 indicates that someone, God, the author or editor, sees Israel as in need of a very specific sort of governance. Verse 1 in 1 Samuel 10 is longer in the LXX; the second passage connects to the contents of the following verses: *You shall rule over the people of the Holy One and you will save them from the hand of their enemies all around. Now this shall be the sign to you that the Holy One has anointed you ruler over God's own heritage. . . .*

In Acts 13:16, Paul addresses the public assembly as "Men of Israel," as is common in his speeches in Acts. There is no reason to imagine women were excluded from the public square or from his exhortation as he welcomes women believers and leaders in the early church, including in Acts (see 1:14; 9:2, 36–41; 16:13–14; 17:4, 12, 34; 18:2; 21:9). His rhetoric is idiomatic and reveals his own gender hierarchies. The Greek of verse 17 uses God's "high hand," an expression found throughout the LXX to render the Hebrew "outstretched arm" (see Exodus 6:6; Deuteronomy 4:34, etc.). In verse 22 Paul (or the author of Acts) reworks Samuel's, not God's, description of David from 1 Samuel 13:14: "*The* HOLY ONE *has sought out a man after God's own heart and the* HOLY ONE *has appointed him to be ruler over God's people.*" The flexibility with which Acts represents Samuel is a helpful reminder that ancient readers and hearers were not literal readers or reciters, were comfortable with multiple versions, and learned readers like Jesus, Luke, and Paul adapted and reinterpreted the texts as the prophets often did with the Torah. More recently, the translators of the CEB turned to the Targum to render the description as: *a man who shares my desires.*

Matthew 4:4 follows Deuteronomy 8:3 in word order, "not by bread alone" comes first and both texts use words that can mean a person or humanity as the subject. While "devil" and "Satan" are grammatically male, grammatical gender does not reflect ontological gender, if the literary or literal devil/Satan, as one prefers, can even be said to possess or embody gender. Thus, I translate it in neutral terms. (However, the creation of gendered humanity in the image of God invites reflection on God and gender.)

Preaching Prompts

Most of the Hebrew Scriptures were written in a henotheistic world, one which acknowledged multiple gods, where one was chosen above all others signaled by expressions such as "God of gods," and the emphasis on not making God jealous by choosing other gods. The psalm is in this tradition: God is revered among all other gods in verse 4 and moves beyond it in declaring other gods idols in verse 5.

As Paul rehearses Israelite history, he hearkens back to Israelite migration to Canaan and the claim that God despoiled other nations and gave Israel their land. Joshua presents this period as one of successive genocides vanquishing the Canaanites, including women and children at God's direction. Judges undermines these claims by pointing out the original inhabitants were still present and still hostile, hence the need for judges. (Compare Joshua 24:11 and Judges 3:5–6.) Even with an understanding of the conquest as more literary than literal, its scripturality became justification for the despoliation and decimation of native peoples here and around the world and colonization, occupation, and enslavement. The ongoing discussions about migration in the US make it difficult to gloss over these texts.

The description—Samuel's, Paul's, Luke's, God's—of David as "a man after God's heart" has troubled many readers given David's rapacious violence, such as his extermination of women and men (though no mention of children) in Canaanite cities not engaged in hostilities as a way to prove his loyalty to a Philistine king in 1 Samuel 27:8–12 (while lying that he was killing women and men from Judah and its allies) and David's rape of Bathsheba. (Rape is indicated by her abduction; he sent men to take, not solicit her. Further, neither God nor Samuel charge her with adultery.) The texts agree that God sought a man after, "according to" in Hebrew, God's heart. David's conduct very much raises the question whether God found such a one in him.

PROPER 13 (CLOSEST TO AUGUST 3)

1 Samuel 15:1–3, 8, 10–17, 24–25; Psalm 7:1–8, 17; Romans 2:1–11; Matthew 5:21–26

1 Samuel 15:1 Samuel said to Saul, "I was sent by the Dread God to anoint you ruler over
God's people, over Israel; now then, hearken to the call of the words of the Inscrutable
God: 2 Thus says the Sovereign of heaven's vanguard, 'I will punish Amalek for what they
did to Israel, setting against them in their ascent from Egypt. 3 Now go and smite Amalek, and
put to holy destruction all they have; do not spare them and put them to death from woman
to man and from infant to nursing baby and from ox to sheep, from camel to donkey.'"

8 Saul seized Agag ruler of the Amalekites alive, and put to holy destruction all the people at the edge of the sword.

10 The word of the Sovereign God to Samuel was: 11 "I regret that I crowned Saul
as ruler, for he has turned away from me, and my commands he has not instituted." Then
Samuel was angry, and he cried out to the God Who Hears, all night. 12 And Samuel rose
early in the morning to meet Saul, and it was told to Samuel: "Saul went to Carmel, where
he erected a monument for himself, then turned around and passed by, going down to Gil-
gal." 13 Now, Samuel came to him and Saul said to him, "Blessed are you by the Holy One
of Old; I have instituted the command of the Holy One of Sinai." 14 Then Samuel said,
"What is this sound of sheep in my ears, and the sound of cattle I am hearing?" 15 And Saul
said, "They brought them from the Amalekites, for the people spared the best of the sheep
and the cattle to sacrifice to the Holy One your God; but the rest we have put to holy
destruction." 16 Then Samuel said to Saul, "Stop! Let me tell you what the Ancient One
said to me last night." Saul replied, "Speak."17 Samuel said, "Though you are small in your
own eyes, are you not the head of the tribes of Israel? The Holy One anointed you ruler
over Israel."

24 Saul said to Samuel, "I have sinned; for I have transgressed the utterance of the Dread
God and your words, because I feared the people and obeyed their voice. 25 Now then, I pray,
pardon my sin, and return with me, so that I may worship the Holy One of Old."

Psalm 7:1–8, 17

1 Faithful One, my God, in you I take refuge;
save me from all my pursuers, and deliver me,
2 lest one [of them] rend me like a lion, dragging [me] away;
with none to rescue.
3 Just One, my God, if I have done this:
if there is iniquity in my hands,
4 if I have repaid one at peace with me with evil
or imperiled my foe without cause,

5 then let the enemy pursue and overtake me,
and trample my life to the ground,
and lay my glory in the dust. *Selah*
6 Rise up, DREAD GOD, in your anger;
be lifted up against the fury of my enemies.
Wake! O my God; you have mandated judgment.
7 Let the assembly of the peoples be gathered around you,
And above it, return on high.
8 The RIGHTEOUS ONE judges the peoples;
acquit me, JUST ONE, according to my righteousness
and according to the integrity in me.
17 I will praise the MOST HIGH on account of God's righteousness,
and sing praise to the Name of the HOLY ONE OF OLD, the Most High.

Romans 2:1 Each of you is without excuse when you pass judgment; for in passing judgment on another you condemn yourself, because you, the judge, are doing the same things.
2 We know God's judgment is on those who in accordance with truth do such things. 3 Do
any of you think when you judge those who do these things and yet do them yourself, you will
escape the judgment of God? 4 Or do you despise the riches of God's kindness and clemency
and patience? Are you unaware that the kindness of God should lead you to repentance? 5 For
through your hard and unrepentant heart you are accumulating wrath for yourself on the day
of wrath when the righteous judgment of God will be revealed. 6 For "God will repay each one
according to their deeds." 7 To those who with patience do good, seeking glory and honor and
immortality, God will give eternal life. 8 But for those who are contentious and disobey the
truth choosing wickedness, there will be wrath and fury. 9 There will be anguish and distress
for every human soul who does evil, the Jew first and also the Greek [or Gentile], 10 but glory
and honor and peace for everyone who does good, the Jew first and also the Greek [or Gen-
tile]. 11 For "God shows no favoritism."

Matthew 5:21 Jesus said, "You have heard that it was said to those of old, 'You shall not
murder,' and 'whoever murders shall be subject to judgment.' 22 But I say to you all that if
you are angry with a sister or brother, you will be liable to judgment, and if you call a sister or
brother an idiot, you will be subject to the council; and if you say, 'You fool,' you will be subject to the hell of fire. 23 Therefore, if you are offering your gift at the altar and you remember that your sister or brother has something against you, 24 leave your gift there before the
altar and go; first be reconciled to your sister or brother, and then come and offer your gift.
25 Come to favorable terms quickly with your accuser while you are on the way with them
or your accuser may hand you over to the judge, and the judge to the court officer, and you
will be thrown into prison. 26 Truly I tell you, you will never get out until you have paid the
last penny.

PROCLAMATION

Text Notes

I choose language to render the divine name that communicates the horror of Samuel's claim that God called for annihilation "from woman to man and from infant to nursing baby," a God who is dread and inscrutable. In 1 Samuel 15:1, the "call" of the words of God is the "sound" or "voice." In the prosecution of holy war called for by God, utter annihilation is sanctified as the ultimate offering to God. People, animals, and sometimes the land itself is "put under the ban"—banned from existence, the living beings slaughtered, the land torn up and often salted to prevent planting. The verb, *haram*, means "ban," "devote" (to God), and "destroy." There is no respite, rescue, or redemption from holy destruction (Leviticus 27:28–29); failure to complete this genocidal action is punishable, they can be shown no mercy or pity (Deuteronomy 7:2).

God expresses regret—not quite repentance—for enthroning Saul in the same terms that Job expresses regret and not repentance for demanding an account of God in Job 42:6.

Romans 2:11 quotes a line found in both Psalm 62:12 and Proverbs 24:12.

Preaching Prompts

Beyond moving the story of Israel's monarchy along, the fall of Saul offers a challenging study on repentance and forgiveness and Saul's unanswered plea for pardon illustrates the difficulty in teasing out the human and divine in the scriptures. The psalmist's assurance that God is a righteous judge echoes throughout the canon and contributes to the dissonance of hearing God call for the slaughter of innocents, including babies at the breast in 1 Samuel (and elsewhere), a stark contrast with the teaching that God shows no favoritism. And then we hear Jesus telling us to reconcile, even if we have to walk out of worship.

One of the most problematic theological claims in the Hebrew Bible is on display in this lesson on the fall of Saul that serves as a literary foil for the selection of the beloved David, the genocidal God of the "Old Testament" often set in opposition to the loving God (and Jesus) of the New Testament. Needless to say, these claims and their underlying theology require frank discussion and thoughtful engagement, not least for what they signify about God. An important caveat is that these texts are retrospective and the bulk of them are ahistoric; Joshua is particularly notorious in this regard with eighteen of nineteen Canaanite cities claimed as utterly destroyed showing no evidence of destruction or not having been occupied at all in the relevant timeframe. (See the very helpful charts and discussion in Frank Frick's chapter on Joshua and Judges in *A Journey through the Hebrew Scriptures*.) A rare moment of grace in this story is that even though it marks God's rejection of Saul, Samuel seems not to have given up on him. More significantly, he gets angry (at God?) and pours out his heart, all night long. Yet we should remain troubled by Saul's fate and the purported fate of the Amalekites and the claims made in God's name by God's prophet.

There are women missing from the telling of Saul's fall from grace; he has a primary wife, Ahinoam the daughter of Ahimaaz (1 Samuel 14:50) and two daughters, Merab and Michal (1 Samuel 14:49). He also has a low-status wife, Rizpah. His rise and fall affected them all, not least because it brought David into their orbit, leading to the engagement of both daughters, marriage (and abandonment) of one, and ultimately the death of Merab's children and those of Rizpah, at the word of David (2 Samuel 21:8–9). In the other texts, women are subsumed in the people, congregation, and believers.

Paul's quote and affirmation of the verses that God shows no favoritism is both scripture and regularly in conflict with portions of scripture. Paul is a useful teacher in exegetical method (if not always its fruit). We as readers and hearers choose which texts and interpretations we normalize. Jesus does this and more in the broader tradition when he says, "It is written, but I say unto you . . ." Paul chooses a portrait of God from the scriptures that is just.

Lastly, Jesus's admonition about reconciliation is explicitly egalitarian, applicable to women and men. If read in light of the patriarchy that abounds in the church and the wider world, there are men who need to leave their gift at the altar and do the work of reconciliation with their sisters.

PROPER 14 (CLOSEST TO AUGUST 10)

1 Samuel 17:1–7, 12–16, 24–27; Psalm 108:1–6, 11–13; Ephesians 6:10–17; Matthew 5:43–48

1 Samuel 17:1 Now the Philistines gathered their encampments for war; they were gathered at Socoh, which is part of Judah and they encamped between Socoh and Azekah, in Ephes-dammim. [2] And Saul and the Israelites were gathered and encamped in the valley of Elah and they organized ranks to engage the Philistines. [3] Now the Philistines were standing on this hill and the men of Israel were standing on this other hill with a valley between them. [4] And there went out from the camp of the Philistines a man apart [a champion], Goliath was his name, of Gath; his height was six cubits and a span [over nine feet tall]. [5] A helmet of bronze was on his head and he was clothed in scale armor; the weight of the bronze armor was five thousand shekels [or one hundred twenty-five pounds]. [6] And greaves of bronze were on his legs, and a javelin of bronze between his shoulders. [7] The shaft of his spear was like a weaver's beam and the iron tip of his spear weighed six hundred shekels [or fifteen pounds] and his shield-bearer went before him.

12 Now David was the son of this Ephrathite man of Bethlehem in Judah, and his name
was Jesse, and he had eight sons. And the man was, by the days of Saul, old and going as
mortals do. 13 Now the three eldest sons of Jesse set out and followed Saul to the battle; the
names of his three sons who went to the battle were Eliab the firstborn, Abinadab his second,
and the third, Shammah. 14 David was the youngest; the three eldest followed Saul. 15 David
would come and go back from Saul to feed his father's sheep at Bethlehem. 16 And the Philistine came forward morning and evening and took his stand for forty days.

24 And all the men of Israel in seeing the man, fled from his presence and were very afraid.
25 The Israelites said, "Do you all see this man who is coming forward? He is coming forward
to insult Israel. What will happen is, the man who smites him, the king will make rich—great
riches!—and he will give him his daughter and make his family free in Israel." 26 David said to
the men who were standing with him, "What shall be done for the man who smites this Philistine and takes away the reproach from Israel? For who is this uncircumcised Philistine that
he should defy the ranks of the living God?" 27 The people answered him according to those
spoken words, "Thus shall it be done for the man who smites him."

Psalm 108:1–6, 11–13

1 My heart is fixed God;
let me, even with my glory, sing praise and hymn.
2 Wake the harp and lyre!
I will wake the dawn.
3 I will give thanks to you, ANCIENT ONE, among the peoples,
and I will sing praises to you among the nations.
4 For higher than the heavens is your faithful love,
and your trustworthiness extends to the clouds.
5 Be exalted above the heavens, God,
and let your glory be over all the earth.
6 That those whom you love may be delivered,
save with your right hand and answer me.
11 Have you not rejected us God?
For you do not go out with our armies God.
12 Grant us help from the adversary,
for human deliverance is worthless.
13 Through God we shall triumph;
and God will trample our adversaries.

Ephesians 6:10 Finally, be strengthened in the Redeemer and in the strength of his power.
11 Put on the armor of God, so that you may be able to stand against the schemes of the devil.
12 For our struggle is not against blood and flesh, but against the rulers, against the authorities, against the overlords of this darkness, against the spiritual [forces] of evil in the heavenly

[realms]. [13] Therefore take up the armor of God, so that you may be able to resist on that evil day, and having done everything, to stand. [14] Stand therefore, and fasten the belt of truth around your waist, and put on the breastplate of righteousness. [15] Bind on your feet preparedness to proclaim the gospel of peace. [16] With all this, take the shield of faith, with which you will be able to quench all the flaming arrows of the evil one. [17] Take the helmet of salvation, and the sword of the Spirit, which is the word of God.

Matthew 5:43 "You all have heard that it was said, '*You shall love your neighbor and hate your enemy.*' [44] Yet I say to you all: Love your enemies and pray for those who persecute you, [45] so that you may be children of the One in heaven who begot you; for the sun—which belongs to God—rises on the evil and on the good, and God rains on the righteous and on the unrighteous woman or man. [46] For if you all love those who love you, what reward do you have? Do not even the tax collectors do the same? [47] And if you greet only your sisters and brothers, what more are you doing than others? Do not the Gentiles do the same? [48] Be perfect, therefore, as your heavenly Sovereign is perfect.

PROCLAMATION

Text Notes

Often what Biblical Hebrew designates a "mountain" as in 1 Samuel 17:3 would qualify as a "hill" elsewhere. Goliath is characterized as "a man between the armies." "Champion" is an elliptical, not literal choice; the surviving solo fighter would be the de facto champion. In the LXX Goliath is just over six feet tall. The tip of his spear is a "flame" in verse 7. Verses 12–31 are missing from the LXX, which is not simply a translation, but a translation from a different Hebrew text than the text that gave rise to the MT. The discovery of the Dead Sea Scrolls (DSS) established that among the most ancient manuscripts were versions corresponding to both Hebrew MT and Greek LXX and readings unique to the DSS. "Free in Israel" in verse 25 suggests the victor will be exempt from military or civil service projects, which were generally compulsory. "Forty days" (or "forty nights and days") is idiomatic for a good long time like "a month of Sundays," which we would never render literally as twenty-eight weeks.

Psalm 108 is composed of two other psalms: Psalms 57:7–13 provide verses 1–5 and 60:5–13 yield verses 6–13. Each of the three is attributed to David. Clearly these lines were firmly associated with him; however, it is not unheard of for psalmists to borrow the content of their psalms from within and without the biblical canon. It is unlikely David, or any other Iron Age shepherd girl or boy, would be literate. Literacy was the provenance of royalty and those who served them. David's rapid ascent to the throne, including a significant period of mercenary service, does not seem to allow time for his schooling. "Triumph" in verse 13 is "make/do [as a] warrior;" I follow the JPS translation here.

Unlike the way many of us may have learned this passage from Ephesians, there is no "whole" armor of God; the adjective is lacking. The "armor of God" here consists of a few pieces; perhaps it would be hubris to imagine wearing all of God's armor or perhaps God has parts and armor that we could not imagine or describe. Ephesians 6:12 has a couple of adjectives without their nouns, supplied in brackets. The translation "overlord" in the same verse comes from Markus Barth in the *Anchor Bible* commentary on Ephesians; the underlying word, *kosmokratōr*, "world-controller" or "world-dominator," applies to supernatural and human subjects. "Waist" and "loins" are the same word in verse 14; the former seems the better fit here.

Preaching Prompts

Deliverance from enemies is one of the major hallmarks of God's fidelity in the Hebrew Scriptures, invoked by the first lesson and psalm, and that language remains powerful in a world with interpersonal and international enmity. Women and their children were often invisible in these conflicts except as markers of brutality or valiant women like Deborah, Jael, and Judith. Yet there are mothers, wives, sisters, daughters, aunts, nieces, and grandmothers connected to each undifferentiated man in the Israelite and Philistine armies and there are David's mother and sisters, Zeruiah and Abigail, who will appear later in 2 Samuel 17:24 and 1 Chronicles 2:15–16. It is worth asking how women in the text and its world experienced such deliverance; salvation of their town, protection from captivity and abuse come to mind. While no less bloody a world, the New Testament doesn't proffer pitched battles with the occupying Romans or an upstart champion to knock them down a peg. The author turns to incorporeal enemies, the powers behind the thrones on earth and in heaven. Against these, we don the armor of God as David did that of Saul and God bridges the gulf between the infinite and the finite. And Jesus calls us to affirm our shared humanity with those with whom we are at enmity.

The David and Goliath story has become an archetype of the unlikely victor overcoming great odds. The story exists in a variety of forms in the Hebrew Bible: 1) the familiar story in 1 Samuel 17:1–58, 2) 2 Samuel 21:19 where Elhanan son of Jaare-oregim, also of Bethlehem kills (another?) Goliath whose spear shaft is also a weaver's beam, and 3) 1 Chronicles 20 where another Elhanan, this time son of Jair, killed Lahmi, the brother of Goliath, who possessed yet a third weaver's beam spear shaft. The first and second Goliaths are from towns spelled with the same consonants, suggesting different versions of the same story. Similarly the fathers of the two Elhanans from the second and third stories are variations of the same name. None of these later stories are fleshed out as well as the first. The variances point to the flexibility of storytelling and scripture and the comfort of ancient readers with hearing multiple, competing versions.

Jesus quotes the common wisdom, which is a combination of the command to love your neighbor (from Leviticus 19:18) and its interpretive corollary, hate your enemies, cited together as an equally authoritative text. This is a useful reminder that interpretations are just as authoritative as primary texts, often holding the weight of scripture. As is the case for Jesus in Matthew before his transforming encounter with the Canaanite mother, his language about the Gentiles presents them as negative examples in stereotypical terms, an opportunity to discuss the ways in which human biases are present in the text. The call to love enemies is also a call to love those from whom we are separated by societal and cultural structures like race, class, and gender. "Enemies" are just the most extreme example of the radical limitlessness of our love.

FEAST OF THE EVER-BLESSED VIRGIN MARY, AUGUST 15

Judith 13:18–20; Canticle 15, the Magnificat (Luke 1:46–55); Revelation 21:1–7; Luke 1:26–38

Judith 13:18 Uzziah said to Judith, "O daughter, you are blessed by the Most High God
above all other women on earth, and blessed be the Holy God, who created the heavens and
the earth, who has guided you to cut off the head of the leader of our enemies. 19 Praise of
you will never depart from the hearts of women and men who remember the power of God.
20 May God do these things for you as an eternal exaltation, and may God visit you with
blessings, because you did not withhold your life when our nation was humiliated, rather
you rallied against our demise, walking straight before our God." And all the people said,
"Amen. Amen."

Canticle 15, the Magnificat, Luke 1:46–55

46 "My soul magnifies the Holy One,
47 and my spirit rejoices in God my Savior,
48 for God has looked with favor on the lowliness of God's own womb-slave.
Surely, from now on all generations will call me blessed;
49 for the Mighty One has done great things for me,
and holy is God's name.
50 God's loving-kindness is for those who fear God
from generation to generation.
51 God has shown the strength of God's own arm;
God has scattered the arrogant in the intent of their hearts.
52 God has brought down the powerful from their thrones,
and lifted up the lowly;

53 God has filled the hungry with good things,
and sent the rich away empty.
54 God has helped God's own child, Israel,
a memorial to God's mercy,
55 just as God said to our mothers and fathers,
to [Hagar and] and Sarah and Abraham, to their descendants forever."

Revelation 21:1 I saw a new heaven and a new earth, for the first heaven and the first earth
had passed away, and the sea was no more. 2 And I saw the holy city, the new Jerusalem,
descending heaven from God, prepared as a bride adorned for her beloved. 3 And I heard a
loud voice from the throne saying,

"Look! The home of God is among the woman-born.
God will dwell with them as their God;
they will be God's peoples,
and selfsame God will be with them.
4 God will wipe every tear from their eyes.
Death will be no more;
grief and weeping and pain will be no more,
for the first things have passed away."

5 And the One who was seated upon the throne said, "Look! I am making all things new."
The One also said, "Write, for these words are trustworthy and true." 6 Then the One said
to me, "It is done! I am the Alpha and the Omega, the beginning and the end. I will give to
the thirsty from the spring of the water of life freely. 7 Those who overcome will inherit these
things, and I will be their God and they will be my daughters and sons."

Luke 1:26 In the sixth month the angel Gabriel was sent by God to a town of Galilee, Nazareth, 27 to a virgin betrothed to a man whose name was Joseph, of the house of David. And the
name of the virgin was Mary. 28 And the angel came to Mary and said, "Rejoice, favored one!
The Most High God is with you." 29 Now, she was troubled by the angel's words and pondered
what sort of greeting this was. 30 Then the angel said to her, "Fear not Mary, for you have found
favor with God. 31 And now, you will conceive in your womb and give birth to a son, and you
will name him Jesus. 32 He will be great and will be called the Son of the Most High, and the
Sovereign God will give him the throne of his ancestor David. 33 He will reign over the house of
Jacob forever, and of his sovereignty there will be no end." 34 Then Mary said to the angel, "How
can this be, since I have not known a man intimately?" 35 The angel said to her, "The Holy
Spirit, She will come upon you, and the power of the Most High will overshadow you; therefore the one born will be holy. He will be called the Son of God. 36 And now, Elizabeth your
kinswoman has even conceived a son in her old age, and this is the sixth month for she who was
called barren. 37 For nothing will be impossible with God." 38 Then Mary said, "Here am I, the
woman-slave of God; let it be with me according to your word." Then the angel left her.

PROCLAMATION

Text Notes

In Judith 13:20 Judith's actions are described awkwardly as "rallying against" the "corpse" (understood as the eminent demise) of her people, i.e., taking action to oppose that which would end in their deaths.

Revelation 21 deploys a marriage metaphor which does not require a rigid gender binary or heteronormativity to be effective, so I have translated *aner*, "man," meaning "husband" in verse 2, as "beloved." *Nike* in verse 7 means to "overcome obstacles" or "prevail." To "be victorious" and "conquer" are also within the semantic range; however the latter two choices do not clearly indicate struggle and "conquer" (as in NRSV) seems unnecessarily martial here.

In Mary's languages, Hebrew for prayer and religious texts, and Aramaic for daily life, the Holy Spirit is feminine. The Greek scriptures use the neuter pronoun corresponding to "it." It is not until the production of the Vulgate and other Latin texts that the masculine pronoun is inserted. While the literary language is Greek, the translation choice reflects the underlying Semitic linguistic cultural context. In verse 48 of the Magnificat, Mary uses the same slave language that Hannah does, "woman-slave of God," a common expression across the canon. When used with reference to reproduction, as here, I use womb-slave; the language of slavery pervades the scriptures and forms the rhetoric of the most familiar stories, often without examination. In verse 55 of the Magnificat I have added Hagar as a witness to God's fidelity proclaimed in the verse.

Preaching Prompts

Like Judith, whose name can be translated "Jewish woman," Miriam rendered "Mary" in English (along with other Hebraic names in the Second Testament to sound less Jewish) was a Jewish woman. Where Judith is an older widowed woman when she puts her body on the line to save her people, Mary, named for the prophet Miriam like all of the "Marys," was young and on the cusp of marriage. Each woman has her bona fides established in a lengthy genealogy. Judith's is the longest of any woman in the canon, stretching from the time of Nebuchadnezzar to Simeon, Leah's son by Jacob (Judith 8:1, 9:2), though some argue against her historicity. While Judith's husband is folded into *her* genealogy, "Her husband Manasseh, who belonged to her tribe and family," Mary's genealogy is *Joseph's* genealogy.

The patriarchal genealogy fails to tell the story of Mary and Jesus as descendants of Bathsheba and David, though it does so for Joseph (Matthew 1:1–17, see verses 6 and 16 and Luke 2:4), even while naming Tamar (I), Ruth, and describing Bathsheba as the wife of Uriah but without her name (Matthew 1:3, 5–6). Mary is *presumed* to be from Joseph's tribe, Judah, following the most common marital pattern and likely from a more closely related clan within the tribe. Mary is likely not Joseph's sister, though she could be his cousin; somewhere between Solomon in verse 7 and Matthan, Joseph's grandfather in verse 15, Mary's genealogy is obscured.

Both Judith and Mary have their virtue attested—Judith's piety as a widow (Judith 8:4–6) and Mary's virginity (Luke 1:26ff)—and both will use their bodies in scandalous ways to effect salvation. Judith entices an enemy general who seeks to seduce her—but with a maid present to testify to her virtue—and beheads the man with his own sword (Judith 13:4–10). Mary agrees to the divine pregnancy, risking being ostracized and perhaps stoned for the appearance of breaking faith with Joseph. For some readers there will always be a question of the degree to which Mary was free to refuse. That she affirmatively consents is clear: *let it be with me according to your word*. But could she refuse? Before she consents, Gabriel says: *You will* . . . The timing is crucial, helping readers and hearers grapple with consent issues in the text and the gulfs between ancient and contemporary ethical standards.

Mary and Judith are also linked in the words of blessing "among" and "above other" women in Judith 13:18 and Luke 1:42. Elizabeth, Mary's relative, could have chosen the blessing by drawing from her scriptures, from Judith and from the words of Deborah's blessing on Jael in Judges 5:24: "*most blessed of women . . . of tent-dwelling women most blessed*." (Judith was included in the Greek Jewish Bible and influential where not later canonical). Like her textual sisters, Jael's story is framed by scandal, assassinating an enemy general after welcoming him to hide there; a man who was so well known as a rapist his mother imagines his delay is caused by his proclivities (Judges 4:17–24; 5:24–30). His position at his death, between (not "at" per NRSV) Jael's legs, would seem confirmation.

The blessings of Jael and Judith with their histories of violence worry the innocence of the annunciation with the reminder of the violence to which Mary is at risk now and the violence she will live to see enacted on the body of her son. In the words of another holy person, "*a sword will pierce her soul*" (Luke 2:35).

John (1:1) says, "The Word became flesh and dwelled, *eskēnōsen*, among us." If Jesus is the heir of Bathsheba and David according to the flesh, it is through Mary's flesh, the matrix of the Incarnation that God comes to dwell with us. That verb, *skēnoō*, "to dwell" is also used in the second reading chosen for today: *God will dwell with them as their God*. The Feast of the Ever-Blessed Virgin Mary affords an opportunity to reflect on the ways in which God dwells with us and a model of hospitality.

PROPER 15 (CLOSEST TO AUGUST 17)

1 Samuel 17:55–18:9; Psalm 78:68–72; Romans 1:1–8; John 7:37–44

1 Samuel 17:55 When Saul saw David go out to meet the Philistine, he said to Abner, the commander of the army, "Whose son is this boy, Abner?" Abner said, "By the soul of the king, if I knew . . ." [56] Then the king said, "You ask whose son the stripling is." [57] As David returned from smiting the Philistine, Abner took him and brought him before Saul with the head of the Philistine in his hand. [58] And Saul said to him, "Whose son are you boy?" And David answered, "I am the son of your slave Jesse the Bethlehemite."

[18:1] Now it happened by the time David finished speaking to Saul, the soul of Jonathan was bound to the soul of David, and Jonathan loved him as his own soul. [2] And Saul took David that day and would not permit him to return to the house of his father. [3] Then Jonathan made a covenant with David because he loved him as his own soul. [4] So Jonathan stripped off the robe that was on him and gave it to David and his armor and even his sword and his bow and also his belt. [5] David went out and in all to which Saul sent him, was successful; then Saul placed him over the warriors. And it was good in the eyes of all the people, even in the eyes of the slaves of Saul.

[6] And it was as they were coming back, when David returned from smiting the Philistine, the women came out of all the towns of Israel to sing with the dances to meet King Saul with hand drums, with rejoicing, and with musical instruments. [7] And the women sang in response to each another as they reveled,

> "Saul has killed his thousands,
> and David his ten thousands."

[8] And Saul raged, hot; this saying was evil in his eyes. And he said, "They gave to David ten thousands and to me they gave thousands. There is only the throne left for him!" [9] So it was that Saul eyed David from that day on.

Psalm 78:68–72

68 God chose the tribe of Judah,
Mount Zion, which she loves.
69 She built her sanctuary as the heights,
as the earth which she founded for all time.
70 She chose David her slave,
and took him from the sheepfolds.
71 From following the nursing ewes she brought him
to shepherd her people Jacob [born of Rebekah], Israel, her legacy.
72 David shepherded them with an upright heart,
and guided them with skillful hand.

Romans 1:1 Paul, a slave of Christ Jesus, called to be an apostle, set apart for the gospel of God, [2] the one God promised beforehand through God's prophets [women and men] in the holy scriptures, [3] the gospel concerning God's Son, who was born of the line of David [and Bathsheba] according to the flesh [4] and was made known as the Son of God with power according to the spirit of holiness by resurrection from the dead, Jesus Christ our Savior, [5] through whom we have received grace and apostleship to bring into obedience of faith all the Gentiles for the sake of his name, [6] among them, you all who are called by Jesus Christ.

[7] To all who are in Rome, God's beloved, who are called to be saints:

Grace to you and peace from God our Creator and the Messiah Jesus Christ.

[8] First, I thank my God through Jesus Christ for all of you, because your faith is proclaimed throughout the world.

John 7:37 On the last, the great day of the festival of Booths, Jesus stood and cried out saying, "If anyone thirsts, woman or man, come to me and drink. [38] The one who believes in me, as the scripture has said, 'From their belly shall flow rivers of living water.'" [39] Now he said this about the Spirit, which believers in him were to receive; for as yet there was no Spirit, because Jesus was not yet glorified.

[40] When the crowd heard these words, some said, "This is truly the prophet." [41] Others said, "This is the Messiah." But some said, "Indeed, the Messiah does not come from Galilee, true? [42] Does not the scripture say that the Messiah comes from the line of David and comes from Bethlehem, the village where David lived?" [43] So there was a division in the crowd because of him. [44] Some wanted to arrest him, but no one laid their hands on him.

PROCLAMATION

Text Notes

First Samuel 17:55 and the first five verses of chapter 18 are missing from the LXX. Verse 55 is commonly translated as some version of "By the life (or soul) of the king, I do not know." Others change it to second person, "By your life/soul . . ." Compare NRSV, CEB, and JPS. The rather common idiomatic expression is conditional, introduced with "if"; further, the negative particle "no/not" is missing.

In 1 Samuel 18:1, "by the time" is "when . . ." and in verse 5, the "warriors" are "men of war." The word most often translated "timbrel" is actually a hand drum. Extensive archaeological work, particularly by Carol Meyers, has turned up no images or evidence of the metal or other noisemakers on the drum frames; the final group of instruments in verse 6 are likely sistrums, a handheld percussive instrument that is shaken, in the broad category of a rattle. Saul's rage in verse 8 is expressed with a verb for "burning" modified by "much/greatly."

As Israel's prophets were female and male, I make the gender range in Romans 1:2 explicit. In Romans 1:3 and John 7:42, David is "born/created" of the "seed" of

David, here the line of David and Bathsheba. Paul's address to the Romans seems wider, i.e., to all of Rome including the nascent church, i.e. all of Rome is beloved of God, rather than just to the church as the beloved of God within Rome when the syntax is taken into account.

John 7:2 establishes that "the festival" mentioned is the fall festival of Sukkoth, "Booths" or "Tabernacles" (see Leviticus 23:33–36, 39–43). In the *Jewish Annotated New Testament* commentary, Adele Reinhartz notes the prominent place of water in the ceremony as the backdrop to Jesus's teaching about living water; it would make a dramatic object lesson. The scriptural "citation" of verse 38 is not found in Hebrew, Aramaic, or Greek texts and has only passing similarity to passages such as Isaiah 44:3, Jeremiah 17:13, and Zechariah 14:8. There is a similar verse in the Gospel of Thomas, which may represent an attempt to resolve the discrepancy. "The prophet" of verse 40 is likely the promised "prophet like Moses" in Deuteronomy 18:15, 18. Verse 42 likely refers to Micah 5:2, which provides the basis for the "Little Town of Bethlehem" carol; curiously there is a version in the Dead Sea Scrolls (4QXII^{f}) in which the "ruler" to come does not come from Bethlehem. The division in verse 43 is a "schism," *schisma.*

Preaching Prompts

It is striking that David's mother is missing from the narratives that introduce him, perhaps owing to the lack of a barrenness and miraculous pregnancy trope. It is even more odd when considering that his sisters, Abigail and Zeruiah, daughter Tamar (II) and granddaughters, Tamar (III) and Maacah born to Absalom, Mahalat born of his nearly unknown son Jerimoth (2 Chronicles 11:18) and Solomon's daughters Taphath and Basemath are all named. (David has other unnamed daughters in 2 Samuel 5:13.) The rabbis provided a name for his mother in the Babylonian Talmud, Nizbeth (or Nitzevet) bat Adael (*b. Baba Bathra* 91a).

John's claim "that there was yet no Spirit" in verse 39 represents at one level the author's interpretation of Jesus's words and not the words of Jesus himself, an interpretation that is quite at odds with most understandings of the Trinity (albeit itself a postbiblical understanding) and the scriptures themselves.

Lectionaries often focus on David stories because of the messianic title, Son of David. The Messiah, *meshiach*, "Anointed One" from the verb *m-sh-ch*, Christ/*christos* in Greek, is a person chosen or designated by God to serve (primarily as monarch, priests were anointed as well). David (2 Samuel 22:51; Psalm 18:50) and the Persian monarch Cyrus (Isaiah 45:1) are called "God's messiah" in the First Testament; correspondingly, the word used in the LXX in each case is *christos*, making David and Cyrus God's christs. The tradition of translating *meshiach* as "anointed in the Hebrew Scriptures but "Christ" in the second created the misunderstanding that Jesus was the only bearer of the title.

Prophetic texts spoke of a messianic monarch who would save or redeem Israel (and sometimes the world); that redemption was understood as national deliverance from occupation and oppression, hence the question when Jesus would restore the monarchy (Acts 1:6). In order for the reinstituted monarchy to be legitimate, the monarch/messiah would need impeccable lineage, thus the resort to the line of David. Early references to the Messiah as the descendant of David include Psalm 132:11, and invoking his father, "the stump of Jesse" in Isaiah 11:1–5. In the pseudepigrapha "messiah," "monarch," and "Son of David" come together in the Psalms of Solomon 17:21. Verse 32 of the same chapter calls this monarch "Lord Messiah" (see also 3 Enoch 35:5). Yet just as Jesus taught that the reign and realm which he ushered forth was entirely different than the monarchies of this world (John 18:36), so I suggest we hear Jesus as the son and heir of David in different terms. David is not just Israel's beloved monarch of old, but he was also a broken man who broke others while wrestling to live in the light of God's love. When the Messiah is named as the Son of Bathsheba and the Son of David, the fragile fallible humanity that is also the Messiah's lineage is fully present, pregnant with incarnational possibilities.

PROPER 16 (CLOSEST TO AUGUST 24)

1 Samuel 14:49–51; 18:17–21, 29; Psalm 62; Romans 12:9–21; Matthew 7:15–20

1 Samuel 14:49 Now the sons of Saul were Jonathan, Ishvi, and Malchishua, and the names of his two daughters: the name of the firstborn was Merab, and the name of the younger, Michal. 50 The name of Saul's wife was Ahinoam daughter of Ahimaaz and the name of the commander of his army was Abner son of Ner, Saul's uncle. 51 Kish was the father of Saul and Ner the father of Abner was the son of Abiel.

18:17 Then Saul said to David, "Look, here is my older daughter Merab; I will give her to you as a wife; only be my valiant warrior and fight the battles of the HOLY ONE." For Saul said [to himself], "Let me not raise a hand against him rather let the hand of the Philistines do it." 18 Then David said to Saul, "Who am I and what is my lineage, my ancestral house in Israel, that I should be son-in-law to the ruler [of Israel]?" 19 But at the time for giving Merab the daughter of Saul to David, it happened that she was given to Adriel the Meholathite as a wife.

20 Now [at the same time] Saul's daughter Michal loved David. Saul was told, and the matter was all right in his eyes. 21 So Saul said [to himself], "Let me give Michal to David that she may be a snare for him and that the hand of the Philistines may be against him." So, Saul said to David a second time, "Through the second shall you be my son-in-law this day."

29 And Saul became the enemy of David every day from then.

Psalm 62

1 Only with God is my soul quiet;
from her is my salvation.
2 Only she is my rock and my salvation, my stronghold;
I shall never be shaken.
3 How long will you all attack a person,
destroying them—all of you—
as you would a leaning wall, a tottering fence?
4 Truly, from their lofty position they plan to drag them down.
They take pleasure in falsehood;
they bless with their mouths,
but within they curse. *Selah*
5 For God alone is my soul silent,
from her is my hope.
6 Only she is my rock and my salvation, my stronghold;
I shall never be shaken.
7 With God is my deliverance and my honor;
rock of my strength, my refuge, is in God.
8 Trust in her at all times, O people;
pour out your heart before her;
God is a refuge for us. *Selah*
9 The woman-born are only futile,
the children of earth, false;
in the scales they ascend,
less than a single breath.
10 Trust not in oppression,
and set not your heart on robbery;
if force bears fruit, do not set your heart on it.
11 Once has God spoken;
twice have I heard this:
that power belongs to God.
12 Faithful love belongs to you, Most High.
For you repay to each one according to their work.

Romans 12:9 Let love be sincere. Abhor what is evil, cling to what is good. [10] Love one
another as family; lead the way in showing honor to one another. [11] In zeal not idle, fervent in
spirit, serving the Messiah. [12] In hope rejoice, in suffering endure, in prayer persevere. [13] Take
part in meeting the needs of the saints; practice hospitality.

[14] Bless those who persecute you; bless and do not curse them. [15] Rejoice with those who
rejoice and weep with those who weep. [16] Live in harmony with one another; do not think

highly [of yourself], sit with the lowly; do not claim to be wiser than you are. [17] Do not repay anyone evil for evil but, contemplate what is good in the sight of all persons. [18] If possible for you, live peaceably with all. [19] Do not avenge yourselves beloved, rather leave room for the wrath [of God]; for it is written, "Vengeance is mine, I will repay, says the Holy One." [20] On the contrary, "if your enemies hunger, feed them; if they thirst, give them drink; for by doing this you will heap burning coals on their heads." [21] Be not overcome by evil, rather overcome evil with good.

Matthew 7:15 "Beware of false prophets, who will come to you all in sheep's clothing but inside are rapacious wolves. [16] By their fruits you will know them. Are grapes gathered from thorns, or from thistles, figs? [17] Thus, every good tree bears beautiful fruit, but the rotten tree bears wicked fruit. [18] A good tree cannot bear wicked fruit, nor can a corrupt tree bear beautiful fruit. [19] Every tree that does not bear beautiful fruit is cut down and thrown into the fire. [20] Thus you will know them by their fruits.

PROCLAMATION

Text Notes

In 1 Samuel 14:49 Merab is Saul's firstborn, though her brothers are listed previously. "Father's family" is translated "ancestral house" in 18:18 and "my life" as "my lineage."

The psalmist uses strong language invoking murder; however since it applies equally to a wall and a fence, I use "destroy." While verses 2 and 6 in the psalm are identical, verses 1 and 5 which precede them are only partially identical. In verse 9, the same word means both "futile" and "breath." (*Chevel* gives rises to "vanity of vanities" from Ecclesiastes.) "Force" in verse 10 of the psalm is *chayil,* which is also "warrior" and "army" and a warrior's might or heart or accumulated wealth (through their martial abilities).

Romans 12:16 uses a verb that means "condescend" to describe Paul's instruction that Christians spend time with the "lowly." I translate it "sit with" here. Verse 18 ends abruptly with "the wrath," without specifying divine wrath. Yet the following verses quoting Deuteronomy 32:35 and Proverbs 25:21–22 make clear that God's wrath is indeed the referent.

In Matthew 7:17 the writer (or speaker) uses a variety of adjectives: good and (a separate superlative) good/beautiful, corrupt/rotten, wicked/evil; many translations reduce the vivid imagery to good and bad fruit and trees.

Preaching Prompts

Valorization of David is often paired with demonization of Saul. I like to invite my hearers and readers to resist the urge to identify with David as God's beloved and to read with Saul as a person who struggled and failed and who groped for God and experienced abandonment and perhaps lived with mental illness. I suspect we are all more Saul than David.

Today's first lesson traces some of the tangled relational threads woven through Israel's early monarchy. Saul is presented with a significant attention to his family: these few verses present his wife Ahinoam; her father or ancestor, Ahimaaz; her children with Saul, Merab their firstborn, their daughter Michal, their sons together Jonathan, Ishvi, and Malchishua; Saul's father, Kish; Saul's uncle Ner (1 Chronicles 8:33 and 9:39 rewrite the genealogy to connect Saul to an earlier Ner, making Ner the father rather than brother of Kish); and Saul's great-grandfather Abiel.

The royal lady will not be heard from again (Israelites did not use the title "queen"; later the Judeans would adopt "Great Lady" for the king's mother, usually translated Queen-Mother). Her daughters, as was common in monarchies until relatively recently, were bartered for political advantage, in this case to David, who remains a force in their lives after the broken engagement (Merab) and forced dissolution (Michal). Michal's love for David sours when she is ripped from the arms of her second husband, who loves her; he weeps openly as she is taken back to David (2 Samuel 3:15–16). Later, David uses Merab's children to pay a blood debt, along with Saul's other children by his low-status wife, Rizpah (2 Samuel 21:8–9).

In the midst of these machinations there is a story of unrequited love; Michal is the only woman in scripture whose love for a man, not her son, is noted. In contrast, the psalm and second lesson offer reflections on the kind of love that does not barter or betray. Though the psalm's dedicatory language invokes David, it is in keeping with the aims of the lectionary to ask if these words of scripture apply to Michal and Saul and to us. The Gospel offers words to govern all our lives and loves—and arguably theology and biblical interpretation. Know a tree—a person, a love, a theology, a biblical interpretation—by its fruits.

PROPER 17 (CLOSEST TO AUGUST 31)

1 Samuel 25:14–19, 23–25, 32–34, 42–43; Psalm 25:4–12; 1 Corinthians 7:1–9; Matthew 5:38–42

1 Samuel 25:14 To Abigail, wife of Nabal, one of the boys reported: "Look! David sent messengers out of the wilderness to greet our lord; and he screamed at them. 15 Yet the men were very good to us, and we were not put to shame, and we never missed anything all the days we were with them when we were in the field. 16 They were a wall to us even by night and also every day; we were with them, keeping the sheep. 17 Now know this and see what you can do; for evil against our master and against all his house has been resolved; he is worthless, no one can speak to him."

18 Then Abigail hurried and she took two hundred loaves, two skins of wine, five prepared sheep, five measures of parched grain, one hundred clusters of raisins, and two hundred
fig cakes and she loaded them on donkeys. 19 And Abigail said to her boys, "Go on before me;
I am coming after you." And her husband Nabal she did not tell.

23 And Abigail saw David and she hurried and got down from the donkey, fell before
David on her face, bowing to the ground. 24 She fell at his feet and said, "Upon me my lord,
the iniquity; please let your slave-woman speak in your ears and hear the words of your slave.
25 Please my lord, do not set your thought on this worthless man Nabal, for as his name, thus
is he; Nabal [meaning Disgrace] is his name, and he is a disgrace; now I, your slave, did not see
my lord's boys whom you sent."

32 Then David said to Abigail, "Blessed be the Holy One, the God of Israel, who sent
you to meet me today! 33 Blessed be your discernment, and blessed be you, who have kept me
today from coming for blood and saving me from my own hand. 34 Surely as the Holy One
the God of Israel lives, who has restrained me from hurting you, unless you had hurried and
come to meet me, truly by the light of daybreak there would not have been left to Nabal anyone urinating against a wall."

42 [Later after Nabal's death,] Abigail hurried and got up and mounted a donkey with
five of her girls at her heels; she went after the messengers of David and she became his wife.
43 David also married Ahinoam of Jezreel; both of them became his wives.

Psalm 25:4–12

4 Make known to me your ways, Ageless God;
teach me your paths.
5 Guide me in your truth, and teach me,
for you are the God of my salvation;
for you I wait all day long.
6 Remember your maternal love, O Womb of Life,
and your faithful love,
for they have been from of old.
7 The sins of my youth and my transgressions remember not;
according to your faithful love remember me,
for the sake of your goodness, Gracious One.
8 Good and upright is the Fount of Wisdom,
therefore she instructs sinners in the way.
9 She guides the humble in what is just,
and teaches the humble her way.
10 All the paths of the Wisdom of the Ages are faithful and true
for those who keep her covenant and her decrees.
11 For your Name's sake, Loving God,
pardon my guilt, for it is great.

12 Who are they that fear the HOLY ONE OF OLD?
She will teach them the way that they should choose.

1 Corinthians 7:1 Now, about what you have written: It is good for a man not to take hold
of a woman. 2 But because of sexual immorality, each man should have his own woman and
each woman her own man. 3 For the wife, the husband should do his duty and likewise the
wife for her husband. 4 For the wife does not have authority over her own body, rather the
husband does; likewise the husband does not have authority over his own body, yet the wife
does. 5 Do not ever defraud each another except by agreement for a time to devote yourselves
to prayer, and then come together again so that Satan may not tempt you because of your lack
of self-control. 6 This I say as a concession, not a command. 7 I wish that all were as I myself
am. But each has their own gift from God, indeed one to one and another to another.
8 To the unmarried and the widows I say that it is good for them to remain so. 9 But if
they are not showing self-control, they should marry; for it is better to marry than to burn.

Matthew 5:38 [Jesus said,] "You all have heard that it was said, 'An eye for an eye' and 'a
tooth for a tooth.' 39 But I say to you: Do not set yourself against the wicked. But when someone strikes you on the right cheek, turn the other to them also. 40 And when someone wants
you to be judged and take your coat, let your other clothing go as well. 41 And when someone
forces you to go one mile, go the second mile too. 42 Give to those who ask from you, and
those who want to borrow from you, do not refuse."

PROCLAMATION

Text Notes

In the Samuel text, "bless" is used to signify a greeting, indicating common forms of greeting such as, "May God bless you" (see Ruth 2:4). In verse 16, "even by night and also every day" translates "even night and even days." My translation of this verse is indebted to Everett Fox's translation in *The Schocken Bible, Volume II, The Early Prophets*. Nabal is *ben belial,* "the son of worthlessness." In verse 25, Abigail begs David not to "set his heart to[ward]" Nabal. His name encodes all sorts of bad behavior from impiety to sacrilege, to disorderly conduct and sexual assault. Some understand the "wall pisser" of verse 35 to be a euphemism for soldier like "jarhead" or "leatherneck."

To "wait" in Psalm 25:4 also includes hoping; the psalmist waits with expectation. God's maternal love in verse 6 emanates from her womb, which provides the grammatical root for this love.

Neither Hebrew nor Greek has distinct words for wives or husbands. Both languages use the expressions "her man" and "his woman" to indicate conjugal relationships. In 1 Corinthians 7 Paul first says that each *woman or man* should have their own spouse. Then using the same wording, he means that each *wife or husband* should do their duty by their spouse. Paul uses *anthropos,* which means "human" and "man" for man and *aner*, male person, for "husband" while using the most common term for women, *gune*, for both women and wives. Having used *anthropos* for male initially, it is not clear whether Paul means "all males" or "all people" have their own gift of God in verse 7.

The "eye for an eye" teaching occurs in Exodus 21:24, Leviticus 24:20, and Deuteronomy 19:21. "The wicked" in Matthew 5:39 can be translated as "evil (itself)" or a "wicked/evil person" or, "a person who does evil/wickedness." The verb in verse 39 can also mean do not "oppose" or "resist."

Preaching Prompts

At this phase of his life, David is a thug, robbing and extorting people for cash crops and currency on the hoof. Nabal is a vile person, a nasty drunk, a difficult if not abusive husband, but that does not entitle David to his goods; he is not yet king. Nabal had a cultural obligation to provide hospitality but that should not merit a death sentence. Yet David vowed that he would have killed them all if Abigail had not brought him the goods. He and Abigail ride off into the sunset after the death of husband. He then pulls over somewhere and picks up another woman. One purpose of this story in its original context was to emphasize David's youth, strength, and virility. He will have seven wives when he has Bathsheba abducted and will continue collecting them. One wonders what Paul would have made of David and his sexual conduct. For all that David is idolized and idealized in and out of the text, he is a vivid example of the limitations of men, monarchs, and monarchy.

Unlike David in Samuel, the psalmist has lived long enough to be self-aware, grateful for God's mercies, and penitent. She—or perhaps he if David later in life—depends on God's teaching, *torah*, to guide her choices.

In 1 Corinthians 7, Paul proscribes the choices of the community when it comes to marriage but allows for different life patterns while promoting his own celibate estate. He is a "naturalist," desiring believers to remain in their current estate, including marriage, virginity, and, more problematically, slavery (verse 22–23). Paul lays out his preferred pattern of partnering, describing an egalitarian marriage with each belonging to the other, yet within his hierarchal and specifically patriarchal world it is doubtful there was true equality.

Religious proclamations that individuals do not have the right to control their own bodies are dangerous. Paul's narrowing of women's bodily autonomy provides sanctified cover for abusive relationships. His teaching does correspond with Jewish teaching that spouses owe each other sexual pleasure; Jewish tradition is particularly emphatic that husbands owe their wives sexual pleasure based in part on Sarah's response to her predicted pregnancy, that she would again experience "pleasure" [literally "moisture"] in Genesis 18:12.

Jesus's rejection of "an eye for an eye" opens this section that reads as a nonviolent resistance manual and is consistent with rabbinic teaching that called for financial restitution in cases of bodily injury. Jesus says to yield to those who strike or force you and to give to those who ask and to those who take. That was Abigail's strategy and it saved her life and the lives of everyone on her estate. However, like Paul's teaching in 1 Corinthians 7, it can be easily twisted by those with power to victimize the vulnerable. The longer chapter builds towards developing a maturation, "perfection," that imitates the bearing of God our Progenitor. This posture calls for the humility the psalmist recognized in those God teaches her way.

PROPER 18 (CLOSEST TO SEPTEMBER 7)

1 Samuel 27:1–3, 8–12; Psalm 72:1–4, 12–14, 18–19; Romans 2:12–16; Matthew 18:1–7

1 Samuel 27:1 David said to his heart, "Now, one day I shall be swept away by the hand of
Saul; there is nothing better than that I escape to the land of the Philistines, then Saul will despair
of seeking me any further within the border of Israel and I shall escape out of his hand." 2 So David
got up and went over, he and six hundred men who were with him, to Achish son of Maoch, ruler
of Gath. 3 And David stayed with Achish at Gath, he and his troops, each man with his household, and David with his two wives, Ahinoam of Jezreel, and Abigail of Carmel, wife of Nabal.
8 And David and his men went up and raided on the Geshurites, the Girzites, and the
Amalekites, for they were the inhabitants of the land from of old on your way to Shur and on
to the land of Egypt. 9 Then David smote the land and there was neither woman or man living; and he took sheep and cattle and donkeys and camels and clothing and would return and
come back to Achish. 10 Then Achish would ask, "Against whom did you all raid today?" And
David would say, "against the Negeb of Judah," or "against the Negeb of the Jerahmeelites," or
"against the Negeb of the Kenites." 11 Neither woman nor man David left living to be brought
back to Gath, saying, "Lest they tell about us, and say, 'Thus did David.'" Thus was his custom
all the days he lived in the country of the Philistines. 12 Now Achish trusted David saying,
"He has made himself an abhorrent stench in the nostrils of his people, in Israel; so he shall be
my slave for all time."

Psalm 72:1–4, 12–14, 18–19

1 God, give the ruler your justice,
and your righteousness to a ruler's son.
2 May the [next] ruler judge your people with righteousness,
and your afflicted ones with justice.
3 May the mountains raise up well-being for the people,
and the hills, righteousness.

4 May the ruler do justice for the poor of the people,
grant deliverance to those born in need
and crush the oppressor.
12 For the ruler delivers the needy when they call,
the oppressed and those who have no helper.
13 The ruler has pity on the poor and the needy,
and saves the lives of the needy.
14 From oppression and violence the ruler redeems their life;
and precious is their blood in the sight of their ruler.
18 Blessed be the FOUNT OF JUSTICE, the God of Israel,
who alone does wondrous things.
19 Blessed be her glorious name forever;
may her glory fill the whole earth.
Amen and Amen.

Romans 2:12 All who sin lawlessly will also perish lawlessly, and all who have sinned with
regard to law will be judged by law. 13 For it is not those who hear the law who are righteous
before God, but the doers of the law who will be made righteous. 14 When Gentiles, who
do not have the law, naturally act according to the law, these [women and men], not having
the law, are a law to themselves. 15 They demonstrate that the essence of the law is written
on their hearts, which their own conscience proves true, and their conflicting thoughts will
either accuse or excuse them 16 on the day when God will judge the hidden things of women
and men, according to my gospel, through Jesus Christ.

In the scripture below, the gender of the child is unknown and grammatically neutral. Readers may wish to specify a gender to spur reflection.

Matthew 18:1 In that hour [that Jesus taught about taxes] the disciples came to Jesus and
asked, "Who then is the greatest in the realm of the heavens?" 2 Jesus called a [girl] child,
whom he placed among them, 3 and said, "Truly I tell you, lest you all be changed and become
like children, you all will never enter the realm of the heavens. 4 Whoever humbles themselves
like this [girl] child is the greatest in the realm of the heavens. 5 Whoever receives one such
child in my name receives me.

6 "But if anyone puts an enticement to sin before one of these little ones who believe
in me, it would be better for you if a great millstone were fastened around your neck and
you were drowned in the depth of the sea. 7 Woe to the world because of enticement to sin!
Enticements to sin are bound to come, but woe to the one by whom the enticement comes!

PROCLAMATION

Text Notes

The text continues to refer to Abigail as the "wife"—not "widow"of Nabal (in spite of NRSV and CEB) as it will for Bathsheba, though in the latter case it certainly highlights David's transgression.

Throughout Psalm 72 I use "the ruler" for the monarch and his son and the many masculine pronouns for clarity and for the broader utility of this psalm beyond male monarchs given the presence female regents and sovereign monarchs in Judah. In verses 2 and 12, the people are afflicted (or oppressed) through a poverty that is imposed on them through unjust means, hence punishment of "the oppressor" in verse 4; Hebrew's lexicon of poverty has different words for different contexts. "Those born in need" replaces "children/sons of the needy" in the same verse. Hebrew uses "soul" for both the essence of a person's life, what we in the West tend to call a soul, and a person's life. The language of saving and redeeming in Psalm 72:13–14 refers properly to lives; a leader's economic policies are matters of life and death. In verse 15, the "essence" of the law is the "work" of the law.

The adverb *anomos*, "lawlessly," in Romans 2:12, is formed from the word "law," *nomous*, with the "*a*" prefix negating the noun, as in "moral/amoral." Law here is not concrete, "the law," and suggests law broadly rather than Israelite law or Torah specifically, though the latter would be included in the former. "Women and men" replaces "humanity," *anthropos*, in verse 16.

Matthew 18 begins "in that hour" (often translated as "at that time"), connecting it with the previous unit. The question, "Who then . . ." also points back: Given the way monarchs behave on earth, taxing other people's children, how does it work there? Who then is the greatest there? See Matthew 17:24–27. In Matthew 18:3 Jesus says that we must *be* changed, "be turned"; the passive is important, we cannot do it on our own (vs. "change" and "turn" in NRSV CEB). "Enticement" captures the scandalous element of *skandalizo* in Matthew 18:6–7. "Stumbling block" is a common euphemism; however the verb articulates providing the opportunity for sin, including temptation.

Preaching Prompts

David has been anointed ruler of Israel before his family, in 1 Samuel 16:13, yet Saul still reigns. It is left to David to seize the throne himself, however he will not raise his hand against the anointed of God, see 1 Samuel 26:6–12 and 2 Samuel 1:11–16. ("Anointed" is *mashiach*, messiah; monarchy was a messianic enterprise in ancient Israel.) Saul views David's popularity as a threat and has been seeking to kill him (1 Samuel 19:1–2, 11–15). It is in this period that David becomes a mercenary marauder in the employ of the Philistine ruler. David is supposed to decimate his own people for his overlord; instead he chooses peoples and clans that are related to or coresident with Judah. He will be able to say he never touched a hair on the head of his "own" people. He did, however, conduct a series of massacres against noncombatant peoples, murdering women and men alike—murder is a strong word and reflects my ethical assessment given these peoples were not at war and had not engaged in any hostile acts. No mention is made of the children's fate. David is an Iron Age monarch-in-training and monarchy has ever been a brutal occupation. The framing of Jesus as the Son of David and of God as the supreme monarch are intended to convey power, authority, and majesty, but cannot erase the uglier legacies invoked with monarchal language, making Jesus's insistence that his realm, God's realm, is of an entirely different nature than earthly monarchies.

With this background, Psalm 72 reads as a heartfelt prayer for a rising monarch from a declining monarch who knows the pitfalls of power because he has stumbled. The psalm is addressed "to" or "for," (not "of" or "by") Solomon; the mentions of Sheba in verses 10 and 15 recall the visit of Sheba's queen to Solomon. The monarch in the psalm is a far cry from the young David; this ruler is attentive to the poor and needy, the oppressed, and delivers them *from* violence (verses 12–14).

While not addressing monarchs or monarchy specifically, Romans 2 focuses on the deeds, and even secret thoughts, of all people, righteous or unrighteous; here God is Judge and all are subject to judgment. For Paul there is an inward sense of morality, of what is "lawful" for all people, so God's judgment is just whether people know or follow Israel's laws or not.

The lessons conclude with a Gospel reading in which Jesus turns hierarchy on its head. The disciples accept the prevailing royal metaphor envisioning God in a realm that mirrors the monarchies of the world in which there would be a vizier or chief of staff (as Joseph was to Pharaoh). Bathsheba served this role for Solomon from a throne he had installed at his right hand (1 Kings 2:19). The disciples want to know the pecking order and where they fit. Would they have the power and prestige they lack in this world in the next? Instead, Jesus calls them to be as the young child, perhaps a young girl, he places in their midst. Greatness is not measured in monarchal power or conquest; it is the heart, hope, trust, and imaginative capacity of children. A vision of God surrounded by child-hearted saints merits new language, mother rather than monarch, kindergarten teacher rather than king. I have suggested that the child Jesus calls be read as a girl given the gender and power dynamics of the age; in our time, one might choose to preach the child as nonbinary or trans: *Whoever receives one such child in my name receives me.*

PROPER 19 (CLOSEST TO SEPTEMBER 14)

1 Samuel 30:1–8, 17–19; Psalm 13; Hebrews 2:10–13; Matthew 18:10–14

1 Samuel 30:1 And it was that when David and his men came to Ziklag on the third day
[after being dismissed by the Philistine ruler], the Amalekites raided the Negeb and Ziklag.
They smote Ziklag and burned it with fire. 2 And they took captive the women who were in
it, from young to old; they did not kill any, rather they led them away and went their way. 3 So
when David and his men came to the city, they found it burned and their wives and daughters
and sons taken captive! 4 Then David and the people who were with him raised their voices
and wept, until there was no more strength in them to weep. 5 Now the two wives of David
had been taken captive, Ahinoam the Jezreelite and Abigail the wife of Nabal the Carmelite.
6 David was in great distress; for the people said to stone him, because the souls of all the people were embittered on account of their daughters and sons and David strengthened himself
in the Holy One his God.

7 Then David said to Abiathar the priest, the son of Ahimelech, "Bring to me the ephod."
So Abiathar brought the ephod to David. 8 And David questioned the Holy One of Old
asking, "Shall I pursue this band? Will I overtake them?" God answered him, "Pursue, for you
shall surely overtake and you shall surely rescue."

17 So David smote them from twilight until the evening of the morrow. None of them
escaped, except four hundred young men who mounted camels and fled. 18 And David rescued all who the Amalekites took; David rescued his two wives. 19 None was missing, whether
young or old, daughters or sons, spoil or anything that they took for themselves; David
brought back everything.

Psalm 13

1 How long, Holy One? Will you forget me forever?
How long will you hide your face from me?
2 How long will I counsel myself,
sorrow in my heart, every day?
How long shall my enemy be exalted over me?
3 Look! Answer me, Faithful One my God!
Enlighten to my eyes lest I sleep [into] death.
4 Then my enemy will say, "I have prevailed over him";
my foes will rejoice because I am shaken.
5 Yet I trusted in your lovingkindness;
my heart shall rejoice in your salvation.
6 I will sing to the Womb of Life,
because she has poured goodness on me.

Hebrews 2:10 It was fitting for God because of whom and for whom all that is, is, in bringing many daughters and sons to glory, to make the pioneer of their salvation perfect through sufferings. [11] For the one who sanctifies and those who are sanctified are all of one. For this reason Jesus is not ashamed to call them sisters and brothers, [12] saying,

"I will proclaim your name to my brothers and sisters,
in the midst of the assembly I will praise you."

[13] And again,

"I will put my trust in God."

And again,

"Here am I and the children whom God has given me."

Matthew 18:10 [Jesus said,] "See to it that you do not treat one of these little ones with contempt. I say to you all that their angels in the heavens see the face of my Abba who is in the heavens all day [every day]. [12] What do you all think? If a person had one hundred sheep and one of them wandered off, would they not leave the ninety-nine on the mountain and go in search for the one that wandered off? [13] If they find it, truly I tell you all that they rejoice over it more than over the ninety-nine who did not wander off. [14] In the same way, it is not the will of your Abba who is in the heavens that one of these little ones should be lost."

PROCLAMATION

Text Notes

The seized women (and likely girls) in 1 Samuel 30:2 and 19 are either "from young to old" or "from small to great." Given the explicit mentions of daughters in verse 6, I read this in terms of age with Fox, Alter, the CEB, and the Targum, rather than in terms of status "low-born and high-born alike" as in JPS. In the LXX, men are included among the abducted. The ephod is a priestly garment worn over the regular garment. It held the divination tools, Urim and Thummim; the breastplate with stones for each tribe was attached to the front. Traditionally one asked yes or no questions as did David here. However, God seems to speak to David apart from divination beyond yes and no. While normally worn and used by a priest, Gideon made an unsanctioned ephod in Judges 8:27. David's use of the ephod here and in 2 Samuel 6:14 suggests a priestly role for David in his own eyes and those of some of his biographers, which extended to his sons in 2 Samuel 8:18 (see 2 Samuel 6:18 where David offers sacrifice and the note on verse 14 in the same chapter in the *Jewish Study Bible*).

"Counsel myself" in Psalm 13 is the somewhat awkward "put counsel in my soul." In verse 3 the psalmist demands, using the imperative, that God look at her and really see her. The expression "lest I sleep death" lacks a preposition in the text. "Prevail" in verse 4 is "to be able" but clearly has the sense of prevailing in a struggle. An alternate text for Psalm 13:6 might be: *I will sing to the* WOMB OF LIFE, *for she has weaned me.* The verb *gamal* means "to wean, or repay" (wages, consequences, actions, thus goodness or punishment); the verb shares its root with "came" which is a homophone, there being some overlap between q/k and g sounds in Semitic languages.

In Hebrews 2:10 the text only acknowledges "sons," similarly "brothers" in verse 11. The referent for "one" in verse 11 is unspecified. NRSV adds "Father," i.e., *of one Father*; the Aramaic Peshitta adds "nature," *of one nature.* I have also left "one" unmodified and without capitalization to allow for multiple readings. Verse 12 cites Psalm 22:22; verse 13 cites Isaiah 8:17 and 18.

While the Gospel uses masculine language for the shepherd, women like Rachel, Zipporah and her seven sisters, and the female poet in the Song of Songs were also shepherds; a reader might want to acknowledge the reality of the text and with notice to the assembly, read it with feminine pronouns. In verse 10, "all day" is supposed to indicate perpetuity, I have added "every day" as an option to better make the point.

Preaching Prompts

Today's lessons focus on children—their vulnerability and their inherent value to God. First, David, who has made a name for himself slaughtering women and men and either killing or taking their children captive (the text neglects their fate), has his family carried off into captivity along with the families of his men. Understandably they all break down and cry at their loss and at the thought of their fate: enslavement and physical and sexual abuse. The scene is vivid and their pain palpable.

After turning to God for strength, David and his men mount a successful rescue. The psalm provides a suitable prayer that fits the moment. Every moment without their wives and children was a "How long, O God" moment. The plea to not let enemies triumph is apt. The psalmist trusts in God's deliverance and rejoices in it at the end. In the Epistle, believers are God's children as is Jesus, and as David teaches, even a mercenary warlord loves his children and will do anything to save them, how much more God.

The Epistle folds together several texts from differing contexts to make its point, affording an opportunity to reflect on the ways we and our forebears interpreted the First Testament in our respective contexts. In Psalm 22:22 a soul in distress prays for and receives deliverance and promises to give all praise to God; in the LXX version that praise is before siblings lacking in Hebrew. The author of Hebrews puts the psalm on the lips of Jesus—he prayed a bit of it during the crucifixion. This reading may stem from that or simply imagine Jesus speaking the words of scripture, reinterpreting them for the moment. This is midrashic exegesis, not literal.

In Isaiah 8:17–18, Isaiah is waiting for God to resolve the war between Judah and a combined Israel and Assyria. His prophecies to Ahaz have taken peculiar form:

the presence and names of his children, Shear Jashub (7:3) and Maher Shalal Hash Baz (8:1) and Immanu El (7:14), likely also his child. The conception of the last of the three in chapter 8 was Isaiah's rather unorthodox response to God's word to him. For the author of Hebrews, Isaiah furnishes more language for Jesus: "trust" God's ability to save and sanctify her children and the image of God's children as prophetic signs just as Isaiah's were. This type of exegesis permits us to think about how we read these passages in our time, adapting them to our context without negating their original contexts.

Matthew 8:10 is one of very few texts that suggests people, here children, have their own angels who commune with God on their behalf. In the Gospel, the "little ones" may be minor children or new believers young in faith or a combination of both. Here the lost sheep parable has a twist; it is not just about wandering away but being driven away, linked with a warning command not to despise or look at/treat with contempt these little ones. In the worlds of the scriptures, children were not always valued beyond signs of fecundity and prosperity, even with the occasional narrative that values an individual child. These texts together emphasize that we are called *as* children *with* children into the arms of God and our elder sibling, Jesus.

PROPER 20 (CLOSEST TO SEPTEMBER 21)

2 Samuel 1:17–27; Canticle Mater Tua Leaena (Ezekiel 19:1–3; 10–14); Revelation 21:1–7; Matthew 5:1–9

2 Samuel 1:17 David keened this lamentation over Saul and over Jonathan his son. 18 Then
he taught the Bow [Song] to the women and men of Judah; it is written in the Book of Jashar.
He said:

19 The splendor of Israel upon heights lays slain!
How the mighty have fallen!
20 Tell it not in Gath,
proclaim it not in the streets of Ashkelon,
lest the daughters of the Philistines rejoice,
lest the daughters of the uncircumcised exult.
21 Hills of Gilboa,
let there be neither dew nor rain upon you,
nor offering-laden fields.
For there the shield of the mighty was abhorred,
the shield of Saul, anointed with oil no more.
22 From the blood of the slain,
from the fat of the mighty,

the bow of Jonathan did not turn back,
and neither did the sword of Saul return empty.
23 Saul and Jonathan, beloved and delightful.
In life and in death they were not parted;
they were swifter than eagles,
they were stronger than lions.
24 Daughters of Israel, weep over Saul,
who clothed you with scarlet, in luxury,
who overlaid your garments with adornments of gold.
25 How the mighty have fallen
in the midst of battle!
Jonathan upon your heights lies slain.
26 I grieve over you, my brother, Jonathan;
a great delight were you to me;
your love to me was wonderful,
more than the love of women.
27 How the mighty have fallen,
and the weapons of war destroyed!

Canticle Mater Tua Leaena (Ezekiel 19:1–3; 10–14)

Ezekiel 19:1 All of you, raise a keening for the royal seed of Israel, 2 and say:

What a lioness was your mother among lions!
Among young lions she lay, raising her cubs.
3 She raised up one of her cubs; who became a young lion,
who learned to catch prey, who devoured the woman-born.
10 Your mother was like a vine in a vineyard planted by the waters,
fruitful and full of branches from abundant water.
11 She had mighty branches for a ruler's scepter;
she grew tall, her height among the clouds,
and was seen because of her height
and because of her many branches.
12 Then she was uprooted in a rage, she was thrown to the ground,
the east wind withered her fruit, they were stripped off;
her strongest stem was withered, then consumed by fire.
13 Now she is planted in the wilderness,
in a dry and thirsty land.
14 Now fire has gone out from her staff, and has devoured her branches, her fruit,
now there is no mighty branch within her, no scepter for ruling.

This is a keening-lament, and it is used for lamentation.

Revelation 21:1 I saw a new heaven and a new earth, for the first heaven and the first earth
had passed away, and the sea was no more. 2 And I saw the holy city, the new Jerusalem,
descending heaven from God, prepared as a bride adorned for her beloved. 3 And I heard a
loud voice from the throne saying,

> "Look! The home of God is among the woman-born.
> God will dwell with them as their God;
> they will be God's peoples,
> and this selfsame God will be with them.
> 4 God will wipe every tear from their eyes.
> Death will be no more;
> grief and weeping and pain will be no more,
> for the first things have passed away."

5 And the One who was seated upon the throne said, "Look! I am making all things new."
The One also said, "Write, for these words are trustworthy and true." 6 Then the One said
to me, "It is done! I am the Alpha and the Omega, the beginning and the end. I will give to
the thirsty from the spring of the water of life freely. 7 Those who overcome will inherit these
things, and I will be their God and they will be my daughters and sons.

Matthew 5:1 Now when Jesus saw the crowds, he went up the mountain and sat down; his
disciples came to him. 2 Then he opened his mouth and taught them, saying:

> 3 "Blessed are the poor in spirit, for theirs is the majesty of the heavens.
> 4 "Blessed are those who mourn, for they will be comforted.
> 5 "Blessed are the meek, for they will inherit the earth.
> 6 "Blessed are those who hunger and thirst for righteousness, for they will be filled.
> 7 "Blessed are the merciful, for they will receive mercy.
> 8 "Blessed are the pure in heart, for they will see God.
> 9 "Blessed are the peacemakers, for they will be called children [daughters and sons] of God.

PROCLAMATION

Text Notes

The Book of Jashar, referenced in 2 Samuel 1:18, is lost to us; it is also mentioned in Joshua 10:13, where another poetic composition, a war epic, is said to be preserved in it, suggesting a collection of poetic text. The title, *yashar*, means "upright"; hence it is likely "The Book of the Upright." The verb and noun forms of "lament" or "keen" in verse 17 are homophones of keen, *q-y-n*, as are the nominal forms in Ezekiel 19:1 and 14. The repetition in 2 Samuel 1:17 is more literally "David keened a keening."

Context suggest that the "Bow" which David calls to be taught to the people of Judah is his lament. The word "song" is missing, supplied by most translators. Some understand the Bow as a call to greater skill in archery in the face of their losses; the Targum and KJV translate David commanded them to learn "to draw/ use the bow," common in older translations (Wycliffe, Geneva [to shoot], Bishops and Douay). A few drop the bow, yielding "teach" an unspecified "it," the LXX (Wycliffe and RSV).

I have selected the phrase *Mater Tua Leaena*, "Your Mother, A Lioness," from Ezekiel 19:1 as the title for the canticle. Its central figure is described as a lioness and a tree in feminine language throughout (compare CEB with NRSV, which shifts to "it" in verses 11ff counter to the Hebrew). It is a lament over the decline and fall of the Judean monarchy, that last vestige of a self-governing Israel; the individual cubs are the sons of Josiah, enthroned and dethroned at the whims of their conquerors, Nebuchadnezzar and Pharaoh Neco. The lioness, singular, conflates the last two queen mothers, Nehusta and Hamutal, or may represent Judah, uncommonly in feminine language (versus the more familiar (male) lion of Judah). Because the fall of Judah did not only affect royal sons, I use the more inclusive "royal seed" in verse 2. For the peril faced by the last princesses of Judah, see Jeremiah 41:10; 43:5–7 and my discussion of them and the queen mothers in *Womanist Midrash*. The translation "vine in a vineyard" comes from a widely accepted correction to the original text, "vine in your blood."

Throughout the *Lectionary* I use "realm of heaven" to avoid an anthropomorphic male hierarchal image of God. I have chosen "majesty" here where the inheritance is not ruling the divine realm but sharing in its glory.

Preaching Prompts

Saul was the major obstacle to David's enthronement, but David refused to kill him because he was the anointed of God, God's messiah (*christos* in the LXX), a point he makes repeatedly (see 1 Samuel 16:6; 24:6, 10; 26:9, 11, 16, 23; 2 Samuel 1:14, 16). Saul's death clears the way for David who does not celebrate, but grieves, after killing the young man Saul compelled to kill him so he would not be captured and abused. David grieves and composes a lament, normally composed and performed by women in an apprenticing guild, like those of Philistine women in verse 20 and Israelite women in verse 24 (see the discussion of women's musical and funerary guilds in my *Daughters of Miriam*). The Israelite women would be mourning while the Philistine women would be celebrating, a useful place to discuss the effects of war and foreign policy on women.

The lament emphasizes the import of grieving, no matter who you are, no matter what world-changing events are unfolding. David laments Saul and Jonathan and

Jonathan's love. Curiously David does not name his love for Jonathan; Jonathan is "beloved" in verse 23, passive, no subject. Missing from Saul and Jonathan's funeral are Ahinoam bat Ahimaaz, Saul's wife and Jonathan's mother and her daughters Michal and Mered, Johathan's sisters. His brothers are also missing, as is the second woman with whom Saul had children, Rizpah (see 1 Samuel 14:49–50; 2 Samuel 21:7–8). The portion of Ezekiel used as a canticle is a lament for a royal line; its focus is the mother of monarchs, whether human or figurative, compensating for the lack of royal women in Saul and Jonathan's funeral scene.

All of these texts recognize the need to grieve, that lament is healthy and healing. The Beatitudes promise comfort for the mourner and the second lesson promises the end of death itself. The comfort of the Gospel honors and responds to grief; it does not forestall it.

PROPER 21 (CLOSEST TO SEPTEMBER 28)

2 Samuel 11:2–15; Psalm 38:1–9, 11, 18, 21–22;
Colossians 3:5–11; Matthew 15:10–11, 15–20

2 Samuel 11:2 And it happened near the evening that David rose from his lying-place and went walking about on the roof of the palace and he saw a woman bathing from the roof; the woman was extraordinarily beautiful in appearance. [3] David sent someone to inquire about the woman. It was reported, "Is not this Bathsheba daughter of Eliam, the wife of Uriah the Hittite?" [4] And David sent messengers and he took her, and she came to him, and he lay with her. Then she purified herself after her defilement and she returned to her house. [5] The woman conceived, and she sent and had someone tell David, "I am pregnant."

[6] So David sent word to Joab, "Send me Uriah the Hittite," and Joab sent Uriah to David. [7] When Uriah came to him, David asked after the status of Joab and the status of the people and the status of the war. [8] Then David said to Uriah, "Go down to your house, and wash your feet." Uriah went out of the palace, and after him a gift from David. [9] Now Uriah slept at the entrance of the palace with all the slaves of his lord and did not go down to his house. [10] And they told David, "Uriah did not go down to his house." So David said to Uriah, "Have you not come from a journey? Why did you not go down to your house?" [11] Uriah said to David, "The ark and Israel and Judah dwell in temporary shelters and my lord Joab and the slaves of my lord are at the edge of the field, camping. Should I then go to my house, to eat and to drink, and to lie with my wife? As you live, and as your soul lives, I will not do this thing." [12] Then David said to Uriah, "Stay here this day also, and tomorrow I will send you." So, Uriah remained in Jerusalem that day and the next. [13] Then David called him to dine in his presence and he drank, and David got him drunk. Then in the evening he went out to lie on his couch with the slaves of his lord, yet he did not go down to his house.

[14] And it was in the morning that David wrote a [message] scroll to Joab and sent it in the hand of Uriah. [15] Now in the scroll David wrote, "Set Uriah at the frontline of the most intense battle and pull back from behind him, so he will be struck down and die."

Psalm 38:1–9, 11, 18, 21–22

1 FAITHFUL GOD, rebuke me not in your wrath,
nor chastise me in your fury.
2 For your arrows have descended into me,
and your hand has descended on me.
3 There is no soundness in my flesh
in the face of your indignation;
there is no health in my bones
in the face of my sin.
4 For my iniquities have gone over my head;
like a heavy burden, too heavy for me.
5 My wounds grow stink and rot
in the face of my foolishness.
6 I am bent over and bowed down beyond low;
all day I go around mourning.
7 For my loins are filled with burning,
and there is no soundness in my flesh.
8 I am numb and crushed to the bone;
I groan because of the roaring of my heart.
9 Holy One, before you is all my longing;
my sighing is not hidden from you.
11 My lovers and friends stand back from my plague,
and my near ones stand far off.
18 Now will I confess my iniquity;
I shudder on account of my sin.
21 Forsake me not, SAVING ONE;
be not far from me my God.
22 make haste to help me,
Holy One, my salvation.

Colossians 3:5 Put to death, therefore, whatever part of you that is of the earth: sexual immorality, impurity, passion, evil desire, and greediness which is idolatry. [6] Because of these [things] the wrath of God is coming on the spawn of disobedience. [7] In these things you all also once followed, when you were living in that way. [8] But now you all must put away all anger, wrath, wickedness, slander, and bad language from your mouth. [9] Do not lie to one another, seeing that you have stripped off the old self with its deeds. [10] And you all have clothed yourselves with the new self, which is being made new in knowledge according to the image of its creator. [11] There is no longer Greek and Jew, circumcised and uncircumcised, barbarian, Scythian, slave and free, rather Christ is all and in all.

Matthew 15:10 Jesus called the crowd saying to them, "Listen and understand: [11] It is not what enters the mouth that defiles a woman or man rather, it is what exits the mouth that defiles a person."

[15] Then Peter said to him, "Explain to us this parable." [16] So Jesus said, "Are you all also still lacking understanding? [17] Do you not see everything that enters the mouth goes into the stomach and exits into the sewer? [18] But what comes out of the mouth comes forth from the heart and this is what defiles a woman or man. [19] For out of the heart come evil intentions, murder, adultery, sexual immorality, theft, false testimony, slander. [20] These are what defile women and men, but to eat with unwashed hands does not defile a person."

PROCLAMATION

Text Notes

In 2 Samuel 11:7 *shalom* is used for the welfare check on Joab and the people in the war. Commentators understand the "gift" in verse 8 to be some largess from David's table or holdings, agricultural stuffs, livestock, etc. In verse 11 *succoth* is the plural of "booths" or "shelters"; it is also phonetically the same as the city Succoth, which is how JPS understands it. In verse 13 Uriah's drunkenness is articulated with a verb form that lays the cause at David's feet: *he (made/got) him drunk.*

In verses 6 and 8 of the psalm, I translate the generic intensive adverbial particle *ad-moed* ("until/as far as + "very') contextually, "beyond low" in verse 6 and "to the bone" in verse 8. "Lovers" in verse 11 is often translated as "friends" or "companions" (NRSV, JPS, Alter). However, "my lovers" is a literal rendering of the participle "those-who-love-me" (note the CEB's "my loved ones"). Further, since what is being described is likely a sexually transmitted infection (STI), the romantic and sexual connotations are applicable. The STI reading rests on the description of burning genital sores or wounds: their receipt due to foolishness—not a war injury and David's multipartner sexual history, including with women who also had multiple partners such as Abigail. "Plague" in verse 11 refers to marks or spots on the skin.

"Sexual immorality," *porne* in Colossians 3:5, is a broad brush that generally refers to sex outside of (an appropriate) marriage including adultery, prostitution, and use of prostitutes. The term is also used more broadly: the author of Hebrews calls Esau *pornos*, "sexually immoral" in 12:6. However, no biblical or postbiblical texts attribute inappropriate sexual behavior to him beyond marrying Hittite women against his mother's wishes, Genesis 26:34–35; 27:46. "Evil desire" is not (simply) lust, sexual or otherwise; it is wrong or inappropriate desire for that which is not acceptable.

It is not a condemnation of sexual desire. In verse 8 the root for "slander" is "blaspheme"; at one level blasphemy is slander against God. "Bad language" is broad, including obscenity and talk considered in "poor taste" according to BDAG, where it is bound up with class in Aristotle, the way a slave speaks but not a free "gentleman." (See the entry on *aischrologia* in *A Greek-English Lexicon of the New Testament and Other Early Christian Literature* [known as BDAG].)

Preaching Prompts

In these lessons David's most infamous act, the rape of Bathsheba, is held in conversation with later teaching on the ethical values and character traits that characterize the reign and realm of God. The psalm includes a surprisingly graphic lament over the diseased state of (most likely) David's loins and a confession for having brought it on itself. Colossians associates undesirable characteristics, including sexual immorality, with the earth, a binary reading that often demonizes the flesh as earthly while lauding so-called spiritual or heavenly values. Often that binary acquires gendered characteristics, with women being associated with the flesh and earthliness, as can be seen in some readings of Bathsheba. In the Gospel, Jesus addresses many of the same undesirable characteristics as the Epistle, focusing on their origin in the human heart. He does so using ritual washing before meals as an object lesson, putting him at odds with the Pharisees in the text, a classic rabbinic disputation.

David's violation of Bathsheba's body is treated as a violation of her husband's rights to and over her body and as an offense against God. She is not treated as a victim or survivor. The extolling of her beauty has been weaponized—she (and other women) tempt men with their beauty by existing and conforming to some aesthetic standard. The construction of David's sin as adultery projects blame onto Bathsheba that neither the text nor Nathan assert on God's behalf. Indeed, Bathsheba is not charged with or punished for adultery; no sin is ascribed to her in the text. Rooftops often formed an extra room in Israelite households; Bathsheba's bathing there is also not critiqued in the text as it is in subsequent interpretation. The initial mention of her bathing in verse 2 did not mention "impurity," often read as menstruation though that term is not used. She purifies herself from her impurity, "defilement" here, in verse 4 *after* David rapes her; that is a second cleansing. David's decision to gift (or pay) Uriah for a harm that he may not yet know he has suffered conjures men who after a sexual assault offer their victim money or something valuable for silence or just out of guilt. (For a detailed analysis of the passage, see the chapter on Bathsheba in *Womanist Midrash*.)

The Gospel portion intentionally omits the critique of the Pharisees as anti-pharisaic rhetoric in the Christian scriptures and its interpretation are often unnecessarily anti-Semitic. As always, contextualizing Jesus as a religiously observant

Jewish scholar who respected the Pharisees even while disagreeing with them and agreed more than disagreed is helpful. Consider Jesus's overlooked instruction in Matthew 23:2–3: "*The scribes and the Pharisees sit on Moses's seat; therefore, do whatever they teach you and follow it.*" This injunction affirming the legitimate authority of the Pharisees is the necessary prerequisite for understanding the following more familiar text to break with the Pharisees only when they do not do as they themselves say. Jesus's dissent over ritual washing represents the normative variance in religious practice expected among any group, not a condemnation of the Judaism of his age or the authority of the Pharisees—though other texts will position them differently.

PROPER 22 (CLOSEST TO OCTOBER 5)

2 Samuel 13:1–16, 21–22; Psalm 27:1–14;
1 Corinthians 5:9–11; Matthew 25:31–46

2 Samuel 13:1 Now it was after [the defeat of the Ammonites]. The sister of Absalom, David's son, was beautiful; her name was Tamar and Amnon son of David loved her. 2 Amnon was distressed to the point of sickness over Tamar his sister, for she was a virgin and it seemed impossible in his eyes to do anything to her. 3 Now Amnon had a friend whose name was Jonadab, the son of Shimeah, David's brother, and Jonadab was an extremely astute man. 4 He said to Amnon, "Why are you so poorly, royal son, morning after morning? Will you not tell me?" Amnon said to him, "Tamar, sister of Absalom my brother, I love [her]."

5 Jonadab said to Amnon, "Lie down on your bed and make yourself sick and your father will come to see you, then say to him, 'Please let Tamar my sister come and feed me bread and prepare the food before my eyes so I may see it and eat it from her hand.'" 6 So Amnon lay down and made himself sick and when the king came to see him, Amnon said to the king, "Please let Tamar my sister come and make heart-cakes before my eyes that I may eat from her hand."

7 Then David sent Tamar to the palace saying, "Go to the house of your brother Amnon and prepare food for him." 8 So Tamar went to the house of Amnon her brother; he was lying down. And she took dough and kneaded it and made heart-cakes in his sight and cooked the cakes. 9 Then she took the pan and tipped them out before him, but he refused to eat. Then Amnon said, "Send everyone out [away] from me." So everyone went out [away] from him. 10 Then Amnon said to Tamar, "Bring the food into the room that I may eat from your hand." So Tamar took the heart-cakes she had made and brought them into the room to Amnon her brother. 11 And she brought them to him to eat and he seized her and said to her, "Come, lie with me, my sister." 12 She said to him, "No! Do not my brother! Do not rape me! Such a thing is not done in Israel! Do not commit this sacrilege! 13 And I, where could I go with my shame? And as for you, you would be as one of the outcasts in Israel. Now please, speak to the king; for he will not withhold me from you." 14 He did not want to listen to her voice; he overpowered her, and he raped her and lay with her.

[15] Then Amnon hated her with a very great hatred, for greater was his hatred toward her than his love of her, so Amnon said to her, "Get up! Get out!" [16] But she said to him, "No, this great evil, sending me away, is more than what you did to me." And he would not listen to her.

[21] And the king, David, heard of all these things and he became very angry, yet he would not grieve the spirit of Amnon his son, because he loved him, for he was his firstborn. [22] Now Absalom spoke not to Amnon neither ill nor well for Absalom hated Amnon, because of that deed—he raped Tamar his sister.

Psalm 27

[1] The FIRE OF SINAI is my light and my salvation;
whom shall I fear?
The ARK OF SAFETY is the strength of my life;
whom shall I dread?
[2] When evildoers advance against me
to devour my flesh,
my adversaries and my foes,
they shall stumble and fall.
[3] If a battalion besieges me,
my heart shall not fear;
though war rise up against me,
in this will I trust.
[4] One thing I asked of the FOUNT OF LIFE,
that [one thing] will I seek:
to live in the house of the WOMB OF LIFE
all the days of my life,
to behold the beauty of the WELLSPRING OF LIFE,
and to inquire in her temple.
[5] She will shield me in her shelter
when the day is evil;
she will cover me under the cover of her tent;
she will raise me high on a rock.
[6] Now my head is lifted up
above my enemies all around me,
and I will sacrifice in her tent, joyful sacrifices;
I will sing and make melody to the FOUNT OF JUSTICE.
[7] Hear my cry, FAITHFUL ONE, when I cry aloud,
be gracious to me and answer me!
[8] To you my heart says, "seek my face!"
Your face, JUST ONE, do I seek.

9 Do not hide your face from me.
Do not send your slave away in anger;
you have been my help.
Do not abandon me, do not forsake me,
God of my salvation!
10 If my mother and father forsake me,
the COMPASSIONATE GOD will gather me in.
13 If I but believe, I shall see the goodness of SHE WHO IS FAITHFUL
in the land of the living.
14 Wait for the LIVING GOD;
be strong, and let your heart take courage;
wait for GOD WHOSE NAME IS HOLY!

1 Corinthians 5:9 I wrote to you all in my epistle not to associate with the sexually immoral.
10 Not referring at all to the sexually immoral people of this world, or the greedy and predatory,
or idolaters, since you would be obliged then to go out of the world. 11 But now I write to you
all not to associate with anyone who bears the name of sister or brother who is sexually immoral
or greedy, or is an idolater, a slanderer, a drunkard, or predator. Do not even eat with such a one.

Matthew 25:31 "When the Son of Woman comes in his glory with all the angels, then will
he sit on the throne of his glory. 32 And gathered before him will be all the nations and he will
separate them one from another just as a shepherd separates the sheep from the goats. 33 And
he will put the sheep on his right and the goats at the left. 34 Then shall the one who rules
say to those at his right, 'Come, those blessed by my Abba; inherit the realm prepared for
you all from the foundation of the world. 35 For I was hungry and you all gave me food; I was
thirsty and you all gave me drink; a stranger and you all gathered me in. 36 Naked and you all
clothed me; I was sick and you all cared for me; in prison and you all visited me.' 37 Then the
righteous will answer asking, 'Majesty, when did we see you hungry and feed you, or thirsty
and give you drink? 38 And when did we see you a stranger and gather you in, or naked and
clothe you? 39 And when did we see you sick or in prison and visit you?' 40 And the one who
rules will answer them, 'Truly I tell you all, as much as you all did for one of the least of these
my kindred, you all did it to me.'

41 "Then the one who rules will say to those on the left, 'Go from me, all you who are
accursed, into the eternal fire prepared for the devil and his angels. 42 For I was hungry and
you all gave me no food; I was thirsty and you all gave me no drink; 43 a stranger and you all
did not gather me in, naked and you all did not clothe me, sick and in prison and you all did
not care for me.' 44 Then they also will answer, asking, 'Majesty, when was it that we saw you
hungry or thirsty or a stranger or naked or sick or in prison, and did not take care of you?'
45 Then the ruler will answer them, 'Truly I tell you all, just as you did not do it to one of the
least of these, you all did not do it for me.' 46 And these will go away into eternal punishment,
but the righteous into eternal life."

PROCLAMATION

Text Notes

The Hebrew Masoretic Text is corrected against the Dead Sea Scrolls in academic translations like the NRSV and CEB, as the scrolls are the oldest most complete manuscripts, resulting in some ninety corrections in the NRSV compared to the RSV. Samuel is the most heavily corrected, slightly more than 40 percent, due in part to a number of gaps, including David's rationale for his silence after his daughter's rape: "*but he would not punish his son Amnon, because he loved him, for he was his firstborn.*"

Tamar and Absalom were the children of Maacah, daughter of the ruler of Geshur (2 Samuel 3:3), David's fourth wife. Amnon was the son of Ahinoam (1 Samuel 25:43; 2 Samuel 3:2), David's third wife. The idiom "fell in love" is modern and inappropriate to the ancient world. In 1 Samuel 13:1 Amnon "loves" Tamar using the common verb that refers to love of Jonathan and Michal for David, and that between God and humanity, in both directions. I keep the word "love" rather than "infatuate" (JPS) or even "lust" because Amnon and others use "love" talk as part of their pattern of abuse. It "seemed impossible" is something like "it would take a miracle," using the verb *p-l-'*, to be wondrous or miraculous. His "miracle" comes in the form of Jonadab, David's nephew who facilitates the rape of his own cousin. Jonadab is described as "wise," sometimes translated as "shrewd" or "crafty."

I use "astute" to articulate the nature of Jonadab's "wisdom." He tells Amnon to make himself sick using a causative verb form; the notion of pretense is not expressed but within reason. Jonadab's correct assumption that David will come see about his sick child intimates David's love for his son was well-known and stands in sharp contrast to his avoidance of his raped daughter.

"Feed me" in verse 5 is much more intimate than "give me something to eat" (NRSV, JPS) or "give me some food" (CEB); the shape of the "heart-cakes" is suggested by the verb *l-v-v*, a homophone of "heart." They are described as being "boiled," evoking dumplings or hot-water cornbread. In verse 11 I added the "No!"; the Hebrew "Do not!" does not have the same force in English. "Sacrilege" and "outcast" are the same root whose meaning include outrage and offenses against God, impiety, etc.; it is a homophone of "fool/foolish" but stronger. It serves as a synonym of the rape and description of the rapist.

Psalm 27:8 is often revised in translation to read seek "his" or "God's" face (see NRSV and CEB). However, it is sensible as is: the psalmist longs to be seen by God even as she seeks God's face.

In 1 Corinthians 5:10–11 *harpax* has the primary sense of "rapacious" as an adjective and "robber" as a noun; I use "predator/predatory" to maintain the same root in each case.

Where KJV and RSV use "son of man" throughout both testaments, NRSV has dropped it from the First Testament altogether; CEB follows suit. Instead, they use versions of "mortal (one)," "human one," and "human being." As the title emphasizes humanity (*anthropou* is the word for humanity, the root of anthropology, study of humanity), I use Son of Woman to emphasize the woman-born humanity of Jesus.

Somewhere between the Testaments a decided bias against goats developed; they would continue to be demonized, ultimately becoming a satanic symbol. However, in the Hebrew Scriptures goats and sheep are often represented by the same word, though they are distinguished in the LXX.

Preaching Prompts

The incestuous rape of Tamar II (Tamar I appears in Genesis 38:6ff) is a well-studied text, the most classic treatment in Phyllis Trible's *Texts of Terror*. David's failure to attend to his brutalized daughter stands in sharp relief to his rush to his son supposedly sick in bed. The story bears hallmarks of rape and incest narratives with which modern readers and hearers are familiar: an absent mother figure, an untrustworthy friend or relative, inadequate response from parents and authority figures, and, less frequent, a new cycle of retributive violence. A frank discussion of rape and incest in the text and in the world reading the text can bring back memories of trauma in survivors and it is advisable to have appropriately trained pastoral counselors on hand, trusted counselors in the community to whom you can refer, and resource sheets with contact information for survivor services and helplines.

I have paired Psalm 27 with the account of Tamar's rape, imagining her praying it. Reading through her story, the enemy who came to devour, eat up, her flesh stands out as a stark reminder of the vulnerability of female flesh in the world of the psalm and beyond, combined with an absolute trust in God who remains worthy even when father and brother fail and mother is nowhere to be found.

In the Gospel, the separation of the sheep and goats appears to be by nation rather than individual, contrary to Western understandings of individual salvation. Salvation in the Hebrew Scriptures is corporate, national. Indeed, Jesus uses the plural form of "you" throughout the passage. What might it mean for our individual salvation to be dependent on the judgment of our community, our nation, rather than our own or our individual faith as so often preached in the Protestant tradition? Faith and its profession are not salvific here, rather it is the work of the gospel, the work that Christ did with and for "the least of these" that is salvific.

"The least of these" in the text and in the world that reads and interprets the text includes those living under the structural oppressions of poverty and inequity, those entangled in the criminal justice system—with no thought to guilt or innocence—and those living with illness or perhaps dying. Of course, this gospel is not limited to persons in these circumstances. We can add those ground down by any oppressive system and give thought to who is most precarious on the furthest edge of the margins. That includes persons who do not find themselves in the binary language of the scriptures or its social and familial constructs, those against whom the scriptures have been weaponized. Bearing this in mind, I use "kindred" in verse 39 to replace "brothers (and sisters)" for folks who do not fit into the gender binary of the world of the text and embody profound vulnerability.

When read together, the lessons empower us to say in Jesus's name for rape survivors like Tamar: "*whatsoever you do to Tamar, you do to Me.*" The Epistle challenges us to withdraw our fellowship from the predatory in light of the #MeToo and #ChurchToo movements launched in response to rampant and unadjudicated sexual harassment and abuse. And for those who survive a psalm reheard in light of patterns of sexual violence that have changed little from the Iron Age.

PROPER 23 (CLOSEST TO OCTOBER 12)

2 Samuel 20:1–3, 14–22; Proverbs 8:1–4, 10–17; 1 Corinthians 12:4–11; Matthew 13:54–58

2 Samuel 20:1 Now [among the people] there was by chance a worthless man named Sheba
son of Bichri, a Benjaminite. He sounded the trumpet and cried out,

> "We have no portion in David!
> No share in Jesse's son!
> Every man [back] to his tent, Israel!"

2 Then all the men of Israel left from behind David and went behind Sheba son of Bichri
while the men of Judah clung to their king from the Jordan to Jerusalem. 3 And David came to
his Jerusalem house and the king took the ten low status wives whom he had left to watch the
house and put them under watch in a guardhouse and he provisioned them but did not go to
them. So were they confined until the day of their death, a living widowhood.
14 Then Sheba passed through all the tribes of Israel to Abel of Beth-Maacah and all the
Bichrites assembled and they went behind him. 15 They came and lay siege against him in Abel
of Beth-Maacah; they threw up a siege-ramp against the city and it stood against the rampart.
Joab's people were dismantling the wall to bring it down. 16 Then a wise woman called from the
city, "[All of you!] Listen! Listen! Tell Joab now, 'Come here and I will speak to you.'" 17 So he
drew near to her and the woman said, "Are you Joab?" He answered, "I am." Then she said to
him, "Listen to the words of your slave-woman." He answered, "I am." 18 Then she said, "They
used to say this saying in former times, 'Let them ask at Abel and thus would settle the matter.'
19 I am among the most peaceful and faithful in Israel and you seek to put to death a city and a
mother in Israel. Why would you swallow up the heritage of the MOST HIGH GOD?" 20 Joab

answered, "Far be it! Far be from me it, that I should swallow up or dismantle! [21] The matter is not thus! Rather a man from the hills of Ephraim—Sheba son of Bichri is his name—has raised up his hand against David, against the king; give him up, just him and I will go from the city." Then the woman said to Joab, "Look, his head shall be thrown to you beyond the wall." [22] Then the woman went to all the people with her wisdom. So, they cut off the head of Sheba son of Bichri and then they threw it to Joab. And he blew the trumpet and they dispersed from the city and all went to their homes while Joab returned to Jerusalem to the king.

Proverbs 8:1–4, 10–17

1 Does not Wisdom call,
and Understanding put forth her voice?
2 On the highest heights, beside the way,
at the crossroads she takes her stand.
3 Beside the gates at the entry of the town,
at the opening of the entryway she sings out:
4 "To you, the woman-born, I call,
and my cry is to all earth's children.
10 Take my instruction and not silver,
and knowledge but not choice gold.
11 For better is Wisdom than jewels,
and not even every delight can compare with her.
12 I, Wisdom, dwell with prudence,
and knowledge and discretion I find.
13 The fear of the FOUNT OF WISDOM is to hate evil;
pride and arrogance and the way of evil
and perverse speech I hate.
14 Wise counsel and sound wisdom are mine;
I am Understanding, might is mine.
15 By me royals reign,
and rulers decree what is just.
16 By me governors govern,
and nobles, all who judge rightly.
17 I love those who love me,
and those who seek me diligently shall find me.

1 Corinthians 12:4 Now there are diversities of gifts, but the same Spirit. [5] And there are diversities of ministries, but the same Sovereign. [6] And there are diversities of works, but it is the same God who works all of them in everyone. [7] To each person is given the manifestation of the Spirit for mutual good. [8] To one woman or man through the Spirit is given a word of wisdom, and to another a word of knowledge according to the same Spirit: [9] To another faith by the same Spirit, to another gifts of healing by the one Spirit, [10] to yet another working miracles, to another prophecy, to yet another discernment of spirits, to another families of tongues, to another the translation of tongues. [11] All these are activated by one and the same Spirit, who allots to each one individually just as the Spirit chooses.

Matthew 13:54 Jesus came to his hometown and began to teach the women and men in their synagogue, so that they were astounded and said, "Where did this man get this wisdom and these powers? [55] Is not this the carpenter's son? Is not his mother called Mary? And are not his brothers James and Joseph and Simon and Judas? [56] And are not all his sisters with us? From where then did this one get all this?" [57] And they were offended over him. But Jesus said to them, "Are prophets dishonored except in their hometown and in their own house?" [58] And he did not there do many works of power because of their unbelief.

PROCLAMATION

Text Notes

Wisdom in the Hebrew Scriptures, *chokmah*, is of "heart and hand," and often synonymous with skill; it is never limited to intellectual capacity. In Greek it is more intellectual while retaining transcendent qualities. Each is feminine and often personified as a personified divine character or characteristic of God and identified with *torah*. Greek wisdom, *sophia*, will be conflated with *logos*, and ultimately, Christ.

Sheba addresses the men in his community as decision-makers, set against the woman who will decide his fate. In verse 2, the men of Israel "cling" to David the way Ruth clung to Naomi (Ruth 1:14) and spouses cling to each other (a man to his woman in Genesis 2:24), all using the same verb.

Unions with primary (*isshah*, sing., *nashim*, pl.) and secondary or low-status wives (*pilegesh*, sing., *pilegeshim*, pl.) were all legal marriages producing legally recognized children; however, only the children of a primary wife—category, not sequence—were legal heirs, though nothing prevented voluntary inheritance. These particular women were abandoned by David because his son Absalom—who had his sister's rapist murdered—raped them in 2 Samuel 16:22 as part of his campaign to usurp his father in every way.

In verse 16 "all of you" identifies the plural voice. In the same verse NRSV undercuts the woman's authority by inserting "want to" where she says "I will." Her self-abasement as his "slave-woman" is at odds with the strength of her overall portrayal but reflects a common self-deprecating practice of women and men. The sage sets herself in the tradition of Deborah as "a mother in Israel" (Judges 5:7); multiple translations sever that lineage, changing the conjunction to "city *that is* a mother." In verse 20 Joab says he would never "dismantle" God's heritage while "dismantling" the city wall in verse 15.

In Proverbs 8:4 "woman-born" replaces "people/men" as "earth's children" does "children/sons of humanity." Earth, *adamah*, and *adam*, humanity (or person), share the same root. We are earth-crafted earthlings, humus-sourced humans.

I have made the presence of women in the synagogue explicit in "them/their" in Matthew 13:54; note "all his sisters *with* us" in verse 56. Not only did women participate in religious life at synagogue and temple, inscriptional evidence identifies women in leading positions including *archisynagogos*, "leader of the synagogue" (the same title as the male leaders in Matthew 9:18; Mark 5:36, 38; Luke 8:41; 13:14; see Bernadette Brooten, *Women Leaders in the Ancient Synagogue* and Kate Cooper, *Band of Angels: The Forgotten World of Early Christian Women*). Paul would go on to arrest women and men at synagogues who followed Jesus in Acts 9:2. We don't know how many sisters Jesus had: "all" is more than one and likely more than two.

In verse 56 "carpenter" includes more than wood-working, extending to "building" and "construction" from other materials.

Preaching Prompts

Today's canticle drawn from Proverbs connects the sage-woman of Abel Beth Maacah with the broader wisdom tradition in which Wisdom personified is divine, a characteristic or emanation of God, or some readings, God herself. In the Epistle, wisdom is a gift of the spirit and in the Gospel, wisdom is one of the characteristics that distinguishes Jesus; it is as noteworthy as the miracles he performs. Jesus will identify himself as the child of Wisdom in Luke 7:35 and, in some manuscripts, in Matthew 11:29.

In the first lesson, David is enthroned (2 Samuel 2:4), but not securely. Saul's military commander crowned one of Saul's surviving sons (2 Samuel 2:8–9), who held the larger part of Israel for two years while David ruled Judah. After a lengthy war and his assassination, Israel turned to David (2 Samuel 5:1), but later split to follow his son Absalom (2 Samuel 15:13). The aftermath of Absalom's death at the hand of his uncle Joab, his sister Zeruiah's son, David's military commander and chief enforcer, was another flashpoint (2 Samuel 2:18; 8:16; 1 Chronicles 2:15–16). David's decision to return to Jerusalem after fleeing Absalom's coup, accompanied by loyal Judeans, alienated the northerners (2 Samuel 19:41), leading to a series of uprisings, including the Sheba episode.

David's throne was secured with bloodshed and brutality and at the same time, the fruit of God's promise and anointing. Monarchy is a bloody, messy business, making it a challenging metaphor for God. Indeed, the Gospels eschew the title and while not completely rejecting the concept, completely redefine the concept. While other texts will locate wisdom with the monarch, notably Solomon, this wisdom in this text is that of a woman who uses her wits and her words to minimize the death toll of this unstable monarchy and in the process helps stabilize his reign. The wisdom of

Jesus, like that in the Epistle, reflects the Greek literary context of the Christian Testament and is rooted in his teaching, teaching that transcends expectations based on what his hometown neighbors know about his family of origin. Their astonishment is a bit of a knock on Jesus's family.

English translations of the New Testament regularly diminish the Jewishness of Jesus, his family, and followers by anglicizing their names: Mariam (Miriam/Mary), Iakobos (Jacob/James), Ioseph (Joseph), Simon (Simeon), and Ioudas (Judah/Judas or Jude), but ancestral figures from the scriptures with the same names are not treated that way, i.e., Rebekah's son Jacob does not become "James." Names matter and how and why we change them—particularly for other people—matter tremendously beyond the anti-Jewishness of this practice.

PROPER 24 (CLOSEST TO OCTOBER 19)

2 Samuel 21:1–14; Psalm 94:1–15; 1 Timothy 1:12–17; Matthew 5:38–42

2 Samuel 21:1 Now there was a famine in the days of David for three years, year after year,
and David sought the presence of the MOST HIGH. The HOLY ONE said, "There is bloodguilt on Saul and on his house, because he put the Gibeonites to death." 2 So the king summoned the Gibeonites and spoke to them. Now the Gibeonites were not of the Israelites; they
were the remnant of the Amorites. The Israelites had sworn to spare them, yet Saul sought to
destroy them in his zeal for the Israelites and Judah. 3 David said to the Gibeonites, "What
shall I do for you and how shall I atone that you all may bless the heritage of the HOLY ONE
OF OLD?" 4 The Gibeonites said to him, "We will take no silver or gold of Saul or of his house
and there is no one for us to put to death in Israel." He said, "What do you say that I should
do for you all?" 5 They said to the king, "The man who finished us off and intended to destroy
us that we would not be able to stand in all the territory of Israel, 6 let seven men from his sons
be handed over to us and we will hang them before the DREAD GOD at Gibea of Saul on the
mountain of the LIVING GOD." The king said, "I, myself, will give [them]."

7 But the king had pity on Meribbaal, son of Jonathan the son of Saul because of the oath
of the MOST HIGH that was between them, between David and Jonathan son of Saul. 8 The
king took the two sons of Rizpah daughter of Aiah, whom she gave birth to for Saul, Armoni
and [Mephibbaal called] Mephibosheth, and the five sons of Merab daughter of Saul, whom
she gave birth to for Adriel son of Barzillai the Meholathite. 9 David gave them into the hands
of the Gibeonites and they hung them on the mountain before the CREATOR OF ALL and
they fell, the seven of them, as one. Now they were put to death in the first days of harvest, at
the beginning of barley harvest.

10 Then Rizpah the daughter of Aiah took sackcloth and spread it on a rock for herself,
from the beginning of harvest until rain fell on them from the heavens; she did not allow

the birds of the air to come on the bodies by day or the beasts of the field by night. 11 Now it
was told David what Rizpah daughter of Aiah, the low status wife of Saul, had done. 12 Then
David went and took the bones of Saul and the bones of Jonathan his son from the nobles of Jabesh-gilead who had stolen them from the square of Beth-shan where the Philistines had
hung them up on the day the Philistines killed Saul at Gilboa. 13 And he brought up from
there the bones of Saul and the bones of his son Jonathan and they gathered the bones of
those who had been hung. 14 And they buried the bones of Saul and of his son Jonathan in
the land of Benjamin in Zela, in the tomb of Saul's father Kish and they did all that the king commanded. And God granted entreaty on behalf of the land after that.

Psalm 94:1–15

1 God of vengeance, DREAD GOD,
God of vengeance, shine forth!
2 Rise up, Judge of the earth;
repay recompence on the proud!
3 How long shall the wicked, JUST ONE,
how long shall the wicked exult?
4 They gush, they speak arrogance;
all the workers of iniquity boast.
5 Your people, they crush, FAITHFUL ONE,
and your heritage, they abuse.
6 Widow and immigrant they slay,
and orphans they murder.
7 And they say, "The HOLY ONE, she does not see,
the God of Rebekah's line does not understand."
8 Understand, you ignorant among the people;
fools, when will you become wise?
9 The one who planted the ear, does she not hear?
The one who formed the eye, does she not see?
10 The one who disciplines the nations,
the one who teaches knowledge to the woman-born,
does she not chastise?
11 The ALL-KNOWING GOD knows the thoughts of the woman-born,
that they are but breath.
12 Blessed is the one who you admonish, JUST ONE,
whom you instruct from your teaching,
13 to grant them respite from evil days,
until a pit is dug for the wicked.
14 For the FAITHFUL ONE will not forsake her people;
her heritage she will not abandon.

[15] For to the righteous justice will return,
and after it go all the upright in heart.

1 Timothy 1:12 I give thanks to Christ Jesus our Redeemer, who has strengthened me, because he deemed me faithful and appointed me to ministry. [13] Previously I was a blasphemer, a persecutor, and a violent person. But I received mercy for I acted ignorantly in unbelief. [14] Then the grace of our Redeemer overflowed with the faith and love that are in Jesus the Messiah. [15] This message is trustworthy and worthy of full acceptance, that Jesus the Messiah came into the world, sinners to save, of whom I am the principal. [16] But because of that I received mercy, so that in me principally, Jesus the Messiah would demonstrate all patience making an example to those who would come to believe in him for eternal life. [17] To the eternal Majesty, immortal, invisible, the only God, be honor and glory forever and ever. Amen.

Matthew 5:38 [Jesus said,] "You all have heard that it was said, 'An eye for an eye' and 'a tooth for a tooth.' [39] But I say to you: Do not set yourself against the wicked. But when someone strikes you on the right cheek, turn the other to them also. [40] And when someone wants you to be judged and take your coat, let your other clothing go as well. [41] And when someone forces you to go one mile, go the second mile too. [42] Give to those who ask from you, and those who want to borrow from you, do not refuse.

PROCLAMATION

Text Notes

The Hebrew of 2 Samuel 21:5 is unclear in places; the LXX forms the basis of the translation here. In verse 6 the Gibeonites specify adult sons to hang, literally "dislocate." Some read the form of execution as "impaling" (NRSV and JPS). Alter notes that something akin to crucifixion may have been intended (*The Hebrew Bible: A Translation with Commentary*). What is clear is they were left hanging on the instruments of their deaths. Verse 8 names Michal, Saul's daughter, as the mother of the second group of Saulide hostages. However, since her sister Merab's husband is named (1 Samuel 18:19), and Michal was sequestered by David, there is widespread agreement Merab is meant. The Targums resolves the dissonance by having Michal raise Merab's children.

The names of Rizpah's son with Saul and Jonathan's son with an unknown woman are also confused in verses 7–8, where both are called Mephibosheth. However in 1 Chronicles 8:34 and 9:40, Jonathan's son is Meribbaal; the consonantal text can mean "Baal is my master (or advocate)" or, as vocalized in 1 Chronicles, "one who contends with Baal," a synonym for the honorific bestowed on Gideon, Jerubbaal, in Judges 6:32. (See P. Kyle McCarter's discussion in the *Anchor Bible Commentary* on Samuel.)

A second issue is the name Mephibosheth itself, "from the mouth of shame," highly unlikely to have been chosen by parents. Rizpah's son Mephibosheth was likely actually named Mephibaal, "from the mouth of Baal." The Baal suffix would have been altered by a later editor for pious reasons, however the original referent was not likely the Canaanite deity, but the Israelite God; both were addressed by the same title (Baal's proper name being Haddu). Indeed, Mephibaal is attested in the Old Latin (pre-Jerome) and Lucian's recension of the LXX (see Diana Edelman's entry "Mephibosheth" in the *Anchor Bible Dictionary*). Hosea would try to end the broader confusion by exhorting the people not to use Baal for their God (Hosea 2:16). Since the name Meribbaal is attested in the Masoretic text, I use it for Jonathan's son. And since the name Mephibaal is attested in the broader biblical manuscript tradition, I include it as an option.

In verse 6 of the psalm, *anah*, "abuse," includes "oppression," "humiliation," and physical and sexual violence; in the same verse "orphan" is a fatherless child, hence the frequent pairing of "widow" and "orphan." "Yah," a short form of the divine Name, occurs in verse 7; though traditionally taking masculine verbs, its grammatical form is feminine and in some feminist and egalitarian Jewish contexts, is used with feminine verbs in prayer and liturgy. Also in verse 7, "the God of Rebekah's line" is "the God of Jacob." In verse 11 *chevel* can mean "breath" or "futility."

Paul identifies himself as *hybristen* in 1 Timothy 1:13, meaning both "violent" and "insolent." In verse 17, "eternal Majesty" renders "King of the ages."

Preaching Prompts

These lessons are studies in vengeance, retribution, and reparation. The first lesson is part of a larger cycle of violence and, as is often the case with long-lived conflicts, some of the details of who did what to whom have been lost. Survivors of Saul's violence demand retribution in blood, an eye for an eye. Troublingly, it is God who invokes bloodguilt which can only be satisfied with more bloodshed, but not from the perpetrator, rather the lives of his sons and grandsons would be forfeit. It would be much easier to hold this text in conversation with the Gospel if it were simply David's bloodthirst.

The notion of God as a God of vengeance is ancient and enduring. The psalmist cries out for vengeance while trusting in the rightness of God's actions. Yet concluding God called David's attention to the bloodguilt as a prerequisite for ending the famine might be hasty. God was not amenable to the people's entreaty, "able/willing to be entreated," until the remains of the murdered men were placed respectfully to rest, the answer to Rizpah's unrecorded prayer. The Gibeonites sought vengeance. David sought to be the instrument of that vengeance. He asked the Gibeonites, not God as does the psalmist, how to resolve the blood-debt and unsurprisingly, came up with a very human solution, one that conveniently removed potential claimants for the throne.

Rizpah, the mother of murdered—perhaps lynched—sons, has been a focus of black women's preaching for as long as I can remember. She has lost everything. Her spouse and with him potentially the status that kept her fed, clothed, housed, and safe. In 2 Samuel 3:7, Saul's former commanding general is accused of raping her after Saul's death. And now David has handed her children and those of his own sister-in-law over to death in what could be called an atonement ritual. There was nothing she could do to prevent their deaths and nothing she could say to David in the aftermath. But she could bear witness to her horror and prevent her people and her king from looking away. Animal predation would have resulted in the erasure of her son's bodies in a matter of weeks. By keeping the carrion eaters away, she ensured their slower decomposition, their unburied state an affront to Israelite values (Deuteronomy 21:22–23). Her actions shame David into burying her dead and the bones of Saul and his beloved Jonathan that he had also neglected.

Rizpah is one of the most vulnerable people in the text and one of the strongest. Was the God in whose sight she sat the source her strength? Had she voice, what might she say? One might hear the psalm in her voice, calling the God of vengeance to rise up against the wicked and the proud who murder the fatherless child, concluding in faith that the righteous will receive justice. The Gospel and Epistle offer visions of that justice that include mercy for the violent in Paul's case and an inscrutable and perhaps subversive teaching on the lips of Jesus. Giving up one's over *and* undergarments would leave one publicly naked in the face of one's creditor (see Ulrich Luz's *Hermeneia* commentary on Matthew), perhaps shaming them as Rizpah shamed David. Jesus's teaching on retribution calls for an exploration of the ways in which rhetoric and tone, i.e., provocation or even sarcasm, shape interpretation and the need for nonliteral reading paradigms.

PROPER 25 (CLOSEST TO OCTOBER 26)

1 Kings 1:1–5, 11–18, 29–31; Psalm 61; James 5:1–6; Matthew 6:19–27

1 Kings 1:1 Now King David was old, advancing in days so although they covered him with clothes, he did not get warm. [2] Then his servants said to him, "Let them seek for my lord the king a virgin girl and let her stand in the presence of the king and service him. Let her lie in your bosom and warm my lord the king." [3] So they searched for a beautiful girl throughout the whole territory of Israel and found Abishag the Shunammite and they brought her to the king. [4] Now the girl was very beautiful, and she became the king's service-woman and attended him, yet the king did not know her [sexually].

[5] Then Adonijah son of Haggith exalted himself, saying, "I will reign." He commissioned
for himself chariots and horsemen and fifty men to run ahead of him.

[11] Then Nathan said to Bathsheba, Solomon's mother, "Have you not heard that Adonijah son of Haggith reigns and our lord David does not know? [12] Come now therefore, let me
counsel you please, so that you may save your life and the life of your son Solomon. [13] Come,
go to King David, and say to him, 'Did you not, my lord the king, swear to your slave-woman,
saying: Your son Solomon shall reign after me and he shall sit on my throne? Why then does
Adonijah reign?' [14] Look, while you are still there speaking with the king, I myself will come
after you and confirm your words."

[15] So Bathsheba went to the king's room. Now the king was very old and Abishag the
Shunammite was attending the king. [16] Bathsheba bowed and prostrated herself before the
king, and the king said, "What do you wish?" [17] She said to him, "My lord, you swore to your
slave-woman by the HOLY ONE OF OLD your God, saying: Your son Solomon shall reign
after me and he shall sit on my throne. [18] Yet now, look! Adonijah reigns now and my lord the
king, you know it not.

[29] The king swore and said, "As the ETERNAL ONE lives, who has ransomed my life from
every trouble: [30] As I swore to you by the FAITHFUL ONE, the God of Israel, 'Your son Solomon shall reign after me and he shall sit on my throne in my place.' Therefore, thus shall I do
this day." [31] Then Bathsheba bowed with her face to the ground, and prostrated herself before
the king and said, "May my lord King David live forever!"

Psalm 61

1 Hear my cry God;
be attentive to my prayer.
2 From the end of the earth to you I call,
when my heart is faint.
Lead me to the rock
that is higher than I.
3 For you are a refuge to me,
a strong tower against the enemy.
4 May I abide in your tent for all time,
may I find refuge under the shelter of your wings.
5 For you, God, have heard my vows;
you have granted the heritage of those who fear your name.
6 Grant days upon days for the monarch;
may their years extend to all generations!
7 May they be enthroned for all time in the presence of God;
measure out faithful love and faithfulness to watch over them!
8 Therefore will I always sing praises to your name,
and fulfill my vows day after day.

James 5:1 Come now, wealthy people, weep, wail for the miseries that are coming to you all. [2] Your riches are rotting and your clothes are moth-eaten. [3] Your gold and silver have decayed and their decay shall be a witness against you, and it shall eat your flesh like fire. You all have laid up treasure for the last days. [4] Listen! The wages of the workers who reaped your fields—which you all defrauded them out of—cry out and the cries of the farm workers have reached *the ears of the Commander of heaven's legions.* [5] You all have lived on the earth in self-indulgence and in luxury; you all have gorged your hearts *in a day of slaughter.* [6] You all have condemned, murdered, the righteous one. Does not God resist you?

Matthew 6:19 [Jesus said,] "Do not store up for yourselves treasures upon the earth where moth and corruption consume and where thieves break in and steal. [20] Rather store up for yourselves treasures in heaven, where neither moth nor corruption consumes and where thieves do not break in and steal. [21] For where your treasure is, there also will be your heart.

[22] "The light of the body is the eye. Therefore, if your eye is without guile, the whole of your body will be illumined. [23] But, if your eye is wicked, the whole of your body will be gloomy. If then the light in you is bleak, how great is the gloominess!

[24] "No one can serve two lords [or masters]; for a person will hate the one and love the other or be devoted to the one and despise the other. You cannot serve God and wealth.

[25] "For this reason I tell you all, be not anxious about your life, what you all will eat or what you all will drink, or about your body, what you all will wear. Is not life more than food, and the body more than clothing? [26] Look at the birds of the air; they neither sow nor reap nor gather into barns and yet, your heavenly Provider feeds them. Are you all not of more significance than they? [27] Now then, can any of you by being anxious add to your span of life a single hour?

PROCLAMATION

Text Notes

The virginal girl brought to "service" David is described with a gendered adjective lacking a noun, "as his service-woman." The verbal root has the sense of "being of use." I use "service" with its contemporary sexualized meaning deliberately here. David's sexual impotence is emblematic of his political impotence; procuring the young woman is an attempt to reinvigorate David in every way.

As with all of the Davidic psalms, Psalm 61 has a dedicatory line that means "to" or "for" David. While it might indicate authorship, it may also indicate a dedication or transcription of an oral work. The same grammatical expression in the superscription provides musical instructions "to/for" the worship leader and is not a claim of authorship. As a person raised outside of a royal court, the primary locus for literacy—Israel's priests and prophets were not literate as a rule—David would have been unlikely to have been literate. The psalm reads well as having been composed for David as his death approached. The preservation of the psalm in the communal collection means that it would have been read, prayed, and sung after David's death; therefore I use inclusive language, recognizing that not all successive monarchs were male.

In verse 8 of the psalm, the verb *yeshev* means "to sit" and for a monarch, "enthroned." It also means to dwell. In the context of the psalm, which is a plea for a monarch's life, the petition to "dwell" in God's presence evokes death, while remaining "enthroned" is in keeping with the tone of the psalm.

The Epistle attributed to James peppers snippets of Hebrew Scripture throughout today's reading. Isaiah 5:9 uses the phrase "in the ears of Lord of Hosts," translated in verse 4 as the Commander of heaven's legions. Jeremiah 12:3 includes the phrase "in the day of slaughter" from verse 5. James 5:2 uses "rust" to describe the tarnishing of gold and silver; "decay" fits better without ascribing rust to metals that do not in fact rust. (There is a similar issue in Matthew 6:19 where a separate noun describes the process of consumption by rust or blight or eating food.) I follow the translation of Luke Timothy Johnson for the question form of that latter phrase of verse 6 (see his *Anchor Bible Commentary* on James). The subject, "God," is elicited from the masculine singular verb and the presence of God earlier in the passage.

In Matthew 6:22 the eye, representing the ethical status of a person, is in one of two states, *haplous*, "aboveboard, single, without guile, sincere, straightforward, i.e., without a hidden agenda," according to the *A Greek-English Lexicon of the New Testament and Other Early Christian Literature* (BDAG) or *poneros*, wicked/evil. While NRSV and CEB choose a binary reading, "healthy" and "unhealthy," I maintain the nonbinary nuance. For verse 23, *skotos*, the root of the adjectives in the second sentence, has a semantic range that includes "shadow," "gloom," and "bleakness." My practice is to avoid dark/light binaries wherever possible.

Preaching Prompts

Monarchy is for the world that generated and canonized the scriptures, the primary way people think about society and governance and therefore, God's relation to and organization of the world. As postmonarchal people, many Americans romanticize monarchy even as we firmly reject it for ourselves. That romance is often around royal trappings: wealth, jewels, pomp and circumstance, power, privilege, and more recently, princesses. David's decline exacerbated the struggle for his royal power and position that characterized David's early reign and reemerged after his rape of Bathsheba. As he lay dying, none of those things matter anymore, not even the pursuit of women. He is unexpectedly chaste, literally impotent in all ways. A contemporary reading of the desperate attempt to revitalize David may note that there no discussion of whether Abishag or her family consented to her use or whether their child was simply taken from them for the king's harem. David is not even concerned with his lack of a designated successor. He is fully occupied with dying.

The psalm, whether composed for or by David, makes clear that with the approach of death, none of the accouterment of royalty matter. The Epistle and Gospel each proclaim the temporal nature of things, particularly wealth and privilege. The Hebrew Scriptures do some ethical and class critique on the accumulation of wealth, particularly that of Solomon. The Epistle has a similar ethical concern; there, the *plusioi* (same root as plutocrats) employ wage-theft to further enrich themselves. Contemporarily, undocumented agricultural workers and returning citizens (from incarceration) are particularly vulnerable to wage-theft. James also sets the corruptly wealthy in opposition to "the righteous one," Jesus, setting them in opposition to God; thus, the murder of Jesus is laid at the feet of the powerful across religious and ethnic lines.

In the Gospel, Jesus, who can lay claim to majesty on earth and in heaven, rejects the lure of wealth, seeing in it a seductive enslaving snare. Moreover, Jesus bids us trust God for all we need in light of the abundant provision of nature. On closer examination, this is a challenging text because all persons do not have what they need, neither did they in his time. Similarly, between his time and ours, the natural world has seen depredation and extinctions and environmental crises. An overliteral reading of Jesus's words here would seem to undermine God's provision or ability to provide. Indeed, Jesus was most certainly aware of the poor, underhoused, and under-resourced in his time. Perhaps the text might speak to trust in God who knows our need *and* our lack, a trust that is not based on whether we or the poor among us in fact have what we need. And at the same time, this text does not free us from responsibility of sharing the burden for each other's needs. Jesus's words about being anxious remain true; anxiety does not change our material condition. An important caveat, Jesus does not condemn anxiety or the people who live with it.

FEAST OF ALL SAINTS, NOVEMBER 1

Isaiah 25:1, 4a, 6–10a; Psalm 67; Romans 15:7–13; Matthew 27:50–56

Isaiah 25:1 Holy One of Old, you are my God;
I will exalt you, I will praise your name,
for you have worked wonders,
ancient counsel, faithful and trustworthy.
4 For you are a refuge to the poor,
a refuge to the needy in their distress,
a shelter from the storm and a shade from the heat.
6 The Commander of heaven's legions will make for all peoples on this mountain
a feast of rich food, a feast of well-aged wines,
of rich food prepared with marrow, of refined well-aged wines.

7 And God will destroy on this mountain
the shroud that shrouds all peoples,
the veil that veils all nations.
8 God will swallow up death forever.
Then the SOVEREIGN GOD will wipe away tears from every face,
and will sweep aside the shame of God's people from the whole earth,
for GOD WHOSE NAME IS HOLY has spoken.
9 It will be said on that day,
Look! This is our God; in whom we hope, and who saved us.
This is the CREATOR OF ALL in whom we hope;
let us be glad and rejoice in God's salvation.
10 For the hand of the ANCIENT OF DAYS shall rest on this mountain.

Psalm 67

1 May God be merciful to us and bless us,
show us the light of her countenance and come to us.
2 Let your ways be known upon earth,
your saving health among all nations.
3 Let the peoples praise you, O God;
let all the peoples praise you.
4 Let the nations be glad and sing for joy,
for you judge the peoples with equity
and guide all the nations upon earth.
5 Let the peoples praise you, O God;
let all the peoples praise you.
6 The earth has brought forth her increase;
may God, our own God, give us her blessing.
7 May God give us her blessing,
and may all the ends of the earth stand in awe of her.

Romans 15:7 Accept one another, therefore, just as Christ has accepted you, for the glory of
God. 8 I tell you that the Messiah has become a servant of the circumcised for the sake of truth
to confirm the promises given to the mothers and fathers, 9 and in order that the Gentiles
might glorify God on account of God's mercy. As it is written,

> "*Therefore, I will confess you among the Gentiles,*
> *and sing praises to your name,*"

10 and again it says,

> "*Rejoice, O Gentiles, with God's people,*"

11 and again,

> *"Praise the Most High, all you Gentiles,*
> *and let all the peoples praise God;"*

12 and again Isaiah says,

> *"The root of Jesse shall come,*
> *and the one who rises to rule the Gentiles,*
> *in whom the Gentiles shall hope."*

13 May the God of hope fill you with all joy and peace in believing, so that you may abound in hope by the power of the Holy Spirit.

Matthew 27:50 Jesus cried again with a loud voice and relinquished his spirit. 51 Then,
look! The curtain of the temple was torn from top to bottom in two. And the earth was
shaken, and the rocks were split. 52 And the tombs were opened, and many bodies of the saints
who had fallen asleep were raised. 53 Then after his resurrection they came out of the tombs
and entered the holy city and appeared to many. 54 Now when the centurion and those with
him, who were standing guard over Jesus, saw the earthquake and what took place, they were
terrified and said, "Truly this man was God's Son!"

55 Now there were many women there, from a distance watching; they had followed
Jesus from Galilee and had ministered to him. 56 Among them were Mary the Magdalene, and
Mary the mother of James and Joseph and the mother of the sons of Zebedee.

PROCLAMATION

Text Notes

Division of verses varies among translations for Isaiah 25. I follow the Masoretic Text and Jewish Publication Society here. Similarly, the flexibility of Hebrew tenses can place God's salvific actions in the past or future. The past tense emphasizes God's past faithfulness, laying the ground for a reasonable hope in continuing faithfulness.

Since *pateron* in Romans 15:8 can be inclusive "ancestors" or "fathers" and God's promises were not and are not limited by gender, I use the most inclusive option. In verse 9, Christ takes up the same diaconal ministry with which the women who follow him are credited. Verses 9–12 quote Psalm 18:49, Deuteronomy 32:43, Psalm 117:1, and Isaiah 11:10 from the LXX. There are some variances between the Greek and Hebrew of Deuteronomy 32:43: In the Hebrew text, "the nations, God's people" are called to rejoice while in the Greek the heavens are called to rejoice *with* God's people. (For more on the divergence between the manuscript traditions on this verse, see the annotations and comparisons in *The Dead Sea Scrolls Bible*, ed. Abegg, Flint, and Ulrich.)

The women who "ministered" to Jesus, *diakoneo*, have been understood as providing for Jesus (NRSV), serving him (CEB), and ministering to him (KJV); all are viable, however breadth rather than specificity would seem to be called for.

Preaching Prompts

For the Feast of All Saints, this lectionary turns to declarations of God's faithfulness to all peoples and nations. This passage of Isaiah speaks repeatedly to "all peoples" and "all nations" in verses 6–7, all of whom will benefit from God's death-destroying salvific work. Similarly, in the psalm, God's salvation is for all nations with all peoples invited to join in the praise of God. The Epistle focuses on the acceptance of God's gift of salvation by the Gentile nations. The Gospel takes us back to that saving work in the life and death of Jesus, hinting at the resurrection to come with the resurrection of saints who preceded Jesus in death, at the moment of his death. Meanwhile, the saints who stood bearing witness would become second-class saints in the eyes of many, excluded from ministry, ordination, and leadership based on their gender. Perhaps ironically and almost certainly intentionally, reduction of their ministry to open checkbooks exploits and limits their gifts at the same time.

PROPER 26 (CLOSEST TO NOVEMBER 2)

1 Kings 2:10–24; Psalm 72:1, 5, 8–11, 15, 17; Revelation 15:2–4; Matthew 12:38–42

1 Kings 2:10 And David lay with his mothers and fathers and was buried in the city of David. 11 The days that David reigned over Israel came to forty years: In Hebron he reigned seven years and in Jerusalem he reigned thirty-three years. 12 Thus Solomon sat on the throne of his father David and his rule was extremely well founded.

13 Then Adonijah son of Haggith came to Bathsheba, Solomon's mother. She asked, "Is it in peace that you come?" He said, "Peace." 14 Then he said, "I have something to say to you." And she said, "Speak." 15 So he said, "You know that the realm was mine and all Israel set their expectation on me to reign; however, the monarchy has turned and become my brother's, for it was his from the RULER OF ALL. 16 And now I am asking one thing of you; do not turn me away." And she said to him, "Speak." 17 And he said, "Please speak to King Solomon—he will not turn you away—that he might give me Abishag the Shunammite as my wife." 18 Then Bathsheba said, "Good. I myself will speak to the king for you."

19 So Bathsheba went to King Solomon to speak to him about Adonijah. The king rose to meet her and bowed down to her; then he sat on his throne, and had a throne brought for the king's mother, and she sat on his right. 20 Then she said, "One small request I ask of you; do not turn me away." And the king said to her, "Ask, my mother, for I will not turn you away."

[21] Then she said, "Let Abishag the Shunammite be given to your brother Adonijah for a wife."
[22] Then King Solomon replied and said to his mother, "Now why would you ask Abishag
the Shunammite for Adonijah? Ask for him the monarchy for he is my elder brother and the
priest Abiathar and Joab son of Zeruiah are for him!" [23] Then King Solomon swore by the
HOLY ONE OF OLD, "Thus may God do to me and more, for against his life has Adonijah
spoken this word. [24] Now therefore as the AGELESS ONE lives, who has prepared me and
placed me on the throne of my father David and who has made me a house as God promised,
today Adonijah shall be put to death."

Psalm 72:1, 5, 8–11, 15, 17

1 God, give the ruler your justice,
and your righteousness to a ruler's son.
5 May they reverence the ruler with the sun and before the moon,
from generation to generation.
8 May the ruler have dominion from sea to sea,
and from the River to the ends of the earth.
9 In the royal presence may the foes of the ruler bow down,
and may the desert folk lick dust.
10 May the royals of Tarshish and of the isles
bring tribute to the ruler,
may the sovereigns of Sheba and Seba offer gifts.
11 May all queens and kings fall down before the ruler,
may all nations render service.
15 Long may the ruler live
and receive gold of Sheba;
may prayer be offered for the ruler continually,
all day may blessings be invoked for the ruler.
17 May the name of the ruler endure forever,
may the name of the ruler be perpetuated before the sun;
may all nations be blessed in the ruler;
and may they find the ruler happy.

Revelation 15:2 Now I saw something like a sea of glass mixed with fire and those who had
conquered the beast and its image and the number of its name were standing beside the sea of
glass with harps of God. [3] And they sing the song of Moses, the slave of God, and the song
of the Lamb:

"Great and marvelous are your works,
Holy God Almighty!
Just and true are your ways,
Sovereign of the nations!

[4] Who will not fear the Most High
and glorify your name?
For you alone are holy.
All nations will come
and worship before you,
for your righteous acts have been revealed."

Matthew 12:38 Now some of the biblical scholars and Pharisees said to Jesus, "Teacher, we wish to see a sign from you." [39] But he answered them, "An evil and adulterous generation asks for a sign, but no sign will be given to it except the sign of the prophet Jonah. [40] For just as '*Jonah was in the belly of the beast three days and three nights*,' so for three days and three nights the Son of Woman will be in the heart of the earth. [41] The people of Nineveh will rise up at the judgment with this generation and condemn it, because they repented at the preaching of Jonah and look! One greater than Jonah is here! [42] The Queen of the South will rise up at the judgment with this generation and condemn it, because she came from the ends of the earth to listen to the wisdom of Solomon and look! One greater than Solomon is here!

PROCLAMATION

Text Notes

Adonijah's "something to say" in 1 Kings 2:14 is "a word." The "face" figures prominently in idiomatic expressions in this passage. In verse 15, all Israel sets their "faces," on Adonijah, translated "expectation" here. In verse 16, Adonijah asks Bathsheba not to "turn away [his] face," and recurring with Bathsheba's face in verses 17, 19, and 21.

Adonijah has the support of David's senior military commander Joab and therefore the troops along with the support of the priest Abiathar, who had supported David against Saul and Absalom. Joab is the son of David's sister Zeruiah. Abiathar's support of Adonijah fractured the priesthood into two factions that will remain into the Christian Testament. In the request of verse 16, the verb and its object share the same root, "asked an asking."

In order to provide the widest scope for the psalm as a prayer for future monarchs, "the ruler" is used throughout Psalm 72 in place of "king" and masculine pronouns. Its unfamiliar abundance illustrates the pervasiveness of the masculine language. The MT of Psalm 72:5 urges "fear" of the monarch as of the sun and moon; "reverence," within the semantic range, is a better fit for the regard in which (royal) human and heavenly bodies and persons were held. The LXX has "may the ruler live." "The River," verse 8, generally refers to the Euphrates. Those bowing before the ruler in verse 9 vary among the manuscripts, desert-dwellers and enemies in the MT, Ethiopians and enemies in LXX, administrators (governors, prefects, or eparchs) and enemies in Targum Onkelos, and island folk and enemies in the Peshitta.

The "Song of Moses" referenced in Revelation 15:3 is Deuteronomy 32.

Matthew 12:40 quotes the LXX text of Jonah 2:1, which is 1:17 in the MT and most English language bibles. Throughout this work, the Hebrew and Greek idiomatic expressions for humanity and human mortality, *ben adam* and *hious tou anthropou*, are rendered "son of woman," capitalized when applied to Jesus. Verse 41 uses explicitly masculine language, "men, *andres*, of Nineveh," made inclusive here and in major contemporary translations. The subject of "greater than Jonah/Solomon" in verses 41–42 is lacking. I supply "One," as does CEB; however, NRSV uses "something."

Preaching Prompts

Bathsheba and Nathan have successfully gotten Solomon on the throne, but Adonijah is still a threat. He seemingly grudgingly concedes but is putting a new plan into action: with a royal woman whom he can claim is carrying David's heir, he could rally his supporters. Solomon recognizes the threat. Bathsheba's "good" in verse 18 suggests she knows the outcome of the request that Adonijah should have also known. Monarchy is a bloody business and it is well worth reconsidering whether it suits as a metaphor for God, her abode, or her management style.

The significance of Solomon enthroning his mother in verse 19 and placing her at his right hand, in the place of the royal counsel, cannot be overstated. She becomes the first of a long line of Judean Queen Mothers who serve with their sons in an official capacity, some of whom serve as regent for minor sons. (For more on the Judean and Israelite royal women, see my *Womanist Midrash: A Reintroduction to the Women of the Torah and of the Throne.*)

Psalm 72 is a hopeful psalm suited for the ascendancy of a monarch, perhaps even of Solomon. It may also be retrospective, given its mention of Sheba in verse 15. Monarchy has an enduring mystique in the US in spite of our having overthrown it. The American revolution, in religious terms, was a rebellion against an anointed monarch. This season of reflection on David, prior to commemorating the Advent of the One who is the Son of Bathsheba and the Son of David, is an opportunity to contemplate the continuing relevance of monarchal language and imagery. The reading from Revelation seeks to offer a vision of true majesty, God's, beyond humanity, beyond mortality.

The royal women who connect these readings demonstrate the limits of privilege. Bathsheba and Abishag were both taken for a monarch's pleasure, while Abishag is used as a pawn in the next round of contestation for the throne. Her fate is unknown; she is literarily and politically disposable. On the other hand, the Queen of Sheba has an enduring legacy in the scriptures and religious writings of several religions. Her fame is tied to that of Solomon through her visit and recognition of his wisdom in the biblical texts (1 Kings 10, duplicates in 2 Chronicles 9; Matthew 12:42; Luke 11:31), to conversion from sun worship in the Qur'an (*al-Naml* 27:15ff), to Solomon's philosophy student (Josephus *Antiquities* 8.6.2ff), to a child who is the progenitor of the Ethiopian monarchy. While unnamed in either Testament, she is Bilqis in the Qur'an and Makeda in the *Kebra Nagast*, the Ethiopian national hagiography. Her nation has been identified with the Sabeans on the Yemeni portion of the Arabian Peninsula to eastern Africa generically called "Ethiopia" in antiquity.

In the Gospels the Queen of Sheba will be a witness at the (last) judgment, where her verdict against Jesus's contemporaries will stand as though it were God's. She is more than a person here: she is a symbol of enduring truth that can be recognized by anyone from anywhere, including significantly, by a Gentile woman beyond the bounds of Israel.

PROPER 27 (CLOSEST TO NOVEMBER 9)

1 Kings 5:1–6, 13–14; Psalm 148; Revelation 21:10, 22–27; Matthew 6:28–34

1 Kings 5:1 Now Hiram king of Tyre sent his slaves to Solomon for he heard that they had anointed him king in place of his father; for Hiram had always loved David. 2 Solomon sent word to Hiram, saying, 3 "You know that my father David was not able to build a house for the Name of the ETERNAL ONE his God because of the warfare with which his enemies surrounded him until the MOST HIGH put them under the soles of his feet. 4 Yet now the HOLY ONE my God has granted me respite all around; there is neither adversary nor ill fortune. 5 So look! I propose to build a house for the Name of the HOLY ONE my God, just as the HOLY ONE OF OLD spoke to David my father, 'Your son, whom I will set in your place on your throne, he shall build the house for my Name.' 6 Now then, command that they cut for me cedars from the Lebanon; my slaves will be with your slaves and wages for your slaves will I give you according to whatever you say; for you know there is no one among us who knows how to cut timber like the Sidonians."

13 And King Solomon imposed forced labor out of all Israel and the conscripts were thirty thousand men. 14 Now he sent them to the Lebanon, ten thousand a month in turns; one month were they in the Lebanon, two months at home, and Adoniram was in charge of the forced labor.

Psalm 148

1 Praise the ALMIGHTY!
Praise the EXALTED from the heavens;
praise her on the heights!
2 Praise her, all her angels;
praise her, all her starry warriors!

3 Praise her, sun and moon;
praise her, all you stars of light!
4 Praise her, you highest heavens,
and you waters above the heavens!
5 Let them praise the Name of the MIGHTY GOD,
for she commanded and they were created.
6 She established them forever and ever;
she set boundaries that cannot be crossed.
7 Praise the CREATOR OF ALL from the earth,
sea monsters and all [watery] deeps,
8 Fire and hail, snow and frost,
swirling wind fulfilling her word!
9 Mountains and all hills,
fruit trees and all cedars!
10 Animals wild and tame,
creeping things and winged birds!
11 Queens and kings of the earth and all peoples,
royal seed and all rulers of the earth!
12 Young women and men alike,
aged and young together!
13 Let them praise the Name of the ETERNAL,
for her name alone is exalted;
her glory is above the earth and the heavens.
14 She has raised up a horn for her people,
praise for all her faithful,
for the daughters and sons of Israel who are close to her.
Praise the ALMIGHTY!

Revelation 21:10 Now the angel carried me away in the spirit to a great, high mountain and showed me the holy city Jerusalem coming down from the heavens, from God.

22 I saw no temple in the city, for the Sovereign God, the Almighty with the Lamb is its temple. 23 And the city has no use of sun or moon to shine in it, for the glory of God is its light, and its lamp is the Lamb. 24 And the nations will walk by its light and the queens and kings of the earth will bring their glory into it. 25 And its gates will not be shut by day and there will be no night there. 26 Women, children, and men will bring into it the glory and the honor of the nations. 27 Now there shall not enter it anything unclean or anyone who does what is detestable or untrue, but only those who are written in the Lamb's book of life.

Matthew 6:28 [Jesus asked,] "Now why do you all worry about clothing? Consider the lilies of the field, how they grow; they neither labor nor spin. 29 Yet I tell you all, even Solomon in all his glory was not clothed like one of these. 30 Now if the grass of the field, which is alive today and tomorrow is thrown into the oven God so clothes, will not God do much more for you all of little faith? [31] Therefore do not worry, saying, 'What shall we eat?' or 'What shall we drink?' or 'What shall we wear?' [32] For all these the Gentiles strive and indeed your heavenly Provider knows that you all need all these. [33] But strive first for the reign of God and God's righteousness and all these will be given to you all. [34] So do not worry about tomorrow, for tomorrow has worries of its own. Sufficient is the trouble of this day."

PROCLAMATION

Text Notes

This portion of 1 Kings is numbered differently in Christian and Jewish texts and translations. What is 1 Kings 5:15 in the MT and JPS is 5:1 in NRSV, CEB, KJV, etc.; the LXX follows the Jewish numbering. In verse 1 (Heb v. 15) Hiram's "love" for David should probably be understood as "loyalty," as in CEB; Everett Fox adds "in covenant." Solomon suggests that David was unable to build the temple because he was so busy fighting his enemies. He neglects to mention that God forbade David to build the temple because his hands were so bloody (1 Chronicles 22:6–8, though it should be remembered that Chronicles represents an alternative reflection on Israel's story). In verse 4 (Heb v. 18) "adversary" is *satan*; the term has no evil connotation in the Hebrew Bible, unlike the Pseudepigrapha (and subsequently, the Christian Testament) where the character first becomes God's adversary.

Psalm 148 is written in a plural voice for communal praise. In Psalm 148:2 the "hosts" of heaven, which are both God's warriors and the stars, are translated as "starry warriors." "Swirling wind" in verse 8 provides a more poetic translation than "stormy." *Behemah* in verse 10 can be "cattle" or generic domesticated animals; the scope includes the full breadth from wild to tame so the broader term fits best.

In Revelation 21:26, those who bring glory are unidentified; the subject is included in the verb, inclusive plural. When cities or nations offered tribute in hospitality or conquest, representatives from each section of the populace often participated. The choice of "women, children, and men" rather than the "people" of the NRSV or "they" in the CEB makes the population of heaven visible.

Preaching Prompts

David's time is past. His lineage will endure, though his throne will fall. Solomon inherits a wealthy stable country that he expands. He also inherits the divisions between their familial Judean supporters and the other tribes. In spite of his divinely granted wisdom, he lacks the charisma and savvy of David. His conduct, including his sexual excesses, would be his downfall, shattering the once united monarchy.

Solomon's love for foreign women is often held as his primary failing, but his economic policies devastated his reign.

In the first lesson Solomon conscripts able-bodied men to serve one month away and return for two months at home. Consider the impact on agricultural and pastoral work, the backbones of the Israelite economy. The effect of the conscription was so ruinous that when Solomon's son later tried to reinstitute it under the same taskmaster, the people stoned the overseer in 1 Kings 12:18 (there Adoram, understood to be the same as Adoniram here). As with all economic hardships, Solomon's policies would have been most devasting on women and children. The majesty of human monarchs always comes at a cost and those who pay it are most often those who can least afford it. Samuel's warning to the people of the cost of monarchy in 1 Samuel 8:11–17, understood by many as a retrospective on Solomon, lists all that a monarch would take from their subjects, including their daughters in verse 13.

Also often overlooked is that Solomon's expenditures of human and fiscal capital were to build a series of palaces that dwarfed the temple he built for God, including some for the foreign royal women he married. (One of David's wives was also a foreign royal, Maacah bat Talmi, the mother of Tamar and Absalom, who was the daughter of King Talmi of Geshur.) The temple was sixty by twenty cubits and thirty cubits high (1 Kings 6:2); it took seven years to build (1 Kings 6:38). In contrast he spent thirteen years building his primary residence (1 Kings 7:1); a single hall in it was one hundred by fifty cubits, also thirty cubits high (1 Kings 7:2), a second hall was fifty by thirty cubits (1 Kings 7:6) and there were two more halls (1 Kings 7:7). His proper home was "the same construction" and he made a duplicate for the Egyptian princess he married (1 Kings 7:8). Perhaps, having exhausted his treasury, Solomon paid King Hiram of Tyre with twenty cities in Galilee (1 Kings 9:11).

Majesty links these passages, human and divine. Solomon used the fruits of his majesty to craft an abode for the One whose majesty cannot be contained, though he could not resist extravagantly demonstrating the splendor of his own. To him and to those who might be taken in by such wealth and luxury, Jesus says nothing human-made compares to anything God-made. In the psalm, all the God-made praise true Majesty in a chorus stretching from earth to the heavens. The larger text of Revelation 21 describes the incomparable majesty of God surrounded by luxury of which not even Solomon could imagine, expressed in terms of human treasures, gold and jewels, in verses 15–21, on a scale that dwarfs all of Solomon's constructions put together.

Jesus calls our attention from corruptible treasures to the troubles of the day in which we live in which few have much and many have little, and bids us trust in the God who garbed the world in splendor to meet our daily needs as would any parent and provider. Preachers might also wish to use the first lesson to talk about how congregants use the gifts and resources of their members, to what end, and to whose glory.

PROPER 28 (CLOSEST TO NOVEMBER 16)

1 Kings 11:26–39; Psalm 46; Hebrews 12:18–24, 28–29; Matthew 19:27–30

1 Kings 11:26 Now Jeroboam son of Nebat, an Ephraimite of Zeredah whose mother's name was Zeruah, a widow woman, was a servant of Solomon and he raised a hand against the king. 27 And this was the situation in which he raised a hand against the king: Solomon built the Millo, closing the breach in the city of his father David. 28 Now the man Jeroboam was a valiant warrior, and when Solomon saw that the young man was a hard worker, he appointed him over all the forced labor of the house of Joseph. 29 And it was at that time, as Jeroboam left Jerusalem the prophet Ahijah the Shilonite found him on the road. Now Ahijah had clothed himself with a new garment and the two of them were in the countryside by themselves. 30 And Ahijah seized of the new garment that was upon him and tore it into twelve pieces. 31 Then he said to Jeroboam: Take for yourself ten pieces; for thus says the HOLY ONE, the God of Israel, "Look! I am about to tear the realm from the hand of Solomon, and I will give you ten tribes. 32 One tribe will remain his for the sake of my slave David and for the sake of Jerusalem, the city that I have chosen out of all the tribes of Israel. 33 This is because he has forsaken me and worshiped Astarte the goddess of the Sidonians, Chemosh the god of Moab, and Milcom the god of the Ammonites, and has not walked in my ways, doing what is right in my sight—my statutes and my ordinances—as his father David did. 34 Now I will not take the whole realm from his hand and will make him ruler all the days of his life, for the sake of my slave David whom I chose, who did keep my commandments and my statutes. 35 Yet I will take the realm from his son and give to you the ten tribes. 36 And to his son will I give one tribe so that there will always be a lamp before me for my slave David in Jerusalem, the city that I have chosen for myself, to place my Name. 37 You I shall take, and you shall reign over all that your soul desires; you shall be king over Israel. 38 And it shall be if you will listen to all that I command you and walk in my ways and do what is right in my sight, keeping my statutes and my commandments as David my slave did, I will be with you, and I will build you an enduring house as I built for David, and I shall give you Israel. 39 And I shall punish the descendants of David for this, but not for all time."

Psalm 46

1 God is for us a refuge and strength,
a help in trouble, easily found.
2 Therefore we shall not fear, though the earth should change,
though the mountains quiver in the heart of the sea;
3 its waters roar and churn,
the mountains tremble with its swell.
4 There is a river whose streams make glad the city of God,
the holy habitation of the Most High.
5 God is in the midst of her, she shall not be moved;
God will help her when the morning unfurls.

6 The nations roar, dominions quiver;
God puts forth her voice, the earth melts.
7 The WARRIOR PROTECTRIX is with us;
a stronghold for us is the God of Rebekah's line.
8 Come, behold the works of the FIRE OF SINAI;
see what desolations she has set on the earth.
9 She makes wars cease to the end of the earth;
she breaks the bow, and shatters the spear,
she burns chariots with fire.
10 "Be still and know that I am God!
I am exalted among the nations,
I am exalted in the earth."
11 The WARRIOR PROTECTRIX is with us;
a stronghold for us is the God of Rebekah's line.

Hebrews 12:18 Now, you have not come to that which can be touched, and searing fire,
and darkness, and gloom, and whirlwind, 19 and trumpet sound, and a voice at whose words
hearers begged that not another word be spoken to them. 20 For they could not bear the
command, "*If even an animal touches the mountain, it shall be stoned to death.*" 21 Indeed,
so terrifying was the sight that Moses said, "*I am afraid*" and trembling. 22 But you have
come to Mount Zion and to the city of the living God, the heavenly Jerusalem, and to angels
beyond number in joyful gathering, 23 and to the assembly of the firstborn who are recorded
in heaven, and to God the judge of all, and to the spirits of the righteous made perfect, 24 and
to Jesus, the mediator of a new covenant, and to the sprinkled blood that speaks a better
word than the blood of Abel.

28 Therefore, since an unmovable realm are we receiving, let us grasp the grace by which
we offer to God an acceptable worship with reverence and awe; 29 for indeed our "God is a
consuming fire."

Matthew 19:27 Peter said [to Jesus], "Look, we have left everything and followed you. What
then will we have?" 28 Jesus said to them, "Truly I tell you all who have followed me, at the renewal
[of all things], when the Son of Woman is seated on the throne of his glory, you all shall also sit
on twelve thrones, judging the twelve tribes of Israel. 29 And whoever has left houses or sisters or
brothers or mother or father or children or fields, for the sake of my name, will receive a hundredfold and, will inherit eternal life. 30 But many who are first will be last, and the last will be first.

PROCLAMATION

Text Notes

"Zeruah" of Ephraim, the erstwhile Queen Mother of the schismatic monarch Jeroboam in 1 Kings 11:26, was not likely named *zeru'ah*, "diseased"; rather her name may have been altered to make the pun a slur to label her son as rotten from the womb. Ephraim and Manasseh were the sons of Joseph (see verse 28), traditionally named among the tribes rather than their father.

Verse 5 of the psalm uses the feminine pronoun throughout. Other translations (NRSV, CEB) substitute city, the likely referent, a feminine noun in Hebrew, or change the pronoun to "it," JPS. In verses 7 and 11, "WARRIOR PROTECTRIX" expresses the God who commands the legions of heaven, while "Rebekah's line" replaces her son "Jacob."

Hebrews 12:20 cites Exodus 19:12–13 while verse 21 quotes Deuteronomy 9:19 and verse 29 cites Deuteronomy 4:24 and 9:3. In verse 28 the translation "grasp the grace" is indebted to the James Murdock translation of the Peshitta in the public domain.

Preaching Prompts

According to the prophet Ahijah, God fractured the Israelite monarchy because of Solomon's religious infidelity. God intends to preserve the royal line of David out of fidelity to him. Following the evangelists, the Church will find in Jesus the fulfilment of God's words; however, both will overlook the significant gap between the last Davidide, Zedekiah (2 Kings 24:17–18; 25:1,7), and Jesus. This provides an opportunity to talk about the relationship between the Testaments with nuance, going beyond simplistic fulfillment formulae.

Against the broken monarchy and the fear and chaos it must have unleashed, Psalm 46 presents God who is an unmovable bulwark, stronghold and refuge for her children. In times of political chaos and upheaval those already living on the margins become even more vulnerable, disproportionately women and children. The feminine grammar native to Psalm 46:5 would make it possible for a woman who knew those lines to hear herself as the object of God's care:

God is in the midst of her, she shall not be moved;
God will help her when the morning unfurls.

Lastly, there are two women in and beneath the texts, infamous because of their sons and their claims to a throne: Zeruah, whose true name we may never know, and Mary of Nazareth obscured in the mortal euphemism translated in this volume as "Son of Woman." Where monarchies like Jeroboam's take from their subjects, the followers of Jesus, heir to a realm that transcends all monarchies, gave all to follow him, though apparently not without some second thoughts. To them Jesus proclaims a gospel of reversal, the last will be first and the first shall be last. The gospel also acknowledges that there will be losses when we follow Jesus. Jesus speaks of restoration in simple language that runs the risk of over simplistic interpretation. Jesus does not promise that the relationships we have lost along the way will be restored or replaced—indeed there will be losses—rather what we gain is ultimately worth more, without devaluing our losses.

MAJESTY OF CHRIST (CLOSEST TO NOVEMBER 23)

2 Kings 24:8, 11–17; Psalm 47; Hebrews 1:1–9; Matthew 27:11–14, 27–37

2 Kings 24:8 Jehoiachin was eighteen years old at his reign. He reigned three months in
Jerusalem and the name of his mother was Nehushta daughter of Elnathan of Jerusalem.
11 Now King Nebuchadnezzar of Babylon came to the city while his troops were besieg-
ing it. 12 Then King Jehoiachin of Judah surrendered to the king of Babylon, himself and his
mother and his slaves and his officers and his officials. The king of Babylon took him [cap-
tive] in the eighth year of his reign.
13 He brought out from there the treasures of the house of the HOLY ONE OF OLD and
the treasures of the king's house; he cut up all the vessels of gold in the temple of the HOLY
ONE which King Solomon of Israel had made, just as the HOLY ONE had spoken. 14 Nebuchadnezzar took into exile all Jerusalem, all the officials, all the warriors, ten thousand exiled
women and men, all the artisans, and the smiths; no one remained except the poorest people
of the land. 15 He took Jehoiachin into exile to Babylon; the king's mother, the king's women,
his officials, and the elite of the land he took into exile from Jerusalem to Babylon. 16 The king
of Babylon took into exile to Babylon all the valiant warriors, seven thousand, the artisans
and the smiths, one thousand, all of them strong and fit for war. 17 The king of Babylon made
Mattaniah, Jehoiachin's uncle, king in his place and changed his name to Zedekiah.

Psalms 47

1 All you peoples clap your hands;
shout to God with a joyful sound.
2 For the SOVEREIGN GOD, the Most High, is awesome,
a great governor over all the earth.
3 She subdued peoples under us,
and nations under our feet.
4 She chose our heritage for us,
the pride of Rebekah's womb whom she loves.
5 God has gone up with a shout,
SINAI'S FIRE with the sound of a trumpet.
6 Sing praises to God, sing praises;
sing praises to our Sovereign, sing praises.

7 For God is Sovereign over all the earth;
sing praises with a psalm.
8 God rules over the nations;
God is seated on her holy throne.
9 The nobles of the peoples gather,
the people of the God of Hagar and Sarah;
for to God belong the shields of the earth,
she is highly exalted.

Hebrews 1:1 Many times and in many ways God spoke to our mothers and fathers through
the prophets, female and male.
2 In these last days God has spoken to us by a Son, whom God
appointed heir of all there is, and through whom God created the worlds.
3 The Son is the
brilliance of God's glory and reproduction of God's very being, and the Son undergirds all
there is by his word of power. When the Son had made purification for sins, he sat down at
the right hand of the Majesty on high,
4 having become as much greater than the angels as the
name he inherited is more excellent than theirs.

5 For to which of the angels did God ever say,

"*You are my Child; today I have begotten you*"?

Or this,

"*I will be their Parent, and they will be my Child*"?

6 Then again, when God brings the firstborn into the world, God says,

"*Let all the angels of God worship him.*"

7 On the one hand of the angels God says,

"*God makes winds into celestial messengers,*
and flames of fire into God's ministers."

8 But of the Son God says,

"*Your throne, O God, is forever and ever,*
and the righteous scepter is the scepter of your realm.
9 *You have loved righteousness and hated lawlessness;*
therefore God, your God, has anointed you
with the oil of gladness beyond your companions."

Matthew 27:11 Now Jesus stood before the governor and the governor questioned him saying, "Are you the King of the Jews?" Jesus said, "You say so."
12 And when he was accused by
the chief priests and elders, he did not answer.
13 Then Pilate said to him, "Do you not hear
how many accusations they make against you?"
14 And he did not answer him, not one word,
so that the governor was greatly astonished.

[27] Then the soldiers of the governor took Jesus into the governor's command post, and
they gathered the whole cohort around him. [28] They stripped him and put a scarlet robe on
him. [29] And, having woven a crown from thorns, they put it on his head along with a reed in
his right hand and they knelt before him and mocked him, saying, "Hail, King of the Jews!"
[30] And they spat on him, and took the reed and struck him on his head. [31] After mocking him,
they stripped him of the robe and put his clothes [back] on him. Then they led him away
to be crucified. [32] Now going out, they found a Cyrenian man named Simon; this man they
conscripted to carry his cross.

[33] And coming to a place called Golgotha (which means Skull Place), [34] they offered him
wine mixed with vinegar to drink; but when he tasted it, he would not drink. [35] And when
they had crucified him, "*they divided his clothes*" among themselves by "*casting lots.*" [36] Then
they sat down and keeping watch over him there. [37] Now they placed over his head his charge,
written as, "This is Jesus, the King of the Jews."

PROCLAMATION

Text Notes

Nebuchadnezzar's troops are called "slaves" in 2 Kings 24:11. The king's surrender in verse 12 is articulated ironically with the primary verb of the exodus, *y-tz-ʾ*. Likewise, Nebuchadnezzar "bought out" the riches of the Jerusalem temple in verse 13 just as God brought out the Israelites. The ranks of deportees include women and men. The first accounting includes the Queen Mother, second in authority to the king (listed in that order verse 12) and the entire senior administrative team, which would have likely included women in some roles (indicated by seals from royal women and female administrators before and after the fall of Jerusalem). The second reckoning in verse 14 repeats and numbers the officials and warriors at ten thousand, and craftspersons and smiths; the former would have included women, as potting and weaving were traditionally female occupations. A third reckoning in verse 15 circles back to the surrendering of the Queen Mother and adds the royal women, wives, and other women, including royal daughters and likely the surviving wives of previous monarchs, then repeats the officials a third time and adds all of the nobles. A fourth accounting in verse 16 numbers the warriors at seven thousand and one thousand war-ready artisans and smiths. These different accountings suggest chaos and confusion rather than specificity in spite of the recorded numbers. The broader sense is that everyone who was anyone was exiled except the almost overlooked "poor of the land," tucked away at the end of verse 14, not mentioned again.

In Psalm 46:4, the "pride of Rebekah's womb" is "the pride (or majesty) of Jacob." In verse 6, "the God of Hagar and Sarah" is "the God of Abraham."

In Hebrews 1:1 the explication of prophets as female and male reminds the reader/hearer of the diversity in Israel's prophetic ranks.

"Astonished" in Matthew 27:14 can also mean "impressed." Verse 31 ends "to crucify" with no object; some translations add "him" there. Verse 35 quotes the LXX language for dividing garments and casting lots in Psalm 22:18 exactly.

PREACHING PROMPTS

The liturgical year ends with a reflection on the Majesty of Christ as the Church prepares to begin a new year remembering his first advent while preparing for his next. As the weeks reviewing the rise and fall(s) of Israel's monarchies during Ordinary Time have made abundantly clear, monarchy is as all human institutions, an enterprise that is doomed to fail. Yet monarchy and its conventions has given us language for God, imperfect but familiar as the psalm amply demonstrates. Jesus takes that language and those conventions and inverts them; the reign of God and its majesty are very different from the splendor of the world's sovereigns.

To the fallen Judean monarchy and their Babylonian colonizers and occupiers, Jesus says the poor of the land who were deemed not worth the labor to even deport are at the heart of the reign of God. The majesty of Christ is not found in treasures of temple or palace, burgled and broken apart, but in a crown of thorns beaten in by bullies and in his battered and denuded body. This human, mortal, woman-born Jesus is the glory and majesty of God; in the words of the Epistle to the Hebrews, "*the brilliance of God's glory and reproduction of God's very being.*" That humanness, shared with every girl and woman, boy and man, nonbinary child and adult, is also the majesty of Christ and our own.

APPENDIX

GOD NAMES AND DIVINE TITLES*

Ageless God
Ageless One
All-Knowing God
All-Knowing One
All-Seeing God
Almighty
Ancient Of Days
Ancient One
Ark of Safety
Author of Life
Commander of heaven's legions
Commander of heaven's vanguard
Compassionate God
Creator
Creator of All
Dread God
Eternal
Eternal One
Ever-Living God
Exalted
Faithful God
Faithful One
Fire of Sinai
Fount of Justice
Fount of Life
Fount of Wisdom
Generous One
Glorious One
God Who Hears
God Who is Holy
God who is Majesty
God Who Is Mystery
God Who Is Salvation
God Who Redeems
God Who Saves
God Who Sees
God Whose Name is Holy
Gracious God
Gracious One
Healing One
Holy God
Holy One
Holy One of Old
Holy One of Sinai
Inscrutable God
Just God
Just One
Living God
Loving God
Majestic One
Majesty
Majesty of the Heavens
Merciful God
Mighty God
Mighty One
Most High
Mother of All
Mother of Creation
Mother of the Mountains
Mother of Wisdom

* This list was generated in advance of preparing the manuscript and includes some titles that are not used in this resource but might prove useful for those designing worship and liturgy.

One
One God
One Who Is
Redeemer
Redeeming God
Redeeming One
Righteous God
Righteous One
Rock Who Birthed Us
Rock Who Gave Us Birth
Ruler of All
Ruler of the Multitudes of Heaven
Saving God
Saving One
Sheltering God
She Who Birthed the Earth
She Who Hears
She Who is Delight
She Who is Exalted
She Who is Faithful
She Who is God
She Who Is Holy
She Who is Majesty
She Who Is Mighty
She Who Is Peace
She Who is Strength
She Who is Wisdom
She Who is Worthy
She Who Provides
She Who Saves
She Who Sees
She Who Speaks Life
Sinai's Fire
Source of Life
Sovereign
Sovereign-Commander of winged warriors
Sovereign God
Sovereign One
Sovereign of heaven's vanguard
Sovereign of the vanguard of heaven
The I Am
Too Holy to be Pronounced
Wisdom
Wisdom of the Ages
Warrior Protectrix
Wellspring of Life
Womb of Creation
Womb of Life
You Who Are

Jesus/Christ Names

The Anointed
God-born
Messiah
Rabbi
Redeemer
Savior
Son of Woman
Teacher
Woman-Born

BIBLIOGRAPHY

The Anchor Yale Bible Commentaries. Garden City, NY: Doubleday, 1964.

Abegg, Martin, Peter Flint, and Eugene Ulrich. *The Dead Sea Scrolls Bible: The Oldest Known Bible*. San Francisco: HarperSan Francisco: 1999.

Aland, Barbara, Kurt Aland, et al. *Novum Testamentum Graece*. Stuttgart: Deutsche Bibelgesellschaft, 2017.

Alter, Robert. *The Hebrew Bible: A Translation with Commentary*. New York: W.W. Norton and Company, 2018.

The Anchor Yale Bible Commentaries. Garden City, NY: Doubleday, 1964.

Ariel, Israel. *Carta's Illustrated Encyclopedia of the Holy Temple*. Jerusalem: Coronet Books, 2004.

Barth, Markus. *Ephesians. Introduction, Translation, and Commentary*. The Anchor Bible, vol. 34. Garden City, NY: Doubleday, 1974.

Berlin, Adele, and Marc Zvi Brettler. *The Jewish Study Bible*. 2nd ed. Oxford: Oxford University Press, 2004.

Bloch, Ariel, and Chana Bloch. *The Song of Songs: The World's First Great Love Poem*. Modern Library Classics. New York: Random House, 1995.

Briggs Kittredge, Cynthia, and Claire Miller Colombo. "Colossians." In *Philippians, Colossians, Philemon*, edited by Mary Ann Beavis. Wisdom Commentary, vol. 51. Collegeville, MN: Liturgical Press, 2017.

Brooten, Bernadette. *Women Leaders in the Ancient Synagogue*. Brown Judaic Studies 36. Chico, CA: Scholars Press, 1982.

Byron, Gay L., and Vanessa Lovelace. *Womanist Interpretations of the Bible: Expanding the Discourse*. Atlanta, GA: Society for Biblical Literature, 2016.

Clines, David J. A. *The Dictionary of Classical Hebrew*. Rev. ed. Sheffield: Sheffield Phoenix Press, 2018.

Common English Bible. Nashville, TN: Common English Bible, 2011.

Cooper, Kate. *Band of Angels: The Forgotten World of Early Christian Women*. New York: Overlook Press, 2013.

Danker, Frederick William. *A Greek-English Lexicon of the New Testament and other Early Christian Literature*. 3rd ed. Chicago: University of Chicago Press, 2000.

Edelman, Diana. "Mephibosheth." In *The Anchor Bible Dictionary, Volume 5*, edited by David Noel Freeman et al. New York: Doubleday, 1992.

Falk, Marcia. *The Song of Songs: Love Lyrics from the Bible*. Brandeis Series on Jewish Women. Waltham, MA: Brandeis University Press, 2004.

Fox, Everett. *The Early Prophets: Joshua, Judges, Samuel, and Kings: A New Translation with Introductions, Commentary, and Notes by Everett Fox*. The Schocken Bible, vol. 2. New York: Schocken Books, 2014.

———. *The Five Books of Moses: Genesis, Exodus, Leviticus, Numbers, Deuteronomy: A New Translation with Introductions, Commentary, and Notes*. The Schocken Bible, vol. 1. New York: Schocken Books, 1995.

———. *Give Us A King! Samuel, Saul, and David: A New Translation of Samuel I and II, with an Introduction and Notes by Everett Fox*. 1st ed. New York: Schocken Books, 1999.

Freedman, David Noel. *The Anchor Bible Dictionary*. New Haven, CT: Yale University Press, 1992.

Freeman, Lindsay Hardin. *Bible Women: All Their Words and Why They Matter*. Cincinnati, OH: Forward Movement, 2014.

Frick, Frank. "Israel? A People and a Land: Joshua and Judges." *A Journey Through the Hebrew Scriptures*. Belmont, CA: Wadsworth Publishing, 2002.

Gafney, Wilda. *Daughters of Miriam: Women Prophets in Ancient Israel*. Philadelphia: Fortress Press, 2008.

———. *Nahum, Habakkuk, Zephaniah*. Wisdom Commentary, vol. 38. Edited by Barbara E. Reid. Collegeville, MN: Liturgical Press, 2017.

———. *Womanist Midrash: A Reintroduction to the Women of the Torah and the Throne*. Lexington, KY: Westminster/John Knox Press, 2017.

Henderson, J. Frank, Jean Campbell, Ruth Fox, and Eileen M. Schuller. *Remembering the Women: Women's Stories from Scripture for Sundays and Festivals*. Chicago, IL: Liturgy Training Publications, 1999.

Ilan, Tal. *Mine and Yours Are Hers: Retrieving Women's History from Rabbinic Literature*. Leiden: Brill, 1997.

The Inclusive Bible: The First Egalitarian Translation. Lanham, MD: Rowman and Littlefield, 2007.

Johnson, Luke Timothy. *The Letter of James: A New Translation with Introduction and Commentary*. The Anchor Bible, vol. 37. New York: Doubleday, 1995.

Kol HaNeshamah. Elkins Park, PA: Reconstructionist Press, 2000.

Kraemer, Ross. "Nympha." In *Women in Scripture: A Dictionary of Named and Unnamed Women in the Hebrew Bible, the Apocryphal/Deuterocanonical Books, and the New Testament*, edited by Carol Meyers, Toni Craven, and Ross S. Kraemer. Boston: Houghton Mifflin, 2000.

Lamsa, George. *The Holy Bible from the Ancient Eastern Text: George M. Lamsa's Translations from the Aramaic of the Peshitta*. San Francisco, CA: Harper and Row, 1985.

Levine, Amy-Jill. *Entering the Passion of Jesus: A Beginner's Guide to Holy Week*. Nashville: United Methodist Publishing, 2018.

Levine, Amy-Jill, and Marc Brettler. *The Jewish Annotated New Testament*. New Revised Standard Version. Oxford: Oxford University Press, 2011.

Luz, Ulrich, and Helmut Koester. *Matthew*. Hermeneia series. Minneapolis, MN: Fortress Press, 1971.

Magiera, Janet. *Aramaic Peshitta New Testament Translation: Messianic Version*. San Diego, CA: LWM Publications, 2009.

Meyers, Carol L., Toni Craven, and Ross Shepard Kraemer. *Women in Scripture: A Dictionary of Named and Unnamed Women in the Hebrew Bible, the Apocryphal/Deuterocanonical Books, and the New Testament*. Boston: Houghton Mifflin, 2000.

Moore, Carey A. *Tobit: A New Translation with Introduction and Commentary*. New York: Doubleday, 1996.

Murdock, James. *Murdock's Translation of the Syriac New Testament. Translated into English from the Peshitto Version by James Murdock*. Boston: Scriptural Tract Repository, 1892.

A New English Translation of the Septuagint (and Other Greek Translations Traditionally Included Under That Title). New York: Oxford University Press, 2000.

New Revised Standard Version. Washington, DC: National Council of Churches, 1989.

Newsome, Carol, Sharon H. Ringe, and Jacqueline Lapsley. *Women's Bible Commentary*. 3rd ed: Revised and updated. Louisville, KY: Westminster John Knox Press, 2012.

Page, Hugh. *Israel's Poetry of Resistance: Africana Perspectives on Early Hebrew Verse.* Minneapolis. MN: Fortress Press, 2013.

Rashkow, Ilona. *Taboo or Not Taboo: Sexuality and Family in the Hebrew Bible.* Minneapolis, MN: Fortress Press, 2000.

Scholz, Susanne. *Introducing the Women's Hebrew Bible: Feminism, Gender Justice, and the Study of the Old Testament*. New York: Bloomsbury T & T, 2017.

Smith, Mitzi J. *I Found God in Me: A Womanist Biblical Hermeneutics Reader*. Eugene, OR: Cascade Books, 2015.

Stamm, Johann, Ludwig Köhler, and Walter Baumgarner. *The Hebrew and Aramaic Lexicon of the Old Testament*. Leiden: Brill Academic Press, 1994.

Stein, David. *The Contemporary Torah: A Gender-sensitive Adaptation of the JPS Translation.* Philadelphia: Jewish Publication Society, 2006.

Tal, Abraham. *The Samaritan Pentateuch*. Tel-Aviv: Tel-Aviv University, 1994.

Tanakh: The Holy Scriptures: The New JPS Translation According to the Hebrew Text. Philadelphia: Jewish Publication Society, 1985.

Trible, Phyllis. *God and the Rhetoric of Sexuality.* Overtures to Biblical Theology, no. 2. Philadelphia: Fortress Press, 1978.

———. *Texts of Terror: Literary-Feminist Readings of Biblical Narratives*. Overtures to Biblical Theology, no. 13. Philadelphia: Fortress Press, 1984.

Westbrook, April D. *"And He Will Take Your Daughters . . .": Woman Story and the Ethical Evaluation of Monarchy in the David Narrative*. New York, NY: Bloomsbury T & T Clark, 2015.

Wills, Lawrence M. "Mark." In *The Jewish Annotated New Testament: New Revised Standard Bible Translation*, edited by Amy-Jill Levine and Mark Zvi Brettler. Oxford: Oxford University Press, 2011.

Winter, Miriam Therese. *The Gospel According to Mary: A New Testament for Women*. New York: Crossroad, 1993.

———. *WomanWisdom: A Feminist Lectionary and Psalter: Women of the Hebrew Scriptures, Part One*. New York: Crossroad, 1991.

———. *WomanWitness: A Feminist Lectionary and Psalter: Women of the Hebrew Scriptures, Part Two*. New York: Crossroad, 1992.

———. *WomanWord: A Feminist Lectionary and Psalter: Women of the New Testament*. New York: Crossroad, 1990.

Wisdom Commentary Series. Collegeville, MN: Liturgical Press, 2015.

Witherington, Ben. *A New English Translation of the Septuagint (and Other Greek Translations Traditionally Included Under That Title)*. New York: Oxford University Press, 2000.

SCRIPTURE INDEX

Lightning Source UK Ltd.
Milton Keynes UK
UKHW011705071021
391823UK00002B/2